The New Politics of Beijing–Hong Kong Relations

The New Politics of Beijing–Hong Kong Relations

Ideological Conflicts and Factionalism

Sonny Shiu-Hing Lo

Hong Kong University Press
The University of Hong Kong
Pok Fu Lam Road
Hong Kong
https://hkupress.hku.hk

© 2024 Hong Kong University Press

ISBN 978-988-8805-72-3 (*Hardback*)

All rights reserved. No portion of this publication may be reproduced or transmitted in any form or by any means, electronic or mechanical, including photocopying, recording, or any information storage or retrieval system, without prior permission in writing from the publisher.

British Library Cataloguing-in-Publication Data
A catalogue record for this book is available from the British Library.

Digitally printed

Contents

List of Figures and Tables	vi
Acknowledgments	viii
List of Abbreviations	xi
Introduction	1
1. Chinese Politics and Its Implications for Beijing–Hong Kong Relations	10
2. Ideologies and Factionalism in Beijing–Hong Kong Relations	70
3. Beijing's Comprehensive Jurisdiction, Sino-Western Value Clashes, and Hong Kong Elections from 2021 to 2023: Implications for Taiwan	180
Conclusion	229
Bibliography	255
Index	281

List of Figures and Tables

Figures

Figure 2.1: Pro-Beijing Nationalism and Hongkongism — 99
Figure 3.1: Beijing's Interactions with Hong Kong before the 2020 National Security Law — 186
Figure 3.2: Beijing's New Interactions with Hong Kong after the 2020 National Security Law — 186

Tables

Table 2.1: Ideologies, Factions, and Political, Economic, Social, and Legal Disputes in Hong Kong — 117
Table 2.2: The Evolution of the Legislative Council, 1947–1985 — 159
Table 2.3: The Evolution of the Legislative Council, 1985–2021 — 159
Table 2.4: Main Elements of the 2020 Electoral Reform Amended by the National People's Congress — 163
Table 2.5: How District Council Members Are Removed and Replaced by Pro-Beijing Clients in the Fourth and Fifth Sectors of the Election Committee — 164
Table 3.1: Beijing's Comprehensive Responses to Localist Populism — 181
Table 3.2: Number of Voters and Voter Turnout in Legislative Council Elections, 2008–2021 — 197
Table 3.3: Results of the Legislative Council's Direct Elections in December 2021 — 198
Table 3.4: Results of the Election Committee in Legislative Council Elections, 2021 — 200
Table 3.5: Results of the Legislative Council's Functional Constituency Elections, 2021 — 203

Table 3.6:	New Political Profile of the Legislative Council after the 2021 Elections	206
Table 3.7:	The December 2023 District Council Elections in Hong Kong	212

Acknowledgments

The origin of this book could be traced back to my previous work published in 2008 by Hong Kong University Press on *The Dynamics of Beijing–Hong Kong Relations*. However, political changes in Hong Kong have become rapid and drastic since 2008, thereby necessitating me to propose this new book project to Hong Kong University Press four years ago.

The first draft of this book was completed at a time when the Standing Committee of the National People's Congress passed a decision and elaborated on the new electoral system of Hong Kong in late March 2021. I worked diligently at home, continuously for many weekends and months. The second draft was completed in August 2022 because I waited for the chief executive election in May 2022 and President Xi Jinping's visit to Hong Kong on July 1. The second draft was finished in October 2022 as I decided to incorporate any new developments from the twentieth Party Congress in Beijing. The third draft was completed in January 2024 after taking into account the District Council elections in Hong Kong.

I have to thank the staff of Hong Kong University Press for their staunch support of this project and for having granted me the necessary extension so that I could finish the entire book. I suffered from tinnitus for almost three years, and the extension was extremely helpful to me.

I am also indebted to three reviewers of the Hong Kong University Press for giving me detailed and critical comments on the first and second drafts so that I knew how to revise and improve the whole manuscript in a more solid way.

I am deeply grateful to the managing editor of *Asian Survey* (University of California Press), David Fraser, for granting me the permission to reprint two short articles and one longer article that were published in the journal. I combined the content of the three articles as the middle part of Chapter 2; nevertheless, I rewrote, updated, and expanded substantially all these papers to make the new chapter solid. These three articles were as follows: "Hong Kong in 2020," *Asian Survey* 61, no. 1 (February 2021): 34–42; "Hong Kong in 2019: The Anti-Extradition, Anti-Mainlandization and Anti-Police Movement," *Asian Survey*

60, no. 1 (February 2020): 34–40; and "Ideology and Factionalism in Beijing–Hong Kong Relations," *Asian Survey* 58, no. 3 (2018): 392–415.

I fervently hope that this book can stimulate the readers to deepen their understanding of Beijing–Hong Kong relations from the combined perspectives of political science and history. Since 1982, I have been following and analyzing Hong Kong's political development closely. This is my eighth book on Hong Kong politics. Two of my previous books on Hong Kong—*Competing Chinese Political Visions* and *Hong Kong's Indigenous Democracy*—warned that the city's political development posed a threat to the security of the central authorities in Beijing. I argued that Hong Kong could develop its own style of democracy instead of copying entirely from the Western model. Unfortunately, my arguments and advice were ignored academically and practically. Many of my readers might not understand that my previous books on Hong Kong adopted a realist perspective on not only Beijing's approach to dealing with the city but also on how Hong Kong people could and should cope with democratization. Specifically, the people of Hong Kong can design a political system that strikes a balance between protecting Beijing's national security concerns and moving the polity in a more democratic and accountable fashion. This book is a continuation of my realist analysis and my profound interest in the study of Beijing–Hong Kong relations. Undoubtedly, I support China's sovereignty over Hong Kong and realize the importance of protecting its national security interest. I also hope that mainland China and Taiwan will reunite peacefully one day. As such, I make concrete suggestions on how both sides can perhaps and will hopefully reach a political consensus in the coming years.

Finally, I must dedicate this book to my late mother, Lo Ching Yock, and my late father, Lo Ho Leung. While my mother worried about my political study, my father was neutral in his attitude. In early 1982, when I was an undergraduate student at Canada's York University and tried to specialize in the study of political science, my mother opposed me doing so. She warned me that participation in politics could be a highly dangerous endeavor—a warning that was very true in the case of Hong Kong's recent political development. She mentioned to me again and again that my uncle had participated actively in the Hundred Flowers Campaign in mainland China in 1956, but he was eventually sent to a labor camp for many years—an event leaving an indelible imprint on my late mother. I adhere to my late mother's wish: I study and analyze politics, but I must not participate in politics. As an overseas Chinese born and living in Hong Kong, I maintain the principle of studying, analyzing, and writing on Hong Kong politics from a relatively neutral, distanced, balanced, but critical perspective. I still recall vividly that, on the night of June 30, 1997, my late mother told me that I, as a political analyst, would have to be more moderate and cautious in my remarks from then onward—advice that would have profound impacts on my analyses, comments, and academic writings. I must express my deepest gratitude to my late mother, whose advice remains influential on my mind.

I hope that my readers may appreciate my very diligent work on the study of Hong Kong and its interactions with the mainland and that they may find this book interesting and stimulating.

Sonny Shiu-Hing Lo
January 2, 2024

List of Abbreviations

AAF	Antiquities Advisory Board
ACFTU	All-China Federation of Trade Unions
BHKF	Better Hong Kong Foundation
BLC	Basic Law Committee
BP	Bauhinia Party
BPA	Business Professionals Alliance
CCCHKM	Central Coordination Committee on Hong Kong and Macau
CCP	Chinese Communist Party
CDIC	Central Discipline Inspection Committee
CEPA	Closer Economic Partnership Arrangement
CERC	Candidate Eligibility Review Committee
CGO	Central Government Offices
CIS	Commonwealth of Independent States
CMC	Central Military Commission
COFA	Chinese Overseas Friendship Association
CP	Civic Party
CPPCC	Chinese People's Political Consultative Conference
CPSU	Communist Party of the Soviet Union
CSNS	Committee for Safeguarding National Security
CTU	Confederation of Trade Unions
CUHK	Chinese University of Hong Kong
DAB	Democratic Alliance for the Betterment and Progress of Hong Kong
DP	Democratic Party
DPP	Democratic Progressive Party
EU	European Union
ExCo	Executive Council
FEW	Federation of Education Workers
FHKKLU	Federation of Hong Kong and Kowloon Labor Unions
FTU	Federation of Trade Unions

GBA	Greater Bay Area
GONGOs	Government-Organized Non-Governmental Organizations
HKMAO	Hong Kong Macau Affairs Office
HKMSA	Hong Kong Macau Study Association
HKND	Hong Kong New Direction
HKSAR	Hong Kong Special Administrative Region
HKUST	Hong Kong University of Science and Technology
ICAC	Independent Commission Against Corruption
ICCPR	International Covenant on Civil and Political Rights
KMT	Kuomintang
LegCo	Legislative Council
LP	Liberal Party
LSD	League of Social Democrats
MFA	Ministry of Foreign Affairs
MTR	Mass Transit Railway
NATO	North Atlantic Treaty Organization
NCNA	New China News Agency
NGOs	Non-Governmental Organizations
NPC	National People's Congress
NPP	New People's Party
NTFA	New Territories Federation of Associations
OSNS	Office for Safeguarding National Security (of the Central People's Government)
PAP	People's Armed Police
PLA	People's Liberation Army
PoD	Path of Democracy
PP	Professional Power
PPI	Proletariat Political Institute
PPower	Professional Power
PRC	People's Republic of China
ROC	Republic of China
RTHK	Radio Television Hong Kong
SARS	Severe Acute Respiratory Syndrome
SCNPC	Standing Committee of the National People's Congress
UDHK	United Democrats of Hong Kong
UGC	University Grants Council
UK	United Kingdom
US	United States
USC	University Services Center

Introduction

Since the publication of my earlier book on Beijing–Hong Kong relations in 2008, political transformations in both the People's Republic of China (PRC) and the Hong Kong Special Administrative Region (HKSAR) have necessitated a reassessment of their historical interactions and the rapidly changing external political environment.[1] As such, this book adopts a different approach to understanding Beijing–Hong Kong relations by focusing on the ideological conflicts and factional politics on both sides. Since July 1, 1997, when the sovereignty of Hong Kong reverted from Britain to China, ideological conflicts have increasingly become prominent in Beijing–Hong Kong relations, especially after the mass protests against the Tung Chee-hwa government on July 1, 2003. From 2003 to 2019, as this book will discuss, such ideological clashes became far more serious than ever before—a process complicated by the evolution of different factional politics in both the mainland and the HKSAR. The ideological and power struggles between some Hong Kong people and the PRC resulted in Beijing's deeper and swift intervention in Hong Kong matters after the end of 2019, leading to the victory of the central authorities over the local resistance movement.

This book argues that the promulgation of the national security law by the Standing Committee of the National People's Congress (SCNPC) for Hong Kong on June 30, 2020, was a watershed in Hong Kong's political history. It was arguably both dependent and independent variables in Hong Kong's turbulent political development. The national security law was an outcome of the severe ideological conflicts between the PRC authorities on the one hand and some pro-democracy elites and radical populists in Hong Kong on the other hand, as this book will show. The national security law was also a causal event that ushered

---

1. Sonny Shiu-Hing Lo, *The Dynamics of Beijing–Hong Kong Relations: A Model for Taiwan* (Hong Kong: Hong Kong University Press, 2008).

in the new politics of Beijing–Hong Kong relations, changing the Hong Kong political system from patron-client pluralism to patron-client and paternalistic authoritarianism. By patron-client pluralism, I refer to it as a phenomenon in which Hong Kong's polity from 1997 to late 2019 was marked by the proliferation of the clientelist groups and individuals, who sought political influence from the politically powerful patron, namely Beijing authorities responsible for Hong Kong affairs.[2] However, the rise of a localist movement in Hong Kong's pluralistic polity, including democratic populism and its radical faction, challenged the legitimacy of the HKSAR authorities and the central government in Beijing continuously from 2003 to 2019, leading to the PRC's decision to intervene in Hong Kong affairs by imposing the national security law onto the HKSAR and turning the "one country, two systems" into a PRC-led political system. The imposition of the national security law represented a conservative nationalistic and hardline move made by the central authorities—a hardline action that filtered downward to a forceful implementation of the law by the HKSAR authorities. The effect was to establish a patron-client and paternalistic authoritarian system; it was patron-clientelist because Beijing, as the powerful patron, can select who are the "patriotic" elites governing Hong Kong and who should be excluded from the political system. The political system of Hong Kong is increasingly paternalistic because the central government sees itself like a strict father ruling the Hong Kong son, who was politically "naughty" and behaviorally "rebellious" from 2003 to 2019. The Hong Kong polity is partially "populist" in the sense that the pro-Beijing "patriotic" groups have become the most powerful populist sector directly replacing the democrats and shaping the policy-making process and legislative politics. Yet, compared with the democratic populists in Hong Kong before the promulgation of the national security law in late June 2020, the pro-Beijing and nationalistic populists are now electorally much weaker, although they have been empowered to dominate the entire polity through the top-down control of the electoral system by the central authorities.

Factional politics in the HKSAR was complicated by a temporary alliance between the radical democrats, who sought to lobby the Western democratic states against the implementation of the extradition bill in the latter half of 2019, and some Western democracies like the United States (US) and United Kingdom (UK). The PRC perceived such a temporary alliance as a "conspiracy" by the Western states and some local democrats to "subvert" the political system of Hong Kong, thereby enhancing its determination to impose the national security law on the HKSAR in mid-2020.

The new political system in Hong Kong has been characterized by the official preoccupation with the protection of national security, the arrest and

---

2. For patron-client pluralism, see Lo, *The Dynamics of Beijing–Hong Kong Relations*.

prosecutions of the offenders concerned, a much stronger executive-led branch vis-à-vis a relatively weak but "patriotic" legislature, the elevation of the political influence of pro-Beijing and nationalistic populists, and the exclusion of moderate, radical, and confrontational populists from the Legislative Council (LegCo) since December 2022 and District Councils since December 2023. In short, the SCNPC's promulgation of the national security law for Hong Kong on June 30, 2020, transformed the political system from patron-client pluralism to both patron-client and populist authoritarianism. Patron-client politics are proliferating and deepening in Hong Kong where the new electoral system established a 1,500-member Election Committee in which *guanxi* politics among the patriotic elites have become inevitable. Beijing as the most powerful political patron could decide who became the political kingmakers in the 1,500-member Election Committee, which was responsible for not only choosing forty out of ninety LegCo members in December 2021 but also for selecting the Chief Executive in March 2022.

In September 1982, the concept of "one country, two systems" was proposed by the late PRC leader, Deng Xiaoping, to the late British Prime Minister Margaret Thatcher to deal with the question of Hong Kong's future.[3] China would resume its sovereignty over Hong Kong on July 1, 1997, but the promise of "one country, two systems" would be implemented in the HKSAR, whose economic system and lifestyle would remain unchanged for fifty years. In June 1983, when Deng met with Winston L. Y. Yang from Seton Hall University, the former said that

> after the reunification of the motherland, the Taiwan Special Administrative Region can have its own independence, practice a system different from that of the mainland, and its independent judiciary and right of final judgment need not reside in Beijing. Taiwan can retain its army so long as it does not constitute a threat to the mainland. The mainland will station neither troops nor administrative personnel in Taiwan. Taiwan's party, government and army departments are managed by Taiwan itself. The central government will reserve some seats for Taiwan . . . The systems can be different, but only the PRC can represent China in international affairs.[4]

---

3. Wen Qing, "'One Country, Two Systems': The Best Way to Peaceful Reunification," *Beijing Review*, May 26, 2009, accessed March 24, 2021, http://www.bjreview.com.cn/nation/txt/2009-05/26/content_197568.htm.
4. Wen Qing, "'One Country, Two Systems.'" See also Edward A. Gargan, "Taiwan Could Buy Arms Abroad after Reunification, Deng Asserts," *New York Times*, August 21, 1983, accessed March 24, 2021, https://www.nytimes.com/1983/08/21/world/taiwan-could-buy-arms-abroad-after-reunification-deng-asserts.html.

Obviously, Deng Xiaoping wanted to use the "one country, two systems" to settle the future of Hong Kong and Macau first and to cope with Taiwan's future in the long run.[5]

However, Deng passed away in February 1997 and could not witness the handover ceremony of Hong Kong from Britain to the PRC. Nor could he envisage the turbulent relations between the HKSAR and the PRC after the retrocession period. From the national security perspective of the central government in Beijing, it had to intervene in Hong Kong affairs in view of the increasingly anti-PRC activities in the HKSAR, ranging from the occurrence of the anti-national education campaign in the HKSAR during the summer of 2012 to the Occupy Central Movement from September to December 2014, from the Mong Kok riots in early 2016 to the oath-taking controversies of two young legislators-elect (Yau Wai-ching and Baggio Leung) in October 2016, and from the socio-political movement to oppose the extradition bill in May–December 2019 to the holding of so-called "primary elections" by the local democrats in July 2020.

The crux of the problem is that the more Beijing intervenes in Hong Kong matters, the more resistant the Taiwanese regime and its people become to the concept of "one country, two systems." From the PRC perspective, the central government's intervention in the matters of Hong Kong is undoubtedly positive, as Deng Xiaoping had long remarked. However, from the vantage point of many Taiwanese people, the political development of Hong Kong has provided them a significant lesson for Taiwan, which to them should not and cannot be another HKSAR where the central authorities' intervention has been perceived by the Taiwanese as "negative" rather than positive.

The sudden visit of US House Speaker Nancy Pelosi to Taiwan on August 2, 2022, aroused the tensions between the mainland and Taiwan. The PLA conducted military exercises around the island of Taiwan. Following the military drills that tested the capacity of Taiwan's military to deal with a possible partial military and economic blockade by the PRC, the State Council published a *White Paper on the Taiwan Question and China's Reunification*. The document did not mention that the PLA would not be stationed in Taiwan, reserving the right of the PRC to send the PLA to deal with any "separatists" in Taiwan in case of any military action to recover China's sovereignty over the island. Deng Xiaoping's remark in June 1983 that China would not send military personnel to Taiwan was no longer mentioned in the white paper—an indication that the PRC has silently become more hardline toward Taiwan since Pelosi's highly provocative visit to Taipei.

This book will show that ideological conflicts and factional struggles between some Hong Kong democrats and the HKSAR government and pro-Beijing

---

5. Macau was returned from Portugal to the PRC on December 20, 1999.

forces on the one hand, and between the radical democrats and PRC authorities on the other hand, have triggered far more intervention from the central government in Hong Kong's political development than ever before. Arguably, this result stems partly from the underestimation and miscalculation of most Hong Kong democrats about the nature of the PRC regime and partly from the increasingly dominance of a conservative nationalistic faction in the mainland. The underestimation of many Hong Kong democrats originated from a batch of young and radical localists who were imbued with a very strong sense of Hong Kong identity but who were lacking a profound knowledge of how the mainland's Marxist-Leninist political ideology operates. They participated in peaceful and violent protests in such an intertwined manner that the PRC authorities were angered and forced to intervene as a politically powerful patron. From the Marxist-Leninist perspective, the "one country, two systems" in Hong Kong must respect the Chinese Communist Party (CCP) in the HKSAR and the mainland. Unfortunately, some radical protestors in the 2019 anti-extradition movement disrespected the CCP and the mainland's state-owned enterprises in Hong Kong, utilizing violent activities to plunge the legitimacy of the HKSAR government into an unprecedented crisis. Some of them even went so far as to desecrate China's national flags and attack the Liaison Office's headquarters, seriously challenging the legitimacy of the central government in the HKSAR. On the other hand, the moderate democrats totally miscalculated the intention of the PRC authorities, except for the unprecedented 2010 political compromise between them regarding the ways in which LegCo elections should be designed. The 2010 political compromise came at a time when the PRC side was dominated and ruled by liberal nationalists, notably the former President Hu Jintao, and when the HKSAR side was characterized by not only the split between radical and moderate democrats but also the desire of moderates to negotiate with PRC officials. However, after the summer of 2010, the moderate democrats turned more receptive to the radical faction of the democrats, including the participation in the 2014 Occupy Central movement, and their failure to denounce and abandon violence in the 2019 anti-extradition protests. The result was the intertwined relations between some moderate and radical democrats, whose future would be easily cracked down on by the national security law enacted in June 2020.

Chapter 1 will focus on the literature on the PRC's political development and assess how the features of mainland Chinese politics can be applied to our deeper understanding of Beijing–Hong Kong relations. Chapter 2 will focus on the emergence of various factions inside Hong Kong, ranging from pro-democracy and pro-establishment forces, and inside the PRC, including the gradual shift from the relatively liberal nationalistic faction during the Hu Jintao era to the conservative nationalistic faction in the Xi Jinping era. Chapter 3 will show how Beijing responded to the rapid emergence of radical and localist populism in the HKSAR and how the elections held for the LegCo in December 2022 and those held for District Councils in December 2023 established the foundation of "patriotic" elites ruling Hong Kong—a process paving the way for the implementation of Beijing's "comprehensive jurisdiction" over the HKSAR. The concept of "comprehensive jurisdiction" was first mentioned by Beijing in its white paper on the implementation of the Basic Law of Hong Kong in mid-2014, but it took nine years for its realization through a series of measures, including the imposition of the national security law in mid-2020, the chief executive election in March 2022, the LegCo elections in December 2022, the District Council elections in December 2023, and the scheduled legislation on Article 23 of the Basic Law in 2024.

In the process of implementing the "one country, two systems," there are considerable tensions in the interactions of the two systems, politically speaking. First, while many Hong Kong people and foreign states, especially Western democracies, see the HKSAR as an international city, the PRC authorities have increasingly seen Hong Kong as a mainland Chinese city where its political development should not be shaped and manipulated by external forces. In short, the vision of a cosmopolitan and an international Hong Kong has been clashing with the mainland conception of a Hong Kong whose sovereignty is possessed exclusively by the PRC. From the Western point of view, the Sino-British Joint Declaration that was reached in September 1984 provided the fundamental safeguards for Hong Kong's autonomy vis-à-vis the PRC, and it protects the rights and freedom of the Hong Kong people. As such, it has been argued that China's imposition of the national security law on Hong Kong "violated" the Joint Declaration.[6] However, the PRC Foreign Ministry argued that national security is China's internal affairs and that it does not allow foreign intervention; moreover, "the basic policies regarding Hong Kong declared by China in the Joint Declaration are China's statement of policies, not commitment to the UK or an international obligation as some claim."[7] The tensions in the interactions of the "one country, two systems" are shown in how Western countries and some Hong Kong democrats, especially the young ones, have perceived the importance of "two systems" as opposed to "one country," which, however, has become the constant emphasis of PRC authorities who handle Hong Kong matters.

Second, the identity clashes between Hong Kong as a city with its strong local identity and Hong Kong as a mainland borderland that should have a

---

6. See "Foreign Secretary Declares Breach of Sino-British Joint Declaration," November 12, 2020, accessed January 1, 2024, https://www.gov.uk/government/news/foreign-secretary-declares-breach-of-sino-british-joint-declaration.
7. "Foreign Ministry spokesman Zhao Lijian's Regular Press Conference on June 3, 2020," June 3, 2020, accessed January 1, 2024, http://mw.china-embassy.gov.cn/eng/fyrth/202006/t20200603_5808452.htm.

stronger sense of mainland Chinese national identity have become increasingly prominent. Those who support the persistence of local identity saw Hong Kong's integration into mainland China as "unnecessary" and having "negative" impacts on its society and economy, making the HKSAR more economically dependent on the mainland. But those who champion the mainland Chinese national identity have contended that the Hong Kong people should become more politically "patriotic" and more supportive of the city's socio-economic integration with the mainland, especially the Greater Bay Area.

Third, the clashes between the upsurge in Hong Kong's localism and the rising mainland Chinese assertive nationalism were prominent from 2014 to 2020, leading to (1) the SCNPC action of interpreting the Basic Law on the proper behavior of legislators to take their oath in November 2016, (2) the enactment of the national security law for Hong Kong in June 2020, (3) the SCNPC decision on the allegiance requirements of LegCo members in November 2020, and (4) the SCNPC revamp of Hong Kong's electoral system in March 2021. Such assertive Chinese nationalism became obvious in not only the remarks made by PRC authorities on Hong Kong but also in the ways in which the SCNPC has been intervening in Hong Kong's matters.

Fourth, the tensions between democratic change and national security have become apparent. While many local democrats have seen democratization as natural, inevitable, and negotiable, PRC authorities have regarded democratization as a ploy used by local democrats in collaboration with foreign forces to foster a "color revolution" in Hong Kong and to undermine China's national security.

Fifth, the tensions between the Western conception of democracy and the Chinese notion of democracy have become prominent. Prior to mid-2020, many Hong Kong people yearned for a Western-style democracy in which the entire LegCo should be directly elected and the Chief Executive should be directly elected from universal suffrage without political control from the central authorities. To PRC leaders, the HKSAR should develop its Hong Kong–style democracy instead of copying directly from Western-style democracies. Most importantly, PRC authorities are determined to retain their say and veto over the candidates of chief executive elections. On December 20, 2021, the State Council published a *White Paper on Hong Kong's Democratic Development*, emphasizing that democracy was absent in Hong Kong under British colonial rule and that national security is a prerequisite for democracy in the HKSAR.[8] Without

---

8. "White Paper on Hong Kong's Democratic Development," the State Council's Information Office, December 20, 2021, accessed September 11, 2022, https://www.chinadailyhk.com/article/252582#Full-text:-White-paper-on-Hong-Kong's-democratic-development.

national security, democratic development in Hong Kong is vulnerable to external influences—a situation disallowed by the central authorities in Beijing.

Sixth, while the people of Hong Kong have gotten used to living in a relatively pluralistic political system, such pluralism clashes with the mainland Chinese political culture of paternalism in which the state is like a parent protective of the interests of the children. Before the promulgation of the national security law in June 2020, many Hong Kong people were imbued with a Western concept of human rights, believing that human rights were universal and natural. But to the PRC, the rights enjoyed by the people of Hong Kong have been conferred upon them by the Chinese constitution and the Hong Kong Basic Law. From the PRC perspective, the rights of the people of Hong Kong, such as freedom of speech, of the press, and of association, have their limits in that they have to observe and protect China's sovereignty and national security.

Seventh, the tensions between some Hongkongers' political culture tolerant of protests and dissent and a mainland Chinese elite disposition relatively intolerant of political dissident persist. In the latter half of 2019, some local democrats argued for the establishment of a social reconciliation committee to investigate the anti–extradition bill movement, but the HKSAR government and PRC authorities rejected such a move. After the implementation of the national security law in mid-2020, public protests have almost disappeared, except for a notable exception of a protest by one hundred citizens against a land reclamation plan in Tseung Kwan O district in March 2023, when they were asked to wear numbered tags under tight police surveillance.[9]

Eighth, there were tensions between a mass culture of adopting an open but confrontational approach on the one hand and the PRC political culture of giving face (*mianzi*) to authorities and emphasizing harmony between the state and society on the other. The contentious state-society relations in Hong Kong from 2003 to 2019 made it difficult for PRC authorities to accept politically a weak state vis-à-vis a strong society, especially as the mainland Chinese state has traditionally dominated the society. Ninth, there are contradictions between the Chinese legalism that has been adopted by PRC officials on Hong Kong matters and a more lenient approach advocated by some liberal democrats on how local protestors in 2019 should be handled. Tenth, while PRC authorities attach immense importance to the executive-led polity in Hong Kong, many Hong Kong democrats argued for an executive-legislative relation in which the LegCo could effectively check the power of the executive branch of the government.

---

9. "Hong Kong police make protesters wear numbered tags, carry own cordon line, 100 people maximum, mask free," March 23, 2023, *Hong Kong Free Press*, accessed January 1, 2024, https://hongkongfp.com/2023/03/27/hong-kong-police-make-protesters-wear-numbered-tags-carry-own-cordon-line-100-people-max-mask-free/.

While the democrats went so far as to advocate and support a system with a separation of powers, the mainland authorities have rejected the notion of the separation of powers. To PRC authorities, the Hong Kong polity is characterized by an executive-led system, and there should be "harmony" between the executive, the legislature, and the judiciary.

All these ten contradictions have proven to be increasingly prominent in Beijing–Hong Kong relations since the outbreak of mass protests against the Tung Chee-hwa government on July 1, 2003. All these contradictions were fully illustrated in the clashes between two political systems, one far more pluralistic and tolerant than the other. In a sense, the power struggles between the local democrats and the HKSAR government on the one hand and the radical localists and PRC authorities on the other were ferocious, leading to the final decision of Beijing to intervene in Hong Kong's political development and to defeat its political enemies and factional opponents in the HKSAR.

Many Hong Kong people underestimated the possibility that the PRC's authoritarian political system could be transferred or diffused to the HKSAR across the border easily. Many assumed naively and wrongly that since the PRC treated Hong Kong as a golden goose that can lay eggs, Beijing would not have cracked down on political dissidents in the HKSAR. However, treating Hong Kong as a golden goose laying eggs is one thing, but protecting China's sovereignty, national security, territorial integrity, and national dignity is another issue. In the eyes of the PRC authorities handling Hong Kong matters, the anti–extradition bill movement went beyond their bottom line of political tolerance as it plunged the HKSAR into political chaos, violence, terrorism, and "subversion." The PRC's perception that the 2019 anti–extradition bill movement was mingled with foreign forces was a testimony to the belief held firmly by the ruling CCP that a "color revolution" was emerging in the HKSAR. Hong Kong was perceived as a Trojan horse for foreign countries to "subvert" Hong Kong first and then influence the mainland's political system. As a result, the PRC had to intervene decisively and comprehensively to restore political and social stability. In short, some Hong Kong people have neglected the likelihood of authoritarian diffusion from the PRC to the HKSAR, especially as some of them participated in political activities that went beyond the political red lines tolerated by Beijing.

1
Chinese Politics and Its Implications for Beijing–Hong Kong Relations

The imposition of the Hong Kong national security law by the PRC's National People's Congress into the HKSAR on June 30, 2020, was the most important watershed in Beijing's policy toward Hong Kong after July 1, 1997. Supporters of the national security law have hailed it as a stabilizer returning the society of the HKSAR to normalcy after the anti-extradition protests from June to December 2019. Critics of Beijing's new measure of securitizing Hong Kong have regarded the move as an attempt to change the "one country, two systems" into "one country, one and a half systems."[1]

From an academic perspective, it is necessary to comprehend the dynamics of the new politics of Beijing–Hong Kong relations. In the studies of Hong Kong's politics, local scholars who have focused on Hong Kong's internal political development were relatively uninterested in conducting research on how PRC politics might have influenced Hong Kong.[2] On the other hand, sinologists who have focused on the study of Chinese politics and who have researched Hong Kong draw some linkages between the two.[3] This chapter adopts the second approach

---

1. Charles Parton, "China and Hong Kong: One Country, One and a Half Systems," July 23, 2020, accessed July 24, 2022, https://www.rusi.org/explore-our-research/publications/commentary/china-and-hong-kong-one-country-one-and-half-systems. See also Pieter van Wingerden, "The National Security Law, 'One Country, Two Systems,' and Hong Kong's National Security Apparatus: The Coup De Grace to Hong Kong's Ideological Independence and Democratic Autonomy," *The Yale Review of International Studies*, April 2022, accessed July 24, 2022, http://yris.yira.org/essays/5696.
2. Alvin So, *Hong Kong's Embattled Democracy: A Societal Analysis* (Baltimore: Johns Hopkins University Press, 1999); Ma Ngok, *Political Development in Hong Kong: State, Political Society, and Civil Society* (Hong Kong: Hong Kong University Press, 2007); and Sing Ming, *Hong Kong's Tortuous Democratization: A Comparative Analysis* (London: RoutledgeCurzon, 2004).
3. Lynn T. White, *Democratization in Hong Kong—and China?* (Boulder: Lynne Rienner, 2016); and Richard C. Bush, *Hong Kong in the Shadow of China: Living with the Leviathan* (Washington: Brookings Institution Press, 2016). For a review of these two books, see Ming K. Chan and Kent P. K. Wan, "Uncertain Prospects for Democracy in China's Hong Kong," *Journal of East Asian Studies* 18 (2018): 117–126.

by analyzing the features of Chinese politics first and then exploring how these characteristics shape Beijing–Hong Kong relations. Twelve perspectives are going to be examined for us to understand the changing dynamics of Chinese politics and their implications for Beijing–Hong Kong relations.

This book uses the enactment of the national security law in late June 2020 as both dependent and independent variables. The causes of the national security law were attributable to the political development of both the mainland and the HKSAR. The national security law and its implementation have shaped Hong Kong's political development, including the reform of the electoral system in March 2020, the holding of the new LegCo elections in December 2021, and the holding of the chief executive election in May 2022, when John Lee was the only candidate securing the support of the Election Committee members and the central government in Beijing.

Assertive Nationalism in Chinese Foreign Policy: Implications for Hong Kong

From time to time, the PRC has been displaying assertively nationalistic tendencies in its foreign policies, including in the early 1980s when Beijing began to negotiate with Britain and later Portugal over the return of the sovereignty of Hong Kong and the administrative right of Macau back to China.[4] If assertive nationalism is defined as an ideology of showing nationalistic sentiments in dealing with China's foreign relations and policies, Chang Liao Nien-Chung explained this phenomenon by analyzing the perceptions and preferences of PRC political leaders and elites.[5] To bolster regime legitimacy at home, Chinese leaders skillfully exploit any opportunity to build up the military and to expand the PRC's national interests and its geographical reach.[6] Unlike Chang Liao, who focused on the role of political leaders, Alastair Iain Johnston has paid more attention to the nationalistic sentiment of ordinary citizens and argued that public opinion could influence the way in which the PRC's political elites adopted a nationalistic attitude in their foreign policy-making.[7] However, Zhao Suisheng has cautioned us that while the PRC government made effective efforts to rein in popular nationalism before 2008, it has become more willing to follow

---

4. Allen S. Whiting, "Assertive Nationalism in Chinese Foreign Policy," *Asian Survey* 23, no. 8 (August 1983): 913–933; Abanti Bhattacharya, "Chinese Nationalism and China's Assertive Foreign Policy," *Journal of East Asian Affairs* 21, no. 1 (April 2007): 235–262. On Macau, see Lo Shiu Hing, *Political Development in Macau* (Hong Kong: Chinese University Press, 1995).
5. Chang Liao Nien-Chung, "The Sources of China's Assertiveness: The System, Domestic Politics or Leadership Preferences?" *International Affairs* 92, no. 4 (2016): 817–833.
6. Chang Liao, "The Sources of China's Assertiveness," 817–833.
7. Alastair Iain Johnston, "Is Chinese Nationalism Rising?" *International Security* 41, no. 3 (Winter 2016–2017): 7–43.

popular nationalistic demands for adopting a more confrontational position against Western powers and in dealing with China's maritime territorial disputes with its neighbors.[8] This "strident turn" was attributable to the fact that the government was increasingly responsive to public opinion. Moreover, there was a convergence between the state nationalism and popular nationalism that called for a "more muscular Chinese foreign policy."[9] According to Zhao, the rising Chinese power after 2008 showed that the good old days of passivity in the PRC's foreign policy were gone and that there was a firm belief in the mistreatment and exploitation of China's territorial and sovereign rights by the Western powers and neighbors.[10] Zhao has predicted that if this type of elite and mass nationalism prevails in the foreign policy-making process of a rising PRC, it would make compromises with other countries more difficult than ever before.

Long before the writings of Whiting, Chang Liao, Johnston, and Zhao on assertive Chinese nationalism, sinologist Lucian Pye had identified a crucial weakness of Chinese nationalism in China's domestic governance. Pye wrote:

> The problem with Chinese nationalism is that it lacks the content necessary to constrain partisan leaders. The Communist leaders are able to insist that they represent the nation, and anyone who disagrees with them is by definition "unpatriotic." The lack of any distinction between Chinese nationalism on the one hand and the partisan politics of either Communist or Kuomintang leaders means that all dissenting critics run the risk of being labeled subversive enemies of the Chinese people. In a sense the constraints of nationalism should serve as the basis for the "unwritten constitution" that establishes the arena for partisan politics. In the Chinese case, there is not enough content to what might be called Chinese nationalism to distinguish it from the self-interested position of whoever dominates the system at any moment.[11]

While Pye was sharp in linking Chinese nationalism with the mainland's partisan politics, Zhu Zhiqun wrote in May 2020 that Chinese national pride and patriotism were expressed in the form of "wolf-warrior diplomacy" through the remarks made by PRC Foreign Ministry officials. He has noted that some Foreign Ministry officials resorted to Twitter to make blunt remarks on foreign states, such as spokesman Zhao Lijian pointing boldly in March 2020 to the US army officers who brought COVID-19 to China. Zhu views the "wolf-warrior diplomacy" as a reflection of China's foreign policy change from the dictum of *taoguang yanghui* (adopting a low profile) to President Xi Jinping's emphasis on

---

8. Zhao Suisheng, "Foreign Policy Implications of Chinese Nationalism Revisited: The Strident Turn," *Journal of Contemporary China* 22, no. 82 (2013): 535–553.
9. Zhao, "Foreign Policy Implications of Chinese Nationalism Revisited," 535–553.
10. Zhao, "Foreign Policy Implications of Chinese Nationalism Revisited," 553.
11. Lucian Pye, *The Spirit of Chinese Politics* (Cambridge, MA: Harvard University Press, 1992), 231.

the need for the Chinese Communist Party (CCP) to have "fighting spirits."[12] The new behavior of changing *taoguang yanghui* to *yousuo zuowei* (trying to accomplish something) means that PRC officials make rebuttals and strong remarks to counter the criticisms from foreign states.[13] Zhu points to the phenomenon that "wolf-warrior diplomacy" was "an extension of soaring nationalism at home."[14] He warns that "wolf-warrior diplomacy" entails not only combative words but aggressive actions that aroused the anger and reactions from other countries.[15]

> It is too early to tell whether "wolf-warrior diplomacy" represents the culmination of Chinese diplomacy's transition. As China faces growing external criticisms and demands for reparations over the Coronavirus, it is not inconceivable that Chinese leaders may rein in confrontational diplomacy to create an environment conducive to domestic reconstruction. In fact, wolf-warrior diplomacy is already hurting China's foreign policy, since it has generated pushback, such as Australia's calls for an independent probe into the Coronavirus' origins. China's soft power is weak globally; a belligerent approach will further damage China's global image.[16]

In the context of Beijing's relations with Hong Kong under British rule, assertive nationalism could be easily seen on the PRC side. As early as the outbreak of the PRC's Cultural Revolution, its spillover impacts on Hong Kong could be witnessed. Supporters of the Maoists went on the streets to confront the police in Hong Kong under British rule. The left-wing elites in the New China News Agency (NCNA), the de facto representative office of the PRC government in Hong Kong, were determined to stir up the local leftists in their violent confrontations with the police.[17] Assertive nationalism shaped Beijing's policy toward Hong Kong. A radical faction in the NCNA formulated and implemented the plan of mass protests and confrontation with the British Hong Kong police. After the Maoists broke into the British Embassy compound in Beijing on August 22, 1967, and launched an arson attack at an office of the British charge d'affaires, a moderate faction led by Premier Zhou Enlai in late June and early July 1967 twice persuaded the leftists not to attack the Burmese embassy in Beijing.[18] On August 23, Zhou criticized the rebels for attacking the British diplomatic mission in Beijing and challenged the Maoists on whether they wanted to take back Hong

---

12. Zhi Zhiqun, "Interpreting China's 'Wolf-Warrior Diplomacy,'" *Diplomacy*, March 15, 2020, accessed February 21, 2021.
13. Wang Hongying, "From 'Taoguang Yanghui' to 'Yousuo Zuowei': China's Engagement in Financial Multilateralism," CIGI Papers, no. 52 (December 2014): 1–10.
14. Zhi, "Interpreting China's 'Wolf-Warrior Diplomacy.'"
15. Zhi, "Interpreting China's Wolf-Warrior Diplomacy."
16. Zhi, "Interpreting China's Wolf-Warrior Diplomacy."
17. Gary Cheung Ka-wai, *Hong Kong Watershed: The 1967 Riots* (Hong Kong: Hong Kong University Press, 2009).
18. Gary Cheung, *Hong Kong Watershed*, 113–115.

Kong without consulting the CPP and Chairman Mao Zedong.[19] In early 1968, Zhou ordered the Hong Kong Maoist leaders, namely NCNA director Liang Weilin and deputy Qi Feng, to stop their riots, and he believed that maintaining the status quo was the best solution for breaking the PRC's diplomatic isolation by the West.[20] As a result, leftist leaders of the NCNA, including Liang Weilin and deputies Qi Feng and Liang Shangyuan, terminated their instigative activities in Hong Kong. The PRC's assertive nationalism resurfaced again from 1982 to 1984 when Beijing negotiated with Britain over the future of Hong Kong. Extensive propaganda conducted by the pro-Beijing media in Hong Kong sought to win the hearts and minds of the Hong Kong people, arguing that Hong Kong's sovereignty belonged to China, that the Opium War was humiliating to the Chinese people, and that the retrocession of the British colony to the PRC would be a historical moment of Chinese nationalism.[21]

After the HKSAR was established on July 1, 1997, mainland Chinese assertive nationalism has steadily risen in response to the changing political circumstances of Hong Kong. It reached an apex on June 30, 2020, when the national security law was approved by the NPC. In early July 2003, after half a million people protested, the decision of the HKSAR government under Chief Executive Tung Chee-hwa to postpone the enactment of Article 23 of the Basic Law—which bans acts of subversion, treason, secession, and sedition—led PRC authorities to believe that Hong Kong's society was not "patriotic" enough.[22] Compounding the 2003 mass protest against Article 23 was the emergence of an anti–national education campaign orchestrated by young students, such as Joshua Wong of Scholarism, in the summer of 2012 that eventually brought about the decision of the new C. Y. Leung government to shelve the national education policy and let local schools implement the national education policy or not.[23] Beijing was shocked by the extent of "unpatriotic" attitudes among some Hong Kong people. The success of the anti–national education campaign stimulated the rapid emergence of a localist movement, which culminated in its push for democratization in the form of the Umbrella Movement from September to December 2014.[24]

---

19. Gary Cheung, *Hong Kong Watershed*, 116.
20. Gary Cheung, *Hong Kong Watershed*, 127.
21. Chalmers Johnson, "The Mousetrapping of Hong Kong: A Game in Which Nobody Wins," *Asian Survey* 24, no. 9 (September 1984): 887–909.
22. Sonny Lo, *Hong Kong, 1 July 2003: Half a Million Protestors—The Security Law, Identity Politics, Democracy and China* (Toronto: Canadian Institute of International Affairs, 2004).
23. Klavier Wang Jie Ying, "Mobilizing Resources to the Square: Hong Kong's Anti-Moral and National Education Movement as a Precursor to the Umbrella Movement," *International Journal of Cultural Studies* 20, no. 2 (March 2017): 127–145.
24. Eric Chong King-man, "Student and Youth Activism: The New Youth Groups in Anti-National Education Policy and Occupy Central Movement," in *Interest Groups and the New Democracy Movement in Hong Kong*, ed. Sonny Shiu-Hing Lo (London: Routledge, 2018), 174–205.

The localists are those local Hong Kong people imbued with a very strong local identity and who have seen the influx of mainland tourists to the HKSAR as socially undesirable. In early 2016, a riot in Mong Kok was triggered by a dispute between localists and government officials dealing with hawkers, leading to violent confrontations between localists and the police. These confrontations alarmed the PRC authorities, who thought that the Hong Kong localists were radicals challenging the legitimacy of the HKSAR and central governments. On October 12, 2016, two young legislators-elect, Baggio Leung and Yau Wai-ching, used the term "Chee-na" and showed a banner saying that "Hong Kong is not China" in their oath-taking ceremony at the LegCo. Their behavior provoked the anger of PRC authorities, leading to the November 7th interpretation of the Basic Law's Article 104 by the SCNPC, which said that Hong Kong's legislators-elect must take the oath faithfully and solemnly. On November 15, the court disqualified Leung and Yau from becoming legislators.[25] The SCNPC interpretation represented an act of assertive Chinese nationalism over Hong Kong's radical localism. The eruption of the mass protests against an anti-extradition bill from June to December 2019 alarmed the PRC leaders and authorities, who firmly believed that the nationalistic sentiments of the Hong Kong people were weak and that the national security law would have to be formulated and implemented in mid-2020 to "rectify" the political development of the HKSAR.[26] As such, the PRC's assertive nationalism was reimposed onto the HKSAR in the form of enacting the national security law.

Mainland Chinese Legalism and Implications for Beijing–Hong Kong Relations

Chinese politics have been characterized by legalism that shapes the ways in which the PRC copes with legal reforms and political dissent. In the study of Hong Kong politics, scholars have neglected the political significance of Chinese legalism. Historically, Chinese legalist theorists such as Hanfei and Shang Yang emphasized the utilization of legal measures to strengthen the power of the state.[27] Hanfei advocated that a powerful ruler "should manipulate his subordinates by *fa* [law or rules of regulation] and *shu* [manipulative skills used by

---

25. Editorial, "Following the Basic Law Interpretation, the High Court's Ruling on Leung and Yau Makes People Happy," *Ta Kung Pao*, November 22, 2016, accessed February 21, 2021, http://www.takungpao.com.hk/paper/2016/1122/39949.html.
26. For the strong PRC reactions to the protests in 2019, see Sonny Shiu-Hing Lo, Steven Chung-Fun Hung, and Jeff Hai-Chi Loo, *The Dynamics of Peaceful and Violent Protests in Hong Kong: The Anti-Extradition Movement* (London: Palgrave Macmillan, 2020).
27. Hwang Kwang-Kuo, "Leadership Theory of Legalism and Its Function in Confucian Society," in *Leadership and Management in China: Philosophies, Theories, and Practices*, ed. Chen Chao-Chuan and Lee Yueh-Ting (Cambridge: Cambridge University Press, 2008), 108–142.

the rulers to control subordinates and achieve organizational objectives]".[28] According to Hanfei, the law was not only the standard of the people's behavior but also necessary to be publicized. He advocated the utilization of three main techniques, or *shu*, for a ruler to control and manipulate subordinates: namely (1) assigning competent talents to the right positions, (2) following up the projects and checking the results, and (3) evaluating contributions and rewarding performers accordingly.[29] In general, Chinese legalism has been traditionally characterized by the utilization of law as a governing instrument, the deployment of ruling tactics, and the empowerment of the ruling authorities. Chinese legalism represents the rule by law rather than the Western sense of the rule of law. Western legalism defends the rule of law and argues against the morality of law; nevertheless, Chinese legalism did not really separate morality from law.[30] The fidelity to law, from the perspective of Chinese legalism, was interpreted as the "fidelity to the monarch," which was different from the Western concept of the rule of law.

Peng Liu has argued that the Chinese cultural values of legalism have been combined with socialist and free market values in the PRC leadership.[31] He contended that the PRC leadership has been characterized by a mixture of legalism, socialism, and free market ideas. While Mao Zedong sought to reduce the influence of Confucianism, he adopted the socialist principle of serving the people. Deng Xiaoping combined technical competence with not only reform incrementalism but also the free market idea of stimulating the Chinese economic development.[32] Since Xi Jinping came to political power in the PRC in late 2012, China has been characterized by "the legalist position that new law-based approaches are needed" to deal with ethnic conflicts and maintain domestic stability.[33] New legalists who emerged in the PRC under the Xi Jinping era are "attempting to reshape ethnic-minority policy in order to break free from the everyday protean politics of ethnic relations that is based largely on a negative cycle of violent confrontation and financial compensation."[34]

Adam Tyson and Xinye Wu have argued that these new legalists include President Xi Jinping, Premier Li Keqiang and other members of the Politburo Standing Committee, such as Wang Huning and officials of the security

---

28. Hwang, "Leadership Theory of Legalism," 116.
29. Hwang, "Leadership Theory of Legalism," 120–122.
30. Peng He, "The Difference of Chinese Legalism and Western Legalism," *Frontiers of Law in China* 6 (2011): 645–669.
31. Peng Liu, "A Framework for Understanding Chinese Leadership: A Cultural Approach," *International Journal of Leadership in Education* 20, no. 6 (2017): 749–761.
32. Peng Liu, "A Framework for Understanding Chinese Leadership," 749–761.
33. Adam Tyson and Xinye Wu, "Ethnic Conflict and New Legalism in China," *Nationalism and Ethnic Politics* 23 (2016): 373–392.
34. Tyson and Wu, "Ethnic Conflict and New Legalism in China," 373.

apparatuses, notably former Minister of Public Security Guo Shengkun and the former Secretary of the CCP Committee of Politics and Law Meng Jianzhu.[35] These legalists believed that the CCP needs to "manage all types of conflicts in a consistent and impartial manner, without denying the reality that ethnic conflicts are highly emotive, politically charged issues that give rise to subterfuge, payoffs and trade-offs."[36] The legalists perceived that those ethnic unrests and conflicts were "below" the red line, and they must be handled in accordance with the rule of law. However, conflicts "above" the red line "require degrees of political intervention in the form of consultation, compromise, and compensation."[37] The new legalists in the PRC distinguish the conflicts below from those above the red line, adopting a legalistic position to deal with the former but intervening in the latter politically.

In the case of Hong Kong, the enactment of the national security law in June 2020 and its content demonstrate the legalist tradition of the PRC, whose national security was seen as being threatened by a series of protests in Hong Kong, ranging from the anti–Article 23 movement in mid-2003 to the anti–national education campaign in the summer of 2012 and from the Umbrella Movement in late 2014 to the anti-extradition protests from June to December 2019. The new Chinese legalism was shown in the SCNPC interpretation of Article 104 of the Basic Law in November 2016 over the provocative behavior of oath-taking by Baggio Leung and Yau Wai-ching. Moreover, if legalism is punctuated by the state's clarification and imposition of the political red lines into the target individuals and groups, then the speedy process in which the national security law was imposed in June 2020 and the obedient way in which the HKSAR government implements it have demonstrated the Chinese legalist practices and tradition. Under the Xi Jinping regime, the new legalists in the PRC have believed that the Hong Kong localist movements exceeded the red line of Beijing's tolerance, necessitating the center's decisive and swift intervention in the HKSAR.

Paternalism, Political Culture, and Leninism

The PRC's political tradition of paternalism has shaped how Beijing has been dealing with Hong Kong matters since July 1, 1997.[38] Lucian Pye had long emphasized how the Chinese rulers saw their subjects as sons and daughters under the tutelage, teaching, and supervision of their parents.[39] Since Chinese

---
35. Tyson and Wu, "Ethnic Conflict and New Legalism in China," 387.
36. Tyson and Wu, "Ethnic Conflict and New Legalism in China," 387.
37. Tyson and Wu, "Ethnic Conflict and New Legalism in China," 387.
38. Sonny Shiu-Hing Lo, *The Dynamics of Beijing–Hong Kong Relations: A Model for Taiwan?* (Hong Kong: Hong Kong University Press, 2008).
39. Lucian W. Pye, *The Spirit of Chinese Politics* (Cambridge, MA: Harvard University Press, 1992).

children tend to depend on their parents and suppress their aggressive instincts, dependency relations can be seen in how subjects see their rulers as protective parents.[40] Pye's findings were tested by other scholars who have studied paternalism in the PRC, where paternalistic leadership is composed of authoritarianism, benevolence, and moral leadership.[41] Authoritarianism in China has been shaped by Confucianism and legalism.[42] Confucianism emphasized virtuous rule, while legalism centers on the use of penalties and laws to enhance the power of rulers. The Chinese political culture, according to Pye, is paternalistic and stifles opposition. As he wrote: "Above all else citizens were taught that they should never be aggressive or demanding in their relations with public authorities; and officials were expected to be considerate and understanding of those who were docile and properly dependent."[43]

Pye identifies several features of Chinese political culture, features that can be applied in our study of Beijing's relations with the HKSAR. First, the Chinese political culture is characterized by "the supreme importance of consensus, conformity, and agreement [which] requires a standardized denial of conflicts and unresolved disagreements," although behind the scenes, there are tensions and factional conflicts.[44] The cultural need for conformity, according to Pye, has led to a "profound fear of *luan*, or disorder."[45] In other words, nonconformity must be rectified while stability prevails in Chinese politics. The PRC's intervention in Hong Kong matters after the SCNPC decision in November 2016 has become so prominent that the political conformity of Hongkongers is now a natural response to protect not only Beijing's national security but also themselves.

Second, code words and extensive use of symbolic language are essential for us to understand the Chinese political culture. These code words are used in communicating the sentiments of the ruling cadres and officials through the mass media. Other government officials can pick up these signals and demonstrate their support of the authorities by repeating these code words.[46] Moreover, symbolic language is used by PRC authorities to indicate their strategies and plans. The mix of code words and symbolic language in Beijing's new policy toward the HKSAR embraces words like "patriotism" and "patriots" and the need to protect the Chinese sovereignty and its developmental interest. During President Xi Jinping's visit to Hong Kong on July 1, 2022, he used the term "from

---

40. Pye, *The Spirit of Chinese Politics*, 102–106.
41. Wai Kwan Lau, Zhen Li, and John Okpara, "An Examination of Three-Way Interactions of Paternalistic Leadership in China," *Asia Pacific Business Review* 26, no. 1 (2020): 32–49.
42. Lau, Li, and Okpara, "An Examination of Three-Way Interactions," 32–49.
43. Pye, *The Spirit of Chinese Politics*, 19.
44. Pye, *The Spirit of Chinese Politics*, 197.
45. Pye, *The Spirit of Chinese Politics*, 198.
46. Pye, *The Spirit of Chinese Politics*, 202.

chaos to governance, and from governance to prosperity" to refer to Hong Kong's political development from 2020 to 2022.[47] Chaos took place in the HKSAR in the latter half of 2019, when massive protests against the extradition bill were launched, but governance was restored in Hong Kong once the national security law was implemented in late June 2020. The arrests and punishment of the law-offenders from July 2020 to June 2022 marked the implementation of the national security law by the law-enforcement authorities and the Hong Kong court. The victory of the former Secretary for Security John Lee in the May 2022 chief executive election marked the beginning of a new era during which the HKSAR is expected to integrate closely with the Greater Bay Area, to focus on housing and livelihood issues, to improve its governance continuously, and to bring about economic prosperity.

Third, contending groups and factions are the hallmark of Chinese political culture. Contending groups can develop as intraparty struggles without consensus on issues and policies, and their struggles are often along two lines.[48] Gradually, contending groups develop into factions in which the members share trust and loyalty while identifying common enemies and group security through their personal bonds of acquaintanceship, mutual belongings, and personal connections (*guanxi*).[49] Pye alerted us that Chinese politics operate in an oscillating way, shifting from centralization to decentralization and fluctuating from control (*shou*) to loosening (*fang*).[50]

These pendulums of centralization and decentralization and of control and loosening can be seen in Beijing's policy toward the HKSAR, including the relaxed phenomenon of PRC officials reaching a compromise with some Hong Kong democrats over a blueprint of political reform in May 2010 and the continuously tightened control over the HKSAR after the June–December 2019 protests against the extradition bill. The period from late 2016 to the present can be regarded as the *shou* (tightening or controlling) swing in the pendulum of Chinese politics over Hong Kong affairs.

Fourth, Pye stressed that Chinese politics were characterized by personalized power, namely power based on the scope of the influence of individuals.[51] Power can be transmitted through personal relationships and friendship or *guanxi*. *Guanxi*, to Pye, admits that the inferior can victimize the superior, but there is "much greater use of stratagems in creating feelings of responsibility and obligation on the one hand and indebtedness on the other."[52] The evolution of

---

47. *Wen Wei Po*, July 2, 2022, 1.
48. Pye, *The Spirit of Chinese Politics*, 210.
49. Pye, *The Spirit of Chinese Politics*, 207.
50. Pye, *The Spirit of Chinese Politics*, 209.
51. Pye, *The Spirit of Chinese Politics*, 224.
52. Pye, *The Spirit of Chinese Politics*, 217.

Beijing–Hong Kong relations shows that the PRC's "personalized power" has become prominent since the new LegCo elections in December 2021, when the "patriots" scored an overwhelming victory and when only one "democrat" named Tik Chi-yuen, a former member of the Democratic Party, was elected to the legislature. In the December 2023 District Council elections, members of the Democratic Party were also excluded as they failed to acquire sufficient nominations from the "patriotic" elites. If "patriots" ruling the HKSAR is the new political norm, then their *guanxi* with PRC authorities remains a political asset in the new politics of Beijing–Hong Kong relations.

Fifth, anti-intellectualism is another defining feature of the Chinese political culture. Pye argued that, in China, "there has been conscious and ruthless action by the political class against those with constructive skills who would have been prepared to a large degree to contribute to the building of a more advanced nation."[53] Both the KMT and the CCP, according to Pye, utilized intellectuals politically but struggled against them from time to time, especially the CCP that purged intellectuals through political campaigns in the 1950s and 1960s. Pye observed that "the hard core of political power [in China] has passed from one anti-intellectual political class to another," and that "the successive political classes have been surrounded by the ineffectual clamors of the enlightened, whether intellectuals or specialists, who have been persistently denied access to the realm of real decision making."[54] Although some intellectuals might gain access to the political class, they need to sacrifice their "moral principles" and "rationalistic outlook."[55] Pye pointed to the phenomenon of students and intellectuals injecting themselves "sometimes violently into Chinese public affairs and [this] caused great embarrassment to the political class."[56] Intellectuals have been nationalistic, but they have never been able to "shape the decisions of the nation."[57]

Pye's observations on the political predicament of intellectuals are relevant to the case of Beijing–Hong Kong relations. Hong Kong's intellectuals critical of the HKSAR government and PRC state have been politically marginalized. Local intellectuals participative in politics bear the risks of being excluded from the political class. Other intellectuals who wish to become part of the political class are expected to be loyalists of the HKSAR government and obedient followers of the PRC state.

Steve Tsang has argued that, after the death of PRC leader Deng Xiaoping, the CCP has been making the Leninist political machinery more resilient in dealing

---

53. Pye, *The Spirit of Chinese Politics*, 41.
54. Pye, *The Spirit of Chinese Politics*, 42.
55. Pye, *The Spirit of Chinese Politics*, 42.
56. Pye, *The Spirit of Chinese Politics*, 42.
57. Pye, *The Spirit of Chinese Politics*, 42.

with socio-political challenges.⁵⁸ There are five characteristics of "consultative Leninism," including an obsessive focus on the need to maintain power, continuous reforms designed to pre-empt mass demands for democratization, the sustained efforts at enhancing the CCP's capacity to respond to and lead public opinion, pragmatic economic and financial management, and the promotion of nationalism to replace Communism.⁵⁹ Such "consultative Leninism" has made China's political system resilient in meeting the challenges of economic crises. Most importantly, such political resilience is based on a "ruthless repressive capacity" and is strengthened by the CCP's ability to manipulate public opinion and to instill a sense of patriotism among its citizens. As a result, the CCP can deflect public discontent and consolidate its longevity. Leninism, according to Tsang, resorts to "large-scale repression very sparingly."⁶⁰

Paternalism and Leninism as twin elements of Chinese political culture constitute powerful drivers shaping Hong Kong's new political development. Specifically, paternalism was challenged by some Hong Kong people, especially those young ones, in the anti–national education campaign in 2012, the Occupy Central Movement in late 2014, the oath-taking saga in October and November 2016, and the anti-extradition movement in the latter half of 2019. In response to these challenges from the bottom, a top-down reaction in the form of asserting Leninism, namely the CCP leadership, had to be made. Some core leaders of the Occupy Central Movement were prosecuted and imprisoned for violating the law; Baggio Leung and Yau Wai-ching, whose behavior was deemed as exceeding Beijing's red line of political tolerance, were disqualified from becoming legislators-elect; and the violent protestors and active organizers of the 2019 anti-extradition protests were arrested and prosecuted. All these reactions demonstrate the mixture of Chinese paternalism and Leninism.

The Fear of Color Revolutions and Soviet-Style Collapse: Implications for Hong Kong

One of the most significant features of Chinese politics is the CCP's fear of color revolutions and a Soviet-style collapse. The PRC leaders like Jiang Zemin and Hu Jintao maintained a strong state in economic development.⁶¹ The CCP general secretaries, Jiang Zemin and later Hu Jintao, were both selected by Deng Xiaoping,

---

58. Steve Tsang, "Consultative Leninism: China's New Political Framework," *Journal of Contemporary China* 16, no. 62 (2009): 865–880.
59. Tsang, "Consultative Leninism," 865–880.
60. Tsang, "Consultative Leninism," 865–880.
61. Dali Yang, "China's Developmental Authoritarianism: Dynamics and Pitfalls," in *Routledge Handbook of Democratization in Asia*, ed. Tun-jen Cheng and Yun-han Chu (London: Routledge, 2017), 122–141.

and they all maintained the principle of the CCP's leadership in China's economic development. The CCP embarked on a mission to stimulate economic growth, producing employment and improving the people's livelihoods so that ordinary citizens would not challenge its rule. If legitimacy contains two aspects, namely procedures and performance, as Samuel Huntington had long argued,[62] the PRC under the leadership of Jiang Zemin and Hu Jintao from 1989 to 2012 focused on economic performance to win the hearts and minds of the Chinese people and to avoid a Soviet-style collapse. The long period of "developmental authoritarianism," as identified by Dali Yang, was not without any governing problems; there were dramatic increases in inequality, massive and rampant corruption, severe environmental degradation, and inefficiencies of state enterprises.[63] When Xi Jinping came to power in late 2012, he began to launch assertive anti-corruption campaigns, followed by the reforms of state enterprises, anti-poverty work, and an emphasis on sustainable development. Dali Yang argued that Xi Jinping "has become the standard bearer of a resurgent Chinese neo-authoritarianism," that he has concentrated power in his own hands, and that he has relied on a massive drive to curb corruption, tighten Party discipline, and check the influence of the rich oligarchs.[64] The dual objectives of Jiang, Hu, and Xi are the same: the CCP must maintain its rule and longevity and a Soviet-style collapse must be avoided at all costs.

It is under the context of the prevention of a Soviet-style collapse that we understand the dynamics of Beijing's policy toward Hong Kong, especially during the Xi Jinping era. While the PRC fears a Soviet-style collapse, some Hong Kong protest activists turned a blind eye to the CCP's profound trepidation. In the social media of the HKSAR, such as the Hong Kong Golden Forum, some netizens subjectively advanced their theory of the "China collapse" or *zhibao*, a phenomenon that could be seen in the period before and shortly after the anti-extradition protests in 2019.[65] In the discourse among online citizens, they subjectively popularized folk economics and naively predicted the imminent collapse of the PRC.[66] The *zhibao* discourse reflected how some Hong Kong people perceived the PRC's economic development. It became one of the central beliefs of Hong Kong's localism and mass opposition to the anti-extradition bill from June to December 2019.[67] Although some netizens tried to refute the theory

---

62. Samuel P. Huntington, *The Third Wave: Democratization in the Late Twentieth Century* (Norman: University of Oklahoma Press, 1991).
63. Yang, "China's Developmental Authoritarianism," 124.
64. Yang, "China's Developmental Authoritarianism," 134.
65. Yu Po-sang, "Citizen Curation and the Online Communication of Folk Economics: The China Collapse Theory in Hong Kong Social Media," *Media, Culture & Society* 42, no. 7–8 (2020): 1392–1409.
66. Yu, "Citizen Curation," 1392–1409.
67. Yu, "Citizen Curation," 1392–1409.

of the "China collapse" in social media, the upsurge in this popular belief among some localists was unwise and unfortunate, for the central authorities in Beijing saw such belief and the violent protests from June to December 2019 as strong evidence of attempts being made to not only overthrow the HKSAR government but also undermine Beijing's national security and sovereignty in Hong Kong.

The collapse of the former Soviet Union demonstrated the divergence of the developmental paths adopted by the leader of the Communist Party of the Soviet Union (CPSU), Mikhail Gorbachev, and by Deng Xiaoping. According to Sergei Guriev, Gorbachev did study the Chinese modernization and tried to implement China's agricultural and enterprises reforms.[68] Yet, Gorbachev's reforms were blocked by powerful vested interests. Moreover, Gorbachev's state capacity was weak vis-à-vis the powerful interest groups, which were determined to maintain the status quo. In China, however, the reformers still encounter numerous challenges, including the need for structural reforms, the problem of non-performing loans in state-owned banks, inefficiencies of state-owned enterprises, and a constant guard against a real estate bubble.[69] A glaring difference between Gorbachev and Deng Xiaoping was that while the former unleashed political reforms and liberalization that eventually resulted in the collapse of the CPSU, the latter and his successors, including Jiang Zemin, Hu Jintao, and Xi Jinping, have never undertaken political reforms. As such, the PRC learnt a genuine lesson from the Soviet experiences and is constantly keeping a tight lid on political reform and liberalization. Exactly because of the need to guard against political reform and liberalization, PRC authorities have seen some Hongkongers' push for a Western style of democratization along the lines of having both the chief executive and the entire LegCo elected as highly dangerous and "subversive."

The experience of the former Soviet Union in adopting "ethnoterritorial federalism" has been shunned by the PRC, according to Kimitaka Matsizato.[70] "Ethnoterritorial federalism" is defined as a phenomenon in which nationality groups were granted their administrative territories and subnational governments. While the former Soviet Union employed this practice to connect all the ethnic groups together under a centralized system, China imitated this system selectively and cautiously because of its concern about its "dangerous centrifugal tendency."[71] To apply Matsizato's analysis to Hong Kong, the HKSAR has remained an administrative territory created by the PRC government, which does not see the people of Hong Kong as an "ethnic" group. Most people living

---

68. Sergei Guriev, "Gorbachev versus Deng: A Review of Chris Miller's The Struggle to Save the Soviet Economy," *Journal of Economic Literature* 57, no. 1 (2019): 120–146.
69. Guriev, "Gorbachev versus Deng," 120–146.
70. Kimitaka Matsuzato, "The Rise and Fall of Ethnoterritorial Federalism: A Comparison of the Soviet Union (Russia), China, and India," *Europe-Asia Studies* 69, no. 7 (2017): 1047–1069.
71. Matsuzato, "The Rise and Fall of Ethnoterritorial Federalism," 1047–1069.

in Hong Kong and Macau are Chinese. The "one country, two systems" was designed by Deng Xiaoping and his advisers to woo the Republic of China (ROC) on Taiwan into its political orbit in the long run. Treating the people of Hong Kong as an "ethnic" group would imply a recognition that the Chinese in the HKSAR are like the ethnic minorities in Tibet and Xinjiang, where the ethnic Tibetans and Uighurs are given the official status of the "autonomous regions," different from Hong Kong and Macau.

Moreover, "ethnoterritorial federalism," as Matsizato has accurately observed, was discredited by the collapse of the Soviet Union. The PRC's unitary system persists, and the ruling CCP disallows the existence of an "ethnoterritorial federalism" that would stimulate ethnic nationalism and protests against the central government in Beijing. The CCP rejects federalism, which according to Matsizato refers to "a state formation in which subnational governments retain part of their sovereignty vis-à-vis the federal central government."[72] Due to Beijing's sensitivity to the loss of power of the central government, localities like Xinjiang and Tibet have been given the status of "autonomous regions," whose degree of autonomy is far more limited than the special administrative regions of Hong Kong and Macau. As Matsizato has recognized, "Fully fledged ethnoterritorial federalism [that] guaranteed the cultural development and social promotion of non-Russians in the Soviet Union and the Russian Federation [is] inconceivable in the PRC."[73] In short, China under CCP rule rejects "ethnoterritorial federalism" as a model of political reform for it can stimulate separatist tendencies among ethnic and sub-ethnic groups.

An important article written by Li Lifan in a journal published by the PRC Foreign Ministry in 2011 has been neglected by sinologists and Hong Kong scholars studying Beijing–Hong Kong relations.[74] The Rose Revolution in Georgia in 2003 and the Orange Revolution in Ukraine in 2004 provided the catalysts for PRC scholars to study the dynamics of "color revolutions." It was under this context that Li articulated his arguments that the Western non-governmental organizations (NGOs) trained pro-Western political forces in the name of human rights and democracy, that these NGOs became a tool of Western states to support political opposition and foster transformations in Central Europe and the Middle East, and that the Commonwealth of Independent States (CIS) region was plagued by eight types of NGOs. The eight types of Western-supported NGOs included religious organizations, humanitarian aid and development groups, private foundations, advisory and project-related organizations,

---

72. Matsuzato, "The Rise and Fall of Ethnoterritorial Federalism," 1047–1069.
73. Matsuzato, "The Rise and Fall of Ethnoterritorial Federalism," 1047–1069.
74. Li Lifan, "Evolution of Western NGOs in CIS States after the 'Color Revolution,'" *China International Studies* 29, no. 4 (July–August 2011): 158–170.

advocacy agencies, political think tanks, special associations, and self-help groups.[75] Li found that without organizational, staffing, and financial support from the West, these NGOs in CIS states could not have survived, even though their growth strategies became more practical and diversified. Since the eruption of "color revolution," Western states increased their economic support for the CIS states, including the back-up of NGOs to encourage the region's socio-economic and political integration with the Western system.[76] Many foundations were established to promote political transformations, such as the US-based Eurasia Foundation of Central Asia, the Technical Assistance of CIS, and the European Commission Human Aid Department. They provided economic and humanitarian aid and environmental and gender education and channeled budgets into various NGOs in the CIS region. Under the UN Millennium Development Goals, all these foundations and NGOs worked toward the objective of promoting the concept of Western "democracy" to CIS states. Moreover, a "Community of Democracies" was created in 2007 to support democratic regimes in the CIS region.[77] About 3,000 blogs were established in August 2007 to generate concerns and discourse on a multiplicity of issues in the CIS region, ranging from politics to education, from religion to history, and from economy to development.

Some CIS states reacted to the upsurge in NGOs and their internet blogs by intensifying control over them. Russia shut down many local branches of Western NGOs, believing that Western states utilized them to "overthrow" the Russian state and determining to "prevent the penetration and influence of Western powers."[78] Apart from monitoring Western NGOs, CIS states created their own youth organizations, namely the governmental NGOs, to counter the influence of Western NGOs and implement their own government's policies. Russia established a youth organization named Nashi after the color revolutions to stabilize the society and shape public opinion. Li found that, after the color revolutions, the momentum of Western NGOs' penetration into Central Asia weakened and their strategies became more localized and focused on the promotion of public awareness of democratization. In response to Western NGOs, the CIS states countered them by passing stricter internet laws, prohibiting them from publicizing their activities through the media, and advocating nationalism. Li concluded that with the number of Western NGOs growing at a steady rate, "it is very critical that people can distinguish angels from devils among the NGOs."[79]

The PRC has been deeply concerned about Western NGOs on the mainland and in the HKSAR. In April 2016, the PRC passed the Foreign NGO Law, saying

---

75. Li, "Evolution of Western NGOs in CIS States," 158–170.
76. Li, "Evolution of Western NGOs in CIS States," 158–170.
77. Li, "Evolution of Western NGOs in CIS States," 158–170.
78. Li, "Evolution of Western NGOs in CIS States," 158–170.
79. Li, "Evolution of Western NGOs in CIS States," 158–170.

that foreign NGOs must register with the Ministry of Public Security and that they can work in economics, education, environmental protection, and poverty relief, but they "must not endanger China's national security and societal public interest."[80] Nor can they engage in profitable, political, and religious activities. Moreover, foreign NGOs must be legally established overseas with activities for at least two years and be able to independently bear civil liability. The PRC government is keen to control the activities of foreign NGOs, preventing them from fostering political changes, as with the situation in CIS states. In Hong Kong where foreign NGOs were traditionally active, it is understandable that the PRC government was worried about their activities. By implementing the national security law for Hong Kong, these foreign NGOs can be brought under the deterrent umbrella of national security. Aside from the national security law, the HKSAR government in 2024 plans to legislate on Article 23 of the Basic Law and later a cybersecurity law—laws that will prevent Hong Kong from falling into the danger of any "color revolution."

In the context of Beijing–Hong Kong relations, PRC authorities are deeply concerned about the possibility that the HKSAR is used by foreign states to "subvert" the Hong Kong political system and to change the city into a Trojan horse that would have a boomerang effect on the mainland. If Hong Kong were used as a Trojan horse by foreign states, its political system would be democratized in a way that would make the HKSAR's ruling elites subservient to foreign countries rather than being a loyal servant of the central government in Beijing.[81] This mentality of PRC authorities is understandable in an authoritarian and a resilient Marxist-Leninist political system, especially under the circumstances in which the US has been actively attempting to promote the Western concept and universality of human rights and to foster democratic changes in the developing states of the world.

Resilient and Sustained Authoritarianism in China: Implications for Hong Kong

Xiao Gongqing has argued that the defining features of President Xi Jinping's regime are to mobilize the organizational resources of the CCP, to re-integrate the party and the government, to consolidate the recentralization of political leadership, to ban the discussion of universal values and separation of powers,

---

80. "Fact Sheet on China's Foreign NGO Law," November 1, 2017, accessed January 1, 2021, https://www.chinafile.com/ngo/latest/fact-sheet-chinas-foreign-ngo-law.
81. For the Trojan horse argument, see Sonny Shiu-Hing Lo, *Hong Kong's Indigenous Democracy: Origins, Evolution and Contentions* (London: Palgrave Macmillan, 2015).

and to curb the expansion of political activism of leftists and rightists.[82] At the same time, Xi and his subordinates do not return to the Maoist era, but they have created a Chinese dream aimed at realizing an affluent society (*xiaokang*) and national rejuvenation. What Xi Jinping calls "four comprehensives" includes the need for comprehensively deepening reforms, strengthening party discipline, implementing the rule of law, and realizing a well-off society. President Xi and his subordinates did not make any reference to establishing an egalitarian society through class struggle and the elimination of private ownership. This means that the Xi Jinping regime is not going to return to the Maoist emphasis on egalitarianism, which was Mao Zedong's socialist and communist objective.

President Xi's speech at the conference to commemorate the 200th anniversary of the birth of Karl Marx in May 2018 did not mention the elimination of private ownership. Nor did he talk about the class struggle that was the theme of Mao's emphasis from the 1950s to the 1960s. Instead, Xi stressed that globalization would continue and that the CCP would continue to deepen reforms. Hence, Marxism, according to Xiao, has been selectively "abandoned" by the PRC state under President Xi to achieve modernization, persist in pragmatic reforms, and accelerate the process of establishing an affluent society. However, what Xiao did not know during his writing in 2019 was that President Xi did emphasize the importance of "struggling" against the enemies in his remarks to the Party School in March 2021—evidence showing that the CCP is determined to struggle against its political foes.[83] In Hong Kong, the political enemies of the PRC had to be controlled through the enactment and implementation of the national security law.

While some sinologists have maintained that China's authoritarianism remains "resilient," political scientist Cheng Li has argued that such "authoritarian resilience" is stagnant.[84] Li argued that the corruption scandal of Bo Xilai, a Chongqing city party secretary who was convicted of bribery and abuse of power and sentenced to life imprisonment in 2013, revealed the problems of China's political system, including nepotism, patron-client connections in leadership selection, the elite's "contempt for the law," and the failure among competing factions to reach deals.[85] Li added that factions and interest groups have remained strong in the PRC. According to Li, factional checks and balances within the CCP, dynamic interest groups including the middle class, and China's

---

82. Xiao Gongqing, "China's Four Decades of Reforms: A View from Neo-Authoritarianism," *Man and the Economy* 6, no. 1 (2019): 1–7.
83. "Xi Jinping Mentions Struggles 14 Times in His New Speech at the Party School," March 3, 2021, accessed March 30, 2021, https://www.rfi.fr/tw/.
84. Cheng Li, "The End of the CCP's Resilient Authoritarianism? A Tripartite Assessment of Shifting Power in China," *China Quarterly*, no. 211 (September 2012): 595–623.
85. Li, "The End of the CCP's Resilient Authoritarianism?" 595–623.

rising status become the three factors that can be seized by the PRC leadership to undertake democratic reforms.[86] Li was perhaps over-optimistic at the time of his writing in mid-2012, for the events in Hong Kong, notably the NPC's imposition of the new national security law in late June 2020, proved that factionalism in China was dominated by the Xi Jinping faction, that interest groups checking and balancing the central leadership were weak, and that China's rising status had little to do with how it tackled domestic national security. The PRC has emphasized the importance of maintaining multilateralism in its foreign policy. In brief, China under President Xi is internally authoritarian but externally more liberal and multilateral.

In March 2018, the PRC constitution was amended; it repealed the term limit of the president, who previously could not serve more than two consecutive five-year terms.[87] The amendment was seen as a step forward along the path of "totalitarianism."[88] Commenting on the abolition of the presidential term limit, political scientist Pei Minxin has argued that "Xi cemented his political supremacy" amid elite criticisms of his policy direction and challenges to his power.[89] If factional politics remain the hallmark of Chinese politics, as the late Lucian Pye taught us, then the Xi faction became triumphant in the constitutional amendment in March 2018.

Even before Xi came to power, the Chinese media had traditionally sustained authoritarian rule in the PRC.[90] According to Daniela Stockmann and Mary Gallagher, the Chinese media have been contributing to regime legitimacy and effective rule by propagandizing the experiences of citizens in the legal system. But unlike the "mouthpieces" of other communist regimes, "the marketized media provide more convincing and sophisticated messages that continue to accord with state censorship demands while satisfying readers' interest in real-life stories and problems."[91] The media disseminated information in such a positive way that citizens found the legal system to be a useful channel of dispute resolution and rights protection. Public consciousness of the Chinese legal system was stimulated by the media, prompting them to seek legal reforms. Citizens who rely on the law to redress their grievances are not anti-regime.

---

86. Li, "The End of the CCP's Resilient Authoritarianism," 595–623.
87. Laney Zhang, "China: 2018 Constitutional Amendment Adopted," Global Legal Monitor, March 18, 2018, accessed January 3, 2021, https://www.loc.gov/item/global-legal-monitor/2018-05-18/china-2018-constitutional-amendment-adopted/.
88. Ken Suzuki, "China's New 'Xi Jinping's Constitution': The Road to Totalitarianism," November 27, 2018, accessed January 3, 2021, https://www.nippon.com/en/in-depth/a05803/.
89. Pei Minxin, "Xi Jinping's Dilemma: Back Down or Double Down," China Leadership Monitor, December 1, 2018, accessed January 3, 2021, https://www.prcleader.org/xi-s-dilemma.
90. Daniela Stockmann and Mary E. Gallagher, "Remote Control: How the Media Sustain Authoritarian Rule in China," Comparative Political Studies 44 no. 4 (2011): 436–467.
91. Stockmann and Gallagher, "Remote Control," 436–467.

Stockmann and Gallagher have concluded that the commercialized media can stabilize the CCP regime by portraying the legal system as positive. As a result, the CCP's resilience is a result of the increased sophistication of press coverage in the PRC.

In Hong Kong, the pro-Beijing media, including print, electronic, and social ones, are increasingly becoming the sophisticated mouthpieces of the PRC government's policy toward Hong Kong.[92] Since mid-2020, they have been mobilizing different sectors of the society, ranging from the civil service to business and from education to the youth, to support the central government's policies on the HKSAR. After President Xi delivered his speech in the HKSAR on July 1, 2022, civil servants, pro-Beijing interest groups, and secondary school principals were mobilized to study the content of his speech. The pro-Beijing media, such as *Ta Kung Pao* and *Wen Wei Po*, are increasingly sophisticated in the sense that they function not only as the propaganda machine of the government and Beijing but also as a check against the local government's maladministration by exposing policy problems and administrative malpractices. They continue to expose any scandals of the local democrats and provide a platform for pro-Beijing groups and individuals to voice their views in support of the government.

China's Strong State and Weak Society: Implications for Hong Kong

The literature on Chinese politics has discussed one of its main features, namely a strong state versus a relatively weak civil society. This defining feature of mainland Chinese politics has important implications for Hong Kong. Specifically, the assertive civil society of Hong Kong constituted a real national security threat to Beijing many years before the enactment of the national security law in late June 2020.

While authoritarian regimes like China have established government-organized non-governmental organizations (GONGOs) as "fake civil society organizations" to "stifle true dissent,"[93] the PRC's "consultative authoritarianism" has become more sophisticated in its control over civil society because "the decentralization of public welfare and the linkage of promotion to the delivery of

---

92. One of my former students who worked in a pro-Beijing media organization told me that 90 percent of his political desk was composed of mainlanders and that the staff members enjoyed "one dragon services" like buying cheap electric appliances and other daily necessities through the branch markets affiliated with the pro-Beijing Federation of Trade Unions. His political desk with twenty staff members was led by two mainland editors who assigned duties to reporters, a few of whom were asked to mobilize pro-Beijing clan groups to protest in front of the US Consulate during the anti-extradition movement in the latter half of 2019. Personal discussion with my former student, February 2021.
93. Erica Frantz, *Authoritarianism: What Everyone Needs to Know* (New York: Oxford University Press, 2018), 118–119.

these goods supported the idea of local government-civil society collaboration."[94] Jessica Teets has argued that some autonomy in the Chinese civil society does exist alongside with "indirect tools of state control."[95] The PRC state was concerned about the rise of protests and riots throughout the 2000s. The growing income gaps and unemployment among the migrant population and college graduates heightened the sensitivity of PRC policymakers, whose recent national budgets have showed more spending to maintain stability in the areas of public goods and social welfare. The ultimate political objective is to prevent the emergence of any "color revolution." The local state in China has become, to Teets, more regulatory and consultative through the state's guidance of sanctioned groups. Some degree of "officially tolerated social pluralism" persists.[96]

In the Hong Kong case, the increased state surveillance on local NGOs is natural and inevitable under the new national security law. Since mid-2020, Hong Kong's state-society relations have been mainlandized, although some social groups like business, charity, sports, and women ones are operating quite autonomously. The political red line in the HKSAR is that NGOs must not forge linkages with foreign groups and organizations—a stipulation mentioned in Article 23 of the Basic Law.

Gary King, Jennifer Pan, and Margaret Roberts have found that while censorship in China allows public criticism of the government, it has been silencing "collective expression."[97] Analyzing the content of millions of social media posts from nearly 1,400 different social media services all over China, they have observed that the Chinese government is able to find, evaluate, and remove from the internet that content it sees as objectionable and that such censorship curtails collective action by silencing comments that represent or trigger social mobilization.[98] Unlike the US, where social media are centralized through a few providers, the Chinese social media are fractured across hundreds of local sites. As such, the responsibility for censorship is devolved by the PRC government to the internet content providers, who can be fined or shut down if they fail to comply with government censorship guidelines.[99] To comply with the government's censorship requirements, in 2012, each individual site privately employed up to 1,000 censors. Moreover, between 20,000 and 50,000 internet police (*wang jing*) and internet monitors (*wang guanban*) and an estimated 250,000 to 300,000 "50

---

94. Jessica C. Teets, "Let Many Civil Societies Bloom: The Rise of Consultative Authoritarianism in China," *China Quarterly*, no. 213 (March 2013): 19–38.
95. Teets, "Let Many Civil Societies Bloom," 19–38.
96. Teets, "Let Many Civil Societies Bloom," 19–38.
97. Gary King, Jennifer Pan, and Margaret E. Roberts, "How Censorship in China Allows Government Criticism but Silences Collective Expression," *American Political Science Review* 107, no. 2 (May 2013): 326–343.
98. King, Pan, and Roberts, "How Censorship in China Allows Government Criticism," 326–343.
99. King, Pan, and Roberts, "How Censorship in China Allows Government Criticism," 326–343.

cent party members" (*wumao dang*) were recruited at the central, provincial, and local levels of government to participate in the massive censorship program.[100] King, Pan, and Roberts found that despite the widespread censorship of social media, the probability of censoring netizen criticisms did not increase. The aim of censorship was "to reduce the probability of collective action by clipping social ties whenever any collective movements are in evidence or expected."[101] They observed: "The evidence suggests that when the leadership allowed social media to flourish in the country, they also allowed the full range of expression of negative and positive comments about the state, its policies, and its leaders . . . [T]he Chinese people are individually free but collectively in chains."[102]

If authoritarian resilience is a hallmark of Chinese politics, its sophistication in the co-existence of internet control and criticisms cannot be neglected in Hong Kong, where social media utilized by protest activists to engage in cloud funding during the 2019 anti-extradition movement were either closed down by themselves or controlled effectively by the national security law.[103] In the December 2023 District Council elections, three people were arrested for illegally appealing to voters to refrain from voting.[104] In the new Hong Kong polity after the promulgation of the national security law, the social media are also expected to abide by the national security law and to refrain from being a tool used by any protest organizers to stir up "collective" action.

Andrew Mertha has argued that the Chinese policy-making process remains characterized by "fragmented authoritarianism" in which the actors, such as officials, groups, and the media, are increasingly pluralized and the barriers to entry have been lowered.[105] In February 2007, a "nail house" (*dingzi hu*) in Chongqing stood up in a place where the surrounding land had already been excavated, but the occupant Wu Ping and her husband had continued to stay in her house for three years to fight against local bureaucrats and a land developer who failed to compensate them in the process of negotiating their relocation. Wu's resistance to the government and the land developer came under the spotlight of local and international media. Under these circumstances, the local government in Chongqing was embarrassed and, together with the land developer, accelerated the negotiation for compensation and a relocation package acceptable to Wu and her husband. If fragmented authoritarianism involves incremental policy

---

100. King, Pan, and Roberts, "How Censorship in China Allows Government Criticism," 326–343.
101. King, Pan, and Roberts, "How Censorship in China Allows Government Criticism," 326–343.
102. King, Pan and Roberts, "How Censorship in China Allows Government Criticism," 326–343.
103. For the protestors' use of Facebook, Twitter, Instagram, Telegram, LIHKG, Signal, Twitch. Airdrop and HK.map.live, see Lo, Hung, and Loo, *The Dynamics of Peaceful and Violent Protests in Hong Kong: The Anti-Extradition Movement*, 106–107.
104. Radio Television Hong Kong (RTHK), December 11, 2023.
105. Andrew Mertha, "'Fragmented Authoritarianism 2.0': Political Pluralization in the Chinese Policy Process," *China Quarterly*, no. 200 (December 2009): 995–1012.

changes through bureaucratic bargaining, it is characterized by the entry of the media, journalists, local groups, and individual activists in the Chinese policy-making process. Mertha has concluded that the content of the Chinese policy-making process is increasingly "crowded" with the entry of various actors whose participation contributes to political "pluralization."

Although Hong Kong's polity remains more pluralistic than the mainland's, some democrats need to learn how to oppose and bargain with the local authoritarian regime in a more skillful way than before. If they oppose the central authorities, a loyal opposition has to be created to observe the center's red line of political tolerance. They need to give face to PRC officials, unlike the situation in 2015 when some of them stubbornly opposed the political reform model along the August 31, 2014, parameter delineated by Beijing.

Moreover, if the mainland's authoritarian system has its internally pluralistic aspect, then the sudden decision of Beijing in August 2021 to delay the implementation of the Anti-Sanctions Law in Appendix 3 of the Basic Law of Hong Kong and Macau showed that the pragmatists in the PRC leadership sometimes prevailed over the hardline conservative actors.[106] Specifically, the pragmatic leaders in Beijing did not want to see the negative impacts of the Anti-Sanctions Law on the status of the HKSAR as a financial and monetary center. If the Anti-Sanctions Law were implemented in Hong Kong, there would be a likelihood of cross-border legal cases concerning Article 12, which states that organizations and individuals cannot assist the sanctions adopted by foreign countries on China, and Article 14, which stipulates that any organization and individual who does not implement or conform to the Anti-Sanctions Law would be pursued for their legal responsibilities. Articles 12 and 14, if adopted, would trigger court cases that the central authorities were keen to avoid, while local and foreign bankers in the HKSAR expressed their deep concern about the application of the Anti-Sanctions Law. Due to the anxieties of local and foreign bankers, the central government decided to delay the law's implementation—a positive sign for the continuation of the "one country, two systems" in Hong Kong. Again, the political culture of face came into the picture. Even the pro-Beijing media in the HKSAR played down the incident, although the indefinite delay signaled a significant concession from both economic and political perspectives.

If the PRC is characterized by a strong state and relatively weak society, its authorities naturally saw Hong Kong's much assertive civil society and comparatively weak state years before June 2020 as an "abnormal" situation that should be changed. The 2019 anti-extradition protests constituted a turning point in the

---

106. For details, see Sonny Lo, "The Dynamics of Delaying Anti-Sanctions Law for Hong Kong," *Macau Business*, August 21, 2021, accessed July 25, 2022, https://www.macaubusiness.com/opinion-the-dynamics-of-delaying-anti-sanctions-law-for-hong-kong/.

psyche of PRC authorities, who believed that they had to buttress the relatively weak Hong Kong regime by empowering it with the new national security law in June 2020 and by installing a new electoral system in March 2021. Above all, the Hong Kong civil society, in the minds of PRC officials, had its violent or "uncivil" aspect that had to be controlled, tamed, and punished. As such, strengthening the HKSAR government and weakening the over-active civil society were the priorities of Beijing's policy toward the special administrative region from 2020 to 2022.

Critical and Participative Intellectuals as Potential Enemies of the State

Traditionally, intellectuals have been playing multiple roles in Chinese politics, stimulating the growth of nationalism, supporting the regime, opposing the government, and advising those ruling elites in power. The May Fourth Movement in 1919 witnessed the emergence of nationalistic intellectuals who yearned for a politically and militarily strong China in the midst of foreign imperialism.[107] The PRC during the Maoist era envisaged not only the mobilization of intellectuals to implement state policies, such as the Great Leap Forward Movement, but also their suppression if they criticized the CCP beyond the ruling party's red line, such as the Hundred Flowers Campaign.[108] Post-Mao China has witnessed at least several types of intellectuals: "reformers" like Yan Jiaqi, "radicals" like Fang Lizhi, "mouthpieces" like Liu Binyan, and "cultural iconoclasts" like Liu Xiaobo.[109]

From a securitization perspective, intellectuals may constitute a potential threat to the PRC regime. Based on the Copenhagen school of literature, securitization theorists have argued that security must be understood in terms of a "speech-act," meaning that security threats are identified through political arguments and discourse and that security practices are vulnerable to criticisms and transformations.[110] Under the perception of security threats, mainland intellectuals like Liu Xiaobo and his like-minded intellectuals in Hong Kong can be easily viewed as the enemies of the PRC party-state, especially if they took the action of attempting to change the form of the ruling regime.

Intellectuals, who can be referred as the group of intelligentsias "engaging in the practices of creation and criticism of that knowledge," can be divided broadly

---

107. Jerome B. Grieder, *Intellectuals and the State in Modern China: A Narrative History* (New York: Free Press, 1981).
108. Maurice Meisner, *Mao's China and After: A History of the People's Republic* (New York: Free Press, 1986).
109. Mok Ka-ho, *Intellectuals and the State in Post-Mao China* (New York: Macmillan 1998).
110. Michael C. Williams, "Words, Images, Enemies: Securitization and International Politics," *International Studies Quarterly*, no. 47 (2003): 511–531.

into three types.[111] The first type is coopted by the government, contributing their knowledge, skills, and expertise to better governance. The second type belongs to the critical intellectuals who maintain a distance from the state. Some of these critics verbally criticize the government without concrete action, while other critics may undertake action to seek to change the type of the regime. The third type is those participative intellectuals who engage in social and political participation, advocating their ideas and philosophies in the betterment of the society. While the first group of intellectuals is always the friend of the state, the last one often constitutes a security menace to the regime in power. The second group, namely critical intellectuals, can become a target of China's united front work. Yet, critical intellectuals can be the potential enemies of an authoritarian state if their remarks and actions go beyond the bottom line of political tolerance. In Hong Kong, while many intellectuals have been coopted by the HKSAR government and the PRC authorities, a minority has taken political action and acted like "organic intellectuals," to borrow the term from Antonio Gramsci.[112] These "organic intellectuals" tried to change the society and politics of Hong Kong through peaceful and/or violent means—activities that were naturally seen by the central authorities as politically "subversive." In short, while co-opted intellectuals remain the friends of the PRC's central state and the local state in the HKSAR, critical intellectuals are the targets of a united front, and participative intellectuals constitute the political foes, especially "organic intellectuals" who took action to "subvert" and "usurp" state power. The case of forty-seven political activists who launched a "primary election" in the summer of 2020 is a good example of "organic intellectuals" seeking to "subvert" the power of the local state in the HKSAR.

From the perspective of socialization, the PRC authorities regarded many intellectuals in the HKSAR as the educators who directly and indirectly inculcated a strong anti-mainlandization sentiment among the Hong Kong youth. As such, national security education and national education had to be implemented after the promulgation of the national security law in late June 2020, constituting a two-pronged strategy of re-educating the young students of Hong Kong and instilling a stronger sense of socio-political identity among them, especially as the young students of the HKSAR are expected to develop a more politically "patriotic" attitude toward their motherland and the ruling CCP. Since June 2020,

---

111. Darin David Barney, "The Role of Intellectuals in Contemporary Society," *Transforms: Insurgent Voices in Education* 1, no. 1 (1994): 89–105.
112. For a discussion of the "organic intellectuals" in the HKSAR during the anti–national education campaign in the summer of 2012, the Occupy Central movement in 2014, and the rapid rise of localists from 2014 to 2016, see Sonny Shiu-Hing Lo, "Interest Groups, Intellectuals and New Democracy Movement In Hong Kong," in *Interest Groups and the New Democracy Movement in Hong Kong*, ed. Sonny Shiu-Hing Lo (London: Routledge, 2018), 1–14.

national security education and national education have been implemented in a comprehensive manner at the levels of kindergartens, primary and secondary schools, and tertiary institutions.[113] In short, national security education is combined with national education to instill a greater sense of socio-political patriotism into Hong Kong students toward the PRC, neutralizing and reversing the impacts of the educational efforts made by the critical intellectuals in the HKSAR from 1997 to 2019. The elite and political cultures of some Hong Kong people have to be transformed, from Beijing's perspective, from being critical and action-oriented actors to loyal and "patriotic" citizens supportive of the PRC.

The Drift toward "Neo-Totalitarianism"

Political scientist David Shambaugh has remarked that "Xi Jinping has proven to be a very anti-liberal leader" characterized by "personalization and centralization of control," and that he "has intensified repression evident since 2009."[114] Writing in 2016, Shambaugh argued that "China is today more repressive than at any time since the post-Tiananmen (1989–1992) period."[115] While Shambaugh has not seen the possibility of "the China collapse thesis," he has argued that the PRC is moving toward a process of "political atrophy and decline" in the coming decades.[116] He outlines three scenarios for the PRC's political development. At one extreme, China is moving toward "neo-totalitarianism," which to Shambaugh is by no means a positive pathway. This scenario would be triggered by the failure of "hard authoritarianism" to deliver reforms and achieve social stability. The hardline conservative leaders, according to Shambaugh, would push to close the PRC's doors to the outside and reinstall draconian control measures domestically. But this scenario would not be feasible because the Chinese economy has already been globalized. Furthermore, Shambaugh predicted that citizens would "revolt," while the party and military would likely be split into factions.

It is doubtful whether "neo-totalitarianism" would lead to the PRC's political decline. With the benefit of hindsight, Shambaugh's first scenario of "neo-totalitarianism" appears to emerge in China, but he was partially accurate in his analyses. The case of Hong Kong seems to confirm the PRC's drift toward "neo-totalitarianism," for the Hong Kong protest activists in the 2019 anti–extradition bill movement were arrested, prosecuted, and imprisoned after the enactment of the national security law in late June 2020. However, the drift toward

---

113. For details, see Sonny Shiu-hing Lo and Steven Chung-fun Hung, *The Politics of Education Reform in China's Hong Kong* (London: Routledge, 2022).
114. David Shambaugh, "Contemplating China's Future," *The Washington Quarterly* 39, no. 3 (2016): 121–130.
115. Shambaugh, "Contemplating China's Future," 121–130.
116. Shambaugh, "Contemplating China's Future," 121–130.

"neo-totalitarianism" in the PRC has been partly driven by the outbreak of COVID-19 in early 2020, which made the CCP regime tighten its control over the society on the mainland. As such, the drift toward "neo-totalitarianism" was not, as Shambaugh mentioned, driven by the failure of "hard authoritarianism" to deliver reforms but by the sudden outbreak of COVID-19 in early 2020 and the persistence of the variants of COVID-19, such as Omicron, in the early half of 2022. If China has drifted toward "neo-totalitarianism," its leaders have been deeply concerned about the likelihood that Hong Kong would become a Trojan horse in which foreign forces attempt to support the Hong Kong democrats and protestors, especially in the anti-extradition movement in the latter half of 2019, to "overthrow" the HKSAR government and to "subvert" the mainland.

Yet, the scenario of "neo-totalitarianism" in the PRC has been accompanied by a continuously open-door policy, embracing economic liberalization but tightening political control over the societies of the mainland and Hong Kong. The party and the military have not developed into factions explicitly struggling for power, even though there were reports that the Xi Jinping faction in mid-2022 reached a balance of power with the Li Keqiang faction and that Xi had to rely on anti-corruption to purge some miliary leaders.[117] The People's Liberation Army (PLA) has been characterized by its adherence to the CCP leadership, as stressed by President Xi Jinping who is also the chairman of the Central Military Commission.

The second scenario mentioned by Shambaugh is that attempts at recentralizing the state power in economic reforms would be difficult because once the door of economic modernization was opened, it could not be easily closed. This scenario is applicable to the PRC economy, which remains relatively open, while the Xi Jinping regime has been emphasizing multilateralism in its external economic relations with other countries in the world. As such, the PRC under Xi Jinping is externally multilateral and economically pragmatic but internally "neo-totalitarianism," mainly due to its adherence to the "dynamic zero-COVID policy," which aims to contain the spread of COVID-19 and minimize the number of infected citizens and deaths as far as possible.

Shambaugh has mentioned a third scenario in which the PRC would stay on the authoritarian track, but it would loosen its societal control and liberalize civic life and the political system. This path of "soft authoritarianism" would be a return to the period from 1998 to 2008, when Jiang Zemin and Hu Jintao were the presidents. Under liberalization, the political space for the media, non-governmental organizations, intellectuals, dissent, and social discourse would be enhanced. Shambaugh has added that if this path were pursued, then China

---

117. "Li Keqiang Going South, Xi Jinping Going North: What Signals Are Released?" Yahoo News, August 18, 2022, accessed August 21, 2022, https://tw.news.yahoo.com/.

would perhaps follow the footsteps of some East Asian states in either democratizing its political system gradually, like South Korea and Taiwan, or retaining the features of "soft authoritarianism," like Singapore.

Shambaugh's scenario of "neo-totalitarianism" has been deployed by Xiaoguang Kang to refer to "the administrative absorption of society" in the PRC.[118] Kang has argued that China's "neo-totalitarianism" is characterized by state capitalism, unlimited government, the adherence to Leninism, and a mixed ideology of Marxism and Confucianism and that it strengthens the administrative absorption of the society, including the non-profit sector where laws and policies are tight, such as through the enactment of the Charity Law in 2016. Like Kang, Jean-Philippe Beja has identified the PRC's drift from authoritarianism to "neo-totalitarianism."[119] He observed that by the end of 2015, workers' organizers were submitted to the same treatment as human rights defense lawyers because there was a pattern of arrest, detention, and televised self-criticism where activists acknowledged that they had been used by "hostile foreign forces" to subvert China's socialist regime.[120]

The immediate impacts of China's "neo-totalitarianism" on the HKSAR have been significant. The national security law was imposed on the HKSAR in late June 2020. Under the new law, the PRC authorities have already installed a national security apparatus composed of the police and the legal authorities, who have increasingly become politically and legally powerful. From 2020 to 2023, the arrests, prosecution, and imprisonment of many protest activists involved in the 2019 protests pointed to a trend of how China's "neo-totalitarian" drift made the HKSAR administration tighten its control over the society. From the statist perspective, however, the national security law contributes immensely to the stability and order of the HKSAR. If authoritarianism has diffusion effects from one place to another, the same phenomenon can be seen in Beijing–Hong Kong relations.

The Politics of Authoritarian Diffusion: New Beijing–Hong Kong Relations

Charles Ziegler has found that authoritarian regimes could have diffusion impacts on other states, as with the case in Central Asia.[121] The Central Asian

---

118. Xiaoguang Kang, "Moving toward Neo-Totalitarianism: A Political-Sociological Analysis of the Evolution of Administrative Absorption of Society in China," *Nonprofit Policy Forum* 9, no. 1 (2018): 1–8.
119. Jean-Philippe Beja, "Xi Jinping's China: On the Road to Neo-totalitarianism," *Social Research* 86, no. 1 (Spring 2019): 203–230.
120. Beja, "Xi Jinping's China: On the Road to Neo-totalitarianism," 203–230.
121. Charles E. Ziegler, "Great Powers, Civil Society and Authoritarian Diffusion in Central Asia," *Central Asian Survey* 35, no. 4 (2016): 549–569.

states are characterized by authoritarian persistence, such as the cases of Kazakhstan, Kyrgyzstan, and Tajikistan. Western programs supportive of liberal democracy and civil society encountered resistance from authoritarian leaders in Central Asia. Ziegler has observed that a process of "indirect authoritarian diffusion, in combination with the region's illiberal societies and Western democracy promotion fatigue, undermines the development of civil society and makes authoritarian persistence in Central Asia likely."[122] This indirect impact of authoritarian diffusion in Central Asia was attributable to "the neighborhood effect—the models of Russia and China, which are actively resisting democracy promotion and foreign assistance to their struggling civil societies."[123] Central Asian political cultures and elites are more receptive to authoritarian governance than to the pluralistic nature of liberal democracy. Civil society activists occasionally score victories, but the geopolitical atmosphere favors authoritarian persistence. The clash between a liberal democratic approach to civil society and a more statist perspective on Central Asia is a discourse shaped by the Russian and Chinese authoritarian practices. This authoritarian discourse fits into the experiences and political philosophy of Central Asian leaders. While Kazakhstan and Kyrgyzstan have articulated elements of the Western discourse on liberal democracy and civil society, other Central Asian states like Tajikistan have far less tolerance of the civil society in view of the threat of Taliban resurgence in neighboring Afghanistan. Each Central Asian state has used authoritarian practices to reinforce its control of the society, emulating the Russian example of strongman rule, but "there is only mixed evidence that Moscow is effectively promoting its model in Central Asia."[124] As such, Central Asian states have shown "indirect authoritarian diffusion."

Roman-Gabriel Olar has studied authoritarian diffusion in the Middle East and Latin America, where "state repression and authoritarian interdependence" have been understudied.[125] He argues that "the high costs of repression and its uncertain effect on dissent determine autocracies to adjust their levels of repression based on information and knowledge obtained from their peers."[126] Furthermore, "autocracies' own experiences with repression can offer optimal and incomplete information," while repression techniques from other autocracies "augment the decision-making regarding optimal levels of repression for political survival."[127] Autocracies adjust their levels of repression based on

---

122. Ziegler, "Great Powers, Civil Society and Authoritarian Diffusion in Central Asia," 549–569.
123. Ziegler, "Great Powers, Civil Society and Authoritarian Diffusion in Central Asia," 549–569.
124. Ziegler, "Great Powers, Civil Society and Authoritarian Diffusion in Central Asia," 549–569.
125. Roman-Gabriel Olar, "Do They Know Something We Don't? Diffusion of Repression in Authoritarian Regimes," *Journal of Peace Research* 56, no. 5 (2019): 667–681.
126. Olar, "Do They Know Something We Don't?" 667–681.
127. Olar, "Do They Know Something We Don't?" 667–681.

observed levels of repression in their like-minded regimes. This means that authoritarian regimes can learn from regimes with which they share similar institutions. In short, there is "a strong diffusion effect between institutionally similar regimes."[128]

The insights from Ziegler and Olar have implications for Beijing–Hong Kong relations. First, the PRC as either an authoritarian or a neo-totalitarian regime had a direct rather than "indirect" diffusion impact on the HKSAR, unlike what Ziegler has mentioned in the case of Central Asia. However, Zeigler's observation of the "neighboring" impact of a giant state, like Russia, on Central Asian states is applicable to Hong Kong, which is under the tremendous political influence of its motherland, the PRC. Olar's argument that autocracies can learn from other like-minded regimes does have implications for Hong Kong, which before the enactment of the national security law in June 2020 was arguably a "soft" authoritarian state with occasional repression of dissent. Hong Kong has changed since mid-2020 to a much "harder" authoritarian regime with far more visible and frequent control of dissent, including the arrest and prosecution of the 2019 protest activists and other measures, such as a revamp of the electoral system in March 2021. In brief, the PRC does have an authoritarian diffusion impact on Hong Kong's political system, especially since the imposition of the national security law in late June 2020. Geopolitically speaking, China remains a giant state whose political change and culture have tremendous and direct impacts on Hong Kong's political development.

In a sense, the PRC's political influence on Hong Kong is like Venezuela's diffusion impacts on other Latin American states. Carlos de la Torre has studied the mechanisms of influence, learning, and emulation used by Hugo Chavez to diffuse the Bolivian model of governance across Latin America.[129] Chávez promoted what he depicted as a superior model of a populist transformation by emphasizing constitutional revisions, heavy state intervention in the economy, and anti-imperialism. Chavez's model was emulated by nations like Bolivia and Ecuador that experienced crises of political parties and institutions, but it was not followed by nations where political parties and democratic institutions remained functioning and where the civil society cherished democracy, pluralism, and liberal rights. The high prices of oil allowed Chávez to increase his influence by expanding networks of patronage and trade and by supporting and financing presidential candidates, parties, and social movements in Latin America and the Caribbean. Torre concluded that Chávez was at the apex of his popularity and regional and global influence in the mid-2000s and that the spread of Bolivarian

---

128. Olar, "Do They Know Something We Don't?" 667–681.
129. Carlos de la Torre, "Hugo Chávez and the Diffusion of Bolivarianism," *Democratization* 24, no. 7 (2017): 1271–1288.

populism had anti-democratic repercussions as both a deterrent and a model. The likelihood of a Bolivarian revolution prompted Honduran politicians and the army to remove Manuel Zelaya from office with a coup d'état.[130] In nations where Bolivarian ideologies and strategies were adopted, as in Ecuador, the result was an erosion of democracy toward authoritarianism.

The Bolivian diffusion of authoritarianism has implications for Beijing–Hong Kong relations. If the PRC regime is authoritarian, then its diffusion on the HKSAR can be seen, especially during the Carrie Lam administration whose practices and approaches to dealing with political dissent hardened after the enactment of the national security law in late June 2020. Bolivia's oil resources could dispense its political patronage easily in some Latin American states under its sphere of geopolitical influence, while the PRC has been utilizing the Greater Bay Area (GBA) as a region of enticing the economic support and encouraging socio-economic interactions between Hong Kong and South China—a process of economic integration that accelerates the HKSAR's identity transformation. The PRC's economic patronage of Hong Kong's business elites is combined with the HKSAR's economic integration with the GBA, thereby diluting the Hong Kong identity and mixing it with the mainland identity. Authoritarian diffusion of PRC political practices into the HKSAR has been accompanied by a corresponding process of integrating Hong Kong economically and socially into South China. After all, The HKSAR regime changed the electoral systems for LegCo in 2022 and District Councils in 2023 to benefit the "patriotic" elites—another patronage system parallel to the mainland authoritarian practices.

Hong Kong's economic integration and cooperation with the PRC is similar to how Turkey collaborates with China economically. Gozde Yilmaz and Nilgun Elikucuk Yildirim have argued that Turkey's engagement with the PRC has been characterized by authoritarian cooperation extending beyond the regional backyards of the authoritarian gravity centers and focusing on politico-economic benefits and by interest-driven rather than ideological motivation without an active or intentional autocracy promotion.[131] Hong Kong's integration with China is parallel to how Turkey cooperates with the PRC closely. The case of Sino-Turkish economic cooperation shows that both states are keen to counter the Western pressure for democratization and to strengthen the regime domestically. In this aspect, Hong Kong is similar to Turkey as the ruling authorities of the PRC and HKSAR are keen to resist the Western pressure for democratization and the US-led sanctions against some mainland Chinese and Hong Kong officials for their "responsibility" of imposing and implementing the national security law in

---

130. Torre, "Hugo Chávez and the Diffusion of Bolivarianism," 1271–1288.
131. Gozde Yilmaz and Nilgun Elikucuk Yildirim, "Authoritarian Diffusion or Cooperation? Turkey's Emerging Engagement with China," *Democratization* 27, no. 7 (2020): 1202–1220.

the HKSAR. Gozde and Yildirim have found that infrastructure-driven development policy is an important subset of authoritarian cooperation between Turkey and China. In Hong Kong, infrastructure projects have been playing a crucial role in Hong Kong's socio-economic integration with the mainland, including the completion of the West Rail line and West Kowloon Railway Station in September 2018 and the completion of the Hong Kong–Macau–Zhuhai bridge in October 2018.

Aron Buzogany has found that Hungary's slide into illiberalism was not inspired by Russia under Vladimir Putin.[132] Since 2010, Hungary has undergone political changes and constitutional reforms under the leadership of Prime Minister Viktor Orbán. Its "Eastern opening" policy in the analytical framework of authoritarian diffusion and learning from Russia is important. The Russo-Hungarian relations since 2010 have revealed how Hungary has developed an interest-based policy, which was framed in vague references to ideological affinity with authoritarian regimes. Hungary's interests include energy relations, trade, and balancing the pressure from the European Union (EU), while Russia maintains leverage over the EU through its closer cooperation with Hungary. Hungary as "the receiver state" has been seeing economic cooperation more as conforming with its interests than as a diffusion from "the sender state." Buzogany has challenged the academic assumption that the sender state ideologically diffuses its authoritarian system to the receiver state. The unique interest-based relations between Hungary and Russia are also applicable to Hong Kong's relations with mainland China. It is in Hong Kong's economic interest to interact and integrate with the Greater Bay Area and the mainland, where the vast physical space and technological knowhow can help Hong Kong enhance its economic competitiveness. Economic integration between Hong Kong and the mainland is naturally accompanied by the authoritarian diffusion from the PRC's political practices and correctness onto the HKSAR.

Ahmet Kuru has found that rentier states in Muslim countries that possess oil, gas, and mineral resources can have authoritarian diffusion effects on other states.[133] He argues that the rulers of rentier states do not financially depend on taxation and that the people cannot use taxation as a leverage to make rulers accountable. People in rentier states are dependent on governmental allocation of rent revenue, creating a patron-client relationship and a lack of independent political, economic, and civil society. The means of regional diffusion are mostly the deliberate state policies of using the military, diplomacy, finance, and

---

132. Aron Buzogany, "Illiberal Democracy in Hungary: Authoritarian Diffusion or Domestic Causation?" *Democratization* 24, no. 7 (2017): 1307–1325.
133. Ahmet T. Kuru, "Authoritarianism and Democracy in Muslim Countries: Rentier States and Regional Diffusion," *Political Science Quarterly* 129, no. 3 (2014): 399–427.

propaganda. According to Kuru, Islamists are the main opposition forces in the Arab states, and they have expressed various levels of anti-Westernism—a phenomenon explaining why Western governments did not sufficiently support the Arab uprisings. Although the US and EU countries mostly supported democratization in other regions, especially Latin America and Eastern Europe in the 1980s and 1990s, they have preferred to work with autocrats in the Middle East because of their priorities of protecting Israel, stabilizing the oil supply, avoiding Islamist regimes, and fighting terrorism.[134] As such, the Western linkage cannot propel democratization in the Middle East. Instead, a rapprochement between Arab Islamists and Western countries on a shared democratic vision could create a new regional wave of democratization in the Middle East.

In Hong Kong, the PRC is a "rentier" state that possesses tremendous resources, while the HKSAR must rely on the mainland for the supply of water, food, electricity, tourists, and increasingly, talents, especially as many local people emigrated to other countries from the early half of 2020 to 2023. Hong Kong's natural dependence on the mainland has made it politically vulnerable. Moreover, the anti-Westernism of PRC leaders and officials responsible for Hong Kong have already made the mainland's diffusion impacts on the HKSAR more easy, much more profound, and deeply penetrative. After COVID-19 and its variants faded away in greater China in March 2023, more Hong Kong people have flocked into the Greater Bay Area every weekend, with almost 500,000 people crossing the Shenzhen border in a weekend in December 2023. If China as the rentier state provides tremendous space for the spending, consumption, and leisure of Hong Kong people, the HKSAR's dependence on the mainland has been deepening.

The literature on authoritarian diffusion has implications for the study of Beijing–Hong Kong relations. Regardless of whether China since 2012 has remained authoritarian or shifted to "neo-totalitarianism," its authoritarian diffusion into the HKSAR has become far more prominent than ever before, especially after the enactment of the national security law in late June 2020. If China has gradually shifted from authoritarianism to "neo-totalitarianism" since late 2012, its systemic change has made the HKSAR move from "soft" authoritarianism—occasional repression of dissidents—to "hard" authoritarianism—more frequent and decisive suppression of dissidents. It can also be argued that China's authoritarian diffusion was necessary because the anti-PRC movement in the latter half of 2019 plunged Beijing's national security into an unprecedented crisis in the HKSAR. As such, China's authoritarian diffusion into Hong Kong was a must from the perspective of protecting the central government's national security.

---

134. Kuru, "Authoritarianism and Democracy in Muslim Countries," 399–427.

The PRC: An External and Increasingly Internal Actor of Hong Kong Politics

The academic literature on the role of external actors in democratization can be applied to our deeper understanding of Beijing–Hong Kong relations. Sergiu Buscaneanu has studied the external dimension of democratization by focusing on the role of the European Union (EU).[135] He argued that prior to the 1990s, the studies of democratization were mostly concerned with domestic factors, such as economic development and the complex bargaining practices between the ruling elites and the opposition that facilitated the transition to democratization. The literature in the field of international relations was largely uninterested in the topic of democratization. Hence, a renewed emphasis on the role of external actors in democracy promotion, such as the EU, and in the stabilization and democratization in Central and Eastern Europe was significant. Buscaneanu's insights are relevant to our study of Beijing–Hong Kong relations because China can often be regarded as an "external" actor shaping Hong Kong's domestic politics. However, after July 1, 1997, China has increasingly become an internal actor shaping the political development of the HKSAR due to its exercise of sovereignty over the city.

Bruce Gilley has explored the impacts of the US on democratization in the Middle East.[136] In view of the rapid political change in the Middle East from 2010 to 2012, Gilley found that the US policies under President George W. Bush between 2001 and 2008 were limited, but the American emphasis on the Freedom Agenda had significant impacts on the provision of catalysts to domestic pro-democracy forces unexpectedly. According to Gilley, the Bush Freedom Agenda weakened authoritarian regimes and strengthened their opponents, thereby helping to create conditions for democratic openings. Gilley concluded that while the standard tools of democracy promotion—democracy aid, public diplomacy, and norm diffusion—were usually assumed to operate through emulation, the reality was more about the mobilization of people to fight for their civil liberties and push for political liberalization.

While Buscaneanu and Gilley have seen the external actors as positive, Jakob Tolstrup has regarded it as having both positive and negative impacts on the targeted states.[137] Tolstrup has argued that the literature on political transition and democratization had long been dominated by internal explanatory

---

135. Sergiu Buscaneanu, *Regime Dynamics in EU's Eastern Neighborhood: EU Democracy Promotion, International Influences, and Domestic Contexts* (Switzerland: Springer, 2016), 15–42.
136. Bruce Gilley, "Did Bush Democratize the Middle East? The Effects of External-Internal Linkages," *Political Science Quarterly* 128, no. 4 (2013–2014): 653–685.
137. Jakob Tolstrup, "Studying a Negative External Actor: Russia's Management of Stability and Instability in the 'Near Abroad,'" *Democratization* 16, no. 5 (2009): 922–944.

factors, such as economic performance, civil society, and institutional change—a reflection of Western bias. External actors need to be reconsidered in a more in-depth manner. He contends that Russia's foreign policy in the "Near Abroad" or post-Soviet region was underestimated. Specifically, Russia has direct and indirect negative impacts on the region's political liberalization and democratization. It bolstered the authoritarian regime in Belarus, subverted the democratizing regime in Ukraine, and promoted authoritarian norms regionally through the Shanghai Cooperation Organization. Tolstrup has found that the positive influences of the EU, US, and North Atlantic Treaty Organization (NATO) in the former Soviet republics were counter-balanced and "crowded out" by Russia's negative influences.[138]

Tolstrup has developed his arguments based on the analytical framework designed by Steven Levitsky and Lucan Way.[139] Levitsky and Way emphasized the role of linkages and leverage in the process of democratic change. They wrote:

> Linkages to the West—in the form of cultural and media influence, elite networks, demonstration effects, and direct pressure from Western governments—appear to have raised the costs of authoritarian entrenchment, making the democratization of competitive authoritarian regimes more likely. Where Western linkages were weaker, or where alternative, nondemocratic hegemons (such as Russia and China) exerted substantial influence, competitive authoritarian regimes were more likely either to persist or to move in a more authoritarian direction.[140]

Levitsky and Way have elaborated on the role of linkage and leverage in democratization. They have observed: "When local politicians, technocrats, and business leaders do not expect their government's undemocratic behavior to put their ties to the West at risk, they have less of an incentive to oppose such behavior."[141]

Tolstrup has articulated the concept of gatekeeper elites to enrich our understanding of the roles of linkage and leverage in democratization. He argues that Levitsky and Way's arguments for the primacy of structures are not valid. According to Tolstrup, domestic elites cannot be seen as the objects of external influences. Rather, domestic elites act like gatekeepers holding the key to turn the volume of any external actor's pressure up or down.[142] While Levitsky and Way have proposed that the degree to which Western external actors succeed in

---

138. Tolstrup, "Studying a Negative External Actor," 922–944.
139. Jakob Tolstrup, "When Can External Actors Influence Democratization? Leverage, Linkages, and Gatekeeper Elites," *Democratization* 20, no. 4 (2013): 716–742.
140. Steven Levitsky and Lucan Way, "Elections without Democracy: The Rise of Competitive Authoritarianism," *Journal of Democracy* 13, no. 2 (April 2002): 51–65, especially 60.
141. Steven Levitsky and Lucan Way, "The New Competitive Authoritarianism," *Journal of Democracy* 31, no. 1 (January 2020): 51–65, especially 53–54.
142. Tolstrup, "When Can External Actors Influence Democratization?" 716–742.

promoting democracy in other countries is shaped by leverage (the vulnerability of the targeted states to the external pressure) and linkages (the density of ties between the external actor and the targeted state), Tolstrup has added the notion of gatekeeper elites, who have veto power over the influences of leverage and linkages. Three types of gatekeeper elites are important: political elites, economic elites, and civil society elites. Economic elites are often close to governments, while civil society groups often turn into political parties. The ruling political elites are different from the oppositional elites. The ruling elites refer to the core group controlling the state apparatus, whereas the oppositional elites are those groups openly struggling for political power. Tolstrup has argued that the denser the ties between an external actor and a target state, the easier leverage can be converted into political influence. The stronger the external actor is vis-à-vis the target state, the more influence it will have and the more difficult it will be for gatekeeper elites to cut the linkages. Tolstrup has emphasized the role of the ruling political elites, who monopolize the gatekeeping process and who hold the capacity of orchestrating "a complete close-down of a country" and disarming "other elite groups of their gatekeeper powers."[143] In other words, the "gatekeeping carried out by oppositional elites, civil society elites, and economic elites is contingent upon ruling elites not holding the will and the resources to deprive them of this possibility."[144]

Levitsky, Way, and Tolstrup's insights can be applied to the dynamics of Beijing–Hong Kong relations. In recent years, some Hong Kong–based scholars have relied on the concept of a "hybrid regime" to describe the HKSAR's political development.[145] Nevertheless, the application of typology of regimes into the study of Hong Kong has failed to take into account the China factor and to explain the dynamics of political change in the city, where the political system changed from "soft" authoritarianism to "hard" authoritarianism after the imposition of the national security law in late June 2020.[146] The linkages, leverage, and gatekeeper elites as discussed by Levitsky, Way, and Tolstrup constituted a "color revolution" in Hong Kong in the eyes of the PRC authorities. All such

---

143. Tolstrup, "When Can External Actors Influence Democratization?" 716–742.
144. Tolstrup, "When Can External Actors Influence Democratization?" 716–742.
145. Brian C. H. Fong, "State-Society Conflicts under Hong Kong's Hybrid Regime: Governing Coalition Building and Civil Society Challenges," *Asian Survey* 53, no. 1 (2013): 854–882; Matthew Y. H. Wong, "Party Models in a Hybrid Regime: Hong Kong, 2007–2012," *China Review* 15, no. 1 (Spring 2015): 67–94; Edmund W. Cheng, "Street Politics in a Hybrid Regime: The Diffusion of Political Activism in Post-colonial Hong Kong," *China Quarterly* 226 (June 2016): 383–406. An exception to the literature that failed to consider the China factor is the work of Ying-ho Kwong, "Political Repression in a Sub-national Hybrid Regime: The PRC's Governing Strategies in Hong Kong," *Contemporary Politics* 24, no. 4 (January 2018): 361–378.
146. Edwin A. Winckler, "Institutionalization and Participation on Taiwan: From Hard to Soft Authoritarianism?" *China Quarterly* 99 (September 1984): 481–499.

linkages and leverage had to be cut, while gatekeeper elites had to be identified, arrested, and prosecuted in Hong Kong under the national security law. The literature on "competitive authoritarianism" has exaggerated the "competitive" aspect but fails to admit the powerful role of the China factor as both an external and increasingly internal patron shaping Hong Kong's political development swiftly and powerfully. Furthermore, the ruling elites have been empowered by Beijing through the national security law to overwhelm other elites, including those in the opposition and civil society. All those linkages and leverages related to the West were perceived by PRC authorities as "subverting" the Hong Kong polity. The gatekeeper elites, to the PRC, had to be changed from "unpatriotic" to "patriotic" ones, cutting any linkage and leverage with the Western states in Hong Kong's political development. Indeed, the economic elites in the HKSAR supported the central authorities in the process of maintaining law and order through the imposition of the national security law in late June 2020.

The study of Hong Kong's political development must consider the central role of the PRC, which can be regarded as both a positive and "negative" actor in the democratization of the HKSAR. Positively, it had long stimulated the political participation of the people of Hong Kong well before July 1, 1997, when the territory witnessed the emergence of political groups and activists in anticipation of the idea of "Hong Kong people ruling Hong Kong."[147] After Hong Kong's retrocession to the PRC, Beijing gradually was seen by the democrats as a "negative" actor in the political development of the HKSAR, especially after the mass protests on July 1, 2003, when half a million people took the streets of Hong Kong to oppose the legislation on Article 23 of the Basic Law—a stipulation that necessitates the HKSAR government introducing legislation to ban activities relating to subversion, treason, secession, and sedition. The anti–national education campaign in the summer of 2012 provided another golden opportunity for the young localists, students, parents, and intellectuals to oppose the introduction of a national education curriculum. The HKSAR government backed down and decided to let secondary schools decide whether such a curriculum should be implemented. In 2014, the launch of the Occupy Central Movement from September to December shocked the central government in Beijing, for the local activists were determined to push for the democratization of the political system at the expense of maintaining law and order. In early 2016, the outbreak of the Mong Kok riots was triggered by a dispute between localists and the government over the handling of hawkers, an event followed by the action of two young legislators-elect, Yau Wai-ching and Baggio Leung, to use foul language and the term

---

147. Lo Shiu-hing, "Decolonization and Political Development in Hong Kong: Citizen Participation," *Asian Survey* 28, no. 6 (June 1988): 613–629.

"Chee-na" in their oath-taking ceremony in the LegCo in October.[148] Infuriated by Yau and Leung's behavior, the SCNPC interpreted Article 104 of the Basic Law, requiring all legislators-elect to take the oath faithfully, solemnly, and truthfully. The Hong Kong court eventually stripped Yau and Leung of their seats in LegCo. This oath-taking saga reinforced Beijing's perception that some young Hong Kong people were politically defiant, disrespectful, and "unpatriotic." From June to December 2019, the anti-extradition movement proved to the PRC authorities that the central government would have to impose the national security law onto Hong Kong to rein in the emergent radical localism and curb political activism. From the perspectives of pluralism and democratization, while China played a role in stimulating political participation in Hong Kong before July 1, 1997, it has become a "negative" actor intervening in Hong Kong's political development. From the perspective of maintaining law and order, however, China's tightened control over Hong Kong's radical activists after the oath-taking saga in 2016 was a positive actor stabilizing the local polity and the society.

Since July 1, 1997, the China factor has changed from an external shaper to an internal actor that influences the pace, scope, content, and direction of constitutional reforms in the HKSAR.[149] There are strong grounds for believing that the PRC has increasingly become an internal factor shaping Hong Kong's political development. First, with the rise of assertive nationalism in mainland China, PRC authorities have increasingly seen its sovereignty in "ancient" terms, namely "the idea that there is a final and absolute political authority in the political community, and that no final and absolute authority exists elsewhere."[150] Contrary to this "ancient" concept of sovereignty, the modern notion of sovereignty has been interpreted as "justifying the use of absolute power or symbolizing the actual possession of it."[151] The argument in the "modern" concept of sovereignty is as follows: the political system has become "so complex, its mode of operation so diverse and ramified, its distribution of power so dispersed, that it is impossible and in any case unnecessary to suppose there is an ultimate authority within [the polity]."[152]

However, judging from the remarks and action of the PRC authorities responsible for Hong Kong matters, their concept of sovereignty over the HKSAR remains more "ancient" than "modern." The idea of "one country, two systems"

---

148. For the details of the Mong Kok riot, see Sonny Shiu-Hing Lo, *The Politics of Policing in Greater China* (London: Palgrave, 2016), chap. 7, "The 2016 Mongkok Riot in Hong Kong." For the oath-taking saga, see Benjamin Haas, "Hong Kong Court Bans Pro-Independence Politicians from Office," *The Guardian*, November 15, 2016, accessed February 17, 2021, https://www.theguardian.com/world/2016/nov/15/hong-kong-bans-pro-democracy-politicians-after-beijing-rewrites-oath-law.
149. For this argument, see Lo, *Hong Kong's Indigenous Democracy*, 57.
150. Francis H. Hinsley, *Sovereignty* (London: Cambridge University Press, 1986), 26.
151. Hinsley, *Sovereignty*, 217.
152. Hinsley, *Sovereignty*, 218.

is predicated on the premise that the central government of Beijing has to ideally delegate powers and autonomy to the local government of the HKSAR. Yet, by holding a relatively "ancient" view of sovereignty, the PRC authorities have consistently emphasized that the origin of the "two systems" stems from the powers conferred by the "one country." The imposition of the national security law onto the HKSAR in late June 2020 was illustrative of the phenomenon that "there is a final and absolute political authority in the political community."

Second, this "final and absolute political authority in the political community" of Hong Kong resides in the central government in Beijing, as mentioned long ago in an article written by Cao Erbao, a researcher at the Liaison Office, in 2008.[153] The logic of Cao's arguments was as follows: if the "one country, two systems" was designed by the late PRC leader Deng Xiaoping to divide oneness into two, then the mainland cadres and officials in the HKSAR should exercise the central government's jurisdictions over those sovereignty-related affairs. Cao emphasized that the two systems' power originated from "one country," and that China's unitary system was different from those pluralistic systems that confer "residual powers" to local units. What he meant was that the HKSAR does not have "residual power," a perception commonly held by PRC authorities and many pro-Beijing Hong Kong elites, who have been arguing that the powers and autonomy enjoyed by the HKSAR are granted by the central government in Beijing. The most provocative point made by Cao was that, since the Chinese Communist Party (CCP) is the ruling party on the mainland, its batch of cadres and officials working in Hong Kong should operate as an indispensable, "important," "legitimate," and "open" governing force.[154] Cao's call for the "legitimate" and "open" operation of the CCP cadres and officials in the HKSAR was a manifestation of exercising the "final and absolute political authority in the political community" of Hong Kong.

Cao's argument could be seen as that of legalist theorists who stick to the ancient concept of sovereignty and who believe that China's "comprehensive jurisdiction" over Hong Kong stemmed from the power origin of "one country." Without "one country," the autonomy of the "two systems" cannot be enjoyed. In short, Beijing's policy toward the HKSAR has been since the Xi Jinping era, which began in late 2012, guided by an increasingly pro-center and pro-unitary perspective and an ancient concept of sovereignty in its central-local relations.

Third, the local pro-Beijing elites in the HKSAR have been acting more as agents of the central government than as the representatives of the Hong Kong

---

153. Cao Erbao, "Hong Kong's Governing Forces under the Condition of 'One Country, Two Systems,'" *Study Times*, vol. 422 (January 29, 2008), accessed February 17, 2021, https://www.legco.gov.hk/yr08-09/chinese/panels/ca/papers/ca0420cb2-1389-2-c.pdf.
154. Cao, "Hong Kong's Governing Forces."

people since July 1, 1997, making Hong Kong vulnerable to "direct rule" from the central authorities. In Hong Kong under British rule, the British colonialists relied on local indigenous elites to govern the territory, especially as local elites served as not only the middlemen between ordinary people and the ruling expatriate elites but also the mediators solving disputes among citizens and collecting taxes for the British administration.[155] The British indirectly governed Hong Kong through the utilization and cooptation of local elites while exerting direct rule over the colony through the dispatch of the governor, whose governance was assisted by the top policy-making Executive Council (ExCo), the appointed members of the LegCo, and the elderly representatives of rural villages. Although the LegCo underwent a gradual process of democratization and decolonization since 1985 through the introduction of some elected seats, especially after 1991 when direct elections were first introduced to the legislature, the British colonialists combined indirect with direct rule over Hong Kong. Adnan Naseemullah and Paul Staniland have defined indirect rule as a form of political control in which the state's agents delegate governing authority to local powerholders who act like intermediaries, while direct rule refers to a situation in which the state maintains a monopoly over law, policy, and administration of the population through bureaucrats rather than any intermediary.[156]

The enactment of the national security law in Hong Kong in June 2020 showed that, while the PRC authorities continued to allow local bureaucrats to govern the city, they have administered the "monopoly" of implementing the national security law and co-ruled Hong Kong with the local elites. As such, PRC authorities have combined direct rule with indirect rule over the HKSAR. The local pro-Beijing elites have acted less as intermediaries representing the interests of the Hong Kong people but more as the central government's loyal agents in implementing the policy directive of protecting Beijing's national security interests. The stronger the people's representative role of the intermediary elites, the weaker the tendency of the center's direct rule. In other words, if the intermediary elites act more as the loyal agents of the central authorities than as the representatives of local people, they are unlikely to act as a buffer between the center and the locality, making Hong Kong vulnerable to direct rule from PRC authorities. In fact, the pro-Beijing elites are fragmented, compete against each other, and fail to be united, making themselves a relatively weak buffer and providing an environment favorable to the direct rule of central authorities.

---

155. Law Wing Sang, *Collaborative Colonial Power: The Making of the Hong Kong Chinese* (Hong Kong: Hong Kong University Press, 2009).
156. Adnan Naseemullah and Paul Staniland, "Indirect Rule and Varieties of Governance," *Governance: An International Journal of Policy, Administration, and Institutions* 29, no. 1 (January 2016): 13–30.

The Ideology of Unification as Regime Inclusion: Implications for Hong Kong and Taiwan

Most Western literature on China's policy toward the HKSAR and the local scholarly work on Beijing–Hong Kong relations have ignored the mainland's ideology of unification. The PRC ideology of achieving unification has been articulated by mainland Chinese scholars. Yan Qing and Ping Weibun have traced *dayitong* (great unification) as "the common entity ideology of the Chinese nation."[157] They contend that the unification of the whole of China was the ancient and long-standing ideology of the regimes in the Spring and Autumn periods and the dynasties of Qin, Han, Sui, and Tang. The ideology of unifying or reunifying mainland China was shaped by two factors: "the imperial desire and consciousness of tolerating and embracing nationalities under the Mandate of Heaven" and "the distinction between the Chinese nation at the center and barbarians at the peripheral borders."[158] Yan and Ping argued that the ideology of great unification has been inherited by PRC President Xi Jinping, who has raised the ideas of cultivating the "common entity ideology of the Chinese nation," tracing it to the historical process of forming the Chinese nation and responding to the historical sufferings of the Chinese nation, which underwent painful experiences in the Opium War and the Sino-Japanese wars in 1894 and from the 1930s to 1945.[159] Domestically, the ideology of "great unification" is on the top of the agenda of the Xi Jinping administration.[160] Externally, the PRC government is keen to pursue the objective of creating "a common destiny for the mankind" in which countries in the world would enjoy peaceful and sustainable development.[161] Yan and Ping concluded that the PRC has been proceeding from the stage of "standing up" to the era of foreign invasion to the current phase of getting affluent and consolidating itself along the path of the Chinese renaissance.[162] In short, great unification is the crucial objective of the PRC's vision of the Chinese renaissance, pointing to the need to resolve the question of Taiwan's political future. Since Deng Xiaoping's vision of the "one country, two systems" to deal with the future of Hong Kong and Macau during the 1980s was designed to tackle Taiwan's political future in the long run, this task is now left to the PRC under Xi Jinping's leadership.

---

157. Yan Qing and Ping Weibun, "'*Dayitong*' and the Formation of the Common Entity Ideology of the Chinese Nation," *Minzu lilun yu zhengze* [The theory and policy of nationalities] 5 (2018): 14–18 [a Chinese journal published by the Southwest Nationalities University].
158. Yan and Ping, "*Dayitong*, and the Formation of the Common Entity Ideology," 15.
159. Yan and Ping, "*Dayitong*, and the Formation of the Common Entity Ideology," 17.
160. Yan and Ping, "*Dayitong*, and the Formation of the Common Entity Ideology," 17.
161. Yan and Ping, "*Dayitong*, and the Formation of the Common Entity Ideology," 17.
162. Yan and Ping, "*Dayitong*, and the Formation of the Common Entity Ideology," 17.

Some mainland scholars have elaborated on the concept of great unification along the lines articulated by Yan and Ping. Chen Zhonghai has argued that the idea of great unification stemmed from the assumption that any place disunited from the center of the Chinese mainland would be reunited with the passage of time.[163] He elucidated the "inevitability of reunification after a long period of separation" (*hejiu bifen*), an idea that is held by many leaders of the ancient dynasties of China and by PRC leaders from the Deng Xiaoping era to the Xi Jinping period. Like Chen, who identifies the importance of great unification in the Chinese "renaissance," Shen Zuowei has maintained that the idea of great unification could be found in the political philosophy of Sun Yat-sen, the father of the 1911 revolution in China.[164] Shen has argued that, even though the HKSAR witnessed the brief emergence of "independence" sentiment, which is illegal according to the national security law, the idea of great unification remains critical to how the PRC is dealing with the question of Taiwan's political future.[165] He pinpointed to the need to maintain Hong Kong's "one country, two systems" and "fifty years unchanged" and to insist on the 1992 consensus, which means that both the PRC and the Republic of China (ROC) on Taiwan agree with the principle of "one country" whose interpretation can be up to the two sides.[166] Shen concluded that great unification remains an unfinished task of the Chinese people to fulfill the mission of the late Sun Yat-sen.

While Chen and Shen have explicitly linked the ancient concept of great unification to the PRC's vision of achieving the Chinese dream and renaissance of reuniting with Taiwan, other mainland scholars who discussed great unification are historians arguing that *dayitong* was deeply entrenched in the historical governance of Chinese dynasties. Dong Lin has asserted that the idea of great unification could be attributable to Confucius, who had firmly believed in the necessity of achieving territorial oneness and kinship solidarity, and whose political ideal shaped the governing philosophy of the later Qin and Han dynasties.[167] The idea of great unity, according to Dong, has become "an important ideological motive and emotional bond to maintain the development of the Chinese nation."[168]

Similarly, Yang Nianqun argued that, in the Qing dynasty, there was a tension in the concept of unification between those people who advocated that

---

163. Chen Zhonghai "The Chinese People's Concept of *Dayitong*," *Observations on China's Development* 6 (2017): 62–64 [in Chinese].
164. Shen Zuowei, "Creating a Modern Nation of Great Unification," *Shiji* [Century] 4 (2017): 1.
165. Shen, "Creating a Modern Nation of Great Unification," 1.
166. Shen, "Creating a Modern Nation of Great Unification," 1.
167. Dong Lin, "The Space Concept of Confucius' 'Great Unity' Thought," *Journal of Xinyang Normal University* 38, no. 5 (September 2018): 12–15.
168. Dong, "The Space Concept of Confucius' 'Great Unity' Thought," 15.

unification was a means to make China self-reliant and not to be partitioned by foreign invaders, and those who contended that unification would "suppress" ideological contestation and prolong autocracy in China.[169] The idea of great unification was divided into two main factions in the late Qing dynasty, one advocating a loose "federal" system of unifying China and the other faction arguing for the need to maintain territorial integrity and unity on the mainland.[170] Some reformers, notably Liang Qichao, argued that local-level autonomy should be experimented with in mainland China so that great unification would proceed gradually, but this was a minority view that could not counter the mainstream argument for the need to achieve great unification.[171] Unlike Liang Qichao, conservative reformer Kang Yuowei argued that great unification could and would be achieved through political evolution so that all the separated places would gather together in the form of "a common destiny" or "*datong*."[172] According to Yang, moderate reformers like Kang and Sun Yat-sen increasingly adopted the idea of great unification, which could and would be achieved in an incremental manner.[173]

Yang's conclusion is historical with current political implications. The PRC government is now adopting the idea of great unification through a "moderate" approach while simultaneously experimenting with "local-level autonomy" as articulated by the liberal-minded reformers in the late Qing dynasty. PRC authorities are now articulating the concept of a Taiwan model of "one country, two systems" to appeal to Taiwan for reunification, while Hong Kong and Macau have their own models of "one country, two systems." Moreover, Kang Yuowei's concept of a "common destiny" has recently been rearticulated by Xi Jinping as the creation of a "common destiny for the humankind" for the world—a reformulation of Kang's concept so as to portray China's socialist vision for the world.

Yet, mainland Chinese historians have different interpretations on whether the idea of great unification entails pluralistic or autocratic tendencies. Li Yongqiao argued that, during the Qin dynasty, the policies of Emperor Qin were characterized by administrative centralization, economic planning, the center's political control over localities, and ideological conformity.[174] However, by constructing the Great Wall, the Qin dynasty restricted the "barbarians" outside the wall from being incorporated into the scope of the Chinese nation—a legacy

---

169. Yang Nianqun, "On the Modern Transformation of China's Traditional Unification View," *Journal of the People's University* (in Chinese), no. 1 (2018): 117–131.
170. Yang, "On the Modern Transformation of China's Traditional Unification View," 130.
171. Yang, "On the Modern Transformation of China's Traditional Unification View," 130–131.
172. Yang, "On the Modern Transformation of China's Traditional Unification View," 131.
173. Yang, "On the Modern Transformation of China's Traditional Unification View," 131.
174. Li Yongqiao, "Understanding Qin Shihuang's Implementation of 'Great Unity,'" *Culture Journal* no. 7 (July 2017): 222–230 [in Chinese].

impacting on the boundaries of the following dynasties.[175] The great unity concept of the Qin dynasty entailed the strict control over books and works resistant to the political philosophy of legalism, which was utilized by Emperor Qin to control other thoughts ideologically. Qin Shihuang adopted the policy of "burning books" and excluding pluralistic cultures.[176] Li observed that the Qin dynasty laid down the foundation of China's constitutional political order because of three main features: the power conferred by the Mandate of Heaven on the sovereign to unify the whole Chinese nation; the overwhelming power of the sovereign versus the people, although the sovereign was expected to be moral and virtuous in governance; and the proper hierarchical relations between the rulers and the ruled, who had obligations to each other.[177] With the death of Qin Shihuang, the Qin dynasty's longevity was at stake due to several factors: the sovereign was too powerful "without self-correction capability"; succession politics were mismanaged, with the result of a constant power struggle among the ruling elites; the lack of checks and balances against those officials who held powers; the persistence of societal opposition to the Qin rule; and the attempted return of political elites from the previously ousted dynasties.[178] The authoritarian rule of the Qin dynasty was based on strong personal leadership without laying the foundation of political succession, checks and balances, and social stability.

The practices of "great unification" in the Qin dynasty had profound impacts on the Ming and Qing dynasties. While repressive rule was a hallmark of the Ming dynasty, the Qing dynasty added an element of consolidated governance to the concept of "great unification." The Qing dynasty integrated ethnic groups, such as the Manchus, Mongolians, and Hans, into a united entity.[179] Emperors like Kangxi and Qianlong broadened the concept of *dayitong* to embrace the Chinese and "barbarians," abandoning the geographical restrictions of the Great Wall of China and expanding the dynastic territorial reach to border regions outside the Great Wall.[180] The Qing dynasty set up various administrative mechanisms, notably the customs agency, to govern the border areas led by military generals and administrative chiefs. During the apex of the Qing rule, the regions of Tibet and Xinjiang were integrated territorially and governed smoothly.[181] As such, the heydays of the Qing dynasty delineated "the border and territorial map of China."[182]

---

175. Li, "Understanding Qin Shihuang's Implementation of 'Great Unity,'" 228.
176. Li, "Understanding Qin Shihuang's Implementation of 'Great Unity,'" 222–230.
177. Li, "Understanding Qin Shihuang's Implementation of 'Great Unity,'" 222–230.
178. Li, "Understanding Qin Shihuang's Implementation of 'Great Unity,'" 222–230.
179. Li Zhiting, "A Study of the Political Concept of the Great Unity Advocated by the Emperors of the Qing Dynasty," *Journal of Yunnan Normal University* 47, no. 6 (2015): 1–9 [in Chinese].
180. Li, "A Study of the Political Concept of the Great Unity," 5.
181. Li, "A Study of the Political Concept of the Great Unity," 9.
182. Li, "A Study of the Political Concept of the Great Unity," 9.

Zhang Qiang, a legal expert at Peking University, went so far as to assert that any resolution of China's constitutional development has to tackle the issue of unification first. He has argued that while the PRC government and society have the common objective of achieving "the rule of law," "the constitutional order of the Chinese civilization" has originated from the ancient Chinese practices of firstly "internally governing the mountains and rivers," secondly "externally pacifying the barbarians," and finally "achieving national unification."[183] These ancient practices were common in the unification attempts made by the dynasties, such as Zhou and Qin. Prior to Qin's successful unification of the mainland, a debate occurred over whether a system of setting up provinces and counties or delegating powers by the emperor to local officials should be adopted.[184] The system of delegating powers to local officials was advanced by those who had vested interests, but Emperor Qin Shihuang adopted the system of establishing provinces and counties under a powerful central government. This centralized system of governance in the Qin dynasty, according to Li, was followed by the Qing dynasty, which established an "orthodoxy" of the ideology of great unification. Li concluded: "The ideology of unification became sophisticated via the development of various historical periods, such as the unification idea in pre-Qin dynasty, the unification institutions of Qin dynasty, the unification and orthodox theories of Confucianism, and the theory of distinguishing the civilized ruler from uncivilized one."[185] Under the logic of developing the idea of reunification along all Chinese dynasties, it is natural that the PRC under the leadership of President Xi Jinping is eager to achieve great unification, ensuring Hong Kong's integration with the mainland and targeting Taiwan ultimately.

While mainland scholars have written skillfully to stick to the official line and necessity of achieving unification, Zhang Qianfan, a legal expert at Peking University, has not only advocated the need for constitutionalism in the PRC but also argued that the central government in Beijing should adopt a more "neutral" attitude toward the affairs of the HKSAR, whose autonomy can be realized by adopting "the British monarchical practice of being politically and traditionally neutral."[186] He appealed to the need for the Hong Kong democrats and the central government in Beijing to establish trustful relationships and to reach consensus over the difficult issue of constitutional reforms in the HKSAR. Unfortunately, Zhang's suggestion was not heeded by Hong Kong's mainstream

---

183. Zhang Qiang, "Great Unity Thinking as Constitutional System: Discussion of Ancient China's Constitutional Order under the Idea of Unification," *The Journal of South China Sea Studies* (in Chinese) 1, no. 1 (March 2015): 44–49.
184. Zhang, "Great Unity Thinking as Constitutional System," 46.
185. Zhang, "Great Unity Thinking as Constitutional System," 49.
186. Zhang Qianfan, "An Analysis of the Constitution of 'One Country, Two Systems,'" *Yanhuang Chunqiu*, no. 3 (2016): 12–19 [in Chinese].

and radical democrats, who constantly challenged the political bottom line of the central authorities in the process of democratization from the Occupy Central Movement in 2014 to the anti–extradition bill movement in 2019. Nor was Zhang's advice heeded by PRC authorities, who have been consistently adopting a pro-center perspective and the ancient concept of sovereignty in dealing with the HKSAR.

The historical ideology of unification can be seen as an effort at "regime inclusion," which, according to Kenneth Jowitt, refers to "attempts by party elites to expand the internal boundaries of the regime's political, productive, and decision-making systems, to integrate itself with the unofficial sectors of society rather than insulate itself from them."[187] Such attempts at expanding internal boundaries are naturally seen by critics, adversaries, and opponents as politically nationalistic and aggressive. Efforts at regime inclusion can easily meet with political resistance from those peoples whose regional and local identities are different from the central authorities. As political scientist He Baogang observed sharply and accurately in 2003:

> China now faces a national identity problem, that is, sections of the national population do not identify with the Chinese nation-state in which they live. Tibetans, for example, endeavor to create their own political identity through the reconstruction of a Tibetan cultural and ethnic identity. China's national identity problem also involves the question of reunification with Taiwan. In Taiwan, both the KMT and the DPP governments have refused to reunify with China. The question of Taiwan and Tibet are different cases and require different treatment, but Beijing's response to the two questions—refusing to adopt a democratic approach—is the same. It appears that the Chinese leadership is reluctant to initiate large-scale democratization at the national level. Indeed, Chinese state nationalists oppose democratization, which they see as threatening national unity and control of the territories. In particular, the breakup of the former USSR and the separation of East Timor from Indonesia have reinforced Beijing's fear and resistance to democracy, while China's successful reunion with Hong Kong and Macau has strengthened Beijing's belief that power, not democracy, can unify China.[188]

Officially, the PRC government believes that Tibet and Taiwan are indispensable parts of China. As such, democratization in China, according to He Baogang, "may provide an opportunity for Tibet to either separate from China or establish genuine autonomy, and for Taiwan to either establish an independent state, recognized by the international community, or unify with mainland

---

187. Kenneth Jowitt, "Inclusion and Mobilization in European Leninist Regimes," *World Politics* 28, no. 1 (October 1975): 69–96, especially 69.
188. He Baogang, "Why Is Establishing Democracy So Difficult in China?" *Contemporary Chinese Thought* 35, no. 1 (Fall 2003): 71–92, especially 71.

China."[189] He wrote, "A federal and democratizing China may offer a solution to the Tibet question, and establish a confederation or federation with Taiwan. In this way, it may be possible for China to be both strong and democratic."[190] He Baogang's argument that China's successful reunion with Hong Kong and Macau has enhanced its belief that power rather than democracy can unify China is important. It implies that Beijing adopts the same approach of emphasizing the usage of power to deal with the question of Taiwan's political future, especially in a regime that regards great unification as an essential ingredient of the Chinese renaissance.

If the concept of great unification is applied to Beijing's relations with both the HKSAR and Taiwan, two questions arise. First, although the PRC already reunified with Hong Kong and Macau in 1997 and 1999, respectively, are the PRC's attempts at reunifying Taiwan becoming a factor shaping Beijing's policy toward the HKSAR? The answer is affirmative. Specifically, if the protests against the extradition bill from June to December 2019 were perceived as undermining the PRC's national security, then logically, Beijing's intervention in the HKSAR developments had to be decisive and rapid to prevent Taiwan from becoming another increasingly politically "independent" Hong Kong vis-a-vis a "weak" central government in Beijing. As a result, the PRC used the swift promulgation of the national security law in late June 2020 and the decisive revamp of electoral system in March 2021 in the HKSAR as a demonstration model for Taiwan.

On the other hand, however, since the national security law in Hong Kong was implemented in mid-2020, many Taiwanese people have argued that they would not accept the so-called Taiwan model of "one country, two systems," especially those Taiwanese people supportive of the Democratic Progressive Party (DPP). Except for the supporters of the Kuomintang (KMT or Nationalist Party) who see Taiwan's unification with the mainland as their vision bringing about the ROC's economic prosperity, most Taiwanese people do not find the "one country, two systems" model attractive, let alone reunification with the mainland.

From the perspective of attracting Taiwan into the mainland orbit, the implementation of the national security law in the HKSAR has to be moderately administered to strike a balance between maintaining national security on the one hand and retaining a viable image of "one country, two systems" on the other hand. Arguably, only the core leaders and offenders of the 2019 anti-extradition protests were arrested, prosecuted, and imprisoned. A relatively minimal approach to implementing the national security law has been adopted in the HKSAR to avoid a detrimental impact on China's attempt at achieving its

---

189. He, "Why Is Establishing Democracy So Difficult in China?" 89.
190. He, "Why Is Establishing Democracy So Difficult in China?" 89.

"complete reunification" with Taiwan in the coming years. Of course, from the Western perspective, the imposition of the national security law and its implementation in the HKSAR have remained politically "unacceptable"—a clash of Western and Chinese political cultures. The central-local dynamics in the implementation of the national security law are crucial in maintaining a delicate balance between the protection of national security and the creation of a good image of "one country, two systems" for the people of Taiwan.

Second, is the PRC's idea of "great unification" entailing more "autocratic" or centralized practices as with the previous ancient dynasties, like Qin and Qing, than a "pluralistic" or decentralized mode of central-local relations? At present, the PRC's proposal of exploring a Taiwan model of "one country, two systems," as mentioned by President Xi Jinping in his speech to the Taiwanese people on January 2, 2019, and the *White Paper on the Taiwan Question* in August 2022, deserves our attention in three aspects.[191] First, the *White Paper* does not mention that the PRC will not station its military in Taiwan after reunification—an implication that the central authorities retain the right to station the People's Liberation Army (PLA) in Taiwan in light of the separatist tendency on the island, especially after US House Speaker Nancy Pelosi's visit to Taiwan in early August 2022. Second, the document mentions a stage-by-stage process of negotiation in the event of a Beijing-Taipei dialogue on Taiwan's future. Third, the *White Paper* mentions that, after reunification, Taiwan would be able to envisage the establishment of foreign diplomatic missions and offices there—an implication that Taiwan would be able to enjoy a "high degree of autonomy" after reunification with the mainland. Chapter 3 will examine the scenarios of Beijing-Taipei relations and argue for a stage-by-stage negotiation over Taiwan's political future.

The Theory of Convergence, the China Model, and Dependent Development

The theory of convergence, which was expounded by Alfred Meyer in 1970 to predict the eventually similar path of development between communist systems and Western democracies, can be applied to our understanding of China's developmental path and Beijing–Hong Kong relations.[192] Meyer argued that all

---

191. "Highlights of Xi's Speech at Taiwan Message Anniversary Event," *China Daily*, January 2, 2019, accessed February 17, 2021, https://www.chinadaily.com.cn/a/201901/02/WS5c2c1ad2a310d91214052069.html. See also "The Taiwan Question and China's Reunification in the New Era," The Taiwan Office of the State Council, August 2022, accessed September 11, 2022, http://www.scio.gov.cn/zfbps/32832/Document/1728491/1728491.htm.
192. Alfred G. Meyer, "Theories of Convergence," in *Change in Communist Systems*, ed. Chalmers Johnson (Stanford, CA: Stanford University Press, 1970), 336–337.

industrial societies would share common features, such as a pluralistic society, a participatory and democratic political system, economic affluence, bureaucratization, and the use of merit in judging individual performance in the private and public sectors. Economic and technological modernization would make all industrializing states similar to each other politically. However, this assumption turned out to be problematic. The collapse of the former Soviet Union did not bring about a full-fledged democratic Russia, whose regime remains illiberal and exhibits authoritarian features. China has been maintaining the model of authoritarianism although its economic rise has been constituting a threat to the superpower US. Stephan Ortmann and Mark Thompson have observed: "The ruling elite emphasizes China's 'century of humiliation' and its historic destiny; it seeks to revive conservative Confucianism, puts forth expansive territorial claims, and engages in displays of military power. Its policies are more reminiscent of the 'Prussian path' to modernity and great-power status than of any political model in the contemporary world."[193]

The PRC's trend of converging with the Singaporean model, which is characterized by its economic success, meritocracy, relatively clean government, strong developmental state, and weak civil society, has implications for Beijing–Hong Kong and Beijing–Taipei relations. In Hong Kong, the local democracy movement failed to achieve any breakthrough during the Occupy Central Movement in late 2014. The PRC's strong developmental state can be seen in the enactment of the national security law in June 2020 and the revamp of Hong Kong's electoral system in March 2021. On the other hand, Taiwan's ruling elites, including many supporters of both KMT President Ma Ying-jeou (2008–2016) and DPP President Tsai Ing-wen (2016–2023), have argued that China's democratization is a precondition for Taiwan to consider political dialogue and reunification with the PRC. As such, the developmental path of China to converge with the Singaporean model entails a dampening effect on Hong Kong's democratization and brings about a prolonged delay to Taiwan's willingness to consider reunification. During the 2024 presidential election campaign in Taiwan, KMT presidential candidate Hou You-yi rejected the "one country, two systems" solution for Taiwan. While China converges with the Singaporean model rather than Western capitalist democracies, its model has "negative" impact on the prospects of reunifying with Taiwan.

While China is converging with Singapore economically and politically, other scholars have identified the emergence of the China model of development. According to Daniel Bell, the China model is characterized by political meritocracy that combines an impartial state and the rule of law without the

---

193. Stephan Ortmann and Mark R. Thompson, "China and the 'Singapore Model,'" *Journal of Democracy* 27, no. 1 (January 2016): 39–48, especially 46.

features of Western democratic accountability.[194] Alvin So has pointed to the features of fast economic growth, export-led industrialization, innovation and technological upgrading, poverty reduction, and independent and autonomous development.[195] Unlike Bell, who has emphasized the "virtues" of the Chinese model, and unlike So, who has stressed the practical aspects of development, Pei Minxin has characterized the PRC model as showing the hallmark of "crony capitalism."[196] The developmental state in China has been characterized by the practice of central planning, a strong central government with a huge bureaucracy, the infrastructure of heavy industry, the promotion of industrial policy, the existence of a labor-intensive industry accompanied by import substitutive capital-intensive industry, the high rate of domestic savings, the corporatist control over the society, and the relative autonomy vis-à-vis the capitalists.[197] While the feature of a strong developmental state in the PRC is reminiscent of the relatively strong colonial state in Hong Kong under the British rule in the 1970s and 1980s, the negative features of the Chinese model, notably crony capitalism and bureaucratic corruption, have not been cherished by most Hong Kong people. In fact, the Xi Jinping regime has been avoiding crony capitalism and bureaucratic corruption by maintaining a distance from the red capitalists, checking the power of the business class, and launching a persistent anti-corruption campaign in the private and public sectors, including the military leadership and the military-industrial complex.[198] During the opening of the 20th Party Congress on October 16, 2022, Xi Jinping regarded China's anti-corruption campaign as a necessary move by the CCP to conduct its "self-revolution," to instill a permanent crisis consciousness, and to make the ruling regime continue to be resilient and popular.[199]

An alarming aspect of the developmental state, namely the suppression of political dissidents, has been the most worrisome concern of the Western democratic countries and some pro-democracy Hongkongers, who have found the imposition of the national security law to be disturbing. The next chapter will

---

194. Daniel A. Bell, *The China Model: Political Meritocracy and the Limits of Democracy* (Princeton, NJ: Princeton University Press, 2016).
195. Alvin Y. So, "The Chinese Model of Development: Characteristics, Interpretation, Implications," *Perspectives on Global Development and Technology* 13 (2014): 444–464.
196. Pei Minxin, *China's Crony Capitalism: The Dynamics of Political Decay* (Cambridge, MA: Harvard University Press, 2016).
197. Nikolaos Karagiannis, Moula Cherikh, and Wolfram Elsner, "Growth and Development of China: A Developmental State 'With Chinese Characteristics,'" *Forum for Social Economics* (2020), accessed February 20, 2021, https://doi.org/10.1080/07360932.2020.1747515.
198. Sonny Lo, "China's Military Leadership: Reshuffle, Reform and Redirection," *Macau Business*, December 30, 2023, accessed January 1, 2024, https://www.macaubusiness.com/opinion-chinas-military-leadership-reshuffle-reform-and-redirection/.
199. His speech focusing on anti-corruption was highlighted by Hong Kong TVB News, October 16, 2022.

discuss the impacts of the national security law on the HKSAR. However, from the legalist perspective of maintaining national security, the law was a necessary introduction to stem the tide of any separatist tendency and to curb the rising anti-center forces in the HKSAR from 2012 to 2019.

The literature on dependent development has been rarely applied to study the relations between the PRC and Hong Kong. Dependency theory was advanced by scholars studying Latin America in the late 1960s and 1970s, such as Andre Gunder Frank, who argued that the capitalist states constituted a core that economically exploited the peripheral states in the world.[200] Peter Evans articulated the concept of dependent development, arguing that developing states like Brazil had a relatively strong state that forged a triple alliance between the state capital, local capital, and foreign capital to boost the economy.[201] The insights of Evans were followed up by other scholars studying the political economy of development in South Korea and Taiwan.[202] Sinologists did not employ the theory of dependent development to study the PRC until recently. Jin Zheng and Yuanyuan Fang have argued that, despite China's rapid economic growth from the 1980s to 2010s, there is a fear among Chinese officials and experts that the PRC may be heading toward the "middle-income trap," namely economic stagnation and turbulence, as with Latin American states in the 1980s and 1990s.[203] They have contended that the PRC's heavy dependence on foreign investment and technologies has detrimental impacts on the economy, increasing China's vulnerability and truncating domestic industries. To escape from this trap, China should, according to Zheng and Fang, shift its developmental model from low-end commodity manufacturing to knowledge-based and high-value-added activities. Judging from the recent developments in the Chinese political economy, the mainland state has been shifting toward a new direction as suggested by Zheng and Fang, especially as the US-China economic and technological rivalries have propelled the PRC party-state to alter its strategy of dependent development to a more self-reliant mode of development.

In the context of Beijing's relations with Hong Kong, the former depended on the latter before 1997 as a window for Chinese economic modernization. Hong

---

200. Andre Gunder Frank, *Capitalism and Underdevelopment in Latin America* (New York: Monthly Review Press, 1969). See also Charles Wilber, ed., *The Political Economy of Development and Underdevelopment* (New York: Random House, 1979).
201. Peter B. Evans, *Dependent Development: The Alliance of Multinationals, State and Local Capital in Brazil* (Princeton, NJ: Princeton University Press, 1979).
202. Lim Hyun-chin, *Dependent Development in Korea, 1963–1979* (Seoul: Seoul National University Press, 1985); Thomas B. Gold, "Dependent Development in Taiwan" (PhD thesis, Harvard University, 1981); and Zhen Yuxi, "Dependent Development and Its Sociopolitical Consequences: A Case Study of Taiwan" (PhD thesis, University of Hawai'i, 1981).
203. Jin Zheng and Yuanyuan Fang, "Between Poverty and Prosperity: China's Dependent Development and the 'Middle-Income Trap,'" *Third World Quarterly* 35, no. 6 (2014): 1014–1031.

Kong played a crucial role in investing in China's manufacturing industries, providing capital, expertise, and knowledge in modern management, and attracting foreign capital and guiding it to enter the vast Chinese market. However, these multiple roles of Hong Kong have gradually changed after July 1, 1997, especially as China's economic rise has become prominent since the early 2000s. Hong Kong remains a financial and monetary center for the PRC to absorb foreign capital and knowhow, but the increasingly sour relations between China and the Western democratic countries, especially after the enactment of the national security law in Hong Kong in June 2020, have raised the concern of some foreign investors, who are concerned about whether the freedom of information may be controlled and whether the business environment has already changed.[204]

Objectively speaking, the concerns about business confidence in Hong Kong after the enactment of the national security law in June 2020 might have been exaggerated. First, given the fact that the business elites, both local and foreign, tend to separate business issues from politics, this dichotomy between business and politics fits into the psyche of the PRC authorities responsible for Hong Kong matters. PRC officials exactly try to use the national security law to depoliticize Hong Kong and to maintain economic stability, social order, and the business environment in the city. Social stability has been maintained after the introduction of the national security law in June 2020, especially as protests have become almost non-existent after the outbreak of COVID-19 in early 2020. Second, there is no concrete evidence that foreign business companies relocated massively from Hong Kong to elsewhere, although mass emigration from Hong Kong to other countries (like the UK and Canada) loomed.[205]

From the perspective of dependent development, the rise of China has transformed its economic relations with the HKSAR. China during its early phase of the modernization period from the mid-1970s to late 1990s was characterized by its dependency on Hong Kong's capital, expertise, knowledge, and skills in modern management. With the rapid rise of China since the early 2000s, the competitive edge of Hong Kong vis-à-vis the mainland has been narrowed. The HKSAR remains a financial and monetary center, as well as an offshore platform for the internationalization of the renminbi. Yet, the rapid rise of Shenzhen and China's active promotion of Hong Kong to integrate economically into the

---

204. Stephen Mulrenan, "Business Navigates Hong Kong's New National Security Law," International Bar Association, September 25, 2020, accessed February 18, 2021, https://www.ibanet.org/article/ACD909C3-15D4-4817-8D2A-0EE0D39D3028.
205. An American friend told the author in February 2021 that he had no knowledge of US companies making the decision to relocate their offices from Hong Kong to elsewhere. However, in September 2022, it was rumored that 15,000 out of 80,000 American businesspeople left Hong Kong less because of the national security law but more due to the strict quarantine measures against COVID-19 in the HKSAR.

Greater Bay Area accelerates the twin processes of minimizing the mainland's dependency on Hong Kong and making the HKSAR increasingly dependent economically on the mainland. Since the introduction of the individual mainland visitors' scheme in the summer of 2003, the HKSAR has become increasingly reliant on mainland tourists to boost its economy. The onset of COVID-19 in early 2020 significantly reduced the number of mainland tourists to Hong Kong, leading to a rapid decline in the tertiary sector and a corresponding increase in unemployment.[206] While China was dependent economically on Hong Kong on its economic modernization and development before 1997, Hong Kong has been increasingly economically dependent on and integrated into the mainland after 1997. After the election of John Lee as the chief executive of the HKSAR in May 2022, some businesspeople openly lobbied the government for a more liberal policy toward the attraction of talents from the mainland and overseas, for many occupational sectors, including information technology and education, witnessed an inadequate supply of manpower and skilled employees. In 2023, the HKSAR government announced its scheme of attracting global and mainland talents to work in Hong Kong—a policy supported by Beijing. As such, the HKSAR will depend on the mainland for more talents, some of whom have already migrated to, resided, and worked in the city, for its economic competitiveness in the long run.

The concept of Hong Kong's power dependence was articulated by political scientist Kuan Hsin-chi, and it can be redeployed for us to analyze Beijing-HKSAR relations.[207] Writing in 1991, Kuan predicted that the concept of a "dual state" could not be used in our understanding of Beijing's relation with the HKSAR. Nevertheless, after 1997, as China's intervention in Hong Kong matters has become inevitable and extensive, there are two states in Beijing's relation with Hong Kong, namely the central state side by side with the local state. Emphasizing Hong Kong's "power dependence" in mainland China, Kuan anticipated that,

> as relations between Hong Kong and China grow in intensity and complexity, it is possible for China to remain interventionist with regard to functions which are dear to its heart but to leave Hong Kong to have its own way in many other functions. The crux of the matter is therefore to limit as far as possible the functional areas susceptible to intervention. This is exactly what the Basic Law is supposed to do, i.e., to delineate the boundaries between the "two systems" within "one country." The challenge is to make those delineations work. It is likely that it will be a continuous challenge. Constant vigilance and frantic

---

206. The unemployment rate rose to 7 percent in February 2021.
207. Kuan Hsin-chi, "Power Dependence and Democratic Transition: The Case of Hong Kong," *China Quarterly* 128 (December 1991): 774–793.

efforts are required to transform the innovative but elusive idea of "one country, two systems" into a truly creative and dynamic central-local relationship.[208]

As Beijing–Hong Kong relations "grow in intensity and complexity," the PRC intervention in the HKSAR is inevitable. However, the delineations of the boundaries between "one country" and "two systems" have been increasingly tipped in favor of "one country" rather than "two systems." Perhaps sadly, some radical localists and populists on the Hong Kong side of the "two systems" kept on challenging the political red lines of the "one country" so excessively and incessantly from 2012 to 2019 that the central authorities were eventually provoked and stimulated to intervene in Hong Kong matters more swiftly and decisively than ever before.

Summary of the Twelve Perspectives

This chapter reviews twelve perspectives on Chinese politics with significant implications for Beijing-HKSAR relations. Firstly, the rise of assertive Chinese nationalism could be seen as Beijing's development and its response to the rapidly changing politics of Hong Kong, especially the emergence of localism. Such assertive nationalism was superimposed on Hong Kong's localism, putting a brake on the growth of localist and radical tendencies. Second, if Chinese legalism is characterized by using laws to penalize social and political deviants, it was demonstrated in the SCNPC interpretation of the Basic Law's Article 104 over the behavior of legislators-elect in taking the oath of the LegCo. Legalism was again shown in the enactment and implementation of the national security law for the HKSAR and in the plan of enacting Article 23 of the Basic Law and a cybersecurity law. Third, Chinese paternalism has been combined with Leninism, constituting powerful reactions to the localist activities in the HKSAR and penalizing those activists and protestors involved in the anti-mainlandization and anti-CCP movements. Fourth, the PRC's fear of witnessing a "color revolution" in the HKSAR that might trigger a Soviet-style collapse of the CCP was firmly entrenched in the minds of the mainland authorities responsible for Hong Kong matters, especially the national security personnel on the mainland. The PRC authorities as a powerful patron decided to revamp Hong Kong's political system in March 2021 to exclude all those radicals from penetrating the LegCo and to groom and empower the pro-Beijing political clients. The further exclusion of political "troublemakers" could be seen in the 2023 District Council elections during which some pro-democracy activists failed to acquire the necessary nominations from the pro-government elites. Fifth, the PRC trepidation of Hong

---

208. Kuan, "Power Dependence and Democratic Transition," 792.

Kong being politically utilized by foreign states to change the special administrative region and to subvert the mainland is understandable in an authoritarian mainland polity that remains resilient, sustainable, and strong. Sixth, as the PRC is characterized by a strong state and relatively weak society, its leaders naturally see Hong Kong's assertive civil society and comparatively weak state from 1997 to 2019 as an "abnormity" that should be rectified and transformed. Hence, empowering the post-colonial state in Hong Kong and taming the "over-assertive" civil society in Hong Kong have become the priorities of Beijing, which believes that the national security law and electoral reforms are the most effective panacea. Seventh, traditionally, the critical and participatory intellectuals have become the enemies of the PRC state. Given that many liberal-minded Hong Kong intellectuals have become more critical and participative than ever before, they naturally constitute the potential foes of the HKSAR regime and the mainland's party-state. Objectively speaking, the liberal democrats in the HKSAR contributed much to an unprecedented level of democratization in the city from 1997 to 2019. Unfortunately and sadly, some of them failed to understand the fact that Hong Kong's political development cannot and should not constitute a threat to the center's national security. To reverse the trend of anti-mainlandization, PRC authorities have been determined since the promulgation of the national security law in late June 2020 to implement national security education and national education, instilling a stronger sense of Chinese socio-political identity among the young people of Hong Kong.

Eighth, there have been tendencies in China's authoritarianism to drift toward neo-totalitarianism, as seen in how the mainland party-state mobilized citizens to have strict quarantine measures against the outbreak of COVID-19. This drift meant that the PRC authorities have been adopting a hardline approach to dealing with the HKSAR, bearing in mind how the radical Hong Kong democrats did constitute a national security threat to the central authorities. The radical democrats teamed up with the extreme localists in the anti–extradition bill movement in the latter half of 2019, plunging the HKSAR into an unprecedented crisis of legitimacy and provoking the mainland's necessary intervention. Even worse, a minority of radicals and democrats lobbied the Western democracies against the extradition bill, sparking the PRC's concern that they had become the "agents" of Western "imperialism" to "subvert" the local state in the HKSAR.

Ninth, if authoritarianism can have diffusion effects from one state onto another, as seen in other parts of the world, the PRC's "neo-totalitarianism" has already strengthened the authoritarianism of the HKSAR from "soft" to "hard." From the center's realpolitik perspective, the arrest, prosecution, and imprisonment of the law offenders in the 2019 anti-extradition protests and the 47 democrats who orchestrated the so-called primary elections held for the LegCo in the summer of 2020 were politically necessary, producing an effective deterrence against the resurgence of radical democrats and extreme localists in Hong Kong. In particular, the PRC authorities saw some radical democrats and extreme localists as forging a "conspiracy" with foreign political actors in "subverting" the HKSAR regime and fostering a "color revolution" on Chinese soil.

Tenth, the PRC has increasingly become an internal rather than an external factor in shaping Hong Kong's political development. The internalization of the China factor is politically significant for the "one country, two systems," for it propels the interests of "one country" to be preponderant over that of the "two systems." However, the challenge to Beijing is to keep the implementation of the national security law to a relatively minimal approach to promoting a Taiwan model of "one country, two systems" to the Taiwanese people, many of whom, however, still find the "one country, two systems" politically unattractive. Eleventh, the PRC's ideology of reunification can be seen as "regime inclusion" that necessitates the utilization of political power to stop the penetration of local radicals into the LegCo and to curb foreign influences on the HKSAR. Twelfth, the PRC's path of development does not show any convergence with the Western industrial democracies; rather, the China model is moving toward the Singaporean mode of governance. In the past, the PRC was dependent on Hong Kong for its capital, knowledge, and expertise in the mainland's economic modernization. With the onset of China's rise in the early 2000s, the equation of dependent development has been reversed. Hong Kong is now increasingly economically dependent on the mainland. Politically, Hong Kong's power dependence on the mainland is obvious.

All these perspectives are useful for us to understand the dynamics of the new politics of Beijing–Hong Kong relations. They are mutually reinforcing each other. Assertive nationalism strengthens the adoption of the legalist approach to coping with Hong Kong matters. The ideology of assertive nationalism is combined with legalism, paternalism, and Leninism, consolidating and reinforcing the PRC's fear of a "color revolution" in Hong Kong and its possible side-effects on the mainland's political development. The rivalries between China and the US have made the HKSAR a political pawn, especially as some Hong Kong democrats and radicals were politically close to the US and as they lobbied the US government for Hong Kong's democratization. The predominance of ideologies in the PRC under the leadership of Xi Jinping has meant that Hong Kong's relatively strong civil society must be tamed, and its weak post-colonial state must be empowered. The first solution, from Beijing's perspective, is the enactment and implementation of the national security law. Another solution was to change Hong Kong's electoral system to benefit its political clients, namely the "patriotic" or pro-Beijing elites, so that their power can be entrenched. The third solution is to implement a combined package of national security education and national education, changing the political culture and socialization of the young people in the HKSAR. China's Marxist legalists have adopted a perspective that Hong Kong's superstructure, which entails institutions, values, and education, must be changed from colonialism to Chinese nationalism. As such, electoral reforms had to be introduced to the LegCo and District Councils, the local Hong Kong identity has to be deemphasized and replaced by a national Chinese identity, and "patriotic" and national security education has to be enforced in schools where the political culture of the young people is to be transformed. Yet, the capitalistic economic base of Hong Kong remains unchanged for the benefit of China's economic modernization.

If authoritarian diffusion can be easily seen in other parts of the world, China's authoritarian resilience and its transformation into "neo-totalitarianism" have propelled the Hong Kong regime to change from "soft" to "hard" authoritarianism. The diffusion effects of the mainland's political system onto Hong Kong means that China is not converging with the Western democratic states. Specifically, China is adopting a Chinese model comparable to the Singaporean style of governance. Despite the fact that China is legalist, paternalistic, authoritarian, and perhaps "neo-totalitarian," its implementation of the national security law cannot be "excessive" because of the need to use the Taiwan model of "one country, two systems" to appeal to Taiwan for reunification. Even though many Taiwanese people are uninterested in the "one country, two systems" model, PRC authorities believe in its viability and feasibility. In particular, the Taiwan model of "one country, two systems" has already been delineated in the *White Paper on the Taiwan Question and China's Reunification* in August 2022. Specifically, Beijing does not exclude the possibility of stationing the PLA on the island after reunification, implying that the use of military forces to recover China's sovereignty over Taiwan is not excluded. It also proposes a stage-by-stage process of negotiation with Taiwan, and it allows foreign missions and consulates to be established in Taiwan after reunification. The features of the Taiwan model of "one country, two systems" have therefore emerged. Yet, the way in which China has dealt with Hong Kong after the anti-extradition movement in 2019 does have an impact on how many Taiwanese see the "one country, two systems." So long as most Taiwanese do not find the "one country, two systems" politically attractive, PRC authorities are under pressure to make it more palatable, more liberal, and more acceptable to them.

In the final analysis, the PRC is no longer dependent on Hong Kong economically. Rather, Hong Kong is increasingly dependent on the mainland economically. Politically, Hong Kong's power dependence on the mainland means that the principle of "one country, two systems" focuses more on the protection of China's interests, specifically its sovereignty, development, and national security. Both mainland China and Hong Kong have different legal systems; the common-law system in the HKSAR has to be maintained to give real substance to the elements of the "two systems." After all, the common-law system can and will buttress Hong Kong's capitalistic economic base. Regarding the political dimension, the HKSAR is destined to be an agent following the motherland's whims and directives. If the Hong Kong democrats, mainly the moderates now that the radicals have been purged, failed to push the HKSAR into a more Western path of democratization along the lines of having the whole LegCo directly elected and the chief executive directly elected through universal suffrage, they have to accept the reality that Hong Kong's political reform must proceed in a far more incremental and piecemeal manner than what they previously wanted. As such, a Hong Kong–style of democratization is the only one acceptable to Beijing; it may have a long-term impact of demonstrating how the PRC would be able to reform its mainland polity in a more liberal and democratic way.

Relations between the Twelve Academic Perspectives and Ten Contradictions

The twelve academic perspectives discussed above shape the way in which the ten contradictions in the "one country, two systems," which were examined in the Introduction, have been developing. The ten contradictions include (1) internationalism versus Chineseness in the city's development, (2) local identity versus mainland Chinese national identity, (3) localism versus assertive Chinese nationalism, (4) democratization versus national security, (5) the Western concept of democracy versus the Chinese notion of democracy, (6) pluralism versus paternalism, (7) the elite political culture of tolerating protests and dissent versus that of intolerance due to national security concerns, (8) the mass political culture of openness and confrontation versus that of emphasizing face and harmony, (9) Chinese legalism versus lenient liberalism, and (10) an executive-led system versus a more contentious executive-legislative relationship.

The twelve academic perspectives on Beijing-HKSAR relations embrace (1) the rise of assertive Chinese nationalism, (2) the importance of Chinese legalism, (3) the intertwined nature of Chinese paternalism and Leninism, (4) the PRC's concern about a "color revolution" in the HKSAR, (5) the authoritarian regime's tendency of fearing foreign intervention, (6) authoritarianism's dislike and reversal of a "weak" local state and "strong" civil society, (7) the perception of critical and participatory intellectuals as the central state's enemies, (8) the tendency of the PRC regime to drift toward "neo-totalitarianism," (9) the diffusion of authoritarianism from the mainland across the border to the HKSAR, (10) Beijing as increasingly an internal rather than an external actor in Hong Kong's political development, (11) the ideology of reunification as an inclusive approach adopted by the mainland regime, and (12) the PRC's path of converging with the

Singaporean model of development rather than the model of Western industrialized states.

The emergent and mixed ideologies of assertive Chinese nationalism, legalism, paternalism, and authoritarianism have already made the "one country, two system" move toward Chineseness or Sinification in the city of Hong Kong, although its international status as a financial and monetary center is to be maintained. Similarly, the mainland Chinese national identity has been stressed since the promulgation of the national security law. Localism is seen as harmful to the national security interest of Hong Kong under mainland China's sovereignty. Localism has to be replaced by a stronger Chinese national identity, which can be promoted through a revamp of political institutions, educational content, and national security emphasis. Democratization is bound to proceed in a way that must consider national security interests, meaning that the Chinese concept of democracy is preferred. As such, Beijing's rhetoric is to introduce and enhance the Hong Kong style of democracy, while Western-style democracy is to be denounced and jettisoned. Chinese paternalism is preferred over Western pluralism, while protests and dissent are regarded as undermining national security. Mass political culture is now remade to embrace social harmony and face, while Chinese legalism and the executive-led system are preferred over lenient liberalism and executive-legislative contentions, respectively. The PRC's concern about a "color revolution" and its fear of foreign intervention in the HKSAR have propelled the "one country, two systems" toward a heavy emphasis on the national security interest of the "one country." If securitization—a process of putting Hong Kong's political development under the national security umbrella of the central government in Beijing—has become a trend in Beijing-HKSAR relations since the promulgation of the national security law in late June 2020, then Beijing has become an internal rather than an external actor in Hong Kong politics. As the rise of China means that the PRC is not adopting the Western industrialized model of convergence, its uniqueness in maintaining Chinese nationalism, legalism, paternalism, and authoritarianism is bound to shape Hong Kong's "one country, two systems." In the words of Lucian Pye, mainland Chinese political culture has become triumphant over Hong Kong's political culture since mid-2020.

The challenge of Beijing is how to make the "one country, two systems" attractive to more Taiwanese people, who have been concerned about whether today's Hong Kong would become tomorrow's Taiwan. The ideology of reunification in the psyche of mainland authorities has made national security a top priority in their management of Beijing's relations with Hong Kong. Yet, if the ideology of reunification is replicated in dealing with the question of Taiwan's political future, it will demand perhaps a more innovative, more liberal, and more confederal, if not federal, approach to luring Taiwan back to the mainland's political orbit. Otherwise, the stronger the ideology of reunification, the less attractive the Hong Kong model of "one country, two systems" is to the people of Taiwan. Beijing's authorities responsible for Taiwan affairs have appeared to understand this constraint. As such, they have already designed a Taiwan model of "one country, two systems" for Taiwan. Yet, it remains to be seen how the Taiwan model of "one country, two systems" will be refined further to make it politically attractive to more Taiwanese people in the coming years.

2
Ideologies and Factionalism in Beijing–Hong Kong Relations

This chapter contributes to our deeper understanding of Beijing–Hong Kong relations by focusing on factionalism, an indispensable element in Chinese politics according to the late Lucian Pye. The relations between the PRC and Hong Kong have evolved rapidly since July 1, 1997, demonstrating different dominant factions and their complexities in political interactions. This chapter is going to firstly discuss Chinese factional politics and then examine the emergence of new factions on both the PRC and Hong Kong side, thereby making Beijing's relations with the HKSAR highly fluctuating and conflict-ridden.

Factionalism in Chinese Politics

After the Maoist era, the PRC's reform process began in its first phase from 1978 to 1987, when the moderates (formerly labeled as "capitalists," "landlords," "counterrevolutionaries," and "rightists") tried to construct a new legal order by adopting a new state and Party constitution and by promulgating the codes of criminal law, criminal procedures, and legal procedures.[1] Elections to the local people's congresses were held in 1980, while the NPC began to be more active and assertive in the discussions of national policy through its specialized committees to scrutinize proposed legislation. Yet, political liberalization had its costs, for price reform led to the rise of crime and corruption, and the expression of unorthodox views by intellectuals led to the emergence of a materialistic and vulgar popular culture among ordinary citizens. In response to the emergence of the Democracy Wall movement in 1979, PRC authorities clamped down on it and ushered in a period of political retrenchment, including the criticisms of "bourgeois liberalism" in 1980–1981, a campaign against "spiritual pollution"

---

1. Harry Harding, *China's Second Revolution: Reform after Mao* (Washington: The Brookings Institution, 1987), 74–75.

in 1983–1984, and a crackdown against corruption in 1985–1986.[2] The second phase of political reform began in 1986 as Deng Xiaoping raised it ambiguously. There were talks about the separation of the CCP from the government, the rejuvenation of the CCP and state bureaucracies, and the expansion of citizen participation. The relaxation of the political atmosphere led to an upsurge in demonstrations in November and December 1986 focusing on the improvement of university food and living conditions and tuition fees. Some citizens talked about the need for greater "freedom" and "democracy" in China.[3] The former CCP General Secretary Hu Yaobang supported political liberalization and the retirement of Party elders, and he refused to promote the children of senior cadres and officials. Hu's liberal tendencies were criticized by the Party elders. Intellectuals associated with Hu mobilized students to the streets to make their demands, raising the anger of Party elders, who later ousted Hu from the CCP. Hu was forced to resign his position in favor of Zhao Ziyang.

Harry Harding described the two contentious groups as moderate and radical reformers. Both groups agreed that there was a need for significant changes in the structure of China's political and economic systems. While the radicals were bold and enthusiastic about reforms, the moderates tended to be more cautious and skeptical.[4] The radicals supported a greater role for the market in China's economic reforms, while the moderates such a Chen Yun wanted to restrict the market operation to agricultural goods and a few manufactured commodities. Moreover, radicals welcomed more interactions and cooperation with foreign countries than the moderates. In the political realm, radicals allowed more intellectuals, including artists and writers, to have greater freedom to express themselves, and they hoped that the CCP would reduce its control over not only non-Party organizations but also factories. They favored an expansion in the role of local and national legislatures and the granting of greater freedom to the press. The radical reforms included Premier Zhao Ziyang, who succeeded Hu but who was later ousted in the power struggle between the radical and moderates over the issue of handling student protestors on Tiananmen Square on June 4, 1989. The moderate reformers embraced Peng Zhen, a former chairman of the SCNPC, Hu Qiaomu, an ideologist elected to the Politburo in 1982, and Deng Liqun, a member of the Secretariat with responsibility for the CCP's propaganda work. Unlike the radicals who supported bolder reform measures, the moderates were against total Westernization and saw materialism as being responsible for China's corruption and crime. Some of them, like Hu Qiaomu, went so far as to argue that if Guangdong were modeled on Shenzhen, the result

---

2. Harding, *China's Second Revolution*, 75.
3. Harding, *China's Second Revolution*, 76.
4. Harding, *China's Second Revolution*, 78.

would be the "Hongkongization" of the rest of the PRC.[5] The struggles between radicals and moderates shaped the PRC's political development from the mid-1980s to the early 1990s.

Chinese factional politics evolved in the post–Deng Xiaoping era, with his successor Jiang Zemin building up his Shanghai clique, which had legacies and impacts on Hu Jintao, a successor of Jiang.[6] When Jiang and Hu identified Xi Jinping as Hu's successor, Xi was tactful in building up his support from the Shanghai clique.[7] As Xi succeeded Hu as the CCP general secretary and the chairman of the Central Military Commission in November 2012, he began to establish his own faction and gradually curtailed Hu Jintao's Communist Youth League faction.[8] When Xi was elected as the PRC president in March 2013, he and his faction began to centralize political power. Xi departed from the style of collective leadership of Hu Jintao and former Premier Wen Jiabao and centralized political power by chairing many leading small groups.[9] In March 2018, when the NPC passed an amendment removing the term limit of the president, this move paved the way for President Xi to continue as long as he wishes.[10] A minority view argued that such a removal of the term limit was consistent with the "trinity" rule, namely the same person holding the chairs of the Central Military Commission, presidency, and CCP general secretary, and that the term's change would not have a practical impact.[11] The Xi faction consolidated its power in 2015, when Zhou Yongkang, a former secretary of the Central Political and Legal Affairs Commission, was sentenced to life imprisonment after he was convicted of bribery, abuse of power, and disclosure of state secrets.[12] Zhou was criticized by the PRC media for cultivating his own faction and collaborating with Bo Xilai, a former party-secretary of Chongqing, in an attempt at seizing political power

5. Harding, *China's Second Revolution*, 82.
6. Lowell Dittmer, "Chinese Factional Politics under Jiang Zemin," *Journal of East Asian Studies* 3, no. 1 (January–April 2003): 97–128. David Cohen, "China's Factional Politics," *The Diplomat*, December 8, 2012, accessed February 21, 2021, https://thediplomat.com/2012/12/chinas-factional-politics/.
7. Edward Wong and Jonathan Ansfield, "China Grooming Deft Politician as New Leader," *New York Times*, January 23, 2011, accessed February 21, 2021, https://www.nytimes.com/2011/01/24/world/asia/24leader.html.
8. Srijan Shukla, "The Rise of the Xi Gang: Factional Politics in the Chinese Communist Party," occasional paper, Observer Research Foundation, February 20, 2021, accessed February 21, 2021, https://www.orfonline.org/research/the-rise-of-the-xi-gang/.
9. Alice Miller, "More Already on the Central Committee's Leading Small Groups," *China Leadership Monitor*, no. 44 (July 28, 2014), accessed February 21, 2021, https://www.hoover.org/sites/default/files/research/docs/clm44am.pdf.
10. Suzuki Ken, "China's New 'Xi Jinping Constitution': The Road to Totalitarianism," November 27, 2018, accessed February 21, 2021, https://www.nippon.com/en/in-depth/a05803/.
11. Feng Lin, "The 2018 Constitutional Amendments: Significance and Impact on the Theories of Party-State Relationship in China," *China Perspectives*, no. 1 (2019): 11–21.
12. "China Corruption: Life Term for Ex-Security Chief Zhou," BBC, June 11, 2015, accessed February 21, 2021, https://www.bbc.com/news/world-asia-china-33095453.

at the top level of the Chinese leadership.[13] Factional politics were at play even though President Xi Jinping was gradually consolidating his power base.

Mainland Factions Affecting Hong Kong

Mainland Chinese factions shaped Beijing's policy toward Hong Kong in the past. When Xu Jiatun was appointed by the late CCP General Secretary Hu Yaobang as the director of the New China News Agency (NCNA, later renamed the Liaison Office in 2000) in 1983, he was involved in the PRC's factional politics. Xu Jiatun could be regarded as a softliner having opinion differences with the officials of the Hong Kong Macau Affairs Office (HKMAO).[14] Xu tried to get documents from the HKMAO, the secretary-general (later deputy director) of which, Li Hou, refused to let him obtain them.[15] Xu tried to bypass the HKMAO and went upward to report to the CCP's Central Foreign Affairs Leading Small Group—an action that strained the relations between the NCNA and HKMAO.[16] In 1983, the hardline and softline opinion groups emerged on Hong Kong matters, with the hardliners led by conservative planner Chen Yun arguing that the Chinese enterprises in Hong Kong should not engage in speculative and investment activities and that their foreign exchange should not be deposited in foreign banks.[17] But softliners like Xu disagreed with this view.

Xu was increasingly involved in China's factional struggle. In April 1989, Xu went to Beijing and discussed with Premier Zhao Ziyang how the CCP should handle the student protesters on Tiananmen Square. Both agreed that the Party should address the students' grievances. Xu went so far as to lobby Yang Shangkun, a conservative member of the hardline faction, telling him what he and Zhao thought.[18] After Zhao was removed from the premier position, Xu's situation became precarious. A meeting held by the HKMAO saw Ji Pengfei, the former HKMAO director, asking the Hong Kong and Macau Work Committee to "reflect" on the issues surrounding the Tiananmen incident—an indirect

---

13. Carrie Gracie, "Power Politics Exposed by Fall of China's Security Boss," BBC News, June 11, 2015, accessed March 28, 2021, https://www.bbc.com/news/world-asia-china-33098442.
14. Lo Shiu-Hing, "The Chinese Communist Party Elite's Conflicts over Hong Kong, 1983–1990," *China Information* 13, no. 4 (Spring 1994): 1–14.
15. Xu Jiatun, *Xu Jiatun Xianggang Huiyilu* [Xu Jiatun's Hong Kong memoirs] (Taipei: Lianhebao, 1993), Part 1, 397.
16. John P. Burns, "The Structure of Communist Party Control in Hong Kong," *Asian Survey* 30, no. 8 (August 1990): 749–763, especially 755.
17. *Xu Jiatun Xianggang Huiyilu*, Part 1, 246. On how opinion groups, which are issue-based, may change into factions, which are program-based coalitions, see Jurgen Domes, "Intra-Elite Group Formation and Conflict in the PRC," in *Groups and Politics in the People's Republic of China*, ed. David S. G. Goodman (New York: M. E. Sharpe, 1984), 28–35.
18. *Xu Jiatun Xianggang Huiyilu*, Part 2, 373.

criticism of Xu.[19] In response, Xu said that he would shoulder the responsibility. Meanwhile, the newly appointed CCP general secretary, Jiang Zemin, remarked that Xu had "rightist" tendencies and that he should be stripped of his NCNA director position.[20] Conservative hardliners like Ji Pengfei argued that the Hong Kong Alliance in Support of the Patriotic and Democratic Movement in China should be regarded as "subversive," but Xu resisted and argued that the PRC should continue to conduct a united front work on the people of Hong Kong.[21] Xu's decline after the removal of Zhao Ziyang was obvious; Premier Li Peng and CCP General Secretary Jiang Zemin no longer consulted him.[22] Seeing that his factional leader was struggling, Xu escaped to the US in 1990, and later, he was expelled from the CCP. The case of Xu showed that if mainland officials responsible for Hong Kong affairs were involved in the mainland's factional politics, they could be politically vulnerable especially if their faction lost the fight in the power struggles.

After the publication of the memoirs of Xu Jiatun, there were two significant memoirs published by mainland officials responsible for Hong Kong affairs who revealed the inside politics of the factional struggles, namely Zhou Nan and Li Hou.[23] Zhou Nan, who succeeded Xu, described Xu Jiatun as a "materialistic" cadre asking for financial support from Premier Zhou to build up a company in which Xu's relatives were hired.[24] Yet, the company later became bankrupt. As early as 1987, Beijing had the intention of recalling Xu back to work on the mainland. Zhou revealed that during the Hong Kong people's opposition to the construction of the Daya Bay nuclear power plant in 1987, Xu Jiatun was "afraid" of mass politics and suggested the central government consider changing the site of the nuclear power plant.[25] However, Deng Xiaoping was angry at his concession to public pressure, while Premier Zhou told Xu to ignore public opinion in Hong Kong. As a result, the Daya Bay nuclear power plant went ahead with its construction plan. Another PRC official, Li Hou, the former deputy director of the HKMAO, criticized Xu Jiatun for becoming a "big rightist" who ignored the previous work of the NCNA and who groomed his cronies against those cadres holding different views.[26]

---

19. *Xu Jiatun Xianggang Huiyilu*, 386.
20. *Xu Jiatun Xianggang Huiyilu*, 387.
21. *Xu Jiatun Xianggang Huiyilu*, 395.
22. *Xu Jiatun Xianggang Huiyilu*, 410.
23. Zong Daoyi, ed., *Zhou Nan's Oral Narratives* (Hong Kong: Joint Publishing, 2007); and Li Hou, *Historical Journey of Sovereignty Return* (Hong Kong: Joint Publishing, 1997).
24. Zong, *Zhou Nan's Oral Narratives*, 354.
25. Zong, *Zhou Nan's Oral Narratives*, 354.
26. Li Hou, *Historical Journey of Sovereignty Return*, 211.

From 1990 to 2012, PRC authorities responsible for Hong Kong matters were increasingly hardline. Xu's successor, Zhou Nan (1990–1997), failed to project a popular image among the people of Hong Kong; Zhou gave an impression of constantly confronting the last governor, Christopher Patten, over the scope and pace of democratic reform in Hong Kong.[27] Jiang Enzhu, a former PRC ambassador to the UK, succeeded Zhou as the Liaison Office director from 2000 to 2002. He was a former diplomat and projected a slightly softer image. Jiang's successor, Gao Siren (2002–2009), adopted a low-profile approach in Hong Kong and looked like a mainland bureaucrat relatively distanced from the masses. But Gao's subordinates, including all the deputy directors, voiced relatively hardline views on Hong Kong matters. Gao was succeeded by Peng Qinghua, whose image was more interactive with the people of Hong Kong than Gao's, but who served for a short period from 2009 to 2012.[28] In 2012, Zhang Xiaoming, a former secretary of the HKMAO Director Liao Hui in 1986, succeeded Peng. Zhang's image as the former Liaison Office director was quite hardline, saying that the concept of "separation of powers" was not suitable for the HKSAR and that the powers of the chief executive transcended that of the executive, legislature, and judiciary.[29] Overall, after 1990, it was not obvious that the PRC's factional struggle was shaping Hong Kong's development, mainly because those mainland officials responsible for Hong Kong matters were consistently adopting a hardline approach. However, factional politics and struggles evolved in the HKSAR so rapidly after 1997 that the reactions from the PRC's dominantly hardline faction to Hong Kong's factional development has become a prominent feature in Beijing-HKSAR relations.

During the anti-extradition movement from June to December 2019, there were rumors saying that the Jiang Zemin faction was competing with the Xi Jinping faction in the HKSAR, with the former composed of suspected corrupt businesspeople who hid in Hong Kong and who were even suspected of funding some protestors.[30] Taiwan's reports pointed to the action of the Xi faction to put the blame on the Jiang faction for the mass protests against the extradition bill

---

27. Sonny Shiu-Hing Lo, Steven Chung-Fun Hung, and Jeff Hai-Chi Loo, *China's New United Front Work in Hong Kong: Penetrative Politics and Its Implications* (London: Palgrave Macmillan, 2019), 6.
28. Lo, Hung, and Loo, *China's New United Front Work in Hong Kong*, 7–8.
29. Gary Cheung, "Hong Kong 'Separation of Powers': Why Beijing Is Laying down the Law on Who's in Charge," *South China Morning Post*, September 16, 2015, accessed February 22, 2021, https://www.scmp.com/news/hong-kong/politics/article/1858535/why-beijing-laying-down-law-whos-charge-hong-kong.
30. Paul Lin, "Hong Kong Caught in the Middle," *Taipei Times*, September 7, 2019, 8, accessed February 28, 2021, http://www.taipeitimes.com/News/editorials/archives/2019/09/07/2003721845. During the protests, some people painted the words "small Jiang" outside of MTR stations, such as the one in Mong Kok, which implied "little" Jiang Zemin. The author's observation during the June–December 2019 anti-extradition protests.

in the HKSAR.³¹ Although there was no concrete evidence to prove the validity of this claim, the disappearance of the publishers of the politically sensitive books published by the Causeway Bay Bookstore in the HKSAR from October to December 2015 illustrated Chinese factional politics at play. Lee Po was one of the operators of the Causeway Bay Bookstore, which was owned by the Mighty Current and which published political books on the corruption and sex scandals of CCP officials and cadres. It was difficult for any reader to verify the validity and accuracy of all the claims in the books published by the Causeway Bay publishers. Yet, some books were apparently highly sensitive, dealing with the inside politics of the PRC leadership, private affairs of PRC authorities, security personnel, and military developments.³² Some books exposed the allegedly corrupt deeds of mainland officials, such as the former Politburo Standing Committee member Zhou Yongkang and the former Chongqing party-secretary Bo Xilai, intentionally or unintentionally leading to the PRC government's action of investigating and prosecuting them for corruption. Lee Po disappeared from Hong Kong in December 2015. Many news reports said that he was "kidnapped" from the HKSAR, but Lee later diluted the incident when he returned to Hong Kong in March 2016, saying that he would no longer publish such books and returning to the mainland quickly.³³ Lee's bookstore was taken over by a person named Chan Hin-shing who, according to Hong Kong reports, had a mysterious background.³⁴ With the benefit of hindsight, it was unknown whether some books were written and published by mysterious authors who might have the intention of blackening the image of the dominant factional leaders and members in the PRC.

Gui Minhai, a Swedish citizen and another operator of the Causeway Bay Bookstore, disappeared in Thailand in late 2015, later making a confession on the mainland's television program that he had been involved in a car accident in the PRC. Gui was imprisoned for distributing books on the mainland without the

---

31. "Former China Leader Jiang Zemin and Supporters in Chairman Xi's Sights," July 9, 2019, *Taiwan News*, accessed February 28, 2021, https://www.taiwannews.com.tw/en/news/3741630.
32. The author bought a lot of books published by the Causeway Bay Bookstore, and the ones that touched on President Xi Jinping, his wife Peng Liyun, and the personnel changes in the PLA, the People's Armed Police, and the national security apparatuses were seemingly quite sensitive, for readers found it difficult to verify all the claims. See also Vivenne Zeng, "The Curious Tale of Five Missing Publishers in Hong Kong," Hong Kong Free Press, January 8, 2016, accessed March 1, 2021, https://hongkongfp.com/2016/01/08/the-curious-tale-of-five-missing-publishers-in-hong-kong/.
33. *Apple Daily*, March 25, 2016.
34. Chan expressed his interest in buying the ownership of the Causeway Bay Bookstore as early as November 1, 2015. When Lee disappeared in Hong Kong, the person who told Lee's wife that Lee was safe was Mr. Chan, presumably Chan Hin-shing. Chan also accompanied Lee Po to return to China immediately one day after Lee reappeared in Hong Kong on March 24, 2016. See "Chan Hin-shing Returns to Hong Kong after Holidays and Gives the Clients' Data to Lam Wing-kee," June 17, 2016, accessed March 1, 2021, https://theinitium.com/article/20160617-hongkong-hkbooksellers07/.

permission of PRC authorities until October 2017, when he was released from detention. In early 2018, Gui was arrested again and in February 2020 he was sentenced to ten years for "illegally providing intelligence to overseas."[35] Apart from Gui's disappearance, two other booksellers, Lu Po and Cheung Chi-ping, disappeared when they went to the mainland in October. The final one, Lam Wing-kee, was brought to Ningpo from Shenzhen for investigation but disclosed his experiences after his return on June 16.[36] According to Lam, the booksellers' case led to the investigation by a special task force from the central government, and the security personnel asked him for the details of not only authors but also sources, buyers, and subscribers of the politically sensitive books.[37] Refusing to bring a computer disk that involved the mainland subscribers' information, Lam held a press conference in Hong Kong and revealed his experiences on the mainland. In April 2019, Lam was so concerned about the extradition bill proposed by the HKSAR government that he decided to leave Hong Kong for Taiwan for good.

The disappearance of the booksellers was a highly politically significant event that might involve the PRC's factional politics. First, the anti–Xi Jinping faction might make use of the freedom of press in the HKSAR to publish books detrimental to the legitimacy of the PRC government and the CCP. The books that exposed the corrupt deeds and private lives of CCP officials and cadres attracted many mainland readers. Some of them dared to subscribe to the books, some threw them away after buying and reading them in Hong Kong, and some smuggled them onto the mainland through air and land routes.[38] From the perspective of national security, PRC authorities had strong grounds for confiscating such books and banning them from circulation on the mainland. Second, freedom of the press had its limits in the HKSAR. If those politically sensitive books were distributed in Hong Kong, they were allowed. But if they were sent or brought to the mainland, the cross-border distribution and dissemination of politically sensitive materials could violate the mainland law. Third, the disappearances of the five booksellers had different fates: Gui remains imprisoned in the PRC, Lam left Hong Kong for Taiwan, and the other three protected themselves by adopting a low profile on the mainland and in the HKSAR. While Lam became a whistleblower who had no choice but to leave Hong Kong, Gui's predicament showed

---

35. "Gui Minhai: Hong Kong Bookseller Gets 10 Years Jail," BBC News, February 25, 2020, accessed March 1, 2021, https://www.bbc.com/news/world-asia-china-51624433.
36. *Ming Pao*, June 16, 2016.
37. *Ming Pao*, June 16, 2016.
38. From 2013 to 2015, the author witnessed quite a lot of mainland tourists buying all the politically sensitive books in the bookstores, not only in Hong Kong but also at the Hong Kong international airport. One of my former mainland students even brought a whole box of such books into the mainland, but she told me that all the books were confiscated by the mainland customs authorities. Discussion with my mainland student in April 2015.

that his overseas Chinese status with dual citizenship (Swedish and Chinese) could not protect him from being "brought back" to China for trial, even though he stayed in Thailand. By publishing and distributing politically sensitive books in the PRC, the five booksellers were unintentionally entangled in the national security and factional politics of the mainland.

Some members of the anti-Xi faction appeared to utilize Hong Kong as a platform to publish all kinds of books, including on the scandals of officials and the secret lives of PRC authorities, thereby angering the PRC leadership that had to take action against the booksellers. From the perspective of security and factional politics, Xi's subordinates and supporters might be interested in discovering those mainlanders who were providing sources, buying such books, and subscribing to them for further investigation. The reason was that some mainlanders could be either the members of the opposing faction or the elements who deliberately leaked out inside information to the writers of the politically sensitive books.[39] Factional struggle in China could be one of the crucial factors leading to the disappearance of the five booksellers, who were not aware that by publishing and distributing politically sensitive books on China, they had committed cross-border crime from the PRC's national security perspective.

The fate of Xiao Jinhua, a mainland-born Chinese businessman holding Canadian citizenship, illustrated the factional struggles in the PRC. Xiao in January 2017 disappeared from the Four Seasons Hotel in Hong Kong, and it was believed that he was brought back by PRC authorities to the mainland for investigation for his corrupt activities, for he was regarded as a "white glove" of the Jiang Zemin faction.[40] In August 2022, Xiao was given thirteen years of imprisonment for his illegal activities on the mainland, such as "illegally absorbing public funds, illegal use of funds," and the "breach of trust and bribery."[41] The

---

39. Lam Wing-kee revealed to the Hong Kong media that one of the most sensitive books was about the idea of extending the tenure of office of President Xi Jinping, and that the mainland investigators grilled him in detail about the book's writer and the sources concerned. He later told the Taiwan media that another book on Xi's love affairs got the Causeway Bay Bookstore into trouble, for Gui Minhai had obtained a review document on Xi's performance when he was an official in Fujian province. For details, see "A Review Document of Xi Led to the Event of the Causeway Bay Bookstore," March 2, 2018, accessed March 1, 2021, https://www.rti.org.tw/news/view/id/398149. Lam also named the third book that was regarded as politically sensitive, namely a book on the reorganization of the PLA regions from seven to five. See "Those Banned Books That Have to Be Pursued and Investigated," Post852.com, June 17, 2016, accessed March 1, 2021, https://www.post852.com/161892/.
40. "【中共權鬥】外媒：「江澤民白手套」肖建華最快今月上海受審" [Xiao Jianhua who was a 'white glove' of Jiang Zemin is going to be on trial in shanghai this month], 自由亞洲電台粵語部 [Radio Free Asia], June 10, 2022, accessed September 18, 2022, https://www.rfa.org/cantonese/news/xiao-06102022060216.html.
41. Fong Tak Ho, "Shanghai Court Jails Tycoon Xiao Jianhua for 13 Years for Financial Crimes," Radio Free Asia, August 19, 2022, accessed September 18, 2022, https://www.rfa.org/english/news/china/tycoon-jailing-08192022150411.html. See also Blake Schmidt, "Fortune of Jailed Chinese

Xiao case was important from the perspective of factional politics. If the report about Xiao's close connection with the Jiang Zemin faction was accurate, then the extradition bill prepared by the HKSAR government and supported by the PRC authorities in 2019 could have been targeted at some mainland businesspeople, like Xiao, who allegedly committed commercial and criminal offenses on the mainland but who hid in the HKSAR. In other words, the Xiao case could be a stimulus leading to the formulation of the extradition bill in Hong Kong and to the factional rivalries on the mainland over whether such a bill should be enacted in the HKSAR.

The Emergence of Factional Politics in Hong Kong

Immediately after July 1, 1997, political factions in the HKSAR were consolidating quickly: the pro-government/pro-Beijing faction on the one hand and the pro-democracy faction on the other hand. They had already emerged in Hong Kong's electoral politics throughout the 1990s, especially after the LegCo witnessed the introduction of direct elections in 1991. The controversial policies of the Tung Chee-hwa government from 1997 to 2002 included civil service reform and housing reform, which were introduced with good intentions but were not explained properly to the public. The onset of the Asian financial crisis in late 1997 and early 1998 led to the economic difficulties of some citizens, whose negative equity was exacerbated partly by the property bubbles in the mid-1990s and the collapse of the property market.[42] The housing policy of building 85,000 units annually was announced by Chief Executive Tung Chee-hwa in 1998, but it was shelved without informing the public until June 2000. The outbreak of the severe acute respiratory syndrome (SARS) in the early half of 2003 triggered massive discontent, for the government was seen as sluggish in crisis management, including deficiencies in inter-governmental coordination and government-citizens communication.[43] Most importantly, the Tung administration's plan to introduce legislation on Article 23 of the Basic law—a stipulation that bans subversion, treason, secession, and sedition—in the summer of 2003 aroused public anxiety and huge political opposition. The government did not explain the rationale for the national security bill sufficiently. Nor was the bill's content adequately consulted on. Half a million citizens went onto the streets on

---

Billionaire's Family Survives in Exile," Bloomberg, September 6, 2022, accessed September 18, 2022, https://www.bloomberg.com/news/articles/2022-09-05/jailed-chinese-billionaire-xiao-jianhua-s-family-fortune-survives-in-exile.

42. Lo Wai-chung, "A Review of the Housing Policy," in *The July 1 Protest Rally: Interpreting a Historic Event*, ed. Joseph Y. S. Cheng (Hong Kong: City University of Hong Kong Press, 2005), 337–362.

43. Lee Shiu-hung, "The SARS Epidemic in Hong Kong: What Lessons Have We Learnt?" *Journal of the Royal Society of Medicine* 96 (August 2003): 374–378.

July 1, 2003.[44] The mass protests were politically significant as they symbolized a power struggle between pro-government and pro-democracy factions, but the latter faction scored a resounding victory to force the government to postpone the legislation on Article 23 indefinitely. Yet, Beijing was deeply apprehensive of the way in which the national security bill was withdrawn and postponed, for its security interests were not adequately protected.

The power struggle between the pro-democracy faction and the pro-government faction raised the concerns of PRC authorities. After the July 1 protests, PRC Vice-President Zeng Qinghong received delegations from the pro-government parties, including the Democratic Alliance for the Betterment and Progress of Hong Kong (DAB), the Hong Kong Progressive Alliance, and the Liberal Party, but he did not meet the pro-democracy camp.[45] However, it was the Liberal Party's core leaders, such as James Tien resigning from the top policy-making Executive Council (ExCo), who refused to support the Tung administration, perhaps indirectly leading to the failure of the passage of the national security bill. The PRC authorities tried to conduct a united front work on the Liberal Party because the party represented business interests. On the other hand, they saw the pro-democracy faction as politically "subversive," for the Civil Human Rights Front cooperated with the Article 45 Concern Group to mobilize human rights groups, religious activists, lawyers, teachers, intellectuals, and students to join the mass protests on July 1, 2003. The Catholic Church mobilized its religious supports to protest against the government on July 1, while the pro-democracy *Apple Daily* and some popular radio hosts mobilized members of the public to march on the streets. Shocked by the Hong Kong protests, PRC leaders dispatched some mainland researchers to the HKSAR, trying to discover the reasons why the angry civil society had suddenly exploded.[46]

The emergence of factional politics in the HKSAR was not a sudden event after July 1997. It had existed in Hong Kong under British colonial rule during the 1990s. In 1991, when direct elections were first introduced to the LegCo, the democrats performed impressively in elections and defeated many

---

44. Joseph Y. S. Cheng, "Introduction: Causes and Implications of the July 1 Protest Rally in Hong Kong," in *The July 1 Protest Rally: Interpreting a Historic Event*, ed. Joseph Y. S. Cheng (Hong Kong: City University Press of Hong Kong, 2005), 1–69.
45. Joseph Y. S. Cheng, "Hong Kong Since Its Return to China: A Lost Decade?," in *The Hong Kong Special Administrative Region in Its First Decade*, ed. Joseph Y. S. Cheng (Hong Kong: City University of Hong Kong Press, 2007), 31.
46. The author was invited by a few mainland researchers to talk about the July 1 protests and its causes. One of the researchers later joined a local Hong Kong university to become a researcher. He revealed to the author that a report he wrote back to the central government later was debated in December 2003 over the governance problems of the HKSAR. After the debate, the central government, according to him, realized that the HKSAR leadership might have some problems.

pro-government and pro-Beijing candidates.[47] Among the eighteen directly elected seats in the sixty-member LegCo, the democrats grasped sixteen seats, with the remaining two seats captured by independent candidates. The 1991 direct elections held for the LegCo could be seen as the emergence of factionalism in Hong Kong's electoral politics. The arrival of the last British governor, Christopher Patten, pushed democratic reforms further, alienating PRC authorities and unintentionally making the pro-democracy faction politically vulnerable to being seen as the "enemies" of the post-colonial state after July 1, 1997.[48] From the perspective of PRC authorities, Patten and the local democrats could all be seen as the pro-democracy faction, a legacy that paved the way in which China continued to view the pro-democracy forces as "agents" of the foreign states since July 1, 1997.

Factional politics in the first year of the HKSAR shaped electoral reform. In 1991, when the democrats captured most of the directly elected seats, the direct election method adopted "double seats" and single votes, meaning that there were two candidates in each geographical constituency being elected to the legislature and that each voter cast one ballot for one candidate in a direct election. This electoral system was seen by the pro-government conservative camp as having a "coat-tail" effect of making a more popular candidate help a less popular running partner.[49] Christopher Patten favored the "single seat" constituencies, which would likely favor the more popular pro-democracy camp, but he did not change the electoral system. In 1995, of the twenty directly elected seats, the pro-democracy flagship, namely the Democratic Party, captured twelve seats, whereas the pro-Beijing DAB merely got two seats—a result showing that the electoral system favored the pro-democracy faction. As such, in 1998, the HKSAR government under Tung Chee-hwa's leadership changed the direct election method to a proportional representation system, which was supposed to be beneficial to smaller groups, including the DAB at that time. After 1997, however, the proportional representation system gradually favored other small pro-democracy groups, especially the radical and social democrats, whose upsurge in direct elections could be seen in the 2008 LegCo direct elections during which the League

---

47. For details, see *Votes without Power: The Hong Kong Legislative Council Elections, 1991*, ed. Rowena Kwok, Joan Leung, and Ian Scott (Hong Kong: Hong Kong University Press, 1992). See also Li Pang-kwong, "Elections and Political Mobilization: The Hong Kong 1991 Direct Elections" (PhD thesis, University of London, 1995).
48. For details of Christopher Patten's reform plan and its political ramifications, see Lo Shiu-Hing, "An Analysis of Sino-British Negotiations over Hong Kong's Political Reform," *Contemporary Southeast Asia* 16, no. 2 (September 1994): 178–209.
49. For details, see Lo Shiu-hing and Yu Wing-yat, "The Politics of Electoral Reform in Hong Kong," *Commonwealth and Comparative Politics* 39, no. 2 (July 2001): 98–123.

of Social Democrats captured three seats.[50] In 2012, the League only managed to get its member Leung Kwok-hung re-elected in geographical constituency elections. Shortly after 2012, the League was replaced by the rapidly rising radical localists, whose performance in the 2016 LegCo direct elections was surprising, as will be discussed below. Hence, factional politics on the side of the pro-democracy camp evolved rapidly over time, originally led by the mainstream democrats from 1991 up to 2008 and later marked by the brief emergence of the League from its formation in 2006 to its impressive electoral performance in the LegCo's direct elections in 2008, after which the radical localists emerged and constituted a serious national security threat to the HKSAR government and PRC authorities. The radical localists participated in the anti-national education campaign in the summer of 2012, the Mong Kok riot in early 2016, and most importantly, the oath-taking controversy in October and November 2016. Radical localists turned out to be the most "dangerous" faction challenging the authority and legitimacy of both the HKSAR government and Beijing.

Hong Kong's factional politics became increasingly fragmented after the democratic victory in postponing the enactment of the national security bill in July 2003. Its complexity was due to the rapid rise of the localists, who were imbued with a very strong Hong Kong identity and who were to some extent radical and anti-mainland in their socio-political outlook. The fragmentation of the pro-democracy camp was accompanied by the split within the pro-government and pro-Beijing camp. Due to the fragmentation of political factions in the HKSAR, their interactions with the dominant political faction in the PRC became increasingly significant, problematic, and turbulent after July 1, 2003.

Democratic Reform, Patriotism, and the Interpretation of the Basic Law from 2004 to 2007

The mass protests on July 1, 2003—a political earthquake that led to the Tung Chee-hwa government to delay the passage of the national security bill—triggered the demands of the pro-democracy camp for the direct elections of the chief executive and the LegCo. The push for democratization in the HKSAR gathered momentum in the latter half of 2003. The strategy of the democrats was that, since the mass protests in July 2003 were successful in shelving the national security bill, their call for double direct elections would hopefully exert sufficient pressure on the HKSAR government to speed up the pace of democratic reforms. In response to the pressure from the democrats, the Hong Kong government

---

50. For a detailed discussion of the rise of the League of Social Democrats in Hong Kong politics, see Sonny Shiu-Hing Lo, *Competing Chinese Political Visions: Hong Kong vs. Beijing on Democracy* (Santa Barbara: Praeger Security International, 2010), 164–174.

began to review the content and scope of political reform after the July 1 protests in 2003.

The PRC authorities responded to the demands from the Hong Kong democrats cautiously and negatively. In December 2003, PRC President Hu Jintao met Hong Kong Chief Executive Tung Chee-hwa and Macau Chief Executive Edmund Ho, affirming their work positively. He added that the central government persisted in the implementation of "one country, two systems," "Hong Kong people ruling Hong Kong," "Macau people ruling Macau," the support of the two local governments, and the promotion of long-term prosperity and stability in both Hong Kong and Macau.[51] President Hu praised Tung Chee-hwa, saying that, after the chief executive reported his work in July, he should focus on the improvement of governance, livelihood issues, social stability, and economic development. While Tung's performance legitimacy was questioned by some Hong Kong people, especially the local democrats, he was staunchly supported by Hu, who, according to news reports, stayed in Shenzhen on July 1, 2003, when half a million protestors went onto the streets of Hong Kong. Most importantly, President Hu and the central government backed up the Tung administration by implementing the Closer Economic Partnership Arrangement in the summer of 2003, promoting cooperation between Guangdong and Hong Kong on the one hand and the HKSAR and Shanghai on the other and trying to boost the confidence of the Hong Kong people. The relatively moderate faction led by Hu Jintao tended to focus on the economic aspect and development of the HKSAR.

In response to the discussion over political reform in the HKSAR, President Hu remarked that while the central government attached great importance to the development of Hong Kong's political system, its principle was clear: namely, the political system of the HKSAR must not only be in conformity with the stipulations of the Basic Law but also "begin from the practical circumstances of Hong Kong and develop orderly and gradually."[52] On the issue of political reform, Hu believed that "the Hong Kong society can and will reach a broad consensus."[53] As a relatively softline and pragmatic leader who emphasized the collective leadership with Premier Wen Jiabao, President Hu could be seen as a relatively moderate Chinese leader on Hong Kong matters.

The most interesting response to Hong Kong's political reform came from the four legal experts from the PRC, namely Xiao Weiyun of Peking University, Xu Chongde of Renmin University, and Wu Jianfan and Xia Yong of the Chinese Academy of Social Sciences. In January 2004, Xiao argued that the relationships

---

51. "Hu Jintao Paid High Attention to Hong Kong's Political System Development," in *The Discussion and Dispute over Patriotism (Aiguo Luncheng)*, ed. Ming Pao (Hong Kong: Ming Pao Publisher, 2004), 3.
52. "Hu Jintao Paid High Attention to Hong Kong's Political System Development," 4.
53. "Hu Jintao Paid High Attention to Hong Kong's Political System Development," 4.

between one country and two systems were "holistic," referring to the necessity of the Hong Kong people to talk about "one country."[54] What he meant was that the "one country" empowered the "two systems." Furthermore, the people of Hong Kong should not expect to change the mainland's socialist system, and according to Xiao, any such effort at altering the mainland polity would constitute "subversion."[55] On central-local relations, Xiao contended that while the HKSAR enjoyed a high degree of autonomy, it remained a local regime under the central government's jurisdiction. He argued that, due to the unitary nature of China's political system, Hong Kong did not and would not have residual autonomy, unlike the US federal system.[56] If the powers enjoyed by the HKSAR were conferred by the central authorities, then Beijing would have the power to amend the Basic Law and appoint the chief executive and the related principal officials. Xiao stressed that Beijing had the power of appointing or not appointing the chief executive, a sign of substantial approval rather than a "nominal" one.[57] He added that, if the HKSAR could enjoy "complete autonomy," this would not be in conformity with the Basic Law.[58] Xiao elaborated on his ideas of the political system in Hong Kong, which to him was characterized by an "executive-led" polity with the chief executive playing the dual roles of being the leader of both the HKSAR and its government.[59] He pointed to the inapplicability of the concept of "separation of powers" in the context of Hong Kong, where mechanisms for entrenching the "executive-led" system were in place, such as Article 74 of the Basic Law saying that the act of individual legislators to put forward bills relating to government policy would need the approval of the chief executive. Xiao said this stipulation aimed at restricting the power of legislators to initiate bills.[60] The relationships between the executive and the LegCo, to Xiao, should be characterized by "partnership" rather than confrontation, although the chief executive is empowered to dissolve the LegCo, which in turn can also impeach him or her.[61] The chief executive is accountable to both the central government and the LegCo, but legislators cannot case their vote of no confidence on the chief executive as with the British parliamentary system.[62] Xiao cautioned the people of Hong Kong that the concept of "parliamentary supremacy" in the UK system could not be applied to the HKSAR, where the local courts cannot

---

54. Xiao Weiyun, "The Center Has to Control the Development of Political Reform," in *The Discussion and Dispute over Patriotism*, 20.
55. Xiao, "The Center Has to Control the Development of Political Reform," 21.
56. Xiao, "The Center Has to Control the Development of Political Reform," 22.
57. Xiao, "The Center Has to Control the Development of Political Reform," 23.
58. Xiao, "The Center Has to Control the Development of Political Reform," 25.
59. Xiao, "The Center Has to Control the Development of Political Reform," 26.
60. Xiao, "The Center Has to Control the Development of Political Reform," 27.
61. Xiao, "The Center Has to Control the Development of Political Reform," 27–28.
62. Xiao, "The Center Has to Control the Development of Political Reform," 29.

question the law-making power of the PRC Standing Committee of the National People's Congress.[63] Finally, with regard to Hong Kong's political reform, the central government in Beijing must have the right of participation.[64]

Another mainland legal expert, Xia Yong, concurred with Xiao's position in January 2004, emphasizing that the central government had the power of making initiatives.[65] As with Xiao, Xia focused on the rights enjoyed by the central authorities, including the "high degree of autonomy" conferred by the center on the local government in the HKSAR, the right of interpreting the Basic Law, and one country's foundation of the "two systems."[66] Xia pointed to the Hong Kong people's relatively weak awareness and understanding of the Basic Law, adding that reporters should enrich their knowledge of the mini-constitution.[67] He elaborated on the Basic Law's stipulations that require deeper understanding and more consensus, including Article 45 on the ultimate objective of selecting the chief executive "by universal suffrage upon nomination by a broadly nominating committee in accordance with democratic procedures."[68] Xia noted that the people of Hong Kong had different understandings of the concept of democracy. Yet, without a consensus on democracy, Article 45 could be a factor "simulating divisiveness."[69] Consensus building, according to Xia, would be necessary in the HKSAR. Finally, Xia stressed the need for the people of Hong Kong to insist on not only "one country" and "two systems" but also on a deeper understanding of the Basic Law. As with Xiao, Xia offered a centralist interpretation of Beijing–Hong Kong relations, emphasizing the role of the central government and the importance of understanding the mainland perspective on the Basic Law.

Adopting a centralist perspective, Xu Chongde in February 2004 articulated an argument that universal suffrage might not elect patriots ruling Hong Kong.[70] He cited Deng Xiaoping's remark saying that the main entity of "one country, two systems" is socialist China.[71] According to Xu, Hong Kong's autonomy was conferred upon it by the central government and "could not have unlimited boundaries."[72] For example, those people who advocated "self-determination" in designing political reform and deciding the criteria of patriotism were showing

---

63. Xiao, "The Center Has to Control the Development of Political Reform," 30.
64. Xiao, "The Center Has to Control the Development of Political Reform," 31–32.
65. Xia Yong, "The Right of Making Initiatives in Political Reform Comes from the Center," in *The Discussion and Dispute over Patriotism*, 35.
66. Xia, "The Right of Making Initiatives in Political Reform Comes from the Center," 36–37.
67. Xia, "The Right of Making Initiatives in Political Reform Comes from the Center," 38–39.
68. The Basic Law of the Hong Kong Special Administrative Region," Article 45, accessed March 2, 2021, https://www.basiclaw.gov.hk/pda/en/basiclawtext/chapter_4.html.
69. Xia, "The Right of Making Initiatives in Political Reform Comes from the Center," 39.
70. Xu Chongde, "Can Universal Suffrage Elect Patriots Ruling Hong Kong?" in *The Discussion and Dispute over Patriotism*, 107–112.
71. Xu, "Can Universal Suffrage Elect Patriots Ruling Hong Kong?" 108.
72. Xu, "Can Universal Suffrage Elect Patriots Ruling Hong Kong?" 109.

an "unlimited" behavior.[73] Xu emphasized that the persistence in upholding the principle of "one country" was of utmost importance, but a minority of Hong Kong people adopted a mentality of "using democracy to resist communism" and "opposing China whatsoever" and "confronting with the center"—actions that were "contrary to democracy."[74] He argued that since Hong Kong was part of mainland China, any discussion of democracy had to "respect the choice of 1.3 billion people in our national development" and to "support the central government which represents the fundamental interests of 1.3 billion people."[75] Copying directly from Western democracy would "bring about chaos" in the society of Hong Kong, and it "would not solve the unemployment problem of Hong Kong residents."[76] Xu stressed that "one country, two systems" required "the patriots as the mainstream Hong Kong people to govern Hong Kong," observing Deng Xiaoping's three criteria of "respecting our nation, of supporting the motherland to recover its sovereignty over Hong Kong," and of "not undermining Hong Kong's prosperity and stability."[77] Xu criticized those Hong Kong drafters of the Basic Law who "led the society's political forces, raised the banner of 'democracy,' and argued that the Basic Law stipulated the direct election of the Chief Executive through one person one vote."[78] He pointed to the phenomenon that some legislators in Hong Kong who were also the core leaders of the Hong Kong Alliance in Support of the Patriotic and Democratic Movement in China were "blackening" the image of the HKSAR and making remarks supportive of "Taiwan's independence."[79] Clearly, Xu was a centralist and legalist scholar upholding the center's political power and questioning whether universal suffrage would produce patriots ruling Hong Kong.

The remarks of mainland legal experts, such as Xiao Weiyun, Xia Yong, and Xu Chongde, paved the way for the central government's emphasis that patriots had to govern the HKSAR. After the HKSAR government's political reform task force visited Beijing in early February 2004, Xinhua stressed that Hong Kong's political system should be governed by "patriots."[80] When Chief Secretary Donald Tsang returned to Hong Kong from his Beijing visit to report on the position of the central government, he revealed three main points adopted by the center: (1) the principles governing Beijing's relations with the HKSAR; (2) the development of political reform in Hong Kong should proceed not only in "an orderly

---

73. Xu, "Can Universal Suffrage Elect Patriots Ruling Hong Kong?" 109.
74. Xu, "Can Universal Suffrage Elect Patriots Ruling Hong Kong?" 109.
75. Xu, "Can Universal Suffrage Elect Patriots Ruling Hong Kong?" 109.
76. Xu, "Can Universal Suffrage Elect Patriots Ruling Hong Kong?" 109.
77. Xu, "Can Universal Suffrage Elect Patriots Ruling Hong Kong?" 110.
78. Xu, "Can Universal Suffrage Elect Patriots Ruling Hong Kong?" 111.
79. Xu, "Can Universal Suffrage Elect Patriots Ruling Hong Kong?" 111.
80. "Centre: Hong Kong People Ruling Hong Kong Should Use the Patriots as the Mainstream," Xinhua, February 10, 2004, in *The Discussion and Dispute over Patriotism*, 64–65.

and a gradual manner" but also in accordance with the principle of practical circumstances; and (3) the importance of the remarks made by Ji Pengfei, the former director of the HKMAO, who said in 1990 that "balanced participation" was beneficial to Hong Kong's capitalist system and economic development.[81]

The discussion of patriotism laid the foundation for the Standing Committee of the National People's Congress (SCNPC) to interpret the Basic Law procedurally and legally on the questions of the direct election of the chief executive by universal suffrage and of the direct election of the entire LegCo. On April 6, 2004, the SCNPC interpretation was that Article 7 of Annex I of the Basic Law governing the election method of the chief executive and Article 3 of Annex II of the Basic Law dealing with the election method of the LegCo and its voting on bills and motions included the year 2007.[82] Moreover, the methods of selecting the chief executive and the LegCo might be amended or remained unamended.[83] Most importantly, the SCNPC interpretation focused on the procedures with regard to the amendment of the election methods. It stated:

> [A]ny amendment must be made with the endorsement of a two-thirds majority of all the members of the LegCo and the consent of the Chief Executive and shall be reported to the SCNPC for approval or for record mean the requisite legislative process through which the method for selecting the Chief Executive and the method for forming the LegCo and its procedures for voting on bills and motions are amended. Such an amendment may take effect only if it has gone through the said process, including the approval or recording ultimately given or made by the SCNPC in accordance with law. The Chief Executive of the HKSAR shall make a report to the SCNPC as regards whether there is a need to make an amendment; and the SCNPC shall, in accordance with Articles 45 and 68 of the Basic Law of the HKSAR of the PRC, make a determination in the light of the actual situation in the HKSAR and in accordance with the principle of gradual and orderly progress. The bills on the amendments to the method for selecting the Chief Executive and the method for forming the LegCo and its procedures for voting on bills and motions and the proposed amendments to such bills shall be introduced by the Government of the HKSAR to the LegCo.[84]

---

81. Donald Tsang, "The Center Reiterates That Those Hong Kong People Who Manage Hong Kong Should Love China and Hong Kong," in *The Discussion and Dispute over Patriotism*, 68.
82. "The Interpretation by the Standing Committee of the National People's Congress of Annex 7 of Annex I and Article III of Annex II to the Basic Law of the HKSAR of the PRC," L.N. 54 of 2004, B431, April 6, 2004, accessed March 7, 2021, https://www.basiclaw.gov.hk/en/basiclaw/annex-instrument.html.
83. "The Interpretation by the Standing Committee of the National People's Congress of Annex 7 of Annex I and Article III of Annex II," B433.
84. "The Interpretation by the Standing Committee of the National People's Congress of Annex 7 of Annex I and Article III of Annex II," B433.

Clearly, the SCNPC attached importance to all the procedures, especially the need for the chief executive to report to the SCNPC the need for such an amendment and its own approval for the HKSAR to proceed with any amendment of the Basic Law's provisions. The veto power of the SCNPC was affirmed.

On April 15, 2004, Chief Executive Tung Chee-hwa submitted a report to the chairman of the SCNPC, Wu Bangguo, on whether there was a need to amend the Basic Law regarding the election methods of the chief executive and the LegCo. He reported that when PRC President Hu Jintao met him in December 2003, the president expressed "serious concerns and principled position of the central authorities regarding Hong Kong's constitutional development."[85] Tung delineated the process in which the HKSAR government set up a task force to study constitutional development in January 2004. The task force was led by the chief secretary and included the secretary for justice and the secretary for constitutional affairs. In February 2004, the task force visited Beijing and met the representatives of the HKMAO and the Legislative Affairs Commission of the SCNPC while collecting public opinion in the HKSAR. By the end of March, the task force submitted a report on constitutional development to the HKMAO and the SCNPC. In April, it completed the second report. Chief Executive Tung reported to the chairman of the SCNPC, Wu Bangguo, in April 2004 in the following way:

> In considering how the methods for selecting the Chief Executive in 2007 and for forming the LegCo in 2008 should be determined, we should have regard to the following factors: (1) the HKSAR, in examining the direction and pace of its constitutional development, must pay heed to the views of the central authorities; (2) any proposed amendments must comply with the provisions of the Basic Law. Amendments to the design and principle of the political structure prescribed in the Basic Law must not be lightly contemplated; (3) no proposed amendments shall affect the substantive power of appointment of the Chief Executive by the central authorities; (4) any proposed amendments must aim at consolidating the executive-led system headed by the Chief Executive and must not deviate from this principle of design; (5) development towards the ultimate aim of universal suffrage must progress in a gradual and orderly manner step by step. The pace should not be too fast. The progress should accord with the actual situation in the HKSAR, in order to preserve its prosperity and stability; (6) when considering the actual situation, public opinions, as well as other factors, including the legal status of the HKSAR, the present stage of constitutional development, economic development, social conditions, the understanding on the part of the public of "one country, two systems" and the

---

85. The Standing Committee of the National People's Congress, "Report on whether There Is a Need to Amend the Methods for Selecting the Chief Executive of the HKSAR in 2007 and for Forming the LegCo of the HKSAR in 2008," April 15, 2004, accessed March 7, 2021, https://www.cmab.gov.hk/cd/eng/executive/pdf/cereport.pdf.

Basic Law, public awareness on public participation, the maturity of political talent and political groups, as well as the relationship between the executive authorities and the legislature, must be taken into account; (7) any proposed amendments must enable different sectors of society to be represented in the political structure, and to participate in politics through various channels; (8) any proposed amendments should ensure that consideration would continue to be given to the interests of different sectors of society; and (9) any proposed amendments must not bring about any adverse effect to the system of economy, monetary affairs, public finance and others as prescribed in the Basic Law.[86]

While the HKSAR government's report emphasized the need to respect the power and approval of the central authorities, it stressed the need for constitutional reforms to proceed in "a gradual and orderly manner step by step." Therefore, the report could be seen as the first step made by the HKSAR government to justify the necessity of maintaining the political status quo, followed by the decision made by the SCNPC on April 26, 2004.

The decision adopted by the SCNPC on April 26, 2004, was composed of several elements. First, it reiterated the need for Hong Kong's constitutional reform to "conform to principles such as being compatible with the social, economic, political development of Hong Kong, being conducive to the effective operation of the executive-led system, being conducive to the maintenance of the long-term prosperity and stability of Hong Kong."[87] Second, it asserted that Hong Kong did not have a long democratic history and that the Hong Kong people had exercised their democratic right to select their chief executive since 1997. Third, the decision reminded the people of Hong Kong that out of the sixty members of the LegCo, the number of members returned from geographical constituencies increased from twenty in the first term to twenty-four in the second term and then to thirty in September 2004. As such, the democratic progress in Hong Kong remained to be observed, especially the impact on the executive-led system. Fourth, different sectors of society had different views on how the chief executive should be selected and how the LegCo should be democratized. The SCNPC came up with the observation that the people of Hong Kong "have not come to a broad consensus."[88] It asserted that "conditions do not exist

---

86. "Report on Whether There Is a Need to Amend the Methods for Selecting the Chief Executive," 3–5.
87. "Report on Whether There Is a Need to Amend the Methods for Selecting the Chief Executive," 3–5.
88. "Decision of the Standing Committee of the National People's Congress on Issues Relating to the Methods for Selecting the Chief Executive of the HKSAR in the Year 2007 and for Forming the LegCo of the HKSAR in the Year 2008," adopted by the Standing Committee of the Tenth National People's Congress at its Ninth Session on April 26, 2004, accessed March 7, 2021, https://www.cecc.gov/resources/legal-provisions/full-text-npc-standing-committee-decision-on-issues-concerning-methods.

for the selection of the Chief Executive by universal suffrage upon nomination by a broadly representative nominating committee in accordance with democratic procedures as provided for in Article 45 of the Basic Law and the election of all the members of LegCo by universal suffrage as provided for in Article 68 of the Hong Kong Basic Law."[89] According to the decision made by the SCNPC on April 26, 2004,

> The election of the third Chief Executive of the HKSAR to be held in the year 2007 shall not be by means of universal suffrage. The election of the LegCo of the HKSAR in the fourth term in the year 2008 shall not be by means of an election of the members by universal suffrage. The ratio between members returned by functional constituencies and members returned by geographical constituencies through direct elections, who shall respectively occupy half of the seats, is to remain unchanged. The procedures for voting on bills and motions in the LegCo are to remain unchanged.[90]

Clearly, the SCNPC applied its brake on the progress of democratic reforms in the HKSAR, maintaining the political status quo, emphasizing the need for incremental changes, and setting down the half-half ratio of members returned from functional constituencies and those from geographical constituencies. The idea was to maintain checks and balances on those LegCo members returned from geographical constituencies.

In terms of factional politics, it can be argued that PRC leaders and authorities responsible for Hong Kong matters in 2004 were conservative at that juncture because they maintained the principle of gradual and orderly change to the extent of retaining the status quo in the Hong Kong polity. While the mainland legal experts on the Basic Law were legalists and conservatives, other PRC authorities, including President Hu Jintao and Premier Wen Jiabao, were actually and relatively more "liberal" than their successors, especially in the period after late 2012 as Xi Jinping gradually consolidated his political power and position in the PRC. During the Hu Jintao era, at least the moderates dominated the legalist conservatives in China's policy toward the HKSAR, unlike during the Xi Jinping era in which the legalist conservatives have become the dominant policy makers on Hong Kong matters.

After the SCNPC interpretation of Hong Kong's constitutional development was made in April 2004, Chief Executive Tung Chee-hwa resigned on March 10, 2005, for personal and health reasons.[91] Due to Tung's resignation, a replacement

---

89. "Decision of the Standing Committee of the National People's Congress on Issues Relating to the Methods for Selecting the Chief Executive," E9.
90. "Decision of the Standing Committee of the National People's Congress on Issues Relating to the Methods for Selecting the Chief Executive," E9.
91. "Tung Chee-hwa Resigns as Hong Kong Chief Executive," *China Daily*, March 11, 2005, accessed March 7, 2021, https://www.chinadaily.com.cn/english/doc/2005-03/11/content_424042.htm.

chief executive had to be elected in July 2005. However, the society of Hong Kong had different views on the terms of office of the new chief executive, namely whether it would be five-year term or whether it would serve the remaining months of the chief executive. As such, the HKSAR government led by the acting Chief Executive Donald Tsang reported to the PRC State Council in April 2005, seeking an interpretation of the SCNPC on the matter of the term of office of the new chief executive.[92] In response, the SCNPC interpreted the term of office of the new chief executive as follows:

> [P]rior to the year 2007, when the Chief Executive is selected by the Election Committee with a five-year term of office, in the event that the office of Chief Executive becomes vacant as he (she) fails to serve the full term of office of five years as prescribed by Article 46 of the Basic Law, the term of office of the new Chief Executive shall be the remainder of the previous Chief Executive; and that after 2007, the above mentioned method for selecting the Chief Executives could be amended, and should the office of the Chief Executive then become vacant, the term of office of the new Chief Executive shall be determined in accordance with the amended method for the selection of the Chief Executive.[93]

The 2005 SCNPC interpretation on the term of office of the replacement chief executive was a procedural one without controversies as it only clarified the issue concerned. Factional politics was not involved, either from the PRC or from the HKSAR.

Under Chief Executive Donald Tsang, the HKSAR government continued to study the issue of constitutional reform. In December 2007, Chief Executive Tsang submitted a report to the chairman of the SCNPC, Wu Bangguo, reporting on whether there would be a need to amend the Basic Law's provisions regarding the methods of selecting the chief executive and the LegCo in 2012. In October 2005, the Tsang government suggested that the Election Committee would be expanded from 800 to 1,600 members for the selection of the chief executive in 2007. Moreover, candidates running for chief executive would have to acquire at least 200 nominations, and they would not have political party backgrounds. At the same time, the LegCo would be increased from sixty to seventy members in 2008, and five of the new seats would come from geographical constituencies and five from functional constituencies or 500 members of the eighteen District Councils.[94] Without appreciating the fact that the Tsang administration was at

---

92. "Report to the State Council Concerning the Submission of a request to the SCNPC Regarding the Interpretation of Article 53(2) of the Basic Law of the HKSAR of the PRC," April 6, 2005, accessed March 7, 2021, basiclaw.gov.hk.
93. "Interpretation of Paragraph 2, Article 53 of the Basic Law of the HKSAR of the PRC by the SCNPC," adopted at the 15th Session of the Standing Committee of the Tenth NPC on April 27, 2005.
94. Lo, *Hong Kong's Indigenous Democracy*, 46–47.

least sincere in pushing forward the process of democratic reforms, some local democrats were dissatisfied with the proposed model and wanted to have a faster pace and larger scope of democratic reform on the basis of the SCNPC interpretation in April 2004. The democrats mobilized their supporters to protest against the government's proposals. In response, the Tsang administration made a small concession by proposing to abolish the appointed seats in District Councils gradually from 2008 to 2015. Unfortunately, the democrats were hardliners, and twenty-four of the pro-democracy legislators rejected the reform proposal of the Tsang administration, albeit thirty-four pro-government LegCo members supported it. The proposal failed to get a minimum of forty votes in the sixty-member legislature. After the democratic camp's rejection of Tsang's reform plan, it was labeled by the pro-government and pro-Beijing media as the "political opposition." With the benefit of hindsight, the pro-democracy faction was too hardline and missed a golden opportunity to bargain with the Tsang government. From the perspective of PRC leaders, the Hong Kong democrats opposed the HKSAR government for the sake of opposition without the sincerity of making mutual concessions and compromise. As such, on December 29, 2007, the SCNPC interpreted the Basic Law, saying that the method of selecting the chief executive and the LegCo in the year 2012 would remain unchanged, including the half-half ratio of legislators returned from geographical constituencies and those returned from functional constituencies. Clearly, the PRC authorities were reluctant to make any further concession to the democrats, who in their eyes were obstinate, oppositionist and politically aggressive and greedy.

The local democrats led by the hardline faction continued to exert pressure on the HKSAR government to democratize the political system. In November 2005, the HKSAR government continued the discussions with the community on how to achieve the objective of universal suffrage through a Commission on Strategic Development. A Green Paper on constitutional development was published in July 2007, raising various options on the methods of selecting the chief executive and electing LegCo members.[95] Public consultation on the *Green Paper* lasted from July to October 2007 and the government received 18,200 written submissions with 150,000 signatures.[96] Chief Executive Tsang made the following conclusion:

> There is general expectation within the community that the electoral system of the HKSAR can be further democratized and that the ultimate aim of universal

---

95. *Green Paper on Constitutional Development* (Hong Kong: Constitutional and Mainland Affairs Bureau, July 2007).
96. "Report on the Public Consultation on Constitutional Development and on Whether There Is a Need to Amend the Methods for Selecting the Chief Executive of the HKSAR and for Forming the LegCo of the HKSAR in 2012," December 12, 2007, accessed March 7, 2021, https://www.cmab.gov.hk/doc/issues/Report_to_NPCSC_en.pdf.

suffrage can be attained as early as possible in accordance with the Basic Law. Having considered the views of LegCo, District Councils, organizations and individuals from various sectors, as well as members of the public in totality and, after thorough deliberation, I have come to the view that the community generally hopes that the universal suffrage timetable can be determined early, so as to set the course for Hong Kong's constitutional development. Implementing universal suffrage for the Chief Executive first in 2012 is the expectation of more than half of the public, as reflected in the opinion polls; this expectation should be taken seriously and given consideration. At the same time, implementing universal suffrage for the Chief Executive first by no later than 2017 will stand a better chance of being accepted by the majority in our community . . . As for the models of forming LegCo by universal suffrage and how the functional constituencies should be dealt with, views are still very diverse. However, setting the timetable for implementing universal suffrage for the Chief Executive and LegCo can help promote the ultimate resolution of issues involved. On the basis of the above conclusion, I consider that, in order to realize the aim of universal suffrage as provided for in the Basic Law, there is a need to amend the methods for selecting the Chief Executive and for forming LegCo in 2012.[97]

The HKSAR government led by Chief Executive Donald Tsang made genuine efforts at consulting public opinion on the progress of political reform, and at raising various options and issues in the selection of the chief executive by universal suffrage and the methods of electing LegCo members. Therefore, the HKSAR government under Tsang's leadership was by no means a mouthpiece of the central authorities in Beijing; it made initiatives in dealing with democratization locally with considerable autonomy. In factional terms, it can be argued that the HKSAR government led by Donald Tsang was dominated by a relatively liberal faction.

In November 2009, the HKSAR government put forward another political reform proposal, saying that the LegCo in 2012 would increase from sixty to seventy members, that half of the ten new seats would come from geographical constituencies and half stemming from the directly elected members of District Councils, and that the 2012 Chief Executive Election Committee would increase its members from 800 to 1,200. Yet, a radical faction of the democrats stirred up the political reform controversies; two legislators affiliated with the Civic Party and three lawmakers associated with the Liberal Social Democrats resigned from the LegCo in January 2010. Their resignation led to a so-called "referendum movement" for the voters to express their views on democratic reform. Although all of them were interestingly re-elected to the LegCo on May 16, 2010, the PRC authorities were alienated but under the pressure to come up with a compromise with the moderate faction of the democratic camp. In other words, PRC officials

---

97. "Report on the Public Consultation on Constitutional Development," 7–8.

responsible for Hong Kong affairs attempted to conduct united front work on the moderate democrats, reaching a compromise on the territory's constitutional development. Under the HKSAR's executive-led system, "referendum" was seen as "subversive" by PRC authorities, although it was politically tolerated by the HKSAR government. Moreover, PRC authorities attached importance to the question of face; if the HKSAR government proposed a reform plan with some concessions made to the democrats, then the democratic camp should have been more diplomatic and skillful in accepting the goodwill gesture from the ruling elites.

In the early half of 2010, the democrats were divided into moderates, who were composed of the leaders and members of the Democratic Party, and radicals, who were led by Raymond Wong, Leung Kwok-hung and their Liberal Social Democrats and some leaders of the Civic Party. The moderates led by the Democratic Party, including Albert Ho and Emily Lau, went to the Liaison Office and negotiated with its deputy director Li Gang—an unprecedented move in the history of the HKSAR.[98] Li openly remarked: "We very much hope that we can take a fresh step in realizing electoral reforms for 2012 . . . that will take us a step closer toward universal suffrage."[99] From an objective standpoint, the PRC in the year 2010 was governed by relatively liberal leaders and moderates responsible for Hong Kong matters. Hence, under the circumstances that the radical faction of Hong Kong's democrats launched the so-called "referendum movement," neither the PRC nor the HKSAR government suppressed it. While the HKSAR government tolerated such a movement, the Liaison Office officials began negotiating with the moderate democrats. Of course, it can be argued that, without the radical democrats' action of launching the "referendum movement," PRC authorities might not be keen to go to the negotiating table to bargain with the moderates. In short, the PRC, which was ruled by the relatively liberal leaders like President Hu Jintao and Premier Wen Jiabao, adopted a policy of moderation toward Hong Kong,[100] while the HKSAR political landscape was prominently divided between radicals and moderates in the pro-democracy camp. The divided democrats opened a window of golden opportunity for mutual concessions and bargaining between the relatively liberal PRC officials on the one hand and moderate democrats on the other hand. Such a golden opportunity, as will be discussed in this book later, could not be easily replicated with the passage of

---

98. James Pomfret, "Beijing Breaks Ice with Hong Kong Opposition," Reuters, May 24, 2010, https://www.reuters.com/article/us-hongkong-democracy-idUSTRE64N1ZQ20100524.
99. Pomfret, "Beijing Breaks Ice with Hong Kong Opposition."
100. In December 2009, President Hu told Chief Executive Donald Tsang to handle Hong Kong's constitutional reform in "an appropriate manner." See *South China Morning Post*, December 29, 2009. See also Joseph Y. S. Cheng, "Challenge to Pro-democracy Movement in Hong Kong," *China Perspectives*, no. 2 (July 2011): 44–60.

time, especially from 2019 to 2021 when the PRC was led by relatively hardline, nationalistic and conservative legalists.

In the May 2010 negotiation with PRC authorities, the moderate democrats led by the Democratic Party bargained for a political reform model in which the seventy-member LegCo in September 2012 would have five new members directly elected and another five members nominated by all District Council members and then elected directly by voters who would not have ballots in functional constituencies. This proposed model did not reject the Donald Tsang reform proposal, but constructively added the ingredient of how to implement it. As such, the moderates' proposal had the prospect of achieving a political breakthrough. The moderate democrats also formed an Alliance for Universal Suffrage, which was composed of fifteen legislators and which called for the abolition of all functional constituencies. Indeed, this demand was rejected by both the HKSAR government and Beijing, which had to adhere to the SCNPC's earlier interpretation that the LegCo composition would stick to the half-half ratio of members returned from geographical constituencies and functional constituencies. However, Donald Tsang and his officials agreed to make a minor but crucial concession to the moderate democrats by promising to eliminate the appointed members of District Councils on the condition that the moderate democrats would support the 2012 political reform package. It was reported that Tsang wrote to President Hu Jintao, who eventually approved the concessions made to the moderate democrats—a significant breakthrough attributable to the willingness of the moderate democrats to accept the reform plan, the goodwill from the Tsang administration, and the relatively liberal acumen of the PRC leadership. Eventually, the political reform proposal was approved in LegCo with forty-six members supporting it and twelve voting against it. Ten democrats in the LegCo supported the reform proposal, while radical democrats led by Raymond Wong denounced the moderates as "selling out" the interest of the Hong Kong people.

The PRC's relatively liberal faction, which governed the nation and dealt with Hong Kong matters, was not only tolerant of the "referendum movement" launched by the radical democrats in the HKSAR but also favorable toward a compromise between Liaison Office officials and the local moderate democrats. Critics of the political compromise reached between the Democratic Party and the Liaison Office failed to appreciate the fact that the Hu-Wen leadership in the PRC was relatively liberal compared with the Xi Jinping era that began in late 2012. The presence of a relatively tolerant and liberal regime in the PRC provided a fertile ground for the opportunities of political bargaining between the Hong Kong moderates and mainland officials on the one hand and between the moderates and the HKSAR government on the other. The HKSAR government led by Donald Tsang was fully supported by the PRC authorities responsible for Hong Kong matters. As such, the political reform proposal from Tsang was endorsed by Beijing. Tsang's action of reaching a compromise with moderate democrats on the one hand and lobbying Beijing for agreeing to some concessions was critical in the entire political breakthrough. However, the radical democrats who rejected the Tsang proposal were naturally regarded as the enemies of the local government of the HKSAR and the central state in Beijing. Moderate democrats who accepted the Tsang reform plan and made concessions were viewed as the targets of China's united front work, but they were naturally regarded as "traitors" by radical democrats. A trade-off between the acceptance of China's cooptation and the criticism of being the "traitors" of Hong Kong had to be made by the moderates, who however began to build up some degree of political trust with the HKSAR government and PRC authorities.

The 2010 reform breakthrough was politically significant in another aspect. Many democrats, especially the radicals, began to harbor an illusion that, by exerting pressure on both the HKSAR government and Beijing, democratic reform would be expanded in its scope and accelerated in its pace. This assumption, however, turned out to be highly dangerous and problematic from 2012 to 2019 when the Xi Jinping regime in the mainland became increasingly hardline on Hong Kong matters. Moreover, the successors to Donald Tsang adopted an increasingly less supportive, if not necessarily hardline, approach to dealing with concessions to constitutional reforms in the HKSAR. Even worse, the radical democrats in the HKSAR were, as will be discussed later, divided into separatist and extremists. Due to factional draft from moderates to conservatives on the sides of both the HKSAR government and Beijing, and because of the further extremism of the democratic radicals, the outcome was the narrowing space for any moderates to ponder and advocate a compromise, which was increasingly distant and politically difficult.

Factional Politics in Hong Kong and the PRC from 2003 to 2019

Factional politics evolved in several stages in Hong Kong between 2003 and 2019 and interacted with the mainland's factionalism. From 2003 to the emergence of the anti–national education campaign in the summer of 2012, Hong Kong was characterized by a rapid emergence of localism, which can be defined as a local ideology that elevates Hong Kong's socio-cultural and political identity to the level of becoming more anti-mainland, anti-PRC, and anti-CCP than ever before. If localism is defined as a phenomenon of local-born Hong Kong people imbued with a very strong sense of Hong Kong identity, it did exist in Hong Kong long before 2003. The emergence of Hong Kong identity could be traced back to the 1980s when the local people began to develop a strong sense of localism, which was very different in content compared with the localism in the early 2000s. Hugh Baker wrote in 1983 and described the "Hong Kong man" as those people who were neither British nor Chinese, those who were loyal neither to UK nor to the PRC, and those who spoke Cantonese rather than Putonghua.[101]

Baker's content of the Hong Kong person changed after July 1, 1997; more Hong Kong people learnt to speak Putonghua; many of them have increasingly identified themselves as Chinese. Most significantly, a continuity persisted in the psyche of many Hong Kong people. Their Chinese nationalism was relatively weaker compared to the compatriots in the PRC, for their education and political socialization remained very different. Gradually, relatively strong localism and weak Chinese nationalism in Hong Kong developed into a strong anti-PRC ideology. After the 2012 anti–national education movement, the 2014 Occupy Central movement, the 2016 Mong Kok riot and the 2019 anti-extradition movement, PRC authorities responsible for Hong Kong affairs were determined to introduce the national security law, enforce national security education and exert pressure on the HKSAR government to transform the liberal education studies curriculum into national education so that the Hong Kong people can and will have a greater sense of Chinese identity, both culturally and politically. The Hong Kong people from the 1980s to the early 2000s had a weaker sense of Chinese political identity because they tended to separate cultural identification of being Chinese from the political recognition of the ruling party in the PRC, namely the CCP.[102] The mainland Chinese citizens tended to merge their cultural identity with the political identification of the CCP.[103] From the perspective of citizenship, the Hong Kong version of citizenship that separated cultural from political identity of being Chinese was increasingly at loggerheads with the mainland version of citizenship, which inculcates a mixture of cultural and political identities among the mainlanders.

The separation of cultural identity from political one could be seen in the mass protests against the national security legislation as early as July 1, 2003, when the Tung Chee-hwa government failed to enact the legislation and postpone it indefinitely. Many opponents to the national security legislation were classical liberals who were frightened by the prospects of civil liberties being curbed in Hong Kong.[104] The public fear of the PRC in general and the CCP in particular was pushed to another political extreme in the summer of 2012, when parents, teachers, students and intellectuals opposed the implementation of a national education policy. Partly because of the failure of the HKSAR education

---

101. Hugh D. R. Baker, "Life in the Cities: The Emergence of the Hong Kong Man," *China Quarterly* 95 (September 1983): 469–479, and the quotation came from 478–479.
102. Lo, *The Dynamics of Beijing-Hong Kong Relations: A Model for Taiwan?*
103. This was my observation after teaching and interacting with many mainland Chinese students in Hong Kong from 2008 to 2019.
104. The author's personal observations in the LegCo's public hearings on the national security bill from March to May 2003.

bureaucracy to explain the rationale and content of national education to parents and students, and partly because of the sudden emergence of many young local students to launch a social movement to oppose such policy, the national education scheme was shelved in September 2012, but PRC authorities were alarmed, shocked and alienated. The "success" of the anti–national education policy proved to PRC officials that some Hongkongers were anti-governmental, anti-mainland and anti-CCP, sowing the seeds of further conflicts between some Hongkongers and the central authorities.

The first stage of localism in the HKSAR from 2003 to 2012 was marked by public anxieties and fear over whether the lifestyle and civil liberties enjoyed by the people of Hong Kong would be "mainlandized." In between 2003 and 2012 was the execution of the individual visit scheme by the PRC government in response to the eruption of the Severe Acute Respiratory Syndrome (SARS) in Hong Kong in the early half of 2003. The scheme aimed at reviving the Hong Kong economy and stimulating the city's prosperity. Unfortunately, the HKSAR government did not assess the societal impacts of the large influx of mainland tourists and visitors, whose buying sprees in Hong Kong led to the anger of some localists, who argued that their daily lives were disrupted and daily necessities such as toothpaste and milk powder were grasped by the mainlanders. Some mainland pregnant women went to give birth in local hospitals, depriving local pregnant women of their hospital beds until the HKSAR government and the Hospital Authority decided to control the influx of mainland pregnant women and their easy access to local hospital facilities. Poor government planning and its lack of risk assessment of the mainland visitors' scheme led to the unnecessary social tensions between a minority of local Hong Kong people and some mainland tourists. Sadly, some local and mainland media exaggerated the discriminatory attitudes of a minority of Hong Kong people toward mainland tourists, leading to a tense social atmosphere between Hongkongers and mainlanders.

The Ideological Clash between Localism and Mainland Chinese Nationalism

From the summer of 2012 to late 2019, the relationships between the central government in Beijing and the HKSAR was politically characterized by the clashes of two main ideologies: nationalism on the more pro-mainland-Chinese side and localism on the more pro-Hong Kong side.[105] The politico-ideological spectrum in Beijing–Hong Kong relations can be seen as a continuum, with

---

105. This section is an updated version of my article, "Ideology and Factionalism in Beijing–Hong Kong Relations," *Asian Survey* 58, no. 3 (2018): 392–415. I thank Dr. David Fraser, the managing editor, for allowing me to reprint the article here with my updated revisions.

pro-Beijing nationalism on one end and pro-Hong Kong localist sentiment (Hongkongism) on the other (Figure 2.1). The clashes between these two ideologies contributed to serious factional struggles at two levels: between Beijing and the HKSAR, and between pro-government/pro-PRC forces and pro-democracy camps within Hong Kong. This section examines the complex variants of the nationalistic factions on the pro-Beijing or pro-PRC side, and of the localist factions on the pro-Hong Kong side. It will demonstrate that within this conflict, factional fragmentation on both sides complicated the political, economic, and legal interactions between Beijing and the HKSAR. These two political tendencies—pro-Hong Kong localism and pro-Beijing nationalism—were developing simultaneously after July 1, 1997, making Beijing–Hong Kong relations quite turbulent.[106]

Figure 2.1: Pro-Beijing Nationalism and Hongkongism

High degree of pro-Beijing nationalism   High degree of pro–Hong Kong localism

The inter-organizational bonding of these two major ideological factions differs considerably.[107] The late Lucian Pye alerted us to the importance of *guanxi* (personal connections) in mainland-Chinese politics.[108] The pro-Beijing nationalists, including both conservative and liberal elements, are shaped by their political *guanxi*. At the same time, factional struggles in the HKSAR were bitterly fought between Hong Kong people with varying attitudes toward Beijing's influence on the local politics, economy, society, and legal system. Conflict-ridden dynamics emerged between pro-Beijing nationalism, marked by politically "correct" attitudes toward the PRC regime, and pro–Hong Kong localism, characterized by a strong sense of Hong Kong identity that resists any attempt at "mainlandizing" or "Sinifying" the politics, economy, society, and legal systems of the HKSAR.[109] In a nutshell, ideologies and factionalism were intertwined in the political arena of Hong Kong that interacts with the PRC.

---

106. Factional ties can stem from ideological differences. Robert D. Putnam, *The Comparative Study of Political Elites* (Englewood Cliffs, NJ: Prentice-Hall, 1976), 62.
107. Thanks to the reviewer of my article in *Asian Survey* for this insight.
108. Pye, *The Spirit of Chinese Politics*, 207–217.
109. "Mainlandization" refers to an attempt by Beijing and the Hong Kong elites to make Hong Kong political reforms more dependent on the central government's wishes, its society more akin to mainland society, which emphasizes social harmony and media control, its legal system less independent of the executive branch, and its economy more dependent on mainland tourism and investment. See Lo, *The Dynamics of Beijing-Hong Kong Relations: A Model for Taiwan*.

Pro-Beijing Conservative Nationalists in Command

"Ideologies" refers to the existence and persistence of strong political beliefs, consciousness, and faith.[110] Two types of ideologies stand out that have shaped Beijing's relations with the HKSAR since retrocession to China on July 1, 1997. "Pro-Beijing nationalism" refers to a strong sense of not only patriotic allegiance to mainland China as a nation dominated and led by the Han Chinese, but also political loyalty to the CCP as the legitimate regime governing the entire country. Pro–Hong Kong localism is a very strong local or regional identity in which residents and minorities not only see themselves as belonging to the Hong Kong community they reside in, but also regard outsiders, including mainland immigrants, as a menace to local self-interest.[111] From 1997 to 2020, pro-Beijing nationalism, as exhibited in the remarks of various PRC officials dealing with Hong Kong matters as well as some Hong Kong people, were in severe conflict with pro–Hong Kong localism, which was expressed as political resistance and opposition by some Hongkongers to mainland officials, immigrants, and policies on the HKSAR.

There are two variants of pro-Beijing nationalism: conservative and liberal. Conservative nationalists strongly believe in the need to maintain the HKSAR's political, economic, legal, and social *status quo*. They can be viewed as hardliners, who assert that the interest of the central government is of paramount importance in the model of "one country, two systems." In their eyes, the autonomy enjoyed by the HKSAR is granted by the central government in Beijing; it cannot override the power of the central authorities. Examples of the PRC's conservative nationalists responsible for Hong Kong matters included the four famous mainland legal experts in 2004 (Xiao Weiyun, Xu Chongde, Wu Jianfan and Xia Yong); Zhang Dejiang, a former member of the Standing Committee of the Chinese Politburo from 2012 to 2017; Wang Zhenmin, a legal adviser of the Liaison Office (Beijing's representative agency in the HKSAR); and Rao Geping, a mainland member of the Hong Kong Basic Law Committee (a consultative body dealing with the interpretation of the Basic Law that governs Hong Kong). At present, other hardliners in the PRC policy toward the HKSAR embrace the director of the HKMAO, Xia Baolong, and the director of the Liaison Office, Luo Huining. Xia and Luo were sent by Beijing to replace Zhang Xiaoming in February 2020 and Wang Zhimin in January 2020, respectively.[112] Han Zheng,

---
110. See also H. M. Drucker, *The Political Uses of Ideology* (London: Palgrave, 1974).
111. Indeed, Hong Kong's localist complexities extend to the ethnic minorities, especially the Indian and Pakistani minorities. For example, an Indian businessman Hari Harilela may be seen as localist with a strong Hong Kong identity. He can be regarded as politically pro-Beijing but not a Chinese nationalist. Thanks to the reviewer who asked me to address this example of Harilela.
112. On Xia, see "China Replaces Head of Its Hong Kong and Macau Affairs Office," Reuters, February 13, 2020, accessed March 7, 2021, https://www.reuters.com/article/uk-china-hong

a member of the Politburo Standing Committee and a leader of the Central Leading Small Group on Hong Kong and Macau Affairs since April 2018, can also be regarded as a conservative nationalist who in March 2021 emphasized the importance of having patriots governing Hong Kong and struggling against the "subversive" enemies of the governments of Hong Kong and the PRC.[113]

In May 2017, when Zhang Dejiang reviewed the implementation of "one country, two systems" in the HKSAR, he emphasized the need for the HKSAR to observe the "comprehensive governing power of the central government" and exhorted the people of Hong Kong, including civil servants, to study and understand the Basic Law more deeply.[114] He criticized those Hong Kong people for trying to make the HKSAR "independent" of Beijing. Zhang stressed that the concept of "separation of powers" cannot be applied to the HKSAR. Similarly, Wang Zhenmin criticized some Hong Kong people for adopting a perspective of "total Westernization" in discussing Hong Kong's political development.[115] He complained that the HKSAR is a place where comments and views critical of the PRC were heard every day. Echoing Zhang and Wang, Rao remarked in Macao in April 2017 that the PRC would like to institutionalize the procedures of Article 158 of the Basic Law, which confers the power of interpreting the Basic Law on the SCNPC.[116] From 1997 to 2016, the SCNPC interpreted the Basic Law five times—first in June 1999, over the right of abode of Mainland Chinese in Hong Kong; second in April 2004, with regard to the impossibility of direct election of the chief executive in 2007 and the entire LegCo in 2008; third in March 2005, over the term of office of the new chief executive, as Donald Tsang took over from Tung Chee-hwa in June 2005; fourth, over a case concerning a company that sued the Democratic Republic of the Congo; and fifth in November 2016, over the oath-taking behavior of two legislators-elect in the Legislative Council.[117] From the perspective of the conservative nationalists, the SCNPC interpretations of the Basic Law were necessary and beneficial to the operation of "one country, two systems," for such moves could clarify any gray areas in the relationship between Beijing and the HKSAR.

---

kong-idUKKBN2070CX. For Luo, see Keith Zhai, "China Replaces Head of Hong Kong Liaison Office amid Ongoing Protests," Reuters, January 4, 2020, accessed March 7, 2021, https://www.reuters.com/article/uk-hongkong-protests-china-liaison-idUSKBN1Z30AD.
113. His remarks on patriotism and the need to struggle against the "subversive" elements in Hong Kong were reported in Cable TV News, March 7, 2021.
114. *Wen Wei Po*, May 28, 2017, A6.
115. *Oriental Daily News*, April 23, 2017, A23.
116. *Hong Kong Economic Journal*, May 2, 2017, A12.
117. I thank Professor Albert Chen for the insights in his lecture, delivered to a group of students in a program on political leadership at HKU SPACE on December 5, 2017. See also Lo, *Hong Kong's Indigenous Democracy*, 74–84.

Many Hong Kong democrats might have neglected that Wang Huning, a member of the Standing Committee of the CCP Politburo and a close ideological adviser to President Xi Jinping, had not only advocated "new authoritarianism" to govern the PRC but also warned the people of Hong Kong as early as March 2018 to bear in mind five main issues: (1) the HKSAR should "accurately implement the principle of 'one country, two systems;' (2) Hong Kong must "strictly observe the Chinese constitution and the Basic Law;" (3) the local people "should support the HKSAR government and its policies;" (4) Hong Kong should be integrated into the mainland's national plan of development; and (5) the Hong Kong comrades should increase their "national awareness and patriotic spirit."[118] Wang also warned that the central government would have "zero tolerance of Hong Kong independence"—an emphasis that many radical localists and political observers in the HKSAR ignored.[119] As a mainland-trained political scientist, Wang has believed in the virtue of a centralized mode of governance in the PRC, the need for the forceful political leadership, and the necessity of the central government in Beijing to implement its "comprehensive jurisdiction" over the HKSAR.[120] As a conservative nationalistic adviser to the PRC leadership, Wang's beliefs are politically significant and can represent Beijing's policy line on Hong Kong matters.[121]

Conservative nationalists believe that the enactment of the national security law for the HKSAR in June 2020 was necessary because it could and would stabilize the society and polity of Hong Kong. They perceive those protestors in the 2019 anti-extradition movement, the 2016 Mong Kok riot, the 2012 anti-national education campaign, and the 2003 anti–Article 23 movement as "unpatriotic

---

118. *Ta Kung Pao*, "王沪宁：增强香港同胞的国家意识爱国精神", March 7, 2018, accessed April 2, 2021, http://news.takungpao.com/mainland/focus/2018-03/3549139_wap.html.
119. TVB News, "王滬寧出席港區人大代表小組會 稱中央對港獨零容忍," March 6, 2018, accessed April 2, 2021, https://news.tvb.com/tc/local/5a9e4428e60383796599f9ba/%E6%B8%AF%E6%BE%B3-%E7%8E%8B%E6%BB%AC%E5%AF%A7%E5%87%BA%E5%B8%AD%E6%B8%AF%E5%8D%80%E4%BA%BA%E5%A4%A7%E4%BB%A3%E8%A1%A8%E5%B0%8F%E7%B5%84%E6%9C%83-%E7%A8%B1%E4%B8%AD%E5%A4%AE%E5%B0%8D%E6%B8%AF%E7%8D%A8%E9%9B%B6%E5%AE%B9%E5%BF%8D.
120. Yufan Huang, "中共智囊王滬寧的集權政治見解" [Wang Huning's view of centralized politics], *New York Times Chinese Version*, September 30, 2015, accessed April 2, 2021, https://cn.nytimes.com/china/20150930/c30sino-adviser/zh-hant/; Metro Radio, "王滬寧指國家的命運 與香港息息相關," March 6, 2018, accessed April 2, 2021, metroradio.com.hk. For Wang's beliefs, see Haig Patapan and Yi Wang, "The Hidden Ruler: Wang Huning and the Making of Contemporary China," *Journal of Contemporary China* 27, no. 109 (2018): 47–60.
121. In February 2021, it was reported that Wang's protégé in Shanghai, Xu Wei, took over the leadership of Hong Kong's pro-Beijing Phoenix TV, showing that the dominant Xi Jinping faction has become influential in the HKSAR media. See "【香港要聞】王滬寧、令計劃舊部接管，鳳凰衛視或成港版央視" [Phoenix TV may become the CCTV version of Hong Kong], February 9, 2021, accessed April 2, 2021, https://gnews.org/articles/403740.

subversives" who became the target of political struggles.[122] Xia Baolong, the director of the HKMAO, said on February 22, 2021 that those people who are "anti-China and causing chaos" in Hong Kong must be excluded from participation in the crucial positions in the political structures of the HKSAR.[123] Xia added three criteria of patriotism: (1) those people who "wholeheartedly support the national sovereignty, safety and developmental interests" without blackening the image of the central government and without publicizing the platform of "Hong Kong independence," (2) those who "respect and protect the nation's basic system and Hong Kong's constitutional order" without challenging them, and (3) those who protect Hong Kong's prosperity and stability without becoming "a faction that produces chaos" together with others supportive of violence.[124] Xia appealed to the people of Hong Kong to respect the CCP, which leads the socialist system in China and which was responsible for designing the "one country, two systems" for Hong Kong.[125] During his meeting with Hong Kong's NPC members, Xia named the former boss of *Apple Daily* Jimmy Lai, the former core leader of Demosisto Party Joshua Wong, and one of the three leaders of Occupy Central movement Benny Tai as "extremely bad elements" in "opposing China and creating chaos in Hong Kong," adding that the three people should be "seriously punished."[126]

Xia mentioned a series of Hong Kong's events that prompted the central government to adopt a more hardline policy toward the HKSAR, including the July 2003 protests that forced the delay in the implementation of Article 23 of the Basic Law, the 2012 anti–national education campaign, the 2016 Mong Kok riot, and the 2019 anti-extradition movement.[127] He pointed to the political unacceptability of the action of Hong Kong democrats who used filibustering tactics to delay and obstruct the government bills and policies for six months in the LegCo starting from October 2019—an undesirable phenomenon compounded by the claim made by the "troublemakers" that they would occupy over half of the LegCo seats and half of the position of the Chief Executive Election Committee. Xia

---

122. Remarks made by Han Zheng during the NPC meeting on March 7, 2021, as reported in TVB News, March 7, 2021.
123. *Ta Kung Pao*, February 22, 2021, A1.
124. *Ta Kung Pao*, February 22, 2021, A1.
125. "夏寶龍：愛國就要愛中華人民共和國　不允損中共領導社會主義制度" [Xia Baolong: Loving the country is to love the PRC and the act of undermining the CCP-led socialist system is not allowed], hk01.com, February 22, 2021, accessed April 2, 2021, https://www.hk01.com/%E6%9 4%BF%E6%83%85/590212/%E5%A4%8F%E5%AF%B6%E9%BE%8D-%E6%84%9B%E5%9C% 8B%E5%B0%B1%E8%A6%81%E6%84%9B%E4%B8%AD%E8%8F%AF%E4%BA%BA%E6%B0 %91%E5%85%B1%E5%92%8C%E5%9C%8B-%E4%B8%8D%E5%85%81%E6%90%8D%E4%B 8%AD%E5%85%B1%E9%A0%98%E5%B0%8E%E7%A4%BE%E6%9C%83%E4%B8%BB%E7% BE%A9%E5%88%B6%E5%BA%A6.
126. *Wen Wei Po*, March 2, 2021, A5.
127. *Wen Wei Po*, March 2, 2021, A5.

added and that they would "usurp Hong Kong's governing power" and "subvert the CCP-led system of Chinese socialism with Chinese characteristics."[128] He explicitly said that the people of Hong Kong should not oppose the "one country, two systems" founded by the CCP.[129] In other words, those Hong Kong people who oppose the CCP are "unpatriotic." His arguments against the localists and those Hong Kong people critical of the CCP are representative of the consistent position of the PRC's conservative nationalists.

Some Hong Kong people are conservative nationalists. They include former Chief Executive Tung Chee-hwa, who stepped down in 2004 for personal reasons but who has been playing the role of a united front leader to win the hearts and minds of more Hong Kong people.[130] His Our Hong Kong Foundation is now functioning not just as a think tank in various policy areas but also as an umbrella organization to reach out to interest groups and individuals.[131] While Tung's late father, Tung Chao-yung, was pro-Taiwan, Tung Chee-hwa became politically and economically co-opted by the PRC, whose state-owned Cosco Shipping Holdings eventually bought his shipping fleet, Oriental Overseas International Limited, to expand the mainland Chinese shipping fleet under the PRC's Belt and Road scheme.[132] Tung has a profound sense of patriotism toward China, as epitomized by his frequent remarks that "if China is good, Hong Kong is also good." Other Hong Kong elites who are conservative nationalists include former Secretary for Justice Elsie Leung and former Secretary for Security Regina Ip. They have long advocated for public support for local legislation on Article 23 of the Basic Law, which is designed to ban subversion, treason, sedition, and secession.[133] Ip wanted to run for chief executive in the 2017 election but failed to get

---

128. "Xia Baolong: Comprehensively Implement the Principle of 'Patriots Governing Hong Kong' and Promote the Stable and Smooth Process of Realizing the 'One Country, Two Systems,'" *Ta Kung Pao*, March 2, 2021, A10.
129. "Xia Baolong: Comprehensively Implement the Principle of 'Patriots Governing Hong Kong,'" A10.
130. On Beijing's united front work in Hong Kong, see Christine Loh, *Underground Front: The Chinese Communist Party in Hong Kong* (Hong Kong: Hong Kong University Press, 2010).
131. Our Hong Kong Foundation, "Mr. Tung Chee Hwa, GBM," accessed October 11, 2017, https://www.ourhkfoundation.org.hk/en/node/551.
132. S. C. Yeung, "Cosco Takeover of Orient Overseas Fits a Pattern," *EJ Insight*, July 11, 2017, accessed October 12, 2017, http://www.ejinsight.com/20170711-cosco-takeover-of-orient-overseas-fits-a-pattern/. The Belt and Road scheme is the same as "One Belt, One Road," which refers to China's developmental strategy to revive the land and maritime Silk Roads in the era of Marco Polo. See Allen Au-yeung, "What Is One Belt, One Road Strategy All About?" *South China Morning Post*, January 13, 2016, accessed April 13, 2018, http://www.scmp.com/news/hong-kong/economy/article/1900633/what-one-belt-one-road-strategy-all-about.
133. The central government in Beijing sees the HKSAR government as having the obligation to legislate on Article 23 of the Basic Law to deal with subversion, treason, sedition, and secession. In this way, the national security of the PRC can be protected further even after the enactment of the Hong Kong national security law in late June 2020.

enough support and she terminated her campaign in early March. Her failure to secure Beijing's support reflected the central government leaders' very careful choice of Carrie Lam Cheng Yuet-ngor as the new chief executive, for Lam's public image was not as hardline and conservative as Ip's.[134] Other conservative nationalists in the HKSAR include the former Chief Executive C. Y. Leung and Tam Yiu-chung, the Hong Kong NPC member and the former chair of the pro-Beijing DAB. They are all politically patriotic and relatively conservative, but highly respectable and trusted from the perspective of Chinese nationalism.

The liberal nationalists on the pro-Beijing side are a few mainland officials and some Hong Kong people who tend to support Beijing's less interventionist, more compromising approach to dealing with Hong Kong relations. They include a minority of officials on the mainland side, including the late Xu Jiatun, the former director of the Liaison Office.[135] Others included the former PRC President Hu Jintao and Premier Wen Jiabao, whose remarks on the HKSAR were very moderate and restrained. Those Hong Kong people who can be categorized as liberal nationalists include Jasper Tsang Yok-sing, a former Legislative Council president (2008–2016) and a patriot whose brother Tsang Tak-sing was imprisoned for two years by the British colonial authorities during the 1967 riots in Hong Kong for distributing leftwing leaflets. Tsang formerly tended toward a pro-Beijing conservative nationalist outlook, but he adopted a more neutral and even liberal outlook after becoming the President of the LegCo.[136] In August 2015, Tsang criticized the central government for interfering in Hong Kong affairs without reviewing the implementation of "one country, two systems."[137] This criticism might dilute the central government's support for Tsang to run in the 2017 chief executive election, despite the fact that he was politically trusted from the perspective of Chinese nationalism.[138] In the early phase of the anti-extradition movement in 2019, Tsang appealed to the HKSAR government to

---

134. Sonny Shiu-hing Lo, "Factionalism and Chinese-Style Democracy: The 2017 Hong Kong Chief Executive Election," *Asian Pacific Journal of Public Administration* 39, no. 2 (2017): 100–199.
135. Because Xu was involved in the policy dispute between mainland hardliners, such as former premier Li Peng, and softliners, such as former (and late) premier Zhao Ziyang, in Beijing in 1989, his close relations with Zhao led to his downfall after the June 1989 Tiananmen incident. Lo Shiu-hing, "The Chinese Communist Party Elite's Conflicts over Hong Kong, 1983–1990," *China Information* 7, no. 4 (Spring 1994): 1–14.
136. On this gradual change, see Sonny Lo, *Competing Chinese Political Visions: Hong Kong vs. Beijing on Democracy* (Westport: Praeger Security International, 2010).
137. "'One Country, Two Systems' at Risk, Jasper Tsang Says," Tsang Yok-sing, August 31, 2015, accessed October 11, 2017, https://tsangyoksing.hk/2015/08/31/one-country-two-systems-at-risk-jasper-tsang-says/.
138. Kris Cheng, "Beijing Discouraged Me from Entering Leadership Race, Says Ex-LegCo President Jasper Tsang," Hong Kong Free Press, March 15, 2017, accessed October 11, 2017, https://www.hongkongfp.com/2017/03/15/beijing-discouraged-me-from-entering-leadership-race-says-ex-legco-president-jasper-tsang/.

grant an amnesty to the protests—an idea that was rejected by Chief Executive Carrie Lam and opposed by other pro-establishment elites, including Ip Kwok-him and Ronny Tong.[139]

Other liberal nationalists in the HKSAR include the former secretary for transport and housing, Anthony Cheung Bing-leung, who originally was a moderate democrat but gradually shifted to the pro-government, pro-Beijing camp after resigning from the vice chairmanship of the Democratic Party in 2004. Similarly, Christine Loh joined the HKSAR government as an undersecretary for the environment from 2012 to 2017 after leaving the NGO Civic Exchange, which had been critical of the government's environmental policies. Both Cheung and Loh had originally been quite pro–Hong Kong and arguably localist in political outlook, prior to their transformations to the pro-government and pro-Beijing side. Both had been critical of the policies of the Hong Kong government and Beijing, but after they joined the pro-Beijing liberal nationalist front, their critical perspective ceased.[140] Other democrats who turned to be more nationalistic embraced Tik Chi-yuen, a former member of the Democratic Party (DP), who is the chairman of a centrist group named Third Side after he quitted the DP in September 2015. After the SCNPC approved a new electoral model for the HKSAR on March 11, 2021, Tik remarked openly that his group would like to participate in the future elections to be held for the LegCo. He was the only moderate democrat elected to the 90-member LegCo in December 2021. While political correctness is the hallmark of conservative nationalists in Hong Kong, liberal nationalists sometimes retain their critical attitude toward the HKSAR government and Beijing, but they are vulnerable to being politically coopted.

The PRC's conservative nationalists have dominated the policies of Beijing toward the HKSAR, especially after the July 2003 protests that saw half a million residents take to the streets to decry the proposed Article 23. Following the protests, the central government set up the Central Coordination Group for Hong Kong and Macao Affairs (*Zhongyang Guang Ao Gongzuo Xietiao Xiaozu*). The formation of this committee marked the increasing involvement of Beijing in HKSAR matters. The central authorities saw the mass protests as potentially undermining the legitimacy of the Tung Chee-hwa government and tarnishing the image of "one country, two systems." The group includes mainland officials

---

139. Ip is a member of the pro-Beijing DAB and Tong a leader of the Path of Democracy. Alvin Lum, "Advisers to Hong Kong Leader Carrie Lam Dismiss Idea of Amnesty for All Protestors Involved in Clashes over Extradition Bill," *South China Morning Post*, July 4, 2019, accessed April 2, 2021, https://www.scmp.com/news/hong-kong/politics/article/3017329/advisers-hong-kong-leader-carrie-lam-dismiss-idea-amnesty.
140. Cheung, however, voiced views different from many pro-Beijing elites after he left the government. He said the electoral reform introduced by Beijing in March 2021 was one thing, but the enhancement of the government's capability was another matter unrelated to the new electoral system.

from the Ministry of Public Security, the commerce and trade department, the Liaison Office in the HKSAR, and most importantly the Ministry of National Security.

Beijing's conservative nationalists became far more influential and prominent in Beijing–HKSAR relations after the summer 2012 anti–national education campaign in Hong Kong. On July 1, 2007, when former PRC President Hu Jintao visited the territory, he said he hoped Hong Kong would initiate national education.[141] The HKSAR government duly introduced a policy on national education, which however triggered public outcry and opposition, because many students, parents, and intellectuals perceived such a change as an attempt to "brainwash" young schoolchildren. Compounding the problem was the failure of the HKSAR government to explain the national education curriculum. Hence, when the new Leung Chun-ying government came into office in July 2012, it encountered tremendous public opposition to the national education policy. Just one day before the September 2012 LegCo direct election, Leung announced that the policy would be scrapped, leaving it to secondary schools to decide whether it would be tested or postponed. Leung's announcement was timed to avoid a detrimental impact of the anti–national education movement on the LegCo election results. However, the success of the public opposition shocked PRC officials, who then adopted an increasingly hardline and conservative approach to Hong Kong affairs.[142] In response to Beijing's conservative nationalist surge, the new chief executive, Carrie Lam, announced in her first policy address on October 11, 2017, that the Chinese history curriculum would be made compulsory at the junior secondary school level, so that more young students would be required to study China, with the ultimate goal of enhancing their nationalistic feelings toward the PRC.[143]

After the national education policy was watered down by the HKSAR government in September 2012, the ideology of pro-Beijing conservative nationalism gained further momentum with the establishment in November 2013 of the National Security Commission in the PRC. This move was matched by the sudden emergence of three Hong Kong leaders—legal expert Benny Tai, sociologist Chan Kin-man, and priest Chu Yiu-ming—who planned in March

---

141. Jasper Tsang's speech at the conference on the twentieth anniversary of the HKSAR, Education University of Hong Kong, May 25, 2017. Hu Jintao did not use the term national education in his speech, but he did emphasize the need for the Hong Kong people to "achieve social harmony and stability" through the process of maintaining and strengthening the sentiment of "loving China and loving Hong Kong." See "Hu Jintao's Speech in Hong Kong on July 1, 2007," accessed April 13, 2018, http://www.locpg.hk/2015-03/18/c_127594820.htm.
142. Jasper Tsang remarked that Beijing was shocked by the success of the anti–national education campaign in the HKSAR, but he did not say that the PRC officials have become more hardline since then.
143. *Ming Pao*, October 12, 2017, A10.

2013 to launch the Occupy Central movement to push for the democratization of Hong Kong. Tai had published an article in January 2013, arguing that the democrats needed a seven-step process to push for democratization because the C. Y. Leung government would not make any promise to achieve universal suffrage from 2017 to 2020.[144] These seven steps included (1) the mobilization of at least 10,000 people to occupy the Central district; (2) the participation of opinion leaders such as former officials, religious leaders and academics; (3) the use of non-violent means; (4) the need for persistence and perseverance to sustain the momentum of the movement; (5) the willingness of participants to shoulder the responsibility of surrendering themselves to authorities and facing the charge of any criminal offence; (6) the appropriate timing of the movement to exert pressure on the authorities; and (7) the creation of political pressure through the signing of a declaration by participants.[145] Tai's ideas were later grasped by student activists, who launched class strikes from September 22 to 26, 2014, and protests outside the government headquarters on September 27, followed by an announcement made by Tai that the movement began on the morning of September 28. The movement ended on December 15 peacefully with the organizers, including Tai, Chan and Chu, surrendering themselves to the police. In April 2019, a local court sentenced Tai and Chan Kin-man into 16 months' imprisonment for their "conspiracy to commit public nuisance" during the seventy-nine-day Occupy Central movement.[146] Their sentence was reduced by two months because of their clean record and positive character. Moreover, pro-democracy legislator Shiu Ka-chun and Raphael Wong were imprisoned for eight months for inciting public nuisance. Democrats who adopted a confrontational approach to dealing with political reform ran the risks of being prosecuted and imprisoned.

In the PRC, the concept of national security was simultaneously expanded from political security (the regime legitimacy of the CCP) to embrace other aspects, including economic, public health, cultural, and environmental issues. The National Security Commission and the Central Coordination group saw Hong Kong's democratization as a threat to China's national security, and they regarded political change in the HKSAR as a Trojan horse for foreign countries to foster political transformations there and in mainland China.[147] The CCP regime

---

144. Benny Tai, "The Most Lethal Weapon of Civil Disobedience," *Hong Kong Economic Journal*, January 16, 2013.
145. Tai, "The Most Lethal Weapon of Civil Disobedience."
146. James Pomfret and Jessie Pang, "Four Hong Kong 'Occupy' Leaders Jailed for 2014 Democracy Protests," Reuters, April 14, 2019, accessed March 14, 2021, https://www.reuters.com/article/us-hongkong-politics-idUSKCN1S004R.
147. This Trojan horse perspective could be seen in the remarks of PRC authorities even before the anti–national education movement. See Lo, *Competing Chinese Political Visions: Hong Kong vs. Beijing on Democracy*.

under President Xi Jinping wanted to establish itself securely without the fear of being affected by any "color revolution" fostered by foreign countries, as occurred in the Middle East. From 2014–2015, democratization in the HKSAR became a highly ideological matter. Indeed, it can be said that Beijing under President Xi's leadership has been concerned about many mainland "horses" through which urban socio-political instability could threaten the CCP's "Troy." The ideology of conservative nationalism, which was latent in the PRC's policy toward Hong Kong from 2003 to 2012, has arguably become increasingly prominent since the establishment of the National Security Commission in November 2013.

The Occupy Central movement, launched by the three leaders (Tai, Chan, and Chu) in September to December 2014, was supported by many student activists, including Joshua Wong, who had led an interest group named Scholarism in the successful anti–national education campaign in the summer of 2012. Two years after the anti–national education campaign, in June 2014, the central government in Beijing published a *White Paper* on the implementation of the Basic Law. It emphasized that Beijing retained ultimate power and "comprehensive jurisdiction" over the HKSAR, and that the people of Hong Kong should have a "correct" understanding of the Basic Law and the operation of "one country, two systems."[148] The *White Paper* affirmed the central government's strong support of the HKSAR administration while criticizing some local people for misunderstanding the Basic Law. It said:

> Still some are even confused or lopsided in their understanding of "one country, two systems" and the Basic Law. Many wrong views that are currently rife in Hong Kong concerning its economy, society and development of its political structure are attributable to this. The continued practice of "one country, two systems" in Hong Kong requires that we proceed from the fundamental objectives of maintaining China's sovereignty, security and development interests and maintaining the long-term stability and prosperity of Hong Kong to fully and accurately understand and implement the policy of "one country, two systems," and holistically combine holding the principle of "one country" with respecting the difference of "two systems," maintaining the power of the central government with ensuring the high degree of autonomy of the HKSAR, and letting the mainland play its role as a strong supporter of the HKSAR with improving the competitive edge of Hong Kong. In no circumstance should we do one thing and neglect the other.[149]

---

148. Information Office of the State Council, People's Republic of China, *The Practice of the "One Country, Two Systems" Policy in the Hong Kong Special Administrative Region* (Beijing: Foreign Languages Press, 2014).
149. *The Practice of the "One Country, Two Systems" Policy in the Hong Kong Special Administrative Region*, "'一国两制'在香港特别行政区的实践"白皮书 (英文), June 10, 2014, accessed March 14, 2021, http://www.scio.gov.cn/zfbps/ndhf/2014/Document/1373163/1373163.htm.

The *White Paper* stressed that China's socialism is the mainstay and that Hong Kong's capitalism will stay in the long term, that those people who govern Hong Kong should be patriotic, and that the people of Hong Kong must fully respect the socialist system and its principles in the mainland. On the other hand, the mainland respects and tolerates Hong Kong's capitalism. The implication is that the people of Hong Kong should not intervene in the political system and development of the PRC. The *White Paper* made the following conclusion:

> The deepening exchanges and cooperation between the HKSAR and the mainland call for better communication and coordination, and the concerns of the people should be properly addressed. Meanwhile, it is necessary to stay alert to the attempt of outside forces to use Hong Kong to interfere in China's domestic affairs, and prevent and repel the attempt made by a very small number of people who act in collusion with outside forces to interfere with the implementation of "one country, two systems" in Hong Kong.

The central authorities warned the people of Hong Kong to be sensitive to the likelihood that foreign forces would intervene in the political development of the HKSAR—a fear of "color revolution" that was and is constantly riveting in the minds of PRC authorities responsible for Hong Kong matters.

When the *White Paper* was published in June 2014, it was unclear how the central government would implement its "comprehensive jurisdiction" over the HKSAR. But with the passage of time, the SCNPC's interpretation of the Basic Law has become an important means through which Beijing's "comprehensive jurisdiction" over Hong Kong is exercised. On August 31, 2014, to preempt the Occupy Central movement, the SCNPC made a decision on the Basic Law's stipulation governing the selection of the chief executive in 2017. The SCNPC decided that the candidates allowed to run for the office would be two or three chosen by a majority vote of the members of a Nomination Committee which was responsible for screening and nominating the candidates. This decision nominally paved the way for the election of the chief executive by universal suffrage in 2017, but many local democrats in Hong Kong argued that the arrangement created a "pseudo-democracy" in which the central authorities would retain the power to screen out any politically "unacceptable" candidates through their control of the Nomination Committee.

Although Occupy Central ended in December 2014 partly because of the lack of public opinion support and partly due to the voluntary decision of the movement's organizers, the political atmosphere was by no means conducive to any compromise between the hardline conservative nationalists on the PRC side and the pro-democracy localists on the Hong Kong side. The former President of the LegCo, Jasper Tsang, said in public that both sides misperceived each other before the LegCo's June 2015 vote on a political reform proposal prepared by the

HKSAR government in conformity with the SCNPC's August 2014 decision.[150] Beijing's officials believed that some local democrats would relax their hardline oppositionist stance and support the government's proposal, while the local democrats believed that Beijing would concede to some amendments of the proposal so that it would be passed by the LegCo.[151] Both sides were mistaken. The Beijing side made no concession, expecting that some local democrats would vote for the government's bill, while the latter rejected it in order to maintain their own unity and to avoid being labeled as political "traitors".

Even more alarming was the voting result. Only eight members, mostly from the pro-business Liberal Party (LP), supported the government's political reform package, while the pro-Beijing political party, the DAB, failed to enforce discipline among its members, all of whom left the legislative chamber when the vote began. The DAB tried to walk out to wait for a pro-government legislator, the late Lau Wong-fat, to arrive, but miscommunication between the DAB and LP made some LP legislators stay in the chamber, leading to an embarrassing result in which the pro-Beijing DAB looked like it was supporting the democrats to boycott the government's reform proposal. The rejection of the government's political reform bill showed uncompromising attitudes on both sides, namely Beijing and the local democrats; most importantly, it demonstrated the disarray and the lack of political leadership of the pro-Beijing political forces in Hong Kong. Although the pro-Beijing elites went to the Liaison Office the next day, immediately after the surprising voting result, to explain their embarrassingly disunited action, the entire saga demonstrated the weakness and absence of leadership of the pro-Beijing forces, which were composed of a loose coalition from the DAB, LP, the rural advisory Heung Yee Kuk, and other pro-government legislators. Such a coalition was so weak that nobody could communicate, coordinate, and lead the pro-Beijing forces effectively.

PRC authorities did not see the rejection of the political reform package in June 2015 as a negative outcome. The political status quo was maintained. If the political reform blueprint were approved by the LegCo, a more democratic model would be implemented in the HKSAR. Most importantly, the pro-Beijing forces would have to demonstrate better coordination, communication, and leadership in electoral mobilization. If the 2015 political reform blueprint was rejected in the LegCo partly due to the poor leadership of the pro-Beijing forces, how would they prepare for the direct election of the chief executive through

---

150. For the details of the government's political reform proposal, see "Method for Selecting the Chief Executive by Universal Suffrage: Consultation Report and Proposals, April 2015," accessed April 13, 2018, http://www.2017.gov.hk/filemanager/template/en/doc/report_2nd/consultation_report_2nd.pdf.
151. Tsang said this in response to questions from the audience at the twentieth anniversary conference on the HKSAR, Education University of Hong Kong, May 25, 2017.

universal suffrage, even though two to three candidates running for the chief executive would be screened out by a pro-Beijing Nomination Committee? Arguably, pro-Beijing forces remained so politically weak in 2015 as to make the PRC leadership feel less confident of witnessing the direct election of the Hong Kong chief executive in 2017.

The failure of any compromise in the June 2015 vote in the LegCo was contextually a far cry from the political environment in May 2010, when the moderate democrats (Emily Lau, Albert Ho, and Cheung Man-kwong of the DP) went to the Liaison Office to reach a compromise over Donald Tsang's political reform plan. First and foremost, the 2010 development showed a serious split between the moderates and radicals in the pro-democracy camp, unlike the 2015 situation in which none of the democrats wanted to portray themselves as "traitors." In 2010, the radicals were composed of the Civic Party (CP) and the League of Social Democrats (LSD), whose five legislators (Tanya Chan and Alan Leong of CP and Leung Kwok-hung, Raymond Wong, and Albert Chan of LSD) resigned from LegCo in January and were re-elected again in the LegCo by-elections in May. Their so-called "referendum movement" was criticized by the Liaison Office director, Peng Qinghua, as "intimidating."[152] With the benefit of hindsight, Peng's remarks could be seen as already mild, tolerant, and liberal. It was reported that Chief Executive Donald Tsang wrote to Xi Jinping, the PRC vice president and the Politburo Standing Committee member responsible for Hong Kong matters, lobbying him to consider the political reform plan without the fear that the governability of the HKSAR would be undermined by the radical democrats.[153] As a result, President Hu Jintao approved the political reform proposals submitted by the Donald Tsang administration. The breakthrough in political reform represented the combined outcomes of the "referendum movement" launched by radical democrats, the dialogue between moderate democrats and the Liaison Office, and the lobbying efforts of Chief Executive Donald Tsang. Compared with the democrats divided between the radicals and moderates in 2010, the democrats in June 2015 were far more united in their opposition to the government's political reform plan. In June 2015, both radical and moderate democrats rejected the August 31, 2014, parameters of political reform as delineated by Beijing, which allowed two to three chief executive candidates to run in direct elections after being screened out by the Nomination Committee. Almost all the pro-democracy elites saw the August 31 parameters as "pseudo-democratic."

---

152. Xie Yu, "Hong Kong Opposition Demands 'May Hurt Dialogue,'" *China Daily*, March 12, 2010, accessed March 14, 2021, http://www.chinadaily.com.cn/china/2010npc/2010-03/12/content_9577171.htm.
153. Gary Cheung, "Beijing's U-Turn 'to Thwart Radicals,'" *South China Morning Post*, June 22, 2010, accessed March 14, 2021, https://www.scmp.com/article/717745/beijings-u-turn-thwart-radicals.

Second, the pro-government and pro-Beijing camp was far more fragmented and leaderless in May 2015 than during the situation in June 2010, when it was adopting a wait-and-see attitude to witness and accept whatever compromise that the government could make with the moderate democrats. The split in the pro-Beijing camp in 2015 was compounded by miscommunication and the absence of leadership, leading to a very embarrassing scenario in which only eight members of the LP supported the government's political reform blueprint. The DAB as the most politically reliable pro-Beijing organization failed to demonstrate its leadership, united front work, and effective coordination with other pro-government legislators.

Third, misperceptions between the PRC side and democrats were serious in 2015. As Jasper Tsang unveiled, the PRC side misperceived the democrats, who in turn misunderstood the position of the Chinese officials and the HKSAR government. Emily Lau, who participated in the 2010 dialogue and compromise with the Liaison Office officials, revealed in March 2021 that, after the 2010 breakthrough, there was virtually no contact between PRC officials and moderate democrats.[154] In 2015, Liaison Office Director Zhang Xiaoming and his subordinates lacked sufficient communication with the democrats. Political winds changed drastically from 2010 to 2015, generating a different environment for the interactions between PRC authorities and moderate democrats.

The most important miscalculation of the democrats, both moderates and radicals, in the 2015 rejection of the government's reform blueprint was the mistaken assumption that the PRC officials responsible for Hong Kong matters would remain consistently stable, relatively tolerant, and constantly liberal. In other words, while PRC officials responsible for Hong Kong matters in May 2010, such as Li Gang and Peng Qinghua, were far more liberal and compromising, their successors dealing with the HKSAR in 2015 were comparatively more conservative and hardline, including Liaison Office Director Zhang Xiaoming. The take-it or leave-it approach adopted by Zhang in 2015 was quite different from the more relaxed and negotiable approach adopted by the Liaison Office officials in 2010. Most devastatingly, perhaps, the democrats failed to anticipate that while the PRC authorities handling Hong Kong matters were more open-minded toward the democrats in 2015 than their successors in 2020 and 2021, their successors like Xia Baolong of the HKMAO and Luo Huining from the Liaison Office not only adopted a far more hardline, uncompromising, conservative,

---

154. See hk01 interview with Emily Lau, "專訪｜傳「超區」將取消　劉慧卿：2010年後北京與民主派再無溝通," March 10, 2021, accessed March 14, 2021, https://www.hk01.com/%E6%94%BF%E6%83%85/596924/%E5%B0%88%E8%A8%AA-%E5%82%B3-%E8%B6%85%E5%8D%80-%E5%B0%87%E5%8F%96%E6%B6%88-%E5%8A%89%E6%85%A7%E5%8D%BF-2010%E5%B9%B4%E5%BE%8C%E5%8C%97%E4%BA%AC%E8%88%87%E6%B0%91%E4%B8%BB%E6%B4%BE%E5%86%8D%E7%84%A1%E6%BA%9D%E9%80%9A.

and nationalistic approach to deal with the HKSAR, but also implemented the central directive of promulgating the national security law in Hong Kong and changing the new electoral system since March 2021. In short, the democrats and their advisers in Hong Kong failed to assess and understand the changing dynamics of central-local relations.

The pro-democracy camp failed to see the August 31 parameters of electing the chief executive as a model that should be "pocketed" first and that would have a possible demonstration effect on mainland China's democratization in the long run. The Hong Kong model of democracy was already far more pluralistic than that of any other place in mainland China. Without a far-sighted vision of utilizing a Hong Kong model of democracy to shape China's domestic political development, most pro-democracy elites in the HKSAR adopted a narrow-minded approach to dealing with constitutional reforms in 2014 and 2015, failing to appreciate the fact that the Hong Kong model of democracy was already threatening to the mainland's national security.

While conservative nationalists became more politically dominant on the PRC side, they have also seen their like-minded ideologues rising rapidly in the HKSAR. The Voice of Loving Hong Kong, a pro-Beijing conservative nationalist group formed by businessman Patrick Ko in December 2012, launched mass rallies and a march in support of the C. Y. Leung government and against Occupy Central in October 2014.[155] The pro-Beijing forces formed various groups to oppose the leaders and activists of the Occupy Central movement. Even after the movement ended in December, pro-Beijing conservative nationalists mobilized their members to participate in forums at local universities and severely criticized the democrats, like Benny Tai, who discussed political development and legal issues.[156] Unlike the new pro-democracy groups, which were using cyberspace and the internet to make their voices heard,[157] pro-Beijing conservative nationalist groups originally used conventional street protests, rallies, and marches to counter the pro-democracy forces. The pro-Beijing forces gradually learnt from the democrats, utilizing the internet to broadcast their stance and criticize their political enemies. These conservative nationalists have been groomed by PRC authorities and their united front groups in the society of Hong Kong have grown gradually since July 1, 2003, when the latter witnessed the

---

155. *Apple Daily*, October 6, 2014.
156. See, e.g., the struggle between a pro-Beijing conservative nationalist group, the Cherishing Group, led by Lee Pik-yee, and student activists at the Hong Kong Baptist University's public forum, where Benny Tai and former student activist Nathan Lam were invited to discuss Hong Kong's "authoritarian drift," in *The Stand News*, accessed October 11, 2017, https://thestandnews.com/.
157. Sonny Shiu-hing Lo, ed., *Interest Groups and the New Democracy Movement in Hong Kong* (London: Routledge, 2017).

powerful pro-democracy segment of the civil society. Since then, pro-Beijing united front groups have been expanding rapidly in the HKSAR, including clan and dialect groups (Fujianese, Cantonese, Guangxi, and Chiu Chow), women's groups, district federations, youth associations, religious organizations, and other occupational groups that have been receiving political support and patronage, as well as financial support, from either the PRC authorities or pro-Beijing businesspeople.[158] In a nutshell, the conservative nationalistic faction in the HKSAR has been expanding rapidly since the mass protests in July 2003. Whenever there are politically significant events, such as the SCNPC decision on Hong Kong's new electoral system on March 11, 2021, pro-Beijing groups mobilized their members to gather mass signatures on the streets of the HKSAR, generating and collecting public opinion supportive of Beijing's decision.[159]

In the HKSAR, the conservative nationalists embrace some business tycoons, who firmly believe that democratic change in the territory should be minimal and gradual, who see the localists as stirring up political troubles and challenging the central government's bottom line of tolerance, who regard the PRC as giving Hong Kong and themselves tremendous opportunities for profit, and who denounce the pro-democracy activities, especially the 2014 Occupy Central movement, as detrimental to the stability and prosperity of Hong Kong. Some businesspeople in the HKSAR, such as Jimmy Lai, were liberal-minded and supportive of the pro-democracy forces, but they were the tiny minority.[160] The police arrest and governmental prosecution of Jimmy Lai for his alleged involvement in money laundering and activities that were suspected of undermining national security in late 2020 had a chilling effect on the businesspeople who might financially support the democracy movement and the 2019 anti-extradition movement.

Taiwan's political atmosphere had some indirect influence on Beijing's policy toward Hong Kong's democratization. Following the July 1, 2003, mass protests in Hong Kong against the Tung Chee-hwa regime, Beijing was unwilling to make any concession to Hong Kong's political reform in late 2003 and early 2004, when Taiwan was governed by the DPP under Chen Shui-bian. If Beijing had yielded to the demands for democratization in the HKSAR in late 2003 and early 2004, this might have stimulated the DPP to drift toward a more

---

158. Lo, Hung, and Loo, *China's New United Front Work in Hong Kong: Penetrative Politics and Its Implications*.
159. On March 14, 2021, in Hung Hom district, the author observed that, apart from the DAB members collecting mass signatures, pro-Beijing district organizations, such as the Federation of Fujianese Association and the Chinese Enterprises Association, also sent supporters to do so. Clearly, mass mobilization by pro-Beijing united front groups could be easily discerned.
160. Jimmy Lai was a target of political attacks by the pro-Beijing mass media before, during, and after the 2014 Occupy Central movement.

"pro-independence" or separatist stance. Beijing's minor concession to Hong Kong's electoral reforms in the summer of 2010 took place when Taiwan was governed by the Kuomintang (KMT) under Ma Ying-jeou. This move could be interpreted as Beijing's willingness to adopt a soft-line policy toward Hong Kong at a time when it was more comfortable with Taiwan's regime under the KMT presidency. In 2014 and 2015, Beijing's cautious attitude toward Hong Kong's democratic change could perhaps be explained by its prediction and uneasiness regarding the imminent victory of the DPP in Taiwan's presidential election in January 2016. When it was obvious in 2015 that the DPP, under the leadership of Tsai Ing-wen, stood a much better chance than the internally divided KMT to grasp presidential power in Taiwan, Beijing was concerned that any further democratic opening in the HKSAR would send a "wrong" message to Taiwan. Thus, the PRC's conservative nationalistic authorities not only had to rein in the pace and scope of democratization in the HKSAR but also needed to avoid any demonstration effect of Hong Kong's democratization on Taiwan's possible drift toward separatism. In 2020 and 2021, the PRC's tightened grip on the HKSAR could be partly attributable to the Taiwan DPP's continuation of rejecting the 1992 consensus reached by the CCP and KMT: namely, there is only one China, but for the interpretation of the meaning of one China, it is up to the CCP and the KMT. Hence, Taiwan's political development did appear to have impacts on how Beijing dealt with Hong Kong's democratization.

The Sino-US rivalries in the trade, technology, and military spheres during the Donald Trump administration from January 2017 to January 2021 and the Joe Biden administration victimized the pro-democracy factions in the HKSAR. While some members of the pro-democracy faction in Hong Kong went to the US to lobby the American government boldly but naively against the extradition bill proposed by the HKSAR government, their move could be easily regarded as an activity that undermined the national security of the PRC. Even worse, the label of some Hong Kong democrats fostering "color revolution" in Hong Kong together with the help and support of foreigners, like the American politicians and non-governmental organizations (like the National Democracy Institute and the National Endowment for Democracy), could be easily articulated by PRC authorities and the pro-Beijing elites and media. Some members of the pro-democracy faction were entangled, unfortunately, in the Sino-US geopolitical and economic struggles. Siding with the US, some Hong Kong democrats ran the risk of being criticized as enemies of the PRC party-state. The case of Jimmy Lai, who was arrested and prosecuted by the Hong Kong authorities for violating the national security law and "colluding" with foreign forces, was a good example.

Table 2.1 sums up the political, economic, social, and legal positions of the two ideological factions on the PRC and Hong Kong side, specifically the conservative nationalists and liberal nationalists. While the conservative nationalists

Table 2.1: Ideologies, Factions, and Political, Economic, Social, and Legal Disputes in Hong Kong

Ideological factions	Political	Economic	Social	Legal Disputes
Conservative nationalists (includes Beijing officials and Hong Kong people)	Beijing's interventions and decisions are positive	Integration is natural	Harmony is stressed	SCNPC interpretations and decisions are necessary and positive
Liberal nationalists (includes Beijing officials and Hong Kong people)	Keep interventions minimal	Integration as interdependent	Regulate social conflicts	Interpretations and decisions as beneficial
Nationalistic localists	Advocate a gradual, moderate, compromising approach to political reform and disputes	Integration is natural and inevitable; HKSAR needs to adapt	National education as necessary and beneficial to Hong Kong	Interpretations and decisions as beneficial and inevitable for Hong Kong
Liberal localists (mainstream pro-democracy faction)	Call for direct election of both chief executive and Legislative Council	Integration as harmful to Hong Kong and diluting HKSAR's uniqueness	National education as an attempt to brainwash school children	Interpretations and decisions as detrimental to judicial autonomy of Hong Kong
Marxist localists	Advocate double direct election as soon as possible	Integration is seen as mainlandising Hong Kong, calling for tax reform and income redistribution from the rich to the poor	Oppose national education and see social interaction as a kind of co-optation by the mainlanders	Interpretations and decisions as Beijing's authoritarian move on Hong Kong
Confrontational localists	Utilize protests and even violence to call for political reform	Integration is seen as Beijing's annexation of Hong Kong	See Hong Kong's society as being flooded by mainland tourists and immigrants	Interpretations and decisions as Beijing's totalitarian move against Hong Kong
Separatist localists	See Hong Kong as a "nation" and seek "independence"	Integration is seen as the end of Hong Kong	Hong Kong's unique culture should be maintained	Interpretations and decisions as Beijing's dictatorial move against Hong Kong

Note: The democrats' demand for the direct election of the entire LegCo became politically remote and useless after the electoral reform implemented by the SCNPC in March 2021, although theoretically and practically speaking, the August 31, 2014, decision made by the SCNPC (direct election of the chief executive after 2 to 3 candidates are screened out by the Nomination Committee) remains on paper.

favor a far more interventionist approach to dealing with Hong Kong matters than their liberal counterparts, the former can be seen as the hardliners and the latter can be regarded as the softliners in the new dynamics of Beijing-HKSAR relations.

Hong Kong Localists in Fragmentation and Disarray

The fragmentation among localists in the HKSAR greatly widened the political and ideological spectrum, making political compromise with Beijing's conservative nationalists increasingly difficult from 2012 to 2019. There were five variants of localists in the HKSAR in the 2012–2019 period (Table 2.1): (1) nationalistic localists (traditionally called the pro-Beijing Hong Kong people); (2) liberal localists (who support liberal values and civil liberties); (3) Marxist localists (who see the HKSAR city-state as being captured by the capitalist class at the expense of the poor and the working class); (4) confrontational localists (who used protests to oppose the government—some even participated in the early 2016 Mong Kok riots and the 2019 anti-extradition movement);[161] and (5) separatist localists (who saw Hong Kong as a "nation" and advocated for its "independence").

If "localism" refers to Hong Kong people with a very strong sense of identity, seeing Hong Kong as their homeland and resisting the territory's closer political and economic integration with mainland China, then the first generation of localists (notably Martin Lee and the late Szeto Wah) could arguably be traced back to the 1980s. During that period, some Hong Kong activists resisted the 1982–1984 Sino-British negotiations over Hong Kong's future; in the 1990s, many of them were directly elected to the LegCo under the banner of the United Democrats of Hong Kong (UDHK), a predecessor of the DP. Martin Lee, the founder of the DP, could be seen as a liberal localist in the sense that he used democracy in Hong Kong to resist the increasing influence of the CCP in the HKSAR. Although he and Szeto Wah saw Hong Kong's democracy as a "beacon for China's democratization," Lee was arguably more localist than Szeto. Lee supported the resignation of five democrats in the LegCo's geographical constituencies in January 2010 to act as a kind of "referendum" for Hong Kong's people to support a faster pace of political reform during a by-election in May. Szeto was a liberal nationalist who rejected this idea. Szeto's hope for a democratic mainland China characterized his political stance, which was arguably located in the area

---

161. The Mong Kok riot witnessed some young radicals who confronted and attacked the police force in early 2016. The radical action was mainly due to the political anger of some young people over how the government officials dealt with some hawkers on the night of the riot. For the riot, see Sonny Shiu-Hing Lo, *The Politics of Policing in Greater China* (London: Palgrave, 2016), chap. 8.

between liberal nationalism and liberal localism: nationalistic localism.[162] Szeto loved China culturally but rejected CCP rule; he yearned for a democratic China and saw Hong Kong's democratization as a step toward helping the PRC democratize its authoritarian political system. After Szeto Wah passed away in January 2011, no pro-democracy leader could rein in the increasingly radicalized localist movement in the HKSAR, leading to a scenario in which ideological conflicts took place between extreme Hongkongism and assertively conservative Chinese nationalism.

The anti–national education campaign in 2012 signaled the rapid rise of a new generation of localists, especially young students such as Joshua Wong and his supporters, who eventually took part in the 2014 Occupy Central movement. This young generation was far more action-oriented and openly confrontational than the old generation of localists. As a matter of fact, the September 2012 LegCo direct election witnessed the emergence of the Marxist localists, who were represented by Raymond Wong, "Long Hair" Leung Kwok-hung, and the left-wing LSD. The Marxist localists captured four seats in the 2012 election, which they held until the September 2016 legislative elections, when they were overshadowed by the increasingly separatist localists. In Leung Kwok-hung's Marxist political philosophy, Hong Kong's democratization would have to go through the bourgeois stage, namely the introduction of direct elections for the chief executive and the entire LegCo. His LSD hoped that Hong Kong would be democratized through a "referendum" to check the power of the chief executive, the introduction of a comprehensive retirement protection scheme for all citizens, and the adoption of a new tax system, in which rich people would shoulder more of the tax burden and income redistribution would create a more egalitarian society.[163] The LSD saw the August 31, 2014, parameter delineated by the PRC as politically unacceptable, for citizens should directly nominate the candidates running for the chief executive position. Leung and his supporters vowed to use confrontational tactics inside and outside the legislature to make their demands known. Hence, to the Marxist localists in Hong Kong, bourgeois democratization would a means to achieve a socialist, democratic, and egalitarian society. Yet, the Marxist localists in the HKSAR rejected the CCP rule on the mainland and saw it as an authoritarian regime in need of political liberalization and democratization.

---

162. For the political philosophies of Martin Lee and Szeto Wah, as well as their differences, see Lo, *Competing Chinese Political Visions: Beijing vs Hong Kong on Democracy*.
163. For the platform of the League of Social Democrats, accessed October 12, 2017, http://www.lsd.org.hk/policy-2/. By 2021, its platform appeared to dilute the call for referendum and focused on the direct election of both the chief executive and the entire LegCo; see 政制綱領（內文）—社會民主連線, accessed March 14, 2021, https://www.lsd.org.hk/policy-2/.

While some confrontational localists were determined to use violence in clashes with the police in the Mong Kok riot in early 2016,[164] some separatist localists succeeded in being elected to the LegCo, notably two members of the localist Youngspiration party, Baggio Leung and Yau Wai-ching. Leung and Yau performed provocative acts when they took their oaths in the LegCo in October, leading the SCNPC to interpret the Basic Law over their "improper" behavior.[165] The local Hong Kong court eventually followed the decision of the SCNPC to deprive the two legislators-elect of their seats. In December 2020, Baggio Leung remarked openly that he left Hong Kong and sought asylum in the US.[166] He was regrouping with some overseas Hong Kong political activists, trying to maintain a "lifeboat" for those young Hongkongers who wanted to leave the HKSAR for other parts of the world, and to promote democracy in the HKSAR.[167] Leung appeared to be a separatist localist, maintaining that "we do not need one country, two systems" and that "we do not need the Sino-British agreement."[168] Yet, Hong Kong activists who are in exile find it difficult to propel the democracy movement in the HKSAR, especially after the enactment of the national security law in June 2020.

The political and legal bottom line of Beijing's policy toward the HKSAR was clear: the people of Hong Kong should not and must not advocate independence. The rise of Marxist localists, who used filibustering tactics in the LegCo, had already raised the eyebrows of Beijing's conservative nationalists, who reiterated that the HKSAR should have an executive-led system rather than a legislature-led one and that the Western-style "separation of powers" should not be practiced in Hong Kong.

---

164. Benny Tai, Chan Kin-man, and Chu Yiu-ming advocated non-violent means, such as "love and peace," in the push for democratization, but their Occupy Central movement was arguably confrontational vis-à-vis Beijing. Sonny Shiu-hing Lo, *The Politics of Policing in Greater China* (London: Palgrave Macmillan, 2016).
165. Yau changed the content of the oath, adding terms like "the Hong Kong nation" and the "People's Re-fucking of Chee-na." See "Yau Wai-ching Refers to 'People's Re-fu*king of Chee-na' at Hong Kong LegCo Oath-Taking," accessed April 13, 2018, https://www.youtube.com/watch?v=M9rDqvSP4AY. Leung also changed the oath's content by using the term "the Hong Kong nation" and the "People's Republic of Chee-na."
166. "Ex-Hong Kong Lawmaker Baggio Leung Seeks Asylum in US," AFP, December 11, 2020, accessed March 14, 2021, https://hongkongfp.com/2020/12/11/ex-hong-kong-lawmaker-baggio-leung-seeks-asylum-in-us/.
167. Martin Greene and Chris Chang, "Interview with Former Hong Kong Legislator Baggio Leung," Taiwan News, February 27, 2021, accessed March 14, 2021, https://www.taiwannews.com.tw/en/news/4137938.
168. Greene and Chang, "Interview with Former Hong Kong Legislator Baggio Leung."

The transformation of the localist factions in the HKSAR from the dominance of the liberals to the rapid emergence of the young student faction and Marxist segment in 2012, and then to the sudden rise of the separatist forces from 2013 to 2016, was shaped by the closer economic integration between Hong Kong and the mainland. As this policy deepened under the Donald Tsang administration from 2004 to 2012, the influx of many mainland tourists and immigrants into the HKSAR aggravated societal tensions between some mainlanders and the confrontational/separatist localists. Both types of localists saw the influx of mainlanders as a sign of Sinification, or mainlandization, of the HKSAR. The Civic Party, a political group that emerged from the opposition to the legislation on Article 23 of the Basic Law in mid-2003, carried the banner of opposing mainlandization in its 2012 LegCo election campaign. A few other liberal localists also fought mainlandization, such as Gary Fan of the Neo-Democrats from 2012 to 2016, when he was a directly elected legislator. Mainlandization, which could be articulated as an academic concept, was unfortunately turned into a political weapon by the localists to oppose the PRC.

These localist sentiments were understandable, as more and more mainland tourists went to Hong Kong to shop for all kinds of daily necessities, and rich pregnant women from the mainland flocked to the HKSAR's public hospitals to give birth, often at the expense of the hospital beds available for local pregnant women. Hence, the rise of localist forces could be attributable to the massive increase in human interactions between Hong Kong and the mainland. Some mainlanders were stereotyped as "uncivilized," "impolite," and "uncultured" by a minority of localists. The argument that Hong Kong was a "nation" emerged rapidly among a group of localists, who perceived its culture as unique and who saw economic integration and social interaction with the mainland as "harmful" to the HKSAR.

The rise of the confrontational localists was a complex phenomenon attributable to at least two factors. First, as Beijing's conservative nationalist faction increasingly dominated its policy toward Hong Kong from 2014 to 2015, some young Hong Kong localists adopted a more confrontational attitude toward the HKSAR government, which they regarded as a "puppet" of Beijing. The eruption of the Mong Kok riot in early 2016 followed the sudden disappearance of several publishers of the Causeway Bay Bookstore, which published books on the corruption, sex scandals, political struggles, and personal secrets of PRC officials. As mentioned before, these books, which were brought back to the mainland by some mainland visitors in Hong Kong and which were arranged by the publishers to be mailed to the PRC, antagonized PRC authorities. The publishers included Lee Po, Lam Wing-kee, and Gui Minhai in late 2015.[169] Lee disappeared from Hong Kong, Lam vanished in Shenzhen, and Gui was "kidnapped" from Thailand back to the PRC. In the wake of these disappearances, many young localists found themselves increasingly distrustful of the mainland regime. Lee later returned to Hong Kong and eventually issued a public denial that he had been "kidnapped" to China by mainland agents. Lam, however, complained publicly that he was arrested on the mainland for publishing and mailing political books on China. On a mainland TV program, Gui publicly repented his involvement in a traffic accident long ago. Yet, in the minds of the confrontational localists who participated in the Mong Kok riot, the disappearance of the book publishers in late 2015 was not only politically unacceptable and socially intimidating but also sounding a death knell to "one country, two systems."

Ultimately, the legitimacy of the PRC's rule over Hong Kong was seriously questioned by the young localists. Although the Mong Kok riot was triggered in part by the mishandling of street hawkers by HKSAR government officials, the anger shown by many confrontational localists reflected their disgust at the suspected intrusion of mainland agents into the territory to abduct Lee Po. Some confrontational localists arrested by the Hong Kong police were sentenced to imprisonment by the local court, but overall, the Mong Kok riot could be seen as a strong reaction of confrontational localists to the alleged kidnap of Lee Po and the sudden disappearance of his associates. With regard to the publishers, the tide of conservative nationalism in the PRC jeopardized the traditional freedom of the press in Hong Kong because "incorrect" political magazines and books tended to infuriate mainland political leaders, security personnel, and conservative nationalists. However, by distributing and mailing politically sensitive books to the mainland, the publishers of the Causeway Bay Bookstore could be regarded as committing cross-border crime.[170] Freedom of publication had its limits in the HKSAR. If the books published by the Causeway Bay Bookstore were unintentionally involved in a mainland faction opposed to the dominant and ruling Xi Jinping faction, it was arguably logical that Lee and his associates had exposed themselves to being investigated and detained by the mainland security authorities. However, in the eyes of the separatist localists in the HKSAR, the PRC should not interfere with Hong Kong's civil liberties, including the freedom of publication. The book publishers' disappearances showed the

---

169. Lee held a British passport but publicly said in a mainland television program that he had abandoned his British citizenship. Gui held a Swedish passport, but he was detained by the PRC authorities for being involved in a car accident long ago. For details, see Lo, *The Politics of Policing in Greater China*.
170. Sonny Lo, "'New' Cross-Border Crime between Hong Kong and China," Asia Dialogue, August 2, 2016, accessed March 14, 2021, https://theasiadialogue.com/2016/08/02/new-cross-border-crime-between-hong-kong-and-china/.

complexities of factional politics within China and the radical localist faction's strong reaction to their arrests.

Political Climate Change

The political climate in Beijing-HKSAR relations from 2012 to 2021 was totally different from that in the summer of 2010, when DP members, who could be seen as liberal localists, went to the Liaison Office and reached a compromise on the scope and pace of reforms in the LegCo.[171] In mid-2010, the liberal localists dominated the pro-democracy faction, while the Beijing side was not only relatively liberal in political outlook but also eager for political compromise with the democrats. One can argue that the Beijing officials responsible for Hong Kong affairs in the summer of 2010 were closet liberals, but in fact, President Hu Jintao at that time was relatively softline in his political outlook on Hong Kong's democratic change. In the PRC under Hu Jintao, civil society groups were tolerated and some degree of political pluralism could be seen, unlike the shrinking political space that ushered in the beginning of the Xi Jinping era.[172] Moreover, Elsie Leung, the former Hong Kong secretary for justice, acted as an intermediary between the Hong Kong democrats and the Chinese officials of the Liaison Office—assistance that was lacking in the deadlock over political reform in mid-2015, shortly after the end of the Occupy Central movement. Leung acted as a middle person who bridged the communication gap between PRC authorities and Hong Kong's moderate democrats. An unprecedented political compromise was reached in the summer of 2010, but indeed, the liberal localists, notably the DP members, were severely criticized by the Marxist localists, who regarded them as "traitors" to the pro-democracy camp.

The image of the liberal localists as being too soft toward Beijing did cost them politically in the 2012 LegCo elections, in which the Marxist localists won more seats than ever before. The hardline and united position adopted by the localists, ranging from liberals to Marxists and from confrontationalists to separatists, in rejecting the 2015 political reform package proposed by the HKSAR government and endorsed by Beijing led to the victory of separatist localists in the 2016 legislative election. Hence, the irony of Hong Kong's political development from 2012 to 2016 was that if the localists took a hardline and uncompromising approach to the HKSAR government, which was often seen as a staunch

---

171. Jasper Tsang emphasized the very different political climate in the summer of 2010 as compared with the summer of 2015, when the political reform bill prepared by the HKSAR government was rejected by the legislature.
172. Chloe Froissart, "Changing Patterns of Chinese Civil Society: Comparing the Hu-Wen and Xi Jinping Eras," in *Routledge Handbook of the Chinese Communist Party*, ed. Willy Wo-lap Lam (London: Routledge, 2017), 352–370.

supporter of Beijing, they were more likely to benefit in legislative elections. The softer their position, the more likely they would lose their seats, as with the DP candidates in the 2012 legislative election. This pattern of electoral politics pointed to the deliberately hardline stance adopted by many localists prior to the 2016 legislative elections, thus making any political compromise with Beijing's conservative nationalists in the summer of 2015 very difficult. Even worse, the victory of localists in the 2016 LegCo elections led to the politically provocative and overconfident behavior of Baggio Leung and Yau Wai-ching during their swearing-in ceremony.

Table 2.1 sums up the positions of the different ideological factions toward the political, economic, societal, and legal disputes in Hong Kong. It can be argued that with the passage of time, while the ideological factions on the pro–Hong Kong localist side became increasingly differentiated, fragmented, and radicalized, the pro-Beijing side shifted from dominance by the liberal nationalists in the summer of 2010 to the preeminence of the conservative nationalists from 2013 to 2022. Since the CCP's nineteenth Party Congress in October 2017, ideologies have continued to be critical in shaping Beijing's relations with the HKSAR, even though Beijing's officials responsible for Hong Kong matters changed. Key appointments included former Liaison Office director Zhang Xiaoming as director of the Hong Kong and Macao Affairs Office and Wang Zhimin of the Macau Liaison Office as director of the Hong Kong Liaison Office in September 2017. Both projected a strong image of being hardline on Hong Kong matters—a continuity that persisted until their removal in early 2020, when PRC authorities became even more hardline and thought that the two had miscalculated the situation in Hong Kong during the 2019 anti-extradition movement.[173] Zhang was demoted to be a deputy director of the HKMAO, while Wang became a vice president of the Central Institute for Party History and Literature Research. Their apparent demotions were politically unprecedented in the history of PRC officials handling Hong Kong matters, apart from the expulsion of Xu Jiatun from the CCP in 1994 after his escape to the US.

The crux of the problem in the HKSAR from 2016 to 2020 was that some radical and moderate democrats kept on challenging the red lines of PRC authorities. They were either politically naïve or deliberately testing the Chinese bottom line of tolerance. The anti-extradition movement plunged the HKSAR into social disorder. Beijing was furious as its sovereignty and national security were undermined. The PRC national flags were desecrated by radicals; the Liaison Office headquarters were attacked by violent mobs; the LegCo was occupied by mobs

---

173. Zhang was demoted as the HKMAO deputy director in February, a month after Wang's dismissal. See "HKMAO Chief Zhang Xiaoming Demoted," RTHK, February 13, 2020, accessed April 2, 2021.

on July 1, 2019; the national day on October 1 was full of violent activities on the streets; the offices and branches of pro-Beijing organizations were attacked by arsonists and violent protestors; the Mass Transit Railway (MTR) stations were burnt; the Hong Kong international airport and its nearby roads were occupied by protestors; campuses at the Chinese University of Hong Kong (CUHK) and Polytechnic University became battlegrounds between violent protestors and the police; and foreign governments spoke out in opposition to the extradition bill, which was designed by the HKSAR government in collaboration with Beijing to deal with not only a Taiwanese murder case but also the money-laundering activities of at least some 300 mainland business people in Hong Kong.[174] To Beijing, all these protest activities exceeded the bottom line of its political tolerance.

Factional Rivalries in the 2019 Anti-extradition, Anti-mainlandization, and Anti-police Movement

The anti-extradition movement in Hong Kong began in June 2019 and evolved in July into protests against police power and the mainlandization of the territory.[175] The bill triggered a series of protests from March to June 2019, culminating in a mass action occupying and vandalizing the LegCo on July 1. The occupation of the LegCo by protestors was politically unacceptable to the central government in Beijing, for they painted anti-CCP and anti-PRC slogans on the walls of the LegCo buildings. After all, the LegCo represented one of the top political institutions in the HKSAR, where its police were arguably too weak to expel the protestors from the LegCo building. Instead of dispersing the protestors from inside and outside the LegCo building, the police withdrew from the LegCo and allowed protestors to enter it and ransack its offices, creating chaos and humiliation for the central government's sovereignty over Hong Kong. The protests took a turn for the worse on the night of July 21, when some triad members openly attacked ordinary citizens in the Yuen Long MTR station and when some violent protestors defaced the national emblem on the Liaison Office building. The next day, PRC officials and HKSAR Chief Executive Carrie Lam denounced the attack at the Liaison Office building, but Lam shied away from discussing the police's handling of the triad attack, which spawned a public outcry because of news

---

174. It is ironic that at the time of writing in March 2024, Chan Tong-kai, the boy who allegedly murdered a Hong Kong girl in Taipei and escaped back to Hong Kong, is still residing in the HKSAR without being sent to Taiwan for trial. For the details of the protests, see Lo, Hung, and Loo, *The Dynamics of Peaceful and Violent Protests in Hong Kong: The Anti-Extradition Movement*.
175. I thank Dr. David Fraser for allowing me to reprint my article for this section. Sonny Shiu-Hing Lo, "Hong Kong in 2019: The Anti-Extradition, Anti-Mainlandization and Anti-Police Movement," *Asian Survey* 60, no. 1 (February 2020): 34–40. I revised and updated this article in this section.

reports that some police had prior knowledge of it and that triads were involved in the clashes with some anti-extradition protestors. Many protesters demanded that the government set up an independent commission of inquiry looking into excessive police use of teargas and their inaction in the Yuen Long triad attack. Lam and her principal officials, with the support of PRC authorities, refused to make any concessions, stimulating the protests to continue. At the same time, the imbalance in the use of force by the police triggered more protests. The weakness of the Hong Kong government was fully exposed, fueling protests in the following four months. The mixture of violent and peaceful protests continued in Hong Kong throughout August, culminating in a clash between police and protesters in the Prince Edward MTR station on August 23 and protesters' accusations of "police brutality" in the San Uk Ling Holding Center, where some arrested protesters were detained and allegedly "abused." Some protesters and netizens accused the police of causing the disappearance of a few protesters inside the Prince Edward MTR station, but the police called this fake news aimed at delegitimizing the police force. The holding center stopped its operation after its existence was publicized. Throughout the protests, accusations and fake news erupted, causing social chaos.

The Hong Kong protests raised the alarm of the central government in Beijing, which sent the People's Armed Police (PAP) to nearby Shenzhen, Guangdong Province, by the end of August. This was a political warning from Beijing that more forceful intervention from the mainland would be necessary if the HKSAR was out of control. On September 4, Carrie Lam announced that the extradition bill was withdrawn. However, the protesters continued to demand that the HKSAR government not use the term "riot" to refer to the June and July protests, that the arrested protesters should be released from prison, that Hong Kong should have universal suffrage to select the chief executive, and that an independent commission should be established to review police actions. The government did not back down and invoked the Emergency Regulations to enact an Anti-Mask Law on October 4, banning face masks at protests, which however triggered riots on the same night and the next morning when mainland banks and organizations, as well as the MTR railway, were attacked by violent protesters.

To worsen the situation, the US government intervened in the affairs of the HKSAR. On October 15, the US House of Representatives passed the Hong Kong Human Rights and Democracy Act, which was later supported by the Senate and signed by President Donald Trump. The riot on the night of October 4 and the morning of October 5 showed to the central government that it would have to adopt more decisive measures to cope with the Hong Kong crisis, especially as the US attempted to use the Hong Kong Human Rights and Democracy Act to exert pressure on the HKSAR government.

The act coincided with the increased intensity of the protests in Hong Kong in November, when the police entered the Chinese University of Hong Kong (CUHK) to counter and arrest some protesters; later, they arrested 1,100 protestors in a twelve-day siege at the Polytechnic University. On November 24, the District Council elections were held, and an unprecedented turnout of 71 percent led to the democrats capturing 388 seats and seventeen of the eighteen District Councils. The pro-Beijing forces merely obtained eighty-nine seats; their defeat represented the unpopularity of the government. Yet, the election results did not appease the anger of many protestors, who had been adopting the guerrilla tactics of mobilizing flash mobs to occupy streets, to attack pro-Beijing and pro-government shops, banks, and organizations, and to confront the police. To the PRC authorities, the Hong Kong crisis was politically unacceptable because the localists, both peaceful and violent, attempted to seize political power by capturing most directly elected seats in the District Councils, where some local conservative nationalists opposed the November elections being held.

On November 20, when PRC President Xi Jinping visited Macau during the twentieth anniversary celebration of the Macau Special Administrative Region, he criticized foreign countries for interfering with China's "one country, two systems." He implicitly referred to the US and various European countries that opposed the extradition bill. On the night of December 24, Hong Kong protestors again confronted police on the streets of Mong Kok and Tsim Sha Tsui, as well as at a shopping mall in Yuen Long. The protests, however, turned much smaller in scale and infrequent in number in early January 2020, and they tapered off after the outbreak of COVID-19 in the HKSAR in March 2020. At this juncture, the PRC authorities grasped the golden opportunity to draft the national security law in secrecy until it was reported in May that such a law would be proposed and enacted by the NPC in June.

The anti-extradition protests turned out to be a tragic event, confirming to the PRC authorities that foreign countries, like the US, intervened in Hong Kong matters at a time when social and political chaos took place. The mainland image of the HKSAR as a Trojan horse for foreign countries to "subvert" the Hong Kong polity turned out to be corroborated by what happened in the latter half of 2019. Many protestors went too far politically without knowing that their radical and violent actions exceeded the political bottom line of tolerance by Beijing.

Factionalism and the Origins of the Extradition Bill

Although the extradition bill had its explicit objective of dealing with the Taiwanese murder case, there were reports saying that the PRC government staunchly supported it for the sake of tackling the money-laundering activities of some 300 mainland businesspeople in Hong Kong. Hong Kong's Financial

Secretary Paul Chan said in June 2019 that the bill was designed to fight money laundering.[176] Another report said that after mainland businessman Xiao Jianhua was arrested in Hong Kong in January 2017 for money laundering, the PRC's Central Discipline Inspection Committee (CDIC) pressured the mainland officials responsible for Hong Kong matters to arrange an extradition agreement with the HKSAR.[177] Compounding this push was the action of the Hong Kong DAB to help the family victims of the girl allegedly murdered by Chan Tong-kai and to lobby the chief executive for the extradition bill.

It can be argued that the bill was proposed by the HKSAR government to help the dominant ruling faction in China to combat the corrupt officials and cadres, some of whom might belong to the anti–Xi Jinping faction. On the other hand, by helping the family victims of the girl allegedly murdered by Chan, the DAB hoped to gain political popularity in the HKSAR months before the November 2019 District Council elections. Yet, the DAB's political opponents, especially the localists, were determined to oppose the bill and label it as an attempt to send the people of Hong Kong to the mainland for political trials ("*song zhong*"). The fear of many ordinary citizens of witnessing a curtailment of their civil liberties resulted in their easy mobilization by the localist factions in the series of protests from June to December 2019. Factional politics in both the PRC and Hong Kong came into play and were intertwined with the push for the bill and its staunch opposition. Unintentionally and coincidentally, the local protestors who opposed the extradition bill formed an apparently loose coalition with the anti–Xi Jinping faction on the mainland, stirring up anti-PRC and anti-CCP sentiments.

The hurried way in which the HKSAR government handled the bill aroused public opposition. At the end of March 2019, three democrats, namely former Chief Secretary Anson Chan, Professional Commons founder Charles Mok, and Civic Party member Dennis Kwok, visited the US and met with Vice President Mike Pence. They expressed their concerns about human rights and autonomy in the HKSAR; US national security officials were alarmed at the extradition bill, which from their perspective could affect the interests of Americans doing business and residing in the HKSAR.[178] In fact, officials in numerous countries

---

176. *Sing Tao Daily*, June 4, 2019.
177. David Lague, James Pomfret, and Greg Torode, "How Murder, Kidnappings and Miscalculation Set Off Hong Kong's Revolt," Reuters, December 20, 2019, https://www.reuters.com/investigates/special-report/hongkong-protests-extradition-narrative/.
178. Owen Churchill and Alvin Lum, "Hong Kong's Former No. 2 Anson Chan Meets Mike Pence in Washington as US Report Criticizes Beijing's 'Intervention' in City's Affairs," *South China Morning Post*, March 23, 2019, accessed December 25, 2019, https://www.scmp.com/news/hongkong/politics/article/3002953/hong-kong-lawmakers-and-former-no-2-hit-us-capital-report. The US National Security Council's senior director for Asian Affairs, Matt Pottinger, met the three democrats.

expressed concern about whether the extradition bill would be utilized by the PRC to "kidnap" their citizens in the HKSAR. This recalled the case of the publishers at the Causeway Bay Bookstore like Lee Po, Gui Minhai, and Lam Wing-kee, who disappeared from Hong Kong, Thailand, and Shenzhen, respectively, in late 2015 after publishing books critical of mainland officials. Foreign business chambers and diplomats voiced their concerns to the HKSAR government. Some Hong Kong businesspeople were afraid that the bill, if enacted, would endanger their personal safety, especially those who had previously "bribed" mainland officials to facilitate business transactions. Genuine concerns about civil liberties in Hong Kong emerged locally and globally.

In late May 2019, the Hong Kong General Chamber of Commerce expressed its fear of the bill to Secretary for Security John Lee in a closed-door meeting, during which the government was asked to raise the extradition threshold to include only offences punishable by jail terms of at least seven years, rather than three years as proposed. Moreover, the local business elites also said that rendition requests from the mainland would have to come from the central government, not local authorities. They argued that the Hong Kong court must consider human rights and humanitarian factors before approving extradition requests from the mainland.[179] On May 30, Lee announced that the scope of extraditable offences could be raised to those punishable by sentences of three years to seven years. In addition, the Supreme People's Procuratorate and the Supreme People's Court of the PRC would be the mainland bodies issuing extradition requests. The local business chambers welcomed the concessions, but the legal community was still dissatisfied.

The Law Society asked the government to extend the consultation period, while the Bar Association led a protest by 3,000 lawyers on June 6. The protest sparked marches on June 9 of almost a million protestors against the extradition bill, although the police claimed that only 270,000 people participated. The HKSAR government insisted that the bill would go through the LegCo on June 12 for the second-reading debate. On June 12, hundreds of thousands of protestors went to the LegCo to demonstrate against the bill, but the police fired teargas. The LegCo announced a delay in the second reading of the bill. Police Commissioner Stephen Lo said that the protestors initiated a "riot"; his remarks angered many protestors, who demanded that the government retract its description of protestors as "rioters." On June 15, Carrie Lam delayed the proposed extradition bill. Yet, protestors were unhappy with her refusal to withdraw

---

179. Jeffie Lam, "Influential Hong Kong Business Body Calls for Extra Safeguards in Government's Controversial Extradition Bill," *South China Morning Post*, May 27, 2019, accessed December 25, 2019, https://www.scmp.com/news/hong-kong/politics/article/3012007/influential-hong-kong-business-body-calls-extra-safeguards.

it and continued to protest. After the occupation of the LegCo by protestors on July 1, Lam made a concession on July 9 by saying that the bill was "dead." Still, many protestors were dissatisfied with her "ambiguous" stance. On September 4, Lam announced that the bill was formally withdrawn. The reluctance of Lam's administration and of Beijing to withdraw the bill from June to early September spurred tremendous public opposition. When the bill was withdrawn, the blend of peaceful and violent protests developed their momentum and could not be terminated.

From Anti-extradition to Anti-police, Anti-mainlandization, and Anti-authoritarianism

The accidental death of Chow Tsz-lok, a university student in Cheung Kwan O where police chased the protestors on the night of November 8, and the injury of two young students after police officers fired at them from a short distance in October and November, as well as other mysterious deaths of citizens, aroused public suspicions about the "abuse" of police power. The anti-extradition protests turned into a massive and long-term citizen movement against police power after the July 21 triad attacks in the Yuen Long MTR station. The refusal of the Lam administration and Beijing to set up an independent commission of inquiry prolonged this citizen movement to some extent.

Many protestors use illegal slogan to call for a "recovery" of Hong Kong, triggering Beijing's hardline official accusation that the Hong Kong protests were like a "color revolution" aimed at toppling the HKSAR government. The slogan, which was later regarded as having "secessionist meaning" in the case of Tong Ying-kit in August 2021, originated from Hong Kong indigenous leader Edward Leung Tin-kei, who was imprisoned for six years due to his involvement in the 2016 Mong Kok riot and who argued as early as 2016 that the HKSAR was more like Tibet and Xinjiang because Hongkongers were "deprived" of their "sovereignty."[180] Motorcyclist Tong Ying-kit, who drove his motorcycle into a crowd of police with a "subversive" banner, was sentenced to nine years in jail. From the historical and national security perspective, Hong Kong's sovereignty belongs to mainland China. After the SCNPC interpreted the Basic Law in November 2016 and said that legislators-elect should take their oaths respectfully and solemnly, the Hong Kong court disqualified the status of legislators-elect Baggio Leung and Yau Wai-ching. Other localists like Agnes Chow and

---

180. For a detailed discussion of the Tong Ying-kit case, see Suzanne Pepper, "The Tong Ying-kit Case: First Show Trial of Hong Kong's New Mainland-Style Legal Regime," Hong Kong Free Press, August 21, 2021, accessed September 28, 2022, https://hongkongfp.com/2021/08/15/the-tong-ying-kit-case-first-show-trial-of-hong-kongs-new-mainland-style-legal-regime/.

Joshua Wong were disqualified to run in local elections on the grounds that they supported "self-determination," as with the banning of Andy Chan's Hong Kong National Party in September 2018. All these moves by the government were legally justified, but in the eyes of some people, the HKSAR was drifting toward "hard" authoritarianism under the sovereignty of and intervention from the PRC. At the same time, public frustration continued to erupt over a wide range of issues reflecting deeper social problems, such as the critical housing shortage and the huge gap between rich and poor. Objectively speaking, the HKSAR government had been slow and clumsy in tackling social issues like the housing shortage and poverty. The anti-extradition movement became a stimulus for many other dissidents and localists to confront the police, who became a symbol of "authoritarianism" and "mainlandization."

The larger geopolitical problem was that the citizen movement against mainlandization and the police was taken by Beijing as endangering its national security. President Xi Jinping's speech in Macau on December 20, 2019, warned foreign countries against interfering in Hong Kong matters. In the latter half of 2019, pro-Beijing media in the HKSAR lashed out against the "intervention" of Taiwan and US in Hong Kong matters. These included the escape of at least thirty Hong Kong protesters who occupied the LegCo on July 1 to seek refuge in Taiwan, the appeal of some Hong Kong university students to the Taiwanese government to enact a refugee law for Hong Kong dissidents, and the remarks of Taiwanese President Tsai Ing-wen, who spoke out against "one country, two systems" and whose presidential re-election campaign benefited tremendously from the Hong Kong protests. Taiwan's non-governmental organizations, especially the Presbyterian Church and the Taiwan State-Building Party in Kaohsiung, were criticized by the pro-Beijing media in the HKSAR for helping and supporting the Hong Kong protesters. The Taiwan link in the Hong Kong protests turned out to be a national security concern in the eyes of the PRC. The victory of Tsai Ing-wen in the presidential election of Taiwan in January 2020 and the defeat of KMT candidate Han Kuo-yu could be partly attributable to the Taiwanese voters' fear of a phenomenon of making Taiwan another Hong Kong. The anti-extradition movement in Hong Kong in 2019 undermined Beijing's diligent united front work to win the hearts and minds of the Taiwanese people, especially the attempt at wooing them to vote for KMT candidate Han Kuo-yu, whose visit to the mainland, Hong Kong, and Macau in March 2019 as the mayor of Kaohsiung city indicated how PRC authorities embraced and supported him.

During the anti-extradition movement from June to December 2019, the former DAB chairman and LegCo president, Jasper Tsang, openly called for the Carrie Lam government to consider a partial amnesty in which arrested protestors who committed lighter offenses should be pardoned, while those who committed serious offenses should be tried and penalized.[181] But Tsang's remarks appeared to be too liberal to the Lam administration and Beijing. Another reason why Beijing saw the Hong Kong protests as a national security threat was because rumors were rife that the anti–Xi Jinping mainland businesspeople had been funding the protestors. The crowd-funding mechanism utilized by some protestors could easily attract lots of funding support from the public, but it was unknown whether some of the financiers behind the scenes involved some mainland and local businesspeople who were opposed to the PRC's anti-corruption and anti-money-laundering campaigns. The involvement of the US and Taiwan in the Hong Kong protests, directly or indirectly, made the Beijing leadership feel insecure. As such, Minister of Public Security Zhao Kezhi joined the Central Coordination Committee on Hong Kong and Macau as a deputy head.[182] When the new Hong Kong Police Commissioner Chris Tang visited Beijing in early December 2019, he also met Zhao—an indication that the Hong Kong police appeared to be held accountable to the PRC's minister of public security on how the Hong Kong police handled the protests and riots.

The Imposition of the National Security Law in June 2020

Due to Beijing's deep concern about its national security being undermined in Hong Kong, where the anti-extradition protests from June to December 2019 not only challenged the legitimacy of both the central and Hong Kong governments but also constituted an attempt at initiating a "color revolution," a national security law was enacted in late June 2020.[183] The new law aimed at demonstrating its immediate deterrence effects on protestors and dissidents by empowering the Hong Kong authorities to pursue suspected offenders. The results were the escape, arrest, and imprisonment of some local political activists and law offenders. The year 2020 marked the immediate impacts of the national security law on Hong Kong's political development, resulting in the territory's truncated autonomy and exerting some controls over the polity, society, and education.

On May 28, 2020, the NPC of the PRC held a meeting to consider the enactment of a national security law for the HKSAR because the Chinese government firmly believed that Hong Kong's anti-extradition movement of the latter half of

---

181. Hong Kong Cable TV interview with Jasper Tsang, December 24, 2019.
182. When Zhao appeared in a meeting between President Xi Jinping and the new Macau chief executive, Ho Iat-seng, in Beijing in September 2019, there was speculation that Zhao would play an increasingly crucial role in handling the national security of the HKSAR. See William Zheng and Jun Mai, "Is China's Police Chief Playing a New Part in Beijing's Handling of Hong Kong?" *South China Morning Post*, September 13, 2019, accessed March 16, 2021, https://www.scmp.com/news/china/politics/article/3027188/chinas-police-chief-playing-new-part-beijings-handling-hong.
183. I thank Dr. David Fraser for allowing me to reprint and update my article in this section. Sonny Lo, "Hong Kong in 2020," *Asian Survey* 61, no. 1 (February 2021): 34–42.

2019 was marked by the intervention of foreign forces into HKSAR affairs. From June 18 to 20, the NPC released an abstract of the draft national security law. On June 30, the NPC endorsed the promulgation of the law, which was incorporated into Appendix 3 of the Hong Kong Basic Law. It had immediate impacts in the political, social, and educational arenas.

The six chapters of the law cover the duties of the HKSAR government, offenses and penalties, and jurisdictions and legal procedures.[184] Article 1 mandates the "resolute, full and faithful implementation" of the policy of "one country, two systems" and the safeguarding of the PRC's national security. Article 3 states that the HKSAR government has the duty to safeguard national security. Article 4 stipulates that human rights shall be respected and protected in safeguarding national security in accordance with the provisions of the International Covenant on Civil and Political Rights and the International Covenant on Economic, Social, and Cultural Rights. Article 6 points to the "common responsibility of all the people of China" and of Hong Kong to safeguard the PRC's "sovereignty, unification, and territorial integrity." Article 11 says that the chief executive of the HKSAR is accountable to the PRC central government for the implementation of the national security law, while Article 12 establishes the Committee for Safeguarding National Security (CSNS) in the HKSAR. According to Article 15, a national security adviser designated by Beijing sits in the committee meetings. Article 16 says that the Hong Kong police shall set up a department to enforce the protection of national security. Similarly, the Department of Justice shall establish a division responsible for the prosecution of national security cases (Article 18).

Chapter 3 of the law bans secession, subversion, terrorism, and collusion with a foreign country or external elements to undermine national security. A person committing secession, subversion, or terrorism of a grave nature shall be sentenced to either life in prison or a fixed term of not less than ten years (Articles 20, 22, and 25). The same penalties apply to a person who colludes to a grave degree with a foreign country or external elements (Article 29). Article 29 defines collusion as the activities of a person who steals state secrets or who requests and conspires with foreign entities to wage war on the PRC, to disrupt the formulation and implementation of the policies of the HKSAR, to rig or undermine local elections, to impose sanctions on Hong Kong, or to promote "hatred" among Hong Kong residents toward the central government and the HKSAR administration. Article 30 adds that a person who receives funding and support from any foreign organization is forging external collusion.

---

184. "Law of the People's Republic of China on Safeguarding National Security in the Hong Kong Special Administrative Region," accessed November 8, 2020, https://www.gld.gov.hk/egazette/pdf/20202448e/egn2020244872.pdf.

Chapter 4 focuses on jurisdictional issues. Article 41 states that no prosecution shall be instituted in respect of an offense endangering national security without the written consent of the secretary for justice. National security cases within Hong Kong's jurisdictions shall be tried on indictment, and the trial shall be conducted in an open court. Article 44 stipulates that the chief executive shall designate a few judges to handle cases concerning offenses endangering national security and that their term of office is one year. Before making such designations, the chief executive may consult the CSNS and the chief justice. If such a judge makes any statement endangering national security, he or she shall not be designated or shall be removed.

Chapter 5 focuses on the Office for Safeguarding National Security (OSNS) of the Central People's Government in the HKSAR. The OSNS staff shall be dispatched by the central government's national security authorities. While its staff abides by the laws of Hong Kong (Article 50), the office is funded by the central government (Article 51). Article 52 states that the OSNS coordinates with the Liaison Office, the Office of the Commissioner of the Ministry of Foreign Affairs, and the Hong Kong Garrison of the People's Liberation Army in the HKSAR. The OSNS strengthens the management of relations with the organs of international and foreign organizations, including news media and nongovernmental groups (Article 54). Article 55 says that the OSNS has jurisdiction over complex national security cases if the HKSAR government is unable to enforce the national security law or if "a major and imminent threat to national security has occurred."[185]

Immediate Impacts of the National Security Law

Four days after the law was promulgated, the HKSAR government set up the CSNS, whose chairperson is the chief executive and whose national security adviser was Luo Huining, director of the Liaison Office.[186] The Hong Kong police established the National Security Department, whose head was Assistant Commissioner Edwin Lau. The central government established the OSNS, whose director is Zheng Yanxiong, a former mayor and party-secretary of Shanwei (once called Swabue) in Guangdong Province, who took a hardline approach to suppressing protesters in Wukan Village in 2011. The OSNS held its first coordination meeting with the CSNS on July 31, 2020.

Some foreign countries expressed grave concern about the new law. In a press statement released June 30, the former US Secretary of State Michael Pompeo said, "Beijing's paranoia and fear of its own people's aspirations have led

---

185. "Law of the People's Republic of China on Safeguarding National Security in the Hong Kong Special Administrative Region."
186. *Ta Kung Pao*, July 4, 2020, A1.

it to eviscerate the very foundation of the territory's success, turning 'one country, two systems' into 'one country, one system.'"[187] On August 7, 2020, the US government imposed sanctions on eleven officials dealing with HKSAR matters, including the director of the Hong Kong and Macau Affairs Office, Xia Baolong, Liaison Office Director Luo Huining, Chief Executive Carrie Lam, Secretary for Justice Teresa Cheng, Secretary for Security John Lee, and Police Commissioner Chris Tang. The US rescinded Hong Kong's special trading privileges and halted its extradition treaty with Hong Kong. Other countries, including Australia, Britain, Canada, Finland, France, Germany, Ireland, the Netherlands, and New Zealand, also suspended their extradition treaties with the HKSAR.

Hours after the law was passed, the pro-democracy organization Demosisto was disbanded. Its core leaders, namely Joshua Wong, Nathan Law, Jeffrey Ngo, and Agnes Chow, quickly resigned. Nathan Law later fled to the United Kingdom. Wayne Chan Ka-kui, a convenor of the Hong Kong Independence Union, allegedly jumped bail in mid-June and went to the Netherlands and later the United Kingdom.[188] On July 30, Samuel Chu, the son of Reverend Chu Yiu-ming, who was one of the three organizers of the 2014 Occupy Central movement, was under the arrest warrant of the Hong Kong police. Chu was not arrested as he was living and staying in the United States for "inciting secession" and "colluding with foreign powers."[189] Samuel Chu is an American citizen and an activist with the US-based Hong Kong Democracy Council. But Article 38 states that the law applies even to people who are not permanent residents of the HKSAR—an extraterritorial stipulation that has raised tremendous concern among some Hong Kong people and foreigners. Other young people who escaped from Hong Kong included Lau Hong, who was reportedly in the UK, Simon Cheng, a former UK consulate official who is now in the UK, Sunny Cheung, who was reportedly in the UK, and Ray Wong, who was involved in the 2016 Mong Kok riot and escaped to Germany in 2017.[190] On December 3, Ted Hui of the Democratic Party announced that he went into exile after arriving in Denmark. He then quit the party and went to the United Kingdom and stayed there until March 2021, when he arrived in Australia.

While at least 200 young protesters fled Hong Kong for Taiwan from June 2019 to January 2020, on August 23, 2020, twelve who tried to flee on a speedboat

---

187. "On Beijing's Imposition of National Security Legislation on Hong Kong: Press Statement, Michael R. Pompeo, U.S. Secretary of State," June 30, 2020, https://hk.usconsulate.gov/n-2020063001/.
188. *Ta Kung Pao*, October 8, 2020, A1.
189. Kevin Douglas Grant, "China Clampdown: Hong Kong Issues Warrant for Samuel Chu, an American Citizen, Activist and the Pastor's Son," *Sight*, August 30, 2020, https://www.sightmagazine.com.au/features/16930-china-clampdown-hong-kong-issues-warrant-for-samuel-chu-an-american-citizen-activist-and-pastor-s-son.
190. *Ta Kung Pao*, October 8, 2020, A1.

were arrested by the mainland marine police, including Andy Li, an organizer of the Election Observation Mission, which had delegates from 12 countries to observe the November 2019 District Council elections. They were detained in Shenzhen. On December 30, the Shenzhen court sentenced ten Hong Kong people to imprisonment, giving three years to organizer Tang Kai-yin and two years to another organizer, Quinn Moon, and seven months to eight others.[191] Two underaged suspects were returned to the Hong Kong police. The imprisonment of the ten Hongkongers on the mainland was politically significant, as their predicament after the failure to escape to Taiwan represented the cases of *song zhong* (sending back to China), a slogan that had been used by many anti-extradition protestors against the extradition bill in the latter half of 2019. In March 2021, Andy Li and seven other fugitives were returned from the mainland to the Hong Kong police.[192] Apart from their abortive escape from Hong Kong to Taiwan, it was reported in the HKSAR in July 2020 that two groups of protest activists succeeded in their escape to Taiwan, one through the sea route to Kaohsiung and the other to Pingtung. The first group comprised some ten protest activists who succeeded in arriving in Kaohsiung. Another group was composed of five protest activists, whose speedboat eventually ran out of gasoline but drifted to the Dongsha Islands where the Taiwanese coastguard discovered and rescued them.

Chief Executive Carrie Lam announced on July 31 that due to the outbreak of COVID-19, the LegCo elections originally scheduled for September 6 would be postponed for at least a year to 2021. This controversial decision led to public speculation that the HKSAR government was under the instruction of the central authorities to postpone the elections for fear of another pro-democracy victory as in the 2019 District Council elections. During the July 31, 2020, press conference, Lam suddenly mentioned that some people wanted Hong Kong people who resided on the mainland to be able to vote in the LegCo election, implying that the HKSAR government would study the matter and propose cross-border voting by the mainland's Hong Kong residents in future LegCo elections.[193] This announcement was made after twelve pro-democracy candidates preparing for the LegCo elections were disqualified. In mid-July, the pro-democracy candidates organized primaries that witnessed 600,000 people voting for candidates for the LegCo—an action that pro-Beijing media criticized as violating the new national security law. While the primaries turned out to be useless because the

---

191. "Hong Kong Boat Activists: China Jails Group for up to Three Years," BBC News, December 30, 2020, accessed March 16, 2021, https://www.bbc.com/news/world-asia-china-55481425.
192. Li was charged with "colluding with foreign forces" among other offences, and his lawyer was not hired by his family. See "Andy Li's Lawyer Not Hired by Family, Says Sister," RTHK, March 31, 2021, accessed April 2, 2021.
193. Cable TV News, July 3, 2020.

LegCo elections were postponed, most pro-democracy candidates who won the primaries were localists, who were those local Hongkongers advocating maximal autonomy for Hong Kong and who opposed any PRC intervention in Hong Kong's political development. On August 11, after the chief executive and the top policy-making Executive Council invoked the Emergency Regulations to postpone the LegCo election, the SCNPC passed a resolution to extend the sixth LegCo for a term of not less than one year. Two democrats, Eddie Chu and Raymond Chan Chi-chuen, decided to opt out of the extended LegCo. They formally wrote to the LegCo president to quit and resign, arguing that democrats should not participate in a legislature without any mandate from the people of Hong Kong because this would legitimize the CCP's actions. After the November 11 decision made by the SCNPC to disqualify four localist legislators, fifteen other localists and democrats quit the LegCo, except for Cheng Chung-tai of the Civic Passion and medical doctor Pierre Chan, who stayed in the LegCo with the other forty-one pro-government and pro-Beijing legislators.[194] The implication was that the LegCo from November 11, 2020, onward would be dominated by the pro-Beijing lawmakers, who could support and pass government bills and policies easily until the next LegCo elections that would be held in December 2021 under a new electoral system designed by the SCNPC on March 11, 2021.

The national security law has had other ramifications. Some public libraries took a few localist books off the shelves, and pro-Beijing bookstores exercised self-censorship by removing politically sensitive books. Some politically critical books written by localists are now available only in secondhand bookstores. In May 2020, two officials of the Hong Kong Examination and Assessment Authority resigned over the government's criticism of a public examination question that had asked students whether Japan's invasion of China did more good than harm.[195] The PRC state's official news agency, Xinhua, openly commented: "The so-called 'liberal' studies, which were initially designed to encourage students' critical thinking and have been widely promoted, have descended into courses rampant with biased and selective materials, leading students into forming a negative view of the mainland."[196]

The Education Bureau of the HKSAR government intervened by asking the Examination Authority to strike out the question.[197] The government was later

---

194. "Cheng Chung-tai and Pierre Chan Remains in LegCo," *The Standard*, November 11, 2020, accessed March 16, 2021, https://www.thestandard.com.hk/breaking-news/section/4/158912/Cheng-Chung-tai-and-Pierre-Chan-remains-in-Legco.
195. "Two Examination Authority Staff Resigned amid DSE Question Controversy," *Hong Kong Standard*, May 16, 2020.
196. "Hong Kong's University Entrance Exam Question Triggers Outcry, Exposes Education Flaws," Xinhua, May 17, 2020, accessed March 16, 2021, https://www.shine.cn/news/nation/2005178307/.
197. Chan Ho-him and Gary Cheung, "Beijing Blasts 'Poisonous' Hong Kong Exam Question on Whether Japan Did More Good Than Harm to China during First Half of the Last Century

criticized for using the criterion of political correctness to purge officials who were deemed politically liberal and for appointing a pro-Beijing teacher and principal to the authority's examination committee. In July 2020, the HKSAR government announced that secondary schools would implement national security education in April 2021. Secondary school teachers who espoused pro-democracy views became the easy target of criticisms by the pro-Beijing mass media and websites. They were labeled "yellow teachers," like the "yellow judges" who gave relatively lenient sentences to protesters. Secretary for Education Kevin Yeung met the vice-chancellors of local universities, asking them to implement national security education in September 2021.[198] Some university academics decided to introduce lectures on national security in the generic courses in the first year of the undergraduate level, while the liberal studies curriculum was diluted in its political content and was later changed to citizenship and social development. National security education is now required to be implemented in all schools, including kindergartens, primary schools, secondary schools, and international schools in the HKSAR.[199] In the past several years, the liberal studies curriculum was criticized by some pro-Beijing elites and academics for being too political in its content; its reform became inevitable as the curriculum was blamed for its encouragement and politicization of secondary students to participate actively in Hong Kong politics. Although the revamped curriculum would not be named national education, as Yeung said in December 2020, the new Citizenship and Social Development curriculum includes considerable content on China's socio-economic development and the mainland's relations with Hong Kong, and it constitutes *de facto* national education.[200] Some pro-Beijing elites called for the installment of closed-circuit television to monitor how secondary school teach-

---

and Warns of 'Rage' of the Chinese People," *South China Morning Post*, May 15, 2020, accessed March 16, 2021, https://www.scmp.com/news/hong-kong/education/article/3084523/beijings-foreign-ministry-takes-aim-hong-kong-exam.

198. Chan Ho-him, "Hong Kong's Public Universities Should Reflect National Security Law in Curricula by New Academic Year, Be Ready to 'Suppress' Acts That Violate It: Education Minister," *South China Morning Post*, March 3, 2021, accessed March 16, 2021, https://www.scmp.com/news/hong-kong/education/article/3124228/hong-kongs-public-universities-must-reflect-national.

199. Education Bureau Circular No. 3.2021, "National Security: Maintaining a Safe Learning Environment Nurturing Good Citizens," February 2, 2021, accessed April 2, 2021, https://applications.edb.gov.hk/circular/upload/EDBC/EDBC21003E.pdf.

200. For Yeung's claim, see "Kevin Yeung: Doubts on Liberal Studies Revamp 'Unnecessary,'" *The Standard*, December 5, 2020, accessed March 16, 2021, https://www.thestandard.com.hk/breaking-news/section/4/160448/Kevin-Yeung:-doubts-on-liberal-studies-revamp-%22unnecessary%22. Lau Chi-pang, the chair of the committee for renaming the subject of the Hong Kong Examination and Assessment Authority, said openly that the reformed curriculum was just like national education. He also said that the previous liberal studies curriculum was too complex and that it needed to be streamlined. See Sophie Hui and Erin Chan, "Focus on Pluses in Liberal Studies," *The Standard*, February 8, 2021, accessed March 16, 2021, https://www.thestandard.com.hk/section-news/section/4/227346/'Focus-on-pluses-in-liberal-studies.

ers would teach national security education.[201] Some teachers who formerly taught liberal studies decided to adapt to the new curriculum, while a minority decided to quit their jobs.[202] Many teachers expressed their intention to avoid talking about sensitive topics to protect themselves.[203] On the other hand, the government prepared a full set of Chinese history- and culture-related reference books for all the secondary and primary schools in Hong Kong,[204] deepening and broadening the content of national education apart from the need to implement national security education. Overall, while the political red lines delineated by the national security law are clear, its implementation in the educational sphere has ambiguities with the unintended consequences of triggering some personal fear and silent self-censorship. Overall, the entire educational sector has been adapting quickly, cooperatively, and smoothly to the need for national security education and national education since the promulgation of the national security law in late June 2020.

The University Services Center (USC) at the CUHK, which was previously reportedly under the influence of some American researchers in the 1950s and 1960s with a considerable amount of rich archival materials, was under a revamping process after the enactment of the national security law. Although the CUHK authorities claimed that the USC would be integrated into the main library without any political motivation,[205] some critics suspected that the USC's revamp might reduce its significance academically.

Other societal freedoms were affected to some extent. Two sisters who assisted the representative of the Vatican were under house arrest in Hebei province when they visited there.[206] Beijing was reportedly keen to see a local pro-Beijing priest, Peter Choi, become a successor to Bishop Tong Hon. While some mainland priests have been sent to the HKSAR, local Catholics who helped mainland Catholics underground are vulnerable to being monitored.[207] In May 2021, Stephen Chow Sau-yan was appointed by the Vatican to be the bishop of Hong Kong. Chow has been regarded as neither pro-Beijing nor

---

201. *Apple Daily*, March 30, 2021, p. A6, and this idea was criticized by a school principal.
202. One of my former students who taught liberal studies decided to leave Hong Kong for the UK. Personal chat with him in January 2021.
203. Chan Ho-him, "Teachers to Drop Sensitive Subjects," *South China Morning Post*, March 22, 2021, A1.
204. *Wen Wei Po*, March 23, 2021, A6.
205. "Open Letter Relating to Universities Service Centre for China Studies," CUHK, December 30, 2020, accessed January 17, 2021, https://www.cpr.cuhk.edu.hk/en/press/open-letter-relating-to-the-universities-service-centre-for-china-studies-usc/.
206. Greg Torode, "Nuns Arrested as Beijing Turns Up Heat on Church in Hong Kong," Reuters, December 30, 2020, accessed January 17, 2020, https://www.reuters.com/investigates/special-report/hongkong-security-church/.
207. Personal discussion with a Catholic observer, December 2020.

pro-democracy—a relatively neutral Catholic leader who is acceptable to different political stakeholders.[208]

Although Cardinal Joseph Zen remains critical of the Vatican Church's high-ranking officials who have forged closer relations with PRC authorities, he has adopted a low profile since the enactment of the national security law in June 2020. If the Vatican cultivates harmonious relations with Beijing, the Hong Kong Catholic leaders who are relatively autonomous from the PRC's influence will likely be increasingly under the mainland's united front work. On the other hand, some Christian priests who openly supported the 2019 protests and who are critical of the new national security law were named by pro-Beijing media explicitly for their political orientations and "disloyalty." Some of them reportedly left Hong Kong for other places, such as Taiwan.

In March 2021, it was reported that the M+ Museum that would be opened in the West Kowloon Cultural District would have to comply with the national security law by refraining from showing some political artworks prepared by mainland Chinese dissident Ai Weiwei.[209] Some pro-Beijing elites complained about Ai's works after a preview. The chairman of the West Kowloon Cultural District, Henry Tang Ying-yen, said that the art district would abide by the local laws and the national security law. Politically sensitive artworks are perhaps destined to be censored, especially if their content is deemed to be politically incorrect and exceeds the bottom line of political tolerance.

The local mass media are either affected by or showing subtle censorship. Cable TV stopped its program on the PRC reportedly because of financial reasons, but its program was, in the past, critical of and exposed the dark sides of mainland Chinese politics and society. Radio Television Hong Kong (RTHK) was under severe criticism from the government and pro-Beijing elites for having liberal tendencies in its program productions. On March 1, 2021, Patrick Li was appointed by the HKSAR government to replace Leung Ka-wing as the director of broadcasting. Leung was regarded as relatively liberal, but the RTHK under his leadership was criticized by Chief Executive Carrie Lam in February 2021 as "unacceptable," while its management was lambasted by a government report pointing to the lack of accountability and the presence of weak monitoring.[210]

208. "Hong Kong's New Bishop Faces Delicate Balancing Act," Union of Catholic Asia News, December 4, 2021, accessed September 28, 2022, https://www.ucanews.com/news/hong-kongs-new-bishop-faces-delicate-balancing-act/95231.
209. Clarie Selvin, "Hong Kong's M+ Museum Promises to Comply with National Security Law amid Pushback from Pro-Beijing Figures," ARTnews, March 24, 2021, accessed April 2, 2021, https://www.artnews.com/art-news/news/m-plus-museum-hong-kong-ai-weiwei-1234587731/.
210. Kelly Ho, "Hong Kong Government Report Finds 'Deficiencies' in Public Broadcaster RTHK's Editorial Management," Hong Kong Free Press, February 19, 2021, accessed March 18, 2021, https://hongkongfp.com/2021/02/19/hong-kong-govt-report-finds-deficiencies-in-public-broadcaster-rthks-editorial-management/.

The pro-Beijing elites and the police criticized the RTHK for "biased" coverage of the 2019 protests. In March 2021, it was reported that the RTHK censored a few programs for their "problematic" content. Some RTHK staff members complained about the unclear "red line," but Chief Executive Carrie Lam openly praised the work of the new Director Patrick Li. As a government-funded broadcasting corporation, RTHK is expected to toe the official line rather than be constantly critical of the government.

In September 2020, the police announced that only government-registered outlets and internationally well-known foreign media would be recognized, but accreditation from press organizations such as the Hong Kong Journalist Association would no longer be accepted. In other words, some "reporters" from internet radio and websites were no longer allowed to cover any protest activities because they were regarded as illegal news organizations. During the 2019 protests, there were many reporters from large and small media organizations, including the internet media. In the past, membership cards issued by the journalist association were accepted by the police, who in September 2020 decided to tighten the registration system and control those "reporters" who were either "fake" or attempting to "obstruct" the police action of maintaining law and order. In August 2020, the headquarters of the *Apple Daily*, a news organization originally opened by tycoon Jimmy Lai and closed in June 2021, were searched by the police and prosecuted by the government for its alleged involvement in illegal activities, such as money laundering, which allegedly violated national security. From its establishment in 1995 to its demise in 2021, *Apple Daily* turned out to be a strongly pro-democracy media outlet, mobilizing readers and supporters to participate in annual protests after 2003 and utilizing sensational stories and paparazzi photographs to discredit the government. Ideologically, it was increasingly anti-CCP, anti-PRC, and anti-Hong Kong government. Objectively speaking, some mass media professionals and organizations were easily under pressure after the immediate promulgation of the national security law, mainly because they had already deviated from their neutrality to become political actors.

Some pro-Beijing elites argued for the need for judicial reforms, for example, to dispatch Hong Kong's court judges to the mainland for patriotic education, to establish a new sentencing committee to review the "lenient" sentences delivered by some judges, and to reform the composition of the Judicial Officers Recommendation Commission. These suggestions were highly political because some members of the judiciary were seen as too liberal or "yellow." Although the national security law does not bar any foreign judges from serving in the local courts, four local judges who had a track record of having "conservative" rulings were selected to deal with cases concerning national security offenses. The idea of setting up a sentencing committee was interestingly pushed back by the new Chief Justice Andrew Cheung, who said that if litigants were unhappy with the lower court's decision, an appeal to the upper court could be made so that this conventional practice of litigation would continue. Nor did the HKSAR government officials, such as Chief Secretary Matthew Cheung and Secretary for Justice Teresa Cheng, accept the pro-Beijing elite's idea of setting up a sentencing committee. As a result, political pressure exerted by the pro-Beijing elites, especially those from the conservative nationalistic faction, met some resistance from the principal and judicial officials. The local state in the HKSAR encountered pressure from the conservative nationalists, but it refused to intervene excessively in the judicial independence of Hong Kong—a phenomenon showing that judicial independence in the HKSAR persists amid the increasingly politicized environment.

From July 1 to October 18, 2020, the Hong Kong police arrested twenty-eight persons for violating the national security law, and three of them were prosecuted.[211] The Hong Kong America Center, which the pro-Beijing media had accused of being an arm for the US government and of interfering with Hong Kong affairs by holding training sessions for anti-government activists, was closed down in August 2020.[212] In August, Jimmy Lai, the former proprietor of *Apple Daily*, was arrested and charged with suspected collusion with foreign forces. He was later denied bail by a High Court judge on the grounds that he might continue with acts that endangered national security.[213] His case has been watched carefully by foreign countries as he was involved in high-profile visits to the US in the past, especially during the 2019 anti-extradition movement, to lobby the US to promote democratization in Hong Kong.[214] On October 10, some pro-Taiwan activists, who were aware of the red lines delineated by the national security law, decided to cancel a flag-raising ceremony for the national day of the Republic of China (ROC) on Taiwan. On November 5, the police's national security department opened a hotline to allow citizens to report on alleged violations of the national security law. On December 2, 2020, three young political activists—Joshua Wong, Agnes Chow, and Ivan Lam—were sentenced by the magistrate court for organizing and inciting an authorized assembly outside the

---

211. *Ta Kung Pao*, October 18, 2020, A3.
212. *Ta Kung Pao*, August 31, 2020, A6.
213. Kari Soo Lindberg, "Hong Kong Court Keeps Jimmy Lai in Jail on Security Charges," Bloomberg, February 18, 2021, accessed March 16, 2021, https://www.bloomberg.com/news/articles/2021-02-18/hong-kong-court-keeps-jimmy-lai-in-jail-on-security-charges.
214. Candice Chau, "Hong Kong Media Tycoon Jimmy Lai again Refused Bail over Alleged National Security Law Violations," Hong Kong Free Press, February 19, 2021, accessed March 17, 2021, https://hongkongfp.com/2021/02/19/hong-kong-media-tycoon-jimmy-lai-again-refused-bail-over-alleged-national-security-law-violations/.

police headquarters in Wanchai in June 2019. Wong, Chow, and Lam were sentenced to 13.5, 10, and 7 months' imprisonment, respectively.[215]

In May 2022, Secretary for Security Chris Tang told LegCo members that Hong Kong had experienced social chaos in the past two decades, including the illegal Occupy Central movement in 2014, the Mong Kok riot in 2016, and the anti-extradition movement in 2019.[216] He remarked:

> We have even seen the emergence of acts and activities which have seriously undermined the rule of law and public order and endangered national security, including: (1) The rise of activities of "Hong Kong independence" and "self-determination". Some leveraged on "soft resistance" means through the media, arts and culture, etc. to disseminate messages of opposing the central authorities and the HKSAR government, and to incite hatred against the central authorities and the body of power of the HKSAR; (2) Territory-wide large-scale riots, with damage of public facilities in a wide area. Also, some members of external organizations openly raised funds for or donated equipment to the rioters during the riots; (3) Delivery of speeches, words or publications which contain slandering accusations, with a view to inciting the public, glorifying violence, and weakening the concepts of rule of law and law-abiding awareness of the public; (4) Local terrorism, which is growing and increasingly materialized into actions. It includes "lone-wolf" attacks and organizing, planning, and committing local terrorism activities in small groups; and (5) long-term infiltration on all fronts by external elements through grooming local organizations or individuals as agents in Hong Kong, and taking part in activities endangering national security through the agents, including attempting to influence election results with a view to subverting the State power.[217]

Tang added that social order has been restored after the implementation of the national security law. Nevertheless, the five national security risks mentioned above must not be ignored. Furthermore, criminal activities that undermine national security, to Tang, "have gone increasingly underground and become increasingly clandestine, while some lawbreakers have absconded overseas, wantonly colluded with external elements and continued to engage in acts and activities endangering national security."[218] Hence, the HKSAR government is determined to pursue those activists who engage in acts that undermine national security.

---

215. Kelly Ho, "Hong Kong Activist Joshua Wong, Agnes Chow and Ivan Lam Jailed over 2019 'Unauthorized Assembly,'" Hong Kong Free Press, December 2, 2020, accessed March 17, 2021, https://hongkongfp.com/2020/12/02/breaking-hong-kong-activists-joshua-wong-agnes-chow-ivan-lam-jailed-over-2019-unauthorised-assembly/.
216. "LCQ5: Enacting Legislation on Article 23 of the Basic Law," LegCo, May 11, 2022, accessed September 29, 2022, https://www.info.gov.hk/gia/general/202205/11/P2022051100512.htm.
217. "LCQ5: Enacting Legislation on Article 23 of the Basic Law."
218. "LCQ5: Enacting Legislation on Article 23 of the Basic Law."

Four Layers of Autonomy and the Deep State

The enactment of the national security law has had the immediate impact of influencing the degree of autonomy in the HKSAR. Four layers of jurisdiction over various issues are looming. The first layer is the exclusive jurisdiction of the central government over sensitive matters, like the allegedly criminal activities of mainlanders in the HKSAR, as one can recall from the "kidnap" of mainland businessman Xiao Jianhua from the Four Seasons Hotel in January 2017.[219] Xiao's alleged money-laundering activities for the mainland's rich people were reported in *Next Magazine* on February 8, 2017, which said that his relatives bought a lot of properties in Hong Kong for him and that he went to Hong Kong to deal with various investment activities.[220] However, the mainland authorities did not really charge him for money-laundering activities in Hong Kong. Instead, in August 2022, Xiao was imprisoned by a Shanghai court for his activities of "illegally collecting public deposits, using entrusted assets in breach of trusts, and illegal use of funds and bribery."[221] The Xiao case showed that, for mainlanders who commit criminal offenses on the mainland and who may use Hong Kong as a safe haven, they are vulnerable to being "brought back" to the mainland for investigation, prosecution, and imprisonment.

The second layer of the co-jurisdictions of Beijing and the HKSAR embraces the case of twelve Hong Kong people who were prosecuted on the mainland for violating PRC criminal law, and they were eventually sent back to Hong Kong for their alleged violations of the national security law. Another issue overlapping the jurisdictions of Beijing and the HKSAR government is international espionage. Hong Kong has been viewed by PRC authorities as a place where foreign spies were active. As such, the national security law had to be promulgated in June 2020 to deter international espionage. Article 29 says that "a person who steals, spies, obtains with payment, or unlawfully provides state secrets or intelligence concerning national security for a foreign country or an institution, organization or individual outside the mainland, Hong Kong and Macau of the

---

219. He was reportedly accused of laundering money in the HKSAR for rich people on the mainland. See *Next Magazine*, "中南海金手指 追蹤肖建華姊弟幫洗錢網絡," February 8, 2017, accessed January 3, 2021. For the report saying that Xiao's activities involved the family members of rich and powerful people on the mainland, see also "中共權貴家族幾乎全部在香港洗錢" ["Almost all of mainland rich and powerful families laundered money in Hong Kong," June 11, 2018, accessed January 3, 2021, https://www.epochtimes.com/b5/18/6/10/n10472449.htm.
220. "Almost all of mainland rich and powerful families laundered money in Hong Kong."
221. Iris Ouyang, "China Jails Tycoon Xiao Jianhua for 13 Years, Slapping an Unprecedented US$8 Million Fine on His Tomorrow Group," *South China Morning Post*, August 19, 2022, accessed September 29, 2022, https://www.scmp.com/business/banking-finance/article/3189498/tomorrow-groups-xiao-jianhua-sentenced-13-years-prison.

PRC shall be guilty of an offense."[222] According to Secretary for Security Chris Tang, the existing Official Secrets Ordinance (OSO) in the HKSAR provides for the regulation of "espionage," which "covers the prohibition of, among others, acts to approach, inspect, pass over, enter or be in the neighborhood of a prohibited place; compile information that is useful to an enemy; and obtain, collect, record or publish official secrets that are useful to an enemy."[223] Moreover, the OSO also prohibits the unlawful disclosure of protected information—a stipulation similar to the content of Article 29 of the national security law. Chris Tang remarked in January 2022:

> The long-standing position of the HKSAR Government is to combat espionage activities endangering national security in Hong Kong in accordance with the law. Specifically, given that these spies and their agents are all backed by rivals of a national level, actions must be taken to minimize the risks which they may bring about. To avoid impacting investigation work and necessary enforcement actions to be taken in future, we should not disclose further details of our actions. Yet, I can assure [LegCo] members that the police have all along been and will keep on collecting and analyzing intelligence concerning threats to national security in a proactive manner, as well as investigating cases endangering national security rigorously in collaboration with other relevant law enforcement agencies, including conducting intelligence-led operations. Besides, the HKSAR Government will continue to enhance information sharing and operations coordination with the Office for Safeguarding National Security of the Central People's Government in the HKSAR.[224]

In May 2022, Tang said that it is the Hong Kong government's "constitutional obligation to enact Article 23 of the Basic Law, which aims to prohibit any act of treason, secession, sedition, subversion against the Central People's Government, or theft of state secrets, and to prohibit foreign political organizations or bodies from conducting political activities in the HKSAR or from establishing ties with foreign political organizations or bodies."[225]

Once Article 23 is locally enacted, the HKSAR government will have an additional legal instrument to tackle espionage activities and to protect the

---

222. "The Law of the People's Republic of China on Safeguarding National Security in the Hong Kong Special Administrative Region," G.N. (E.) 72 of 2020, accessed September 29, 2022, https://www.elegislation.gov.hk/fwddoc/hk/a406/eng_translation_(a406)_en.pdf.
223. "LCQ2: Espionage Activities Conducted by Foreign Governments in Hong Kong," LegCo, January 26, 2022, accessed September 29, 2022, https://www.info.gov.hk/gia/general/202201/26/P2022012600473.htm.
224. "LCQ2: Espionage Activities Conducted by Foreign Governments in Hong Kong."
225. "The Basic Law of the HKSAR of the PRC," adopted by the NPC on April 4, 1990, and promulgated by Order No. 26 of the PRC President on April 4, 1990, and effective as of July 1, 1997, accessed September 29, 2022, https://www.basiclaw.gov.hk/en/basiclaw/chapter2.html.

national security interest of Beijing, apart from the existing national security law, thereby enhancing Beijing's "comprehensive jurisdiction" over Hong Kong.

The third layer of co-jurisdictions is complex and embraces issues like freedom of speech, of publication, and of expression. Freedom of speech, of publication, and of expression naturally has its limit; it must be exercised in accordance with the national security law. In July 2021, five unionists who produced a series of children books were arrested and charged by the police for having a "conspiracy to print, publish, distribute, display, and/or reproduce seditious publications" under Section 10 of the Crime Ordinance with a maximum penalty of two years' imprisonment.[226] The five members of the General Union of Hong Kong Speech Therapists used cartoon sheep and wolves to refer to Hong Kong and mainland China, respectively. But their cartoons and drawings carried detailed Chinese characters that portrayed the twelve Hong Kong people who tried to flee the HKSAR for Taiwan, but who were arrested, as "heroes."[227] In September 2022, a district court ruled that the five were guilty of "seditious intent" to "brainwash" children, and they were sentenced to 19 months in prison.[228] District Court Judge Kwok Wai-kin remarked that there were four reasons for the length of the sentences, including the high distribution and exposure of the three books, the substantial period of time, the continuation of the conspiracy, and the unstable socio-political situation in which the books were published.[229] He said:

> By identifying the PRC government as the wolves, and the Chief Executive of the HKSAR as the wolves masqueraded as a sheep at the direction of the Wolf-chairman, along the story line told in Book 1, the children will be led into belief that the PRC government is coming to Hong Kong with the wicked intention of taking away their home and ruining their happy life with no right to do so at all... What has happened here is that the publishers of the books clearly refuse to recognize that PRC has resumed exercising sovereignty over the HKSAR, nor do they recognize the new constitutional order in the Region, and lead the children to think that what the authorities both in PRC and HKSAR have done is wrong and illegitimate.[230]

---

226. Sum Lok-kei, "Five Stand Trial for Sedition in Hong Kong over Children's Books about Sheep," *The Guardian*, July 6, 2022, accessed September 29, 2022, https://www.theguardian.com/world/2022/jul/06/hong-kong-sedition-trial-childrens-books-sheep-wolves-china.
227. Candise Chau, "Hong Kong National Security Police Explain Why Children's Picture Books about Sheep Are Seditious," Hong Kong Free Press, July 22, 2021, accessed September 29, 2022, https://hongkongfp.com/2021/07/22/hong-kong-national-security-police-explain-why-childrens-picture-books-about-sheep-are-seditious/.
228. Tommy Walker, "5 in Hong Kong Sentenced to Prison over Sheep Book," VOA News, September 10, 2022, accessed September 29, 2022, https://www.voanews.com/a/in-hong-kong-sentenced-to-prison-over-sheep-book-/6739620.html.
229. Walker, "5 in Hong Kong Sentenced to Prison over Sheep Book."
230. "Therapists Convicted over Seditious Children's Books," RTHK English News, September 7, 2022, accessed September 29, 2022, https://news.rthk.hk/rthk/en/component/k2/1665940-20220907.htm.

This court case has an important implication for freedom of expression, which cannot be exercised in a way that "incites hatred" of the central government.

A question of whether jury should be used in the cases relating to national security was raised in the Tong Ying-kit case and the issue of forty-seven democrats who orchestrated the so-called primary elections in the summer of 2020. In June 2021, the Court of Appeal upheld a decision made by the Court of First Instance of the High Court, which ruled that the Tong Ying-kit case did not need a jury because of "a perceived risk of the personal safety of jurors and their family members."[231] High court judges Jeremy Poon, Wally Yeung, and Johnson Lam added that a jury trial "should not be assumed to be the only means of achieving fairness in the criminal process" and that "when personal safety of jurors and their family members is under threat and due administration of justice may be impaired, there is a real risk that the goal of a fair trial by jury will be put in peril."[232]

In August 2022, Secretary for Justice Paul Lam Ting-kwok ordered a non-jury trial for the case of forty-seven democrats who organized a so-called "primary election" in the summer of 2020 and who were charged with the "conspiracy to subversion."[233] Lam cited the "involvement of foreign elements" as the grounds for not adopting a jury trial.[234] As with the Tong Ying-kit case, the government cited the "personal safety of jurors and their family members" and the "risk of perverting the course of justice if the trial is conducted with a jury."[235] The trial would be heard by three judges appointed by the government to deal with national security cases in accordance with the national security law.

The third layer of co-jurisdiction between Beijing and the HKSAR remains to be unfolded, partly because the local Hong Kong court judges are involved in adjudicating cases of national security offenses and partly because their verdicts are open to question.[236] Since mid-2020, some verdicts and remarks of judges who deal with national security have come under scrutiny by pro-democracy critics on the one hand and pro-Beijing elites and media on the other. A few liberal-oriented and lenient judges were criticized by the "patriotic" elites as

---

231. "Hong Kong Court Upholds Decision for No Jury at First National Security Trial," Reuters, June 22, 2021, accessed September 30, 2022, https://www.cnbc.com/2021/06/22/hong-kong-court-upholds-decision-for-no-jury-at-first-national-security-trial.html.
232. "Hong Kong Court Upholds Decision for No Jury at First National Security Trial."
233. "Non-jury Trial Ordered for Hong Kong's Largest National Security Case: AFP," The Standard, August 16, 2022, accessed September 30, 2022, https://www.thestandard.com.hk/breaking-news/section/4/193545/Non-jury-trial-ordered-for-Hong-Kong's-largest-national-security-case:-AFP.
234. "Non-jury Trial Ordered for Hong Kong's Largest National Security Case: AFP."
235. "Non-jury Trial Ordered for Hong Kong's Largest National Security Case: AFP."
236. Defense Lawyers Argued that the Animal Characters in the Books Were "Fictional" and the Allegations Were "Too Broad." See Walker, "5 in Hong Kong Sentenced to Prison over Sheep Book."

"yellow," while conservative judges were accused of being "harsh." From an objective perspective, as long as court judges make their legalistic decisions on cases relating to national security, some precedents are established—a process testifying to the persistence of the rule of law.

If the rule of law persists and remains basically intact, then the questions of open reporting and bail have been legally contested in court cases involving national security. In August 2022, High Court Judge Alex Lee overturned an earlier ruling by a lower court magistrate, Peter Law, who had disallowed open reports of pre-trial or committal proceedings.[237] Lee's decision was made after a legal challenge was launched by one of the defendants, Chow Hang-tung, who had contended that a full report should be allowed for the sake of protecting and achieving "open justice."[238] Judge Lee's ruling was based on the fact that "Hong Kong is a civilized place . . . with the rule of law" and that "this public debate will not affect the judge's decision."[239] Chow was involved in a case where other leaders of the Hong Kong Alliance in Support of Patriotic and Democratic Movements of China, such as Lee Cheuk-yan and Albert Ho, were charged with "inciting subversion of state power."[240] After Chow, Lee, and Ho were arrested in September 2021, they were denied bail. Magistrate Judge Law had justified the absence of bail on the grounds that open reports of the preliminary inquiry would exert "mental pressure" on witnesses—an argument that was overturned by High Court Judge Lee.[241] The preliminary inquiry involved sixteen boxes of documents and 200 hours of video footage tracing back to 1989. The alliance was disbanded in September 2021 in the wake of the arrest of its leaders and the confiscation of its assets.

Article 42 of the national security law says: "No bail shall be granted to a criminal suspect or defendant unless the judge has sufficient grounds for believing that the criminal suspect or defendant will not continue to commit acts endangering national security."[242] In August 2022, the Court of First Instance granted bail to Albert Ho, a former leader of the alliance and former chairman of the Democratic Party, on the conditions that he paid HK$700,000 as a surety, that he reported to a police station three times a week, that he did not make any speech that could violate the national security law, that he would not meet

---

237. Jessie Pang and James Pomfret, "Hong Kong Court Lifts Reporting Restriction on National Security Case," Reuters, August 17, 2022, accessed October 2, 2022, https://www.reuters.com/world/china/hong-kong-court-lifts-reporting-restriction-national-security-case-2022-08-17/.
238. Pang and Pomfret, "Hong Kong Court Lifts Reporting Restriction on National Security Case."
239. Pang and Pomfret, "Hong Kong Court Lifts Reporting Restriction on National Security Case."
240. Pang and Pomfret, "Hong Kong Court Lifts Reporting Restriction on National Security Case."
241. Pang and Pomfret, "Hong Kong Court Lifts Reporting Restriction on National Security Case."
242. "The Law of the People's Republic of China on Safeguarding National Security in the Hong Kong Special Administrative Region," accessed October 2, 2022, https://www.elegislation.gov.hk/fwddoc/hk/a406/eng_translation_(a406)_en.pdf.

foreign officials, and that he would surrender all travel documents.[243] High Court Judge Jonny Chan added that if Ho committed any acts endangering national security, then "his bail" would be revoked and he would not be able to receive private medical care.[244] Bail appeared to be granted on very exceptional cases. In December 2021, when Patrick Lam and Chung Pui-kuen, two former editors of *Stand News*, were arrested, they were denied bail by the court for they were accused of "conspiring with others to publish or reproduce seditious publications" between July 7, 2020, and December 29, 2021.[245] The police confiscated sixty-two computers, twenty-seven storage devices, and six boxes of documents from *Stand News*, and they would also look into Lam's mobile phone. Court Judge Peter Law remarked that he was unconvinced that Lam and Chung "would not carry out acts endangering national security."[246]

Bail could not be granted in national security cases that were deemed serious. In February 2021, the Court of Final Appeal (CFA) brought Jimmy Lai Chi-ying into custody a week after the government appealed against a decision made by a lower court that had granted him a HK$10 million bail.[247] Five judges in the CFA saw the lower court as applying an "erroneous line of reasoning" and "misconstrued" Article 42 of the national security law.[248] Lai had been arrested in August 2020 when police officers raided the headquarters of the now-defunct *Apple Daily* newspaper. During the anti–extradition bill movement, Lai went to the US and lobbied US officials, including the former Secretary of State Mike Pompeo, for Hong Kong's human rights.

Commenting on the question of bail, the former Secretary of Justice Teresa Cheng said that the CFA ruling on the bail regarding the Jimmy Lai case "stressed the cardinal importance of the primary purpose of the national security law, which explains why there are more stringent conditions to the grant of bail in relation to offences endangering national security."[249] She elaborated on the court's view that "decisions are to whether or not to grant bail, involving a predictive and evaluative exercise, are a 'judicial exercise carried out by the court

---

243. Sarthak Gupta, "Hong Kong Court Grants Bail to Ex-lawmaker in National Security Case," *Jurist: Legal News and Commentary*, August 24, 2022, accessed October 2, 2022, https://www.jurist.org/news/2022/08/hong-kong-court-grants-bail-to-ex-lawmaker-in-national-security-case/.
244. Gupta, "Hong Kong Court Grants Bail to Ex-lawmaker in National Security Case ."
245. "Ex-Stand News Editors Denied Bail," RTHK, December 30, 2021, accessed October 2, 2022, https://news.rthk.hk/rthk/en/component/k2/1626644-20211230.htm.
246. "Ex-Stand News Editors Denied Bail."
247. James Pomfret, "Hong Kong Tycoon Jimmy Lai Denied Bail in National Security Case," Reuters, February 9, 2021, accessed October 2, 2022, https://www.reuters.com/article/us-hongkong-security-idUSKBN2A907P.
248. Pomfret, "Hong Kong Tycoon Jimmy Lai Denied Bail in National Security Case."
249. Secretary for Justice Teresa Cheng, "Prosecutorial Independence Assured," April 15, 2022, accessed October 2, 2022, https://www.news.gov.hk/eng/2022/04/20220415/20220415_121410_161.html.

as an exercise in judgement or evaluation, not the application of a burden of proof."[250] Cheng referred to other common law jurisdictions, such as Canada, Australia, and South Africa, where there is no burden of proof on the prosecution to establish grounds for denying bail, but a burden is put on the accused person to establish why detention is not justified.[251] Lam's successor, Paul Lam, said in August 2022 that stricter bail conditions would apply to offenders under Hong Kong's locally legislated Article 23 of the Basic Law.[252]

The final layer of jurisdiction over Hong Kong's domestic affairs belongs to the HKSAR, including matters such as criminal law, commercial crime, tort, and other issues that do not touch on the "high politics" and national security aspects of Beijing-HKSAR relations. So far, the common law system in the HKSAR works well. In other words, the promulgation of the national security law does not really affect the operation of the entire common law system.

The PRC state has been adopting Chinese legalism as a means to punish those protesters who violated the Hong Kong law, to eliminate some core political opponents and law offenders, to stabilize Hong Kong immediately, and to warn the people of Hong Kong of the dangers of breaching national security. As a loyal agent of the central state, the local state in the HKSAR must protect the national security interest of Beijing. Nevertheless, due to the deep concern of some Hongkongers about civil liberties, the third layer of shared co-jurisdictions between Beijing and Hong Kong, which involve a multiplicity of issues ranging from freedom of speech to court verdicts, will likely continue to be a bone of contention between the HKSAR authorities and some Hong Kong people.

The evolution of ideological conflicts and factionalism between Beijing and Hong Kong has shown that the central state of the PRC can impose its will and whims on the local state in the HKSAR. In a sense, dual states are emerging—the central state and local state—in Beijing–Hong Kong relations. Given the fact that the PRC state has its prerogative over Hong Kong's affairs, and that the local administrative-judicial state needs to implement the national security law and maintain socio-political order in Hong Kong, those dissidents and localists who resist and oppose the dual states are bound to fail. If a "deep state" is defined as those career bureaucrats and law-enforcement officials who protected their power and resisted the policies of the former US President Donald Trump, then

---

250. Cheng, "Prosecutorial Independence Assured."
251. Cheng, "Prosecutorial Independence Assured."
252. Natalie Wong, "Stricter Bail Conditions to Apply to Offenders under Hong Kong's Future National Security Law, Justice Minister Says," *South China Morning Post*, July 17, 2022, accessed October 2, 2022, https://www.scmp.com/news/hong-kong/politics/article/3185585/stricter-bail-conditions-apply-offenders-under-hong-kongs.

another form of "deep state" is emerging in the HKSAR.[253] The mainland security personnel, local police, and legal authorities are now acting as the agents of the increasingly powerful politico-legal apparatus, influencing and shaping the decisions of making arrests and prosecutions. The decisions made by the legal authorities to prosecute lawbreakers are not only legally based on existing law, the Basic Law and the national security law, but also politically implied if prosecutorial decisions can be defined politically as who gets what, when, and how.[254] The government's prosecution of nine democrats (Jimmy Lai, Lee Cheukyan, Margaret Ng, Leung Kwok-hung, Cyd Ho, Albert Ho, Leung Yiu-chung, Martin Lee, and Au Nok-hin) for their organization and participation in an illegal assembly on August 11, 2019, was criticized for having a complex mixture of legal and political considerations.[255] If the politico-legal apparatus remains a feature of the PRC state, it has perhaps loomed in Hong Kong's political system under the national security law.[256]

The deep state is emerging in the HKSAR, but its political content and context are very different from the US circumstances in which bureaucrats resisted the directives from the former US President Donald Trump. The deep state in Hong Kong is composed of legal officials and law-enforcement agencies interacting with their mainland counterparts, who are now stationed in the HKSAR as PRC officials in the OSNS. At the same time, the Liaison Office director (formerly Luo Huining and now, after January 2023, Zheng Yanxiong) is the adviser of the CSNS. The interlocking membership of the director of the Liaison Office in the CSNS and in the Central Coordination Committee on Hong Kong and Macau (CCCHKM) is significant; Zheng is an influential mainland official coping with Hong Kong matters. The head of the CCCHKM is Politburo Standing Committee member Ding Xuexiang, one of the most powerful seven members of the CCP in China. In 2021, the deputies of the CCCHKM included public security minister Zhao Kezhi, united front head You Quan, Politburo member Yang Jiechi, and Vice-Premier Sun Chunlan. Other members included HKMAO Director Xia Baolong, Hong Kong Liaison Office Director Luo Huining, and the Macau

---

253. James B. Stuart, *Deep State: Trump, the FBI, and the Rule of Law* (New York: Penguin Books, 2019), 13.
254. On the relations between prosecutions and politics, see Michael Tonry, "Prosecutors and Politics in Comparative Perspective," *Crime and Justice* 41, no. 1 (August 2012): 1–33.
255. *Apple Daily*, April 2, 2021, A1. The illegal assembly eventually mobilized 1.7 million people, as claimed by the organizers, to participate. One barrister said that "today, it is not a talk about law, as all people know." But another barrister said that, from a purely legal perspective, there were reasons for the court judge to rule that the organizers and core planners were guilty. But from his personal view, he did not want to see those peaceful protest activists to be penalized.
256. Fu Hualing, "Autonomy, Courts and the Politico-Legal Order in Contemporary China," in *The Routledge Handbook of Chinese Criminology*, ed. Liqun Cao, Ivan Sun, and Bill Hebenton (London: Routledge, 2013), 76–88.

Liaison Office Director Fu Ziying. Given the intertwined personnel appointments of Luo as a key member of the CCCHKM and the head of the Hong Kong Liaison Office, as well as the CSNS adviser, he occupied three main positions in Beijing–Hong Kong relations. The fact that the minister of public security and the head of the united front department are also the deputy directors of the CCCHKM demonstrated Beijing's top priority given to security and united front work in Hong Kong and Macau affairs. Yang Jiechi was the PRC foreign minister from 2007 to 2013, while Sun Chunlan was the Vice-Premier assisting the late Premier Li Keqiang in the work of the State Council. In terms of the nomenklatura and rankings of the officials in the CCCHKM, they were of the top level, thereby demonstrating Beijing's deep concerns about foreign affairs, economic development, national security, and united front work in Hong Kong and Macau.

In short, the deep state in the HKSAR includes not only the police-legal apparatuses and high-level officials of both Hong Kong and the mainland, but also the hierarchical but subordinate relations with the CCCHKM, which can be seen as the top-level mechanism of the central state in governing Hong Kong matters. The key institutions of the PRC's political system (CCCHKM, OSNS, HKMAO, and Liaison Office) are interacting, intertwined, and interlocking with the local state apparatuses.

Localist Factions: Losing Their Power Struggle with HKSAR Government and Beijing

At least four types of localists—liberal, Marxist, confrontational, and separatist—were involved in both peaceful and violent protests in the 2019 anti-extradition protests, thereby presenting a golden opportunity for PRC authorities to punish all the suspected lawbreakers by imposing the national security law onto Hong Kong in June 2020. If the liberal democrats denounced the violent activities that involved the confrontationalists and separatists, some of them might have become more politically secure and avoided being prosecuted after the 2019 anti-extradition movement. Unfortunately, some liberal democrats deliberately carved out a division of labor with the violent activists; the former organized and joined peaceful protests, whereas the latter orchestrated violent ones. The victory of the four types of democrats (liberal, Marxist, confrontational, and separatist) in the November 2019 District Council elections was politically unacceptable from the PRC perspective. After they were directly elected, some democrats in District Councils unwisely argued for the investigation of police behavior in the 2019 anti-extradition movement—a move that was regarded by the HKSAR government as not conforming to the terms of reference of District Councils, which remained advisory bodies rather than political organs at the local level. For Beijing, the localist factions went too far after their overwhelming victory in the District Council elections, continuously challenging the legitimacy of the HKSAR government. Drunken with temporary success, the localists sowed the seeds of their own destruction and failure.

In response to the localist electoral landslide in District Council elections, Beijing decided to formulate and design electoral reforms, which were formally approved by the SCNPC on March 11, 2021, to roll back the gradually democratized reforms in the HKSAR after July 1, 1997, to eliminate the influence of the radical localists, and to stabilize the entire political system. From the perspective of some localists, their factional "unity" succeeded in opposing the extradition bill and forcing the HKSAR government to shelve it in September. Yet, the strategic "unity" of the localists factions turned out to be tragic because it stimulated the mainland's conservative nationalists to take the prompt action of cracking down on them by revamping the political system in the HKSAR.

Shortly after the enactment of the national security law in late June 2020, some democrats continued to organize the so-called "primary elections" on July 11 and 12 to choose their representatives who would run in the September 2020 LegCo elections. About 600,000 people cast their "ballots" amid the danger that the organizers of the "elections" would be prosecuted under the national security law. At that moment, neither the democrats nor their core supporters were politically sensitive enough. To make matters worse, Benny Tai and his supporters put forward ten politically "subversive" steps, as follows: (1) democrats had an alternative plan if some of them were disqualified to run in the September LegCo elections; (2) they aimed to achieve the objective of grasping at least thirty-five of the seventy LegCo seats; (3) the democrats would become a majority in the LegCo; (4) the democrats would veto government bills in the LegCo; (5) the LegCo with a majority of democrats would veto the government budget and the chief executive would be forced to dissolve the LegCo; (6) the democrats would run in LegCo elections again and capture over thirty-five seats of the seventy LegCo seats; (7) the LegCo would again veto the financial budget of the government and then the chief executive would resign; (8) the SCNPC would announce that the HKSAR would enter the emergency period, dissolve the LegCo, and replace it with a provisional LegCo; (9) the HKSAR would witness street protests and mass strikes; and (10) Western states would implement political and economic sanctions on the PRC.[257] All these published steps, according to the pro-Beijing media, constituted a "conspiracy" to "paralyze the government, usurp the LegCo, and subvert the political regime."[258]

---

257. "'Primary Elections' Seek to Paralyze the Government, Usurp the Legco and Subvert the Political Regime," in *A Call in the Era of Patriots Ruling Hong Kong: Perfection of Hong Kong's Electoral System* (Hong Kong: Tai Kung Pao, March 12, 2021), a special issue, 10–11.
258. "'Primary Elections' Seek to Paralyze the Government, Usurp the Legco and Subvert the Political Regime," 10–11.

Some democrats went so far as to plan for not only capturing the LegCo but also toppling the HKSAR government—an act that led to the arrest of fifty-three democrats in January 2021 for allegedly violating the national security law.[259] If the plan were revised to get less than thirty-five LegCo seats and to work harmoniously with the HKSAR government on bills and policies proposed to the legislature, the objective of establishing cordial executive-legislative relations could have sent a conciliatory message to PRC authorities. Unfortunately, the continuous radicalization of localist populists even after the promulgation of the national security law in June 2020 proved to be politically subversive and costly. From the perspective of a power struggle, the localist factions continued to struggle for political power with the HKSAR government, the pro-establishment camp, and the central authorities in Beijing. The outcome was to push the dual states—the central state in Beijing and the local state in the HKSAR—to take legal action against the localist activists who organized and planned for the "primary elections."

The HKSAR government on July 31 announced that the LegCo's elections would be postponed partly due to the continuous outbreak of COVID-19 and partly because of the need to protect public safety and health.[260] In early January 2021, fifty-three pro-democracy organizers of the "primary elections" were arrested for allegedly violating the national security law. In February, forty-seven of them were officially charged with "conspiracy to commit subversion" under the national security law.[261] Among the arrested were Benny Tai and former legislators such as Jeremy Tam, Leung Kwok-hung, Roy Kwong, James To, and Joseph Lee. Some District Council members were prosecuted, including Jimmy Sham, Tiffany Yuen, Clarisse Yeung, and Fergus Leung. Although some arrested democrats appeared to be moderates, they participated in the "primary elections" without sufficient political sensitivity that their action violated the national security law.

259. Zen Soo, "Hong Kong Arrest 53 Activists under National Security Law," Associated Press, January 6, 2021, accessed March 28, 2021, https://apnews.com/article/legislature-primary-elections-democracy-hong-kong-elections-25a66f7dd38e6606c9f8cce84106d916.
260. "LegCo General Election Postponed for a Year," HKSAR government's press release, July 31, 2020, accessed March 14, 2021, https://www.info.gov.hk/gia/general/202007/31/P2020073100898.htm.
261. Candise Chau, "47 Democrats Charged with 'Conspiracy to Commit Subversion' over Legislative Primaries," Hong Kong Free Press, February 28, 2020, accessed March 14, 2021, https://www.google.com/search?q=47+Democrats+Charged+with+%E2%80%98Conspiracy+to+Commit+Subversion%E2%80%99+over+Legislative+Primaries&hl=zh-TW&source=hp&ei=imxgY_zHFYX24-EP_9SrwA8&iflsig=AJiK0e8AAAAAY2B6mru7wF6XZ-_14gquayiaRMDP_ozB&ved=0ahUKEwj8tMiB4Yv7AhUF-zgGHX_qCvgQ4dUDCA0&oq=47+Democrats+Charged+with+%E2%80%98Conspiracy+to+Commit+Subversion%E2%80%99+over+Legislative+Primaries&gs_lp=Egdnd3Mtd2l6uAEM-AEC-AEBSIcJUABYAHAAeADIAQCQAQCYATagA-TaqAQEx&sclient=gws-wiz.

According to the PRC position, Benny Tai's plan of preparing the democrats to seize power in both the District Councils and later the LegCo represented a "conspiracy" to "usurp" political power. Xinhua explained why Tai and his associated were prosecuted:

> During the election of the sixth-term LegCo in 2016, Tai launched "Operation ThunderGo" to disrupt the election with "coordinated candidacy" and other political tricks. In 2019, he initiated "Project Storm" to help radicals to seize many seats in the District Councils and incited rioters to harass pro-establishment candidates. In 2020, Tai organized the illegal "primary election" named "35-plus" to rig the election of the seventh-term LegCo. He plotted to manipulate public opinion and assist candidates advocating "mutual destruction" to grab more than half of the seats in the LegCo. If successful, they would indiscriminately veto all major bills of the HKSAR government to paralyze the executive authorities and force the HKSAR Chief Executive to step down. Under the plot, the Hong Kong society would be brought to a complete standstill and foreign countries would impose sanctions against Hong Kong. Tai, a so-called "scholar," repeatedly rigged elections by taking advantage of institutional loopholes. With his assistance, anti-China disruptors entering Hong Kong's power structure spread extremist ideas including "Hong Kong independence," resisted the jurisdiction of the central authorities, and maliciously obstructed the government work.[262]

The democrats who organized the "primary elections" went too far. They persisted in holding the "primary elections" even shortly after the promulgation of the national security law, testing and challenging the bottom line of official tolerance. However, once the national security law was in place, the authorities had to implement it in accordance with the need to protect national security.

On November 11, the SCNPC delineated the principles of disqualifying legislators—an action that prompted the HKSAR government to announce the loss of seats by four legislators, namely Alvin Yeung, Dennis Kwok, Kwok Ka-ki, and Kenneth Leung.[263] The SCNPC decision stated that legislators can lose their seats if they (1) advocate or support "Hong Kong independence," (2) refuse to recognize the fact that China possesses and exercises its sovereignty over the Hong Kong Special Administrative Region (HKSAR), (3) seek foreign or external forces to intervene in HKSAR affairs, and (4) perform acts that do not conform to the requests and conditions of supporting the Basic Law and being

---

262. "What Does Benny Tai's Illegal 'Primary Election' Bring to Hong Kong," Xinhua, March 2, 2021, accessed March 14, 2021, http://www.xinhuanet.com/english/2021-03/02/c_139778675.htm.
263. "HKSAR Government Announces Disqualification of Legislators Concerned in Accordance with NPCSC's Decision on Qualification of Legislators," November 11, 2020, accessed October 3, 2022, https://www.info.gov.hk/gia/general/202011/11/P2020111100779.htm.

loyal to the HKSAR.²⁶⁴ These conditions were, according to the SCNPC decision, applicable to not only those legislators who were disqualified for participation in the Seventh Legislative Council (LegCo) elections originally scheduled to be held on September 6, 2020 (but later postponed due to COVID-19), but also those LegCo members who would participate in future elections. Most importantly, the HKSAR government could announce immediately those legislators (Alvin Yeung, Dennis Kwok, Kwok Ka-ki, and Kenneth Leung) who would lose their eligibility to be LegCo members. In the afternoon of November 11, Chief Executive Carrie Lam said in a press conference that "allowing them to stay in LegCo does not conform to political ethics," that the HKSAR government had the responsibility of managing this matter, that the government requested that the SCNPC handled this matter in accordance with the law, and that Article 104 as interpreted by the SCNPC provided the legal basis.²⁶⁵ In October 2016, after two legislators-elect, namely Baggio Leung and Yau Wai-ching, made provocative and inappropriate remarks during the LegCo's oath-taking ceremony, the HKSAR government initiated a judicial review to question the LegCo's decision to allow the two to retake the oath. The High Court heard the review on November 3, but on November 7, the SCNPC took swift action to interpret Article 104 of the Basic Law to the effect that legislators-elect had to take the oath "solemnly" and "sincerely," an interpretation that would have retroactive effects. Adding onto this November 2016 interpretation was the November 2020 interpretation of how LegCo members could be disqualified. Clearly, the central government in Beijing used the SCNPC interpretations to disqualify legislators-elect in November 2016 and then the existing legislators in November 2020. After the four affected legislators were stripped of their LegCo seats on November 11, 2020, fifteen pan-democratic legislators resigned from the LegCo and said they would submit their resignation letters on the following day. Only two democrats would remain in the LegCo, including Cheng Chung-tai of the localist group named Civic Passion and medical representative Pierre Chan Pui-yin, together with forty-one other pro-government LegCo members.

The SCNPC defined patriotism. If any democrat wishes to run in future LegCo elections, he or she will have to abide by the conditions laid out on November 11: namely (1) refraining from advocating or supporting anything deemed to be separatist, (2) recognizing the fact that China possesses and exercises its sovereignty over Hong Kong, (3) stopping any action to seek foreign or external forces to intervene in the HKSAR affairs, and (4) performing in a way

---

264. "HKSAR Government Announces Disqualification of Legislators Concerned in Accordance with NPCSC's Decision on Qualification of Legislators."
265. TVB News, November 11, 2020.

that is regarded as loyal to the HKSAR.[266] Moreover, any pan-democratic activist elected to the LegCo must take the oath of being a legislator "solemnly" and "sincerely," as the SCNPC interpretation of Article 104 in November 2016 stipulated. The legalization of "patriotism" was an important response from Beijing to the emergence of disobedient and defiant pro-democracy legislators-elect and legislators from late 2016 to late 2020.

Hong Kong's Electoral Reforms: Implications for Factionalism and Chinese Democracy

On March 11, the NPC approved the draft decision of electoral reforms for Hong Kong by 2,895 supportive votes and one abstention, which had tremendous implications for Hong Kong's political development, including the new role of patriotic, democratic, and business factions.[267] The decision was composed of nine stipulations. First, patriots ruling the HKSAR would be the pillar of "one country, two systems" and of "Hong Kong people ruling Hong Kong."[268] Second, a broadly representative Election Committee would be set up and composed of 1,500 members, in which five sectors would be delineated, including a new sector composed of 300 people coming from the LegCo, district-based organizations, and Hong Kong members to the Chinese People's Political Consultative Conference (CPPCC). Third, the chief executive would be selected by the Election Committee and then appointed by the central government. A candidate running for the chief executive election would need to get 188 nominations from the Election Committee and at least fifteen nominated supporters from each of the five sectors. Third, the new LegCo would be composed of ninety members coming from three sectors: Election Committee, functional groups, and direct elections in geographical constituencies. Fourth, a Candidate Eligibility Review Committee (CERC) would be set up to screen the eligibility of LegCo and chief executive candidates and confirm their candidatures. Fifth, the HKSAR government should perfect the screening mechanism to ensure that the eligibility of LegCo candidates will be in conformity with the NPC Standing Committee's interpretation of Article 104 of the Basic Law. Sixth, Annex 1 and Annex 2 of the Basic Law would be amended by the NPC Standing Committee. Seventh, the HKSAR government would organize and arrange election activities after the amendments of Annex 1 and Annex 2. Eighth, the HKSAR chief executive would report to the central authorities on the arrangement and organization of

---

266. Sonny Lo, "Defining Patriotism in Hong Kong: Implications for Political Opposition," *Macau Business*, November 14, 2020, accessed October 3, 2022, https://www.macaubusiness.com/opinion-defining-patriotism-in-hong-kong-implications-for-political-opposition/.
267. *Wen Wei Po*, March 12, 2021, 1.
268. *Tai Kung Pao*, March 12, 2021, 1.

the electoral reforms and activities. Ninth, the NPC decision would be effective from the date of promulgation.

On March 20, President Xi Jinping signed Order No. 75 and Order No. 76 to approve the promulgation of the amended Annex I of the Basic Law and that of the amended Annex II, respectively.[269] The new electoral system of the HKSAR would be characterized by (1) a new LegCo composed of ninety members (forty coming from the Election Committee, thirty from functional constituencies, and twenty from direct elections), (2) five sectors of a 1,500-member Election Committee would come from mostly pro-Beijing groups, (3) the Election Committee would be politically powerful in selecting forty LegCo members and also the chief executive, and (4) the new CERC would screen the candidates for chief executive and LegCo elections by receiving the reports from the police's national security department and from the CSNC.

Table 2.2 sums up the evolution of the LegCo's composition from 1947 to 1985. It shows that more elected members were introduced in 1985, when functional constituencies were first injected into the legislature and their elected representatives articulated the interests of different occupational sectors, such as law, accountancy, engineering, commerce and industry, education, and labor. Table 2.3 illustrates the transformation of the LegCo's composition from 1991 to 2022. If a progressive proportion of directly elected seats in the LegCo was an indicator of democratization, then the electoral reform model amended by the NPC in March 2021 could be regarded a "retrogressive" step back to the colonial era in 1991, when eighteen of the fifty-nine LegCo members (30 percent) were directly elected (Table 2.3). Under the new electoral model amended by the SCNPC in March 2021, only 22.2 percent of the LegCo members (twenty out of ninety) would be directly elected. From the perspective of injecting more directly elected seats as a yardstick of parliamentary democratization, the electoral reform model in March 2021 represented a phenomenon of, to borrow from Samuel Huntington, "reverse democratization."[270] In 2021, the Macau Legislative Council had thirty-three members, of which fourteen were directly elected (42.4 percent), twelve were returned from functional groups (36.4 percent), and seven were appointed by the chief executive (21.2 percent).[271] If the Hong Kong LegCo has ninety members, of which forty would be returned from the new Election Committee, twenty returned from direct elections, and thirty from functional groups, this set-up is even more politically "conservative" than the Macau legislature.

---

269. *Ta Kung Pao*, March 31, 2021, A1 and A24.
270. The term comes from Samuel P. Huntington, *The Third Wave: Democratization in the Twentieth Century* (Norman: University of Oklahoma Press, 1991).
271. *Apple Daily*, March 6, 2021, A3.

However, the transformation of the LegCo composition and its election methods were justified in terms of protecting national security. So long as the localists who are anti-PRC and anti–Hong Kong government can be excluded from the LegCo through the disqualification mechanisms, including the rigorous screening of the CERC, the new electoral design can be regarded as a successful move that strikes a balance between maintaining a Hong Kong–style of democracy and protecting China's national security.

Table 2.2: The Evolution of the Legislative Council, 1947–1985

	Officials	Appointed Unofficials	Elected Unofficials	Total
1947	9	7	–	16
1951	10	8	–	18
1964	13	13	–	26
1973	15	15	–	30
1976	20	22	–	42
1977	21	24	–	45
1980	23	26	–	49
1983	19	29	–	48
1985	11	22	24	57

Source: Norman Miners, *The Government and Politics of Hong Kong* (Hong Kong: Oxford University Press, 1989), p. 124, Table 7.

Table 2.3: The Evolution of the Legislative Council, 1985–2021

	Directly Elected	Functional Seats	Appointed	Election Committee	Total
1991	18 (30%)	21	21	–	60
1995	20 (33.3%)	30	–	10	60
1998	20 (33.3%)	30	–	10	60
2000	24 (40%)	30	–	6	60
2004	30 (50%)	30	–	–	60
2008	30 (50%)	30	–	–	60
2012	35 (50%)	30+5**	–	–	70
2016	35 (50%)	30+5	–	–	70
2022	20 (22.2%)	30	–	40	90

Source: *Apple Daily*, March 12, 2021, p. A8. *South China Morning Post*, March 31, 2021, p. A4.
* The five seats came from the so-called super-seats in which candidates were nominated and selected among District Council members, and then, these candidates would be directly elected by voters.

On March 12, 2021, the deputy director of the HKMAO, Zhang Xiaoming, remarked that the amendments made to the Hong Kong electoral system were aimed at "repairing the loopholes in the legal system and perfecting the system of 'one country, two systems.'"[272] He pointed to the inaccuracy of the narrative that the reforms are "democratic or not." Rather, Zhang said that the reforms are related to the "tug of war between power usurpation and anti-usurpation, between subversion and anti-subversion, and between penetration and anti-penetration."[273] In other words, from the perspective of Chinese officials, Hong Kong's electoral development from 2008 to 2019 showed the politically undesirable phenomenon of radicals infiltrating the LegCo and "subverting" the political system. Electoral reforms aimed at rectifying the political deviations in the past two decades. Zhang added that, through electoral reforms, the government's capability to manage the economy and people's livelihoods would be inevitably improved. What he implied was that when the patriotic elites would govern the HKSAR, more forceful leadership and more down-to-earth policies to improve the people's livelihoods, such as land and housing policy, would have to be implemented. Zhang also added that the objective of achieving universal suffrage had not been changed and that Hong Kong's education sphere would need reforms to rectify the past situation. He remarked that the democrats who are patriotic will be able to participate in the electoral system. On the other hand, the deputy director of the HKMAO, Deng Zhonghua, said explicitly that the aim of the electoral reforms is to "exclude those who are anti-China and causing chaos" in Hong Kong from the political system, which would be "firmly governed by the patriotic people."[274]

During Zhang's three-day visit from March 15 to 17 to Hong Kong to discuss with the patriotic elites the March 11 decision of the NPC, he and his subordinates allowed the consulted elites to express their views toward the composition of the ninety-member LegCo. There were two options mentioned by the mass media: the first option would have forty members coming from the Election Committee, thirty members elected from functional groups, and twenty members from the geographical constituencies; the second alternative would have thirty members from the Election Committee, thirty from functional groups, and thirty from direct elections.[275] On the second day of the consultation, Zhang said that the principle of the draft decision of the NPC, namely the Election Committee selecting a larger proportion of LegCo members, should be adopted.[276] Obviously, the

---

272. *Wen Wei Po*, March 13, 2021, 1–2.
273. *Wen Wei Po*, March 13, 2021, 1–2.
274. *Wen Wei Po*, March 13, 2021, 1–2.
275. Professor Lau Siu-kai openly supported the second option. See his remarks reported on Cable TV News, March 11, 2021.
276. Cable TV News, March 16, 2021.

central authorities had a clear idea of how the LegCo should be reformed, but their visit to Hong Kong aimed at putting up a semblance of listening to the views of the patriotic elites in person. In the entire process of revamping the electoral system in the HKSAR, the central government adhered to the principle of democratic centralism, but the element of centralism carried far more weight than democratic consultation.

The democrats, who traditionally occupied at least half of the directly elected seats in the LegCo, are the main losers in the new electoral system. The new LegCo would have twenty directly elected seats, and given that the democrats usually grasped 50 to 55 percent of the votes in the LegCo's direct elections, they would acquire around, at most, ten directly elected seats. According to the electoral reform plan, while the LegCo direct elections from 1998 to 2016 adopted the proportional representation system in five large geographical constituencies, the new direct election method in December 2021 would have ten geographical constituencies and two candidates would be elected in each constituency, where each voter would have to cast his or her ballot for one candidate. The new electoral system was designed to curb the influence of the democrats even if they might run in the new elections. Moreover, the number of functional constituencies was reduced from thirty-five in 2016 to thirty in 2021, implying that the democrats would likely grasp a very few seats from functional constituencies, most likely in the legal, educational, health, and social work constituencies. However, they would find it relatively difficult to get into the Election Committee. For the candidates competing for the forty seats returned from the Election Committee, each of them would need to acquire ten to twenty nominations from the five sectors of the 1,500-member Election Committee, and each would be required to get the nominated support from two to four members of each sector.[277] Each voter of the 1,500-member Election Committee would be allowed to cast a ballot for forty candidates in order for the vote to be valid, and the highest number of votes obtained by the top forty candidates would be elected to the LegCo through the Election Committee.

The most significant aspect of the electoral reform was to empower the 1,500-member Election Committee, which has several features (Table 2.4). First, it would not only elect the chief executive but also the LegCo members. Second, the memberships from District Councils were abolished, and they are now replaced by the representatives of district-level organizations. Third, a candidate for the chief executive elections would need to obtain 188 nominations and no less than fifteen nominations from each of the five sectors of the Election Committee. Fourth, the Election Committee is now composed of five sectors rather than four sectors as in the past. Fifth, a new sector is composed of 300

---

277. *Wen Wei Po*, March 31, 2021, A2.

members coming from the Hong Kong members of the NPC and CPPCC, as well as representatives of the nation-wide organizations in Hong Kong. Sixth, there would be a convenor empowered to call for meetings on crucial issues. Clearly, as the most powerful political patron in Beijing–Hong Kong relations, the PRC authorities can utilize the Election Committee as a vehicle to reward their political clients and trusted followers, who are going to be the patriotic elites governing the HKSAR. The role of the main convenors in the Election Committee would likely be politically influential; they would appear to be the gatekeepers who can mobilize other members of the Election Committee to support those candidates running for the LegCo elections through the Election Committee.

The removal of all District Council members from the LegCo and the Election Committee was prominent in the new political set-up (Table 2.5). All the original 119 seats in the fourth sector of the Election Committee were from District Councils in Hong Kong, Kowloon, and the New Territories. But under the new electoral system, they are now eliminated. The replacement comes from the District Committees, Fight Crime Committees, and District Fire Prevention Committees, whose members are appointed by the HKSAR government. After the victory of localists in the 2019 District Council elections, the HKSAR government decided not to appoint District Council members to the District Committees—a testimony to their poor relations. As mentioned before, when some pro-democracy District Council members attempted to look into the police handling of the 2019 anti–extradition bill protests, their action actually exceeded and violated the terms of reference of District Councils, which focused on district matters only. The new set-up of the fourth sector of the Election Committee illustrated that the PRC and Hong Kong authorities were displeased with the behavior of District Council members, many of them coming from the localist factions. The new fifth sector of the Election Committee shows that none of its members come from District Councils; it is composed of Hong Kong members of the NPC, CPPCC, and the mainland's nation-wide organizations, such as women and youth, in the HKSAR. From the perspective of patron-client politics, Beijing made sure that its loyal clients and trusted followers would be able to go into the Election Committee and would replace the directly elected District Council members. The politics of excluding the pro-democracy localists and "troublemakers" was prominent in the entire design and set-up of the new electoral system for the LegCo in March 2021.

To ensure that radical localists cannot and would not participate as candidates in LegCo elections, Beijing designed and established the Candidate Eligibility Review Committee (CERC). The committee will receive reports from the police's national security department and from the CSNS, making final decisions on the eligibility of candidates. Candidates who fail the eligibility test will not be allowed to appeal against the decision of the committee. Obviously, the

Table 2.4: Main Elements of the 2020 Electoral Reform Amended by the National People's Congress

Items	Situation in 2016–2020	New Electoral System in 2021
LegCo	A total of 70 seats: 35 from direct elections; 30 from functional groups; and 5 super-seats from candidates nominated by District Council members and directly elected by voters	A total of 90 seats: 20 from direct elections; 30 seats from functional constituencies; 40 seats from the Election Committee; abolition of 5 super-seats
LegCo direct elections	5 geographical constituencies using proportional representation system	10 geographical constituencies; each constituency returns 2 members to the LegCo; each voter votes for one candidate
LegCo functional constituencies	Some sectors had individual votes	The new constituencies include the CPPCC sector, a merged sector combining medicine and health, and sectors like information technology, catering, retail and wholesale, sports/arts/culture, and publication will change from individual votes to group votes
Election Committee	1,200 members; elected chief executive; each candidate needed to acquire not less than 150 nominations from Election Committee members; composed of four sectors	1,500 members; elects chief executive; abolition of all members from District Councils, and they are replaced by representatives of district organizations; a candidate for chief executive needs to get 188 nominations and no less than 15 nominations from each of the 5 sectors of the Election Committee; the Election Committee is composed of 5 sectors, with a new sector composed of 300 members coming from Hong Kong members of the CPPCC and NPC and representatives of the nation-wide organizations in Hong Kong; there will be a convenor who will be empowered to call for a meeting on crucial issues, and each of the 5 sectors will have a certain number of convenors
Candidate Eligibility Review Committee	None, but the election officers played a crucial role as gatekeepers	Reviews the eligibility of candidates running for LegCo and chief executive elections; it will receive reports from the police's national security department and from the CSNS, and its decision will be final and candidate will not be allowed to appeal

Sources: *Wen Wei Po*, March 31, 2021, p. A1 and p. A24; and "Big Electoral Reform: Will C. Y. Leung be a Main Convenor?," HK01, March 30, 2021, accessed April 3, 2021, https://www.hk01.com/%E6%94%BF%E6%83%85/606314/%E9%81%B8%E8%88%89%E5%A4%A7%E6%94%B9%E9%9D%A9-%E6%A2%81%E6%8C%AF%E8%8B%B1%E6%88%96%E4%BB%BB%E9%81%B8%E5%A7%94%E6%9C%83%E7%B8%BD%E5%8F%AC%E9%9B%86%E4%BA%BA-%E8%8C%83%E5%A4%AA-%E5%88%A5%E5%B0%8D%E9%A6%99%E6%B8%AF%E6%8C%87%E6%8C%87%E9%BB%9E%E9%BB%9E.

Table 2.5: How District Council Members Are Removed and Replaced by Pro-Beijing Clients in the Fourth and Fifth Sectors of the Election Committee

Subsector	Number at present	Revised No.	Seats reduced or increased
\multicolumn{4}{c}{The Fourth Sector of the Election Committee}
LegCo members	70	90	Increase by 20
Heung Yee Kuk	26	27	Increase by 1
District Committees; Fight Crime Committees; District Fire Prevention Committees (Hong Kong and Kowloon)	0	76	Increase by 76
District Committees; Fight Crime Committees; District Fire Prevention Committees (New Territories)	0	80	Increase by 80
Representatives of Hong Kong groups on mainland	0	27	Increase by 27
District Councils from Hong Kong and Kowloon	59	0	Decrease by 59
District Councils from New Territories	60	0	Decrease by 60
\multicolumn{4}{c}{The Fifth Sector of the Election Committee}
NPC and CPPCC	87	190	Increase by 103
Nation-wide groups in Hong Kong	0	110	Increase by 110

Source: *Ta Kung Pao*, March 31, 2021, p. A2.
Note: Each of the five sectors has 300 members. The first sector composed of the business sector has seen minimal changes, except for adding 15 seats to the small and medium enterprises. The second sector reduces the seats of those sub-sectors where democrats were previously strong, such as education, social welfare, and health. The third sector increases by 120 seats for the pro-Beijing grassroots organizations and clans' associations.

central government is keen to avoid a scenario in which radical localists like Yau Wai-ching and Baggio Leung win the LegCo elections, as in September 2016. Together with the two disqualification mechanisms of the SCNPC, notably the November 2016 decision and the November 2020 decision, there would be at least three safeguards to prevent the radical localists from entering the LegCo in the future. The PRC authorities believed that Hong Kong from July 1997 to 2020 had loose eligibility requirements for candidates, leaving the difficult task to the election officers responsible for screening the candidates' eligibility. As such, all these new institutional safeguards aimed at plugging the "loopholes" in Hong Kong's elections.

Factions would not fade away in this new electoral system. Instead, factionalism can be expected to persist in both the pro–Hong Kong democratic and pro-Beijing nationalistic camps. The democrats will likely remain divided into hardliners who refuse to participate in elections, the moderates who will be hesitant over running for the direct elections, and softliners who will try to get nominations from the patriotic elites to "share" some power in the political system. As it turned out, in the December 2021 LegCo elections, the softliners participating in elections included Tik Chi-yuen of the Third Side and two members of the Path of Democracy. Hardliners included the members of the radical factions, whereas moderates embraced members of the Democratic Party who did not run for the 2021 LegCo direct elections. In the 2023 District Council elections, even though the moderate democrats tried to run in the elections, most of them, including members of the Democratic Party, failed to get sufficient nominations from the patriotic elites.

The patriotic or nationalistic faction would continue to be divided. The patriots have at least four factions. The first group is composed of diehard loyalists who adhere to the central government's policies and measures. They are regarded by some citizens critically as, to borrow from the term used by mainland political scientist Tian Feilong, "loyalist garbage."[278] Yet, the term "loyalist garbage" entails negative connotations and it led to the criticisms of some "patriotic" elites. Perhaps another term, "uncritical loyalists," may be a better one referring to the "blind patriotism" of some loyalists who appear to be mouthpieces of the central authorities rather than constructive advisers. The second batch of patriotic elites are the moderates trying to bargain with the political center. They can be regarded as the long-term loyal oppositionists playing a key role in the new

---

278. Tian Feilong (田飛龍), "愛國者治港：香港民主的新生" [Patriots ruling Hong Kong: The new life of Hong Kong democracy], *Ming Pao*, March 3, 2021, accessed March 14, 2021, https://news.mingpao.com/ins/%E6%96%87%E6%91%98/article/20210303/s00022/1614528449160/%E6%84%9B%E5%9C%8B%E8%80%85%E6%B2%BB%E6%B8%AF-%E9%A6%99%E6%B8%AF%E6%B0%91%E4%B8%BB%E7%9A%84%E6%96%B0%E7%94%9F%EF%BC%88%E6%96%87-%E7%94%B0%E9%A3%9B%E9%BE%8D%EF%BC%89.

politics of Beijing-HKSAR relations. The third batch are a minority of softliners who are perhaps sympathetic with the "opportunistic" faction of the democrats, but their political future is perhaps limited and under the watchful eyes of PRC authorities. The fourth batch are those mainlanders who migrated to reside in the HKSAR and who are determined to participate in the LegCo's elections, such as Li Shan of the Bauhinia Party.[279] In December 2023, the mainlanders failed to participate in the District Council elections. Very few pro-Beijing "patriotic" elites dared to be softliners supportive of the moderate democrats. Most directly elected candidates in the December 2023 District Council elections turned out to be long-time loyalists, including members of the DAB and the pro-Beijing Federation of Trade Unions (FTU).

The fragmentation of patriotic elites could be seen from March 15 to 17, 2021, when PRC officials led by the deputy director of the HKMAO, Zhang Xiaoming, visited Hong Kong to collect elite opinions on how the LegCo's composition should be reformed.[280] The loyalist faction of the nationalistic camp, notably Ng Chau-pei from the FTU, argued for a composition with fifty legislators returned from the Election Committee, twenty from functional groups, and twenty from geographical constituencies.[281] However, the moderate faction, such as Ronny Tong from the Path of Democracy (PoD), argued for another composition with thirty members returned from the Election Committee, thirty from functional constituencies and thirty from direct elections. Such a difference in opinion was reflective of two varying factions—the FTU being more conservative politically and Tong slightly more liberal in political outlook.

Amid the persistent factional politics among the pro-establishment camp, it remains to be seen how the business factions adapt to the changing political landscape. Traditionally, the business sector has been politically inactive, relying on group participation through the LegCo's functional constituencies and seeing direct elections as the power base of the localists and nationalists. If PRC authorities wish to curb the influence of some big land developers in Hong Kong and change the land policies in favor of the middle-lower classes and the poor, the business sector is likely to be under the pressure of avoiding a "hegemonic" image. When President Xi Jinping visited the HKSAR on July 1, 2022, he asked the HKSAR leadership to distance itself from the "vested interest"—a cryptic remark implying the need for the HKSAR government to maintain its relative

---

279. For details of Li Shan and the implications of the rise of the Bauhinia Party, see Phila Siu and Natalie Wong, "Pro-Mainland Chinese Financiers Based in Hong Kong Launch New Bauhinia Party Aimed at Reforming LegCo, Restraining 'Extremist Forces,'" *South China Morning Post*, December 6, 2020, accessed March 14, 2021, https://www.scmp.com/news/hong-kong/politics/article/3112771/mainland-born-hong-kong-based-financiers-launch-new.
280. *Sing Tao Daily*, March 16, 2021.
281. Cable TV News, March 15, 2021.

autonomy vis-à-vis the business elites. Given the fact that the PRC regime on the mainland is also vigilant over the big businesspeople, such as its attempt at preventing the "monopolistic" operation of Jack Ma's Alibaba,[282] Beijing's policy toward the business elites in Hong Kong is shaped by its decision to maintain a relative autonomy from them, while conducting united front work on the business groups and leaders to ensure that the land and housing policies of the HKSAR government are socially and politically supported.

New Electoral System and Its Implications for Hong Kong, China, and Macau

From 1997 to 2021, the HKSAR government's relative autonomy was weak vis-à-vis the landlord, land developer, and business classes, backing down from time to time on housing and land policies, not to mention any idea of levying more taxes on rich people.[283] The new electoral system has brought more pro-Beijing elites and groups at the grassroots level to the LegCo through the Election Committee, and some of them may advocate for a more "socialist" or welfarist approach to "correcting" the capitalistically "exploitative" features of Hong Kong. If so, the business classes will perhaps encounter more pressure to deal with social inequity, poverty, housing, and tax issues in a more progressive, if not necessarily more socialist, way. After all, PRC authorities hope that Hong Kong's social contradictions can and will be tackled in a more effective way, implying that the LegCo would need to strike a balance between the protection of business interests and that of the poor and the needy.

Because the radical localists have been excluded from participation in the political system, the HKSAR currently has political and social stability. Nevertheless, the late political scientist Samuel Huntington reminded us that political institutions aim at absorbing social forces and turning them into coopted ones—a function that is lost in the newly reformed political system of Hong Kong.[284] The implication is that, if any governance crisis takes place and if any unpopular government policy may attract protests, as with the 2019 antiextradition movement, then such sudden protests would have the real risks of becoming quite violent and unpredictable. Indeed, under the national security law, any person who creates social disorder through protests can and will be

---

282. Lulu Chen and Coco Liu, "China Targets Jack Ma's Alibaba Empire in Monopoly Probe," Bloomberg, December 24, 2020, accessed April 3, 2021, https://www.bloomberg.com/news/articles/2020-12-24/china-launches-probe-into-alibaba-over-monopoly-allegations.
283. Sonny Shiu-Hing Lo, "The Chief Executive and the Business," in *The First Tung Chee-hwa Administration*, ed. Lau Siu-kai (Hong Kong: Chinese University Press, 2002), 289–328.
284. Samuel P. Huntington, *Political Order in Changing Societies* (New Haven, CT: Yale University Press, 1968).

arrested and prosecuted. However, if politics, as Bismarck said long ago, is the art of the possible, it remains to be seen whether the new political system would generate "permanent" socio-political stability. A minority of the excluded localists would still constitute a latent threat to Hong Kong's socio-political stability, for they may wait for the "ripe" time to vent their grievances and anger, reminiscent of the 2019 anti-extradition protests, and to "retaliate" against the relatively "hardline" responses from the HKSAR government and Beijing. From the perspective of risk assessment, the political development of the HKSAR remains volatile and uncertain in the long run, especially if China's political situation turns liberal and if its internal factionalism becomes suddenly prominent.

Positively speaking, the new Hong Kong political system will have implications for mainland China, especially the Greater Bay Area (GBA). Decades later, when the HKSAR will be increasingly integrated socially and economically into the GBA, it can be anticipated that, if China is developing its Chinese-style democracy, the Hong Kong electoral system can and will perhaps be experimented with on the mainland. Specifically, a GBA mayor would likely be elected along the lines of the Hong Kong model of chief executive elections. The existence of a large Election Committee, like the 1,500-member Election Committee in the HKSAR, can perhaps be replicated in the PRC if any city experiments with political reform and gradual democratization. Although the revamped electoral system in the HKSAR in 2021 has been seen by critics and foreign countries, like the US and the European Union, as a "retrogressive" step, it represents a process of "two steps backward, one step forward" because the diluted model of Hong Kong's democracy will ironically have more relevance and applicability to reform the mainland Chinese political system in the long run. If Chinese politics is characterized by a cyclical pattern of control and relaxation, the enactment of the national security law in the HKSAR reflects the current controlling period in Beijing–Hong Kong relations, followed perhaps later by a more relaxed atmosphere in the PRC with immediate political implications for Hong Kong. Any relaxed environment in the form of political liberalization undertaken by the PRC will likely affect not only the HKSAR but also the experimentation of Hong Kong–style democracy on the mainland, especially the GBA.

The revamped political system characterized by the Hong Kong–style democracy of having more control and appointments than elections will likely open the possibility of a directly elected chief executive after the candidates are screened tightly by an Election Committee. If the new electoral system in Hong Kong works well to safeguard the PRC's national security interest, Beijing would likely be open-minded toward the feasibility of the August 31, 2014, model for the HKSAR in the coming years. In other words, the 2014 parameter—two or three candidates for the chief executive election would be screened out by the Election Committee, and then, they would compete for the people's votes through universal suffrage—will perhaps be refloated again in society for deliberation. Such a model would ensure political safety and national security for the PRC because the candidates of chief executive elections will certainly be screened out by the Election Committee and the CERC.

However, two preconditions will likely be needed for the HKSAR to return to the August 2014 parameter: proof showing Hong Kong people's acceptance of the new electoral system and their active participation in it, and China's democratizing and liberalizing atmosphere. If so, a Hong Kong–style model for the chief executive's direct election will likely be much faster than the democratization of the LegCo. While executive-legislative relations are bound to be controlled in favor of the executive branch in accordance with the Basic Law and the PRC's preference, having a chief executive enjoy a popular mandate from Hong Kong voters and safeguard China's national security will arguably provide a strong legitimacy to the executive branch and the central state. A Hong Kong–style democracy along the August 31, 2014, parameter designed by Beijing would perhaps be a realistic possibility, especially if Chinese politics oscillates from political control to relaxation and liberalization in the future.

Critics of the PRC regime have argued that the central authorities in Beijing seek to politically converge the Hong Kong polity with that of Macau.[285] A careful reading of the remarks of the PRC authorities responsible for Hong Kong matters, such as Zhang Dejiang and Wang Zhenmin, indicated that they understood that the HKSAR polity was and is more pluralistic than Macau's and the mainland's; they did not actually seek to Macaunize or mainlandize Hong Kong, and they emphasized the need for Hong Kong people to understand and implement Beijing's interpretations of "one country, two systems."[286] Wang reiterated that if Hong Kong were mainlandized, it would lose the luster of "one country, two systems."[287] Instead of seeking to politically converge Hong Kong's polity with the mainland, the Beijing officials responsible for Hong Kong matters have been trying their best to prevent the intrusion of "Western" aspects of political reform into the HKSAR. When the SCNPC interpreted the pace and scope of political reform in the HKSAR on August 31, 2014, it maintained the "centralist" aspect of democratic centralism, namely a Beijing-controlled Election Committee, which would select two or three candidates for the chief executive election in 2017. This element of "democratic centralism"—a practice in which centralism is constantly more significant than the democratic aspects—could be seen in the March 2021 NPC decision on Hong Kong's electoral reform, which empowered the execu-

---

285. Suzanne Pepper, "A Tale of Two SARs and Beijing's Puzzle: Why Can't Hong Kong Be More Like Macau?" Hong Kong Free Press, May 20, 2017, https://hongkongfp.com/2017/05/20/tale-two-sars-beijings-puzzle-cant-hong-kong-like-macau/.
286. See Wang Zhenmin's remarks in *Ta Kung Pao*, May 1, 2017, A4.
287. *Ta Kung Pao*, May 1, 2017, A4.

tive branch of the HKSAR government and curbed the oppositionists, especially the radical localist factions. "Democratic centralism," which is mentioned in the mainland Chinese constitution, has already been seen in how the chief executive elections in March 2022, the LegCo elections in December 2022, and the District Council elections in December 2023 were conducted. The electoral component has been made subservient to the centralist, controlled, and appointed aspects—a kind of Hong Kong–style democracy perhaps parallel to Chinese-style democracy on the mainland.

Interestingly, Macau followed Hong Kong's disqualification mechanisms and national security law after mid-2020. In July 2021, the Macau Electoral Affairs Commission (EAC) disqualified twenty-one candidates for the September 2021 Legislative Assembly elections, including five candidates (such as Ng Kuok Cheong and Sulu Sou) from the pro-democracy New Macau Association and ten other candidates from the democratic camp.[288] The government regarded the disqualified candidates as failing to uphold the Basic Law and to pledge allegiance to the Macau administration. Some democrats appealed against the EAC's disqualification, but the Court of Final Appeal upheld its decision by saying that the evidence of their failure to support the Basic Law included the action of participating in the "June 4th commemoration" and mourning the late Nobel Peace Prize laureate Liu Xiaobo.[289] On September 12, 2021, the voter turnout was only 42.38 percent, with only 137,281 voters out of 323,907 registered electorates casting their ballots.[290] In the 2017 legislative election, 57.2 percent of the voters cast their ballots. The disqualification of the democrats and the occurrence of COVID-19 curbed the voters' intentions to vote in the 2021 legislative elections.

The implications of the Macau legislative elections were obvious. The political turbulence and the redesign of the electoral system in Hong Kong did have a boomerang effect on Macau, where pro-democracy candidates were immediately affected and disqualified in the September 2021 legislative elections. The dampening voter turnout in Macau had implications for the HKSAR, where the LegCo elections in December 2022 would naturally witness a decline in voter turnout. The previously liberal and relaxed atmospheres in the elections of Hong Kong and Macau became a thing of the past, as the year 2021 was a turning point for both places after the promulgation of the national security law in the HKSAR in June 2020. In 2022, the Macau government consulted public opinion

---

288. *Ta Kung Pao*, May 1, 2017, A4.
289. Lam Kim, "What Implications of the Big Drop of Voter Turnout in Macau Legislative Elections for Hong Kong?" hk01.com, September 12, 2021, accessed October 8, 2022, https://www.hk01.com.
290. Nelson Moura, "2021 Legislative Assembly Election with Lowest Voter Turnout in SAR History," September 12, 2021, accessed October 8, 2022, https://www.macaubusiness.com/2021-legislative-assembly-election-with-lowest-voter-turnout-in-sar-history/.

on the revisions introduced to its national security law enacted in 2009. The Macau national security law was eventually updated in May 2023, expanding the definition of secession to "acts of non-violence" and redefining the theft of official secrets as "violations of official secrets."[291] Hence, Hong Kong's political development from mid-2020 to March 2021 triggered Macau's convergence with the HKSAR in terms of protecting the central government's national security through the disqualification of some pro-democracy candidates and the amendment made to the already approved national security law. The political development of the HKSAR shaped that of Macau.

The decision approved by the NPC in March 2021 represents a new watershed in the political and electoral development of the HKSAR. It can be seen as a phenomenon of "two steps backward, one step forward" with implications for gradual democratization in Hong Kong, mainland China, and perhaps Macau. In Hong Kong, the direct election of the chief executive through universal suffrage would be possible in the long run under two conditions. The people of Hong Kong, especially some democrats, should arguably accept the reality and necessity of the electoral redesign in March 2021 and need to demonstrate their active participation in the legislative elections of the HKSAR. If the pragmatic faction of the democrats does participate in legislative and district elections later and continues to seek the nomination and support of the patriotic elites, it would be possible for them to argue for a "safe" return to the August 31 model in 2014. Of course, if national security in the HKSAR is safeguarded, the central government would likely reconsider the possibility of democratization in Hong Kong along the August 2014 parameter. In the long run, if the HKSAR is integrated more deeply into the Greater Bay Area (GBA), then a new mayor of the GBA would be theoretically and practically possible by imitating the Hong Kong model of an electoral system in the coming decades. Hence, the Hong Kong model of democracy, albeit seemingly "diluted" since March 2021, would arguably have more applicability to the mainland in the coming decades.

If Chinese democracy, as political scientist Andrew Nathan has long argued, is characterized by harmony between the state and individual interests, the supremacy of the state over individuals, and the state's conferment of rights on the individuals,[292] then the 2021 electoral reforms in the HKSAR could be seen as not only a forceful reassertion of the PRC state's power over Hong Kong's radical and localist factions but also as a determination to elevate the patriotic united front to a politically preponderant position. Such a forceful reassertion

---

291. See No. 79/2023, "Amendments to the National Security Legislation," June 5, 2023, accessed January 1, 2024, https://images.io.gov.mo/bo/i/2023/24/despce-79-2023.pdf?_gl=1*zxayk2*_ga*MTIyODE3MzA0MC4xNzA0MTIxMDAz*_ga_VJ4ESSV5N3*MTcwNDEyMTAwMy4xLjEuMTcwNDEyMTA1MC4wLjAuMA.
292. Andrew Nathan, *Chinese Democracy* (Berkeley: University of California Press, 1986).

of the power of Beijing was the means of achieving its "comprehensive jurisdiction" over the HKSAR. The reform model in Hong Kong fits into the features of Chinese-style democracy with significant implications for the PRC's democratization in the long run. Mainland reformers can study the Hong Kong model of democracy and introduce its essential elements of limited pluralism and controlled competition to liberalize and democratize the PRC's political system, especially if the cycle of mainland Chinese politics would perhaps gradually shift from a currently controlling period to a new era of political liberalization.

Under the circumstances in which PRC leaders emphasized the need for patriotic elites to govern the HKSAR after the Fourth Plenum of the nineteenth Party Congress in November 2019, factionalism in Hong Kong has remained politically significant. Those political actors in Hong Kong who wish to augment their political influence, including the business elites and grassroots-level representatives, must join the patriotic united front, jockeying for political positions in the Election Committee and the LegCo, as shown in the December 2021 LegCo elections, and for the elected and appointed positions of the 2023 District Council elections. On the other hand, the pro-democracy Hong Kong people must change their strategies to adapt to the huge political transformations. An overwhelming majority of democrats adopted a wait-and-see attitude and did not participate in the December 2021 LegCo elections, except for a few moderate democrats such as former Democratic Party member Tik Chi-yuen, who was eventually the only democrat elected to the ninety-member LegCo. Tik could be regarded as one of the softliners of the pro-democracy camp, having little room for political maneuvering except for accepting the political reality to voice his minority views in the legislature. Undoubtedly, the hardliners within the pro-democracy camp will continue to resist electoral participation and to express their discontent. It remains difficult for some democrats to transform themselves from ideologues and action-oriented critics to loyal oppositionists, but they must accept the reality that dual states have emerged in Hong Kong politics. The local Hong Kong state was regarded by the central state as relatively weak from 2003 to 2019, and therefore, the PRC state has been reasserting its authority and influence in such a way that Hong Kong is now ruled by "the dual state," namely the local state in the HKSAR and the central state from Beijing.[293]

---

293. Ernst Fraenkel, *The Dual State: A Contribution to the Theory of Dictatorship* (Toronto: Oxford University Press, 1941).

The Dual State and Primacy of Ideologies in Beijing–Hong Kong Relations

The concept of the dual state advanced by Ernst Fraenkel can be academically and partially borrowed for our deeper understanding of the dynamics between the PRC and the HKSAR in the new era of their central-local relations. Specifically, Fraenkel argued that, in the case of the rise of the Third Reich, a "prerogative state" existed side by side with a "normative state," meaning that the National Socialist system in Germany had two layers. The "prerogative state" was "a governmental system which exercises unlimited arbitrariness and violence unchecked by any legal guarantees," while the "normative state" can be seen as "an administrative body endowed by elaborate powers for safeguarding the legal order as expressed in statutes, decisions of the court, and activities of the administrative agencies."[294] Fraenkel argued that the Third Reich's political sphere had a legal vacuum regulated by the dominant officials, who were determined to crush social and political movements resistant to the state.

Fraenkel's concept of a "dual state" can be applied to the relations between the PRC and Hong Kong. The PRC state, through the NPC interpretations of the Basic Law (such as the November 2016 interpretation of Article 104 and March 2021 decision on electoral reforms), exercised its "prerogative" over Hong Kong's political matters, intervening legitimately under Article 158 of the Basic Law. This prerogative is, from the mainland perspective, legitimate; those Hong Kong people who challenged it could be criticized as "unpatriotic." The Hong Kong state is like a "normative" administrative state "endowed by elaborate powers for safeguarding the legal order as expressed in statutes, decisions of the court, and activities of the administrative agencies." The subordinate role of the local Hong Kong state to the supremacy of the PRC's central state became obvious in 2014, when the State Council published the *White Paper* on the "correct" understanding of the Basic Law and emphasized the need for Beijing's "comprehensive jurisdiction" over the HKSAR. Such a subordinate role has become prominent after the promulgation of the national security law in late June 2020 and the overhaul of the electoral system in March 2021. The Hong Kong government has obligations to implement the directives of the central state, which possesses the "prerogative" of enacting the national security law and redesigning the electoral systems for the HKSAR. Furthermore, Fraenkel argued that the administrative and judicial bureaucracy operated subserviently to the prerogatives state that was led by the ruling party and its police apparatus. The Hong Kong situation after the enactment of the national security law resembles a parallel coexistence between the prerogative state in Beijing and the local administrative-judicial

---

294. Fraenkel, *The Dual State*, xiii.

bureaucracy that must implement the national security directives of the central government.

Fraenkel's analysis of Nazi Germany with its ideology of national socialism cannot be applied to the PRC's relations with Hong Kong. Rather, the ideological conflicts between conservative nationalism and localism are far more pertinent to explain Beijing's transformations of the HKSAR. The Marxist-Leninist regime in the PRC has been guided by the need for the CCP to lead the entire country, to develop its economy, to build up its military power, and to rival the Western states, especially the US. Struggling with enemies is an essential feature of Marxism-Leninism. Such enemies in the HKSAR, from the perspective of the mainland's conservative nationalistic leaders, included the localists, some of whom were "anarchists" participating in violent activities.[295] As such, the PRC's central state has to struggle against the Hong Kong enemies, namely some localists and oppositionists who were seen as forming an "alliance" or a "conspiracy" with the Western powers to "subvert" the local state of Hong Kong.

The successful "struggles" of the ruling CCP in its history were emphasized in an important speech delivered by President Xi Jinping to the Central Committee in October 2017—a speech that was republished by the CCP mouthpiece *Qishi* in late September 2022, just two weeks before the twentieth Party Congress. Xi had long emphasized that the CCP engaged in a series of successful struggles against "imperialism, feudalism and bureaucratic capitalism" and that it achieved "national independence, national liberation, national unification, social stability, and new democratic revolution."[296] The CCP's struggles against enemies in its new era from 2012 to the present have been seen in the political development of the HKSAR, which to Beijing was under the heavy influence of Western imperialists and where the "localists" plunged the legitimacy of the Hong Kong government and central authorities into an unprecedented crisis in the latter half of 2019. As such, the CCP, from the political thought of Xi Jinping, had to struggle against the Western imperialistic forces in the context of Hong Kong.

As a neo-Maoist who attaches far more importance to the transformation of superstructure (such as values, culture, and institutions) than the need to accelerate productive forces through the development of the economic base, Xi Jinping has emphasized the CCP's permanent struggles against enemies—a hallmark of revolutionary immortality that distinguishes him from Deng Xiaoping,

---

295. In fact, the anarchists opposed Marxism-Leninism during the May Fourth Movement in China. For details, see Arif Dirlik, *The Origin of Chinese Communism* (New York: Oxford University Press, 1989).
296. Xi Jinping (习近平), "新时代中国共产党的历史使命" ["The historical mission of the Chinese Communist Party in the new era"], 求是网 [qstheory.cn], September 30, 2022, accessed October 9, 2022, http://www.qstheory.cn/dukan/qs/2022-09/30/c_1129040825.htm.

Jiang Zemin, Hu Jintao, Wen Jiabao, and Li Keqiang, who stressed the development of an economic base rather than the changing of the superstructure.[297] Xi Jinping's ideological architect, Wang Huning, is also a neo-Maoist who sees that the political chaos in Hong Kong in 2019 was due to the problematic superstructure, such as the polluted values and the absence of nationalistic sentiment in many young people, the lopsided design of the LegCo's electoral system that favored the radical democrats, and the inability of "patriotic elites" to govern the HKSAR. As such, the superstructure in the HKSAR had to be changed by promulgating the national security law, implementing national security education and national education, redesigning the LegCo's electoral system, and ensuring that the "patriotic elites" can and will govern the HKSAR.

There are strong grounds for believing that the ideologies of pro-Beijing nationalism and Marxism-Leninism-Maoism will persist in Beijing's policy toward the HKSAR. Assertive nationalism has emerged in China since its rapid rise in the early 2000s. "Wolf warrior diplomacy" was adopted by some PRC diplomats in public and in their social media platforms, refuting and "shouting at foreign counterparts" and "insulting foreign leaders" at a time when some foreigners made accusations that COVID-19 originated from China—an action contrary to the low-profile approach adopted by the PRC in the past.[298] However, "wolf warrior diplomacy" gradually faded away after May 2021 when President Xi Jinping told CCP leaders that China should be "open and confident, but also modest and humble" in its communication with foreign countries.[299] The assertive nationalism of PRC leaders and officials have obviously been shaping Beijing's policy toward the HKSAR, adopting a hardline approach to dealing with not only the organizers and activists of the anti-extradition protests in 2019, but also the core leaders of the pro-democracy movement in Hong Kong. As Marxists, PRC officials have seen Hong Kong as vulnerable to Western imperialism. As Leninists, they have regarded the anti–extradition bill movement as a "color revolution" trying to topple the HKSAR government and the CCP on the mainland. As neo-Maoists, Xi Jinping and his supporters have become determined to revamp the Hong Kong superstructure to ensure the dominance of "patriotic elites" in governing the city.

---

297. The discussion of the change in superstructure versus economic base can be found in Stuart Schram, *The Thought of Mao Tse-Tung* (London: Cambridge University Press, 1989).
298. Interview with Peter Martin, "Understanding Chinese 'Wolf Warrior Diplomacy,'" The National Bureau of Asian Research, October 22, 2021, accessed October 9, 2022, https://www.nbr.org/publication/understanding-chinese-wolf-warrior-diplomacy/.
299. Way Weichieh Wang, "China's Wolf Warrior Diplomacy Is Fading," The Diplomat, July 27, 2022, accessed October 9, 2022, https://thediplomat.com/2022/07/chinas-wolf-warrior-diplomacy-is-fading/.

Since 2012, the PRC under the leadership of President Xi Jinping has been emphasizing China's global outreach through the Belt and Road Initiative and stressing the importance of maintaining domestic socio-economic and political stability. Given that the HKSAR is at the borderland of China and that China is extremely concerned about the occurrence of "color revolutions" fomented by foreign countries to subvert the former Soviet Union and some Middle East states, the ideology of conservative nationalism is destined to persist. For the mainland's conservative nationalists, democratic reform in the HKSAR must not provide an opportunity for any foreign states to shape Hong Kong's and the mainland's political systems. Hence, the electoral reforms approved by the NPC in March 2021 were designed to not only roll back the Western-style democratic reforms, but also exclude the localist enemies and restrict the access to power to the pro-Beijing patriotic factions. The "prerogative" state in the PRC had to intervene in Hong Kong politically through legal means, namely the continuous interpretations of the Basic Law, to empower the "normative state" in Hong Kong to carry out the policy of safeguarding China's national security.

Because Hong Kong was under British colonial rule for over 150 years, its political development after July 1, 1997, under the PRC has been viewed as potentially and politically disruptive of the mainland's polity. "One country, two systems" has been evolving in such a way that the PRC (one country) is increasingly apprehensive of whether the Hong Kong political system would be democratized in the Western style of "separation of powers" so that even the mainland polity would be affected. In the minds of PRC authorities, the pro-democracy localists in the HKSAR sought to "Westernize" and "internationalize" the local political system and to "collude" with foreign forces to instigate political protests in Hong Kong, ranging from the 2014 Occupy Central movement to the 2019 anti-extradition movement. To PRC authorities, Hong Kong's political system has a real danger of diverging politically from the mainland. Therefore, PRC authorities had to minimize such political divergence by reconstructing a gigantic Election Committee in March 2021 to apply its brakes on Western-style democratization in the HKSAR.

An article published by *Red Flag*, a leftist mouthpiece in the PRC, in June 2019 amid the anti-extradition protests in Hong Kong revealed how Beijing viewed foreign and especially the American intervention in Hong Kong affairs.[300] It made several arguments illustrative of the position of conservative nationalists. First and foremost, author Lao Xiao pointed to the US intervention in Hong

---

300. Lao Xiao (老萧), "正告美国反华乱港势力：立即住手！——粉碎香港颜色革命，坚决捍卫国家" ["Asking the US and anti-China forces that create chaos in Hong Kong to stop: Dismantling Hong Kong's color revolution and resolutely defending the nation's reunification"], 红旗 [Red Flag Association Website], July 3, 2019, accessed March 14, 2021, http://www.hongqi.tv/zatan/2019-07-03/15616.html.

Kong and the nature of the "color revolution" in Hong Kong's protests. Second, it criticized some Hong Kong court judges for being "lenient" toward the Hong Kong "independence activists" and for siding with Western countries like the US and the United Kingdom. Third, it argued that the HKSAR government lacked emergency powers to deal with not only the 2019 protests but also the 2014 Occupy Central movement. Fourth, it advocated a drastic change in Hong Kong's "superstructure," including the imposition of an emergency law, the expulsion of those court judges who refused to cooperate and defend national interest, the arrest and prosecution of violent protestors, and the expulsion of foreign spies who intervened in Hong Kong affairs.[301] Fifth, it admitted that China's united front work that focused on the local businesspeople had its limitations. Sixth, the Hong Kong capitalist system had its acute social problems, namely the serious gap between the rich and the poor, and the poor people's blaming of the local Hong Kong state and the central state in Beijing.[302] In other words, the Hong Kong government failed to formulate and implement sufficient social welfare policies for the poor and the needy. Seventh, the education system in Hong Kong was "full of people who did not understand China," and this situation was unfavorable to the PRC's integration of Hong Kong. Eighth, Hong Kong had extradition arrangements with some twenty countries, and yet, it did not have an extradition agreement with its motherland. Ninth, without a deep understanding of China's legal system among Hong Kong judicial officials, the HKSAR remained a place where foreign spies were active and undermined the PRC's national security, including Guangdong and other parts of the mainland. Tenth, it was unacceptable for the PRC to witness a phenomenon in which some Hong Kong people went to lobby US politicians against the interests of the HKSAR and China. These people who lobbied foreign countries, according to *Red Flag*, were "traitors."[303] Eleventh, the protestors in Hong Kong made use of ordinary citizens and students as "hostages," attacking the police and government headquarters and participating in "subversive activities" to overthrow the HKSAR administration and to target at the CCP and the PRC government.[304] Twelfth, it criticized Chief Executive Carrie Lam and Police Commissioner Stephen Lo for being weak vis-à-vis the protestors and "surrendering" to them easily.[305] Thirteenth, it pointed to the danger that China's national security and territorial integrity were at stake.

Overall, from the perspective of China's conservative nationalists, the 2019 anti-extradition protests undermined China's national security and territorial

---

301. Lao, "Asking the US and anti-China forces that create chaos in Hong Kong to stop."
302. Lao, "Asking the US and anti-China forces that create chaos in Hong Kong to stop."
303. Lao, "Asking the US and Anti-China Forces that Create Chaos in Hong Kong to Stop."
304. Lao, "Asking the US and Anti-China Forces that Create Chaos in Hong Kong to Stop."
305. Lao, "Asking the US and Anti-China Forces that Create Chaos in Hong Kong to Stop."

integrity, necessitating Beijing's intervention in Hong Kong where the government was weak, where some protestors were seen as collaborating with foreign countries, and where the entire superstructure would necessitate reforms. If the superstructure embraces political institutions from the Maoist perspective, then its institutional design in the HKSAR would have to be altered so that the economic base of Hong Kong would continue to foster prosperity. This Maoist perspective could be seen in the SCNPC decision on Hong Kong's electoral system twenty months after the highly conservative nationalistic arguments had been made by *Red Flag* as early as July 2019.

Summary

Ideological conflicts and factionalism remain the two most important factors shaping the new politics of Beijing–Hong Kong relations. In 2010, when the moderate democrats negotiated with Liaison Office officials on the democratization of the LegCo, the PRC side was characterized by the dominance of relatively liberal nationalists. This mainland political situation could still be seen in August 2014, when the PRC government laid out its parameter for the direct election of the chief executive of the HKSAR. Two to three candidates would be screened out by the Election Committee, and then, they would compete for votes in direct elections in 2017. This model was arguably the most "democratic" one proposed by the PRC side, which maintained the principle of democratic centralism in handling the democratization of Hong Kong. Unfortunately, the Hong Kong localists were ideologically dogmatic and politically united to oppose this model in mid-2015, leading to its failure to be accepted in the LegCo, where the pro-Beijing forces were deeply disunited and uncoordinated without any effective leadership. The failure of the people of Hong Kong to "pocket" the political reform model that grew out of the August 31, 2014, parameter was tragic, propelling the competing pro-democracy and pro-Beijing factions to continuous showdowns. This missed political opportunity of "pocketing" the political reform model in mid-2015 was later proven to have a heavy cost. From the Mong Kok riot in early 2016 to the oath-taking saga in late 2016 and from the anti-extradition movement in the latter half of 2019 to the holding of primary elections in July 2020, the PRC's political arena was ruled by the dominant conservative nationalistic faction. This conservative nationalist faction could not tolerate incessant political provocation and social turbulence in the HKSAR, and it decided to adopt a hardline approach to solving Hong Kong's governance problem. As a result, the national security law was imposed on Hong Kong in late June 2020, leading to the emergence of a deep state in Hong Kong where the law-enforcement authorities turn out to be the most powerful actors in the post-colonial state apparatus. The impacts of the national security law are wide, having profound social and political implications. The most significant impact is to generate great concern, anxiety, and fear among some Hong Kong people and the international community. Some Hong Kong people chose to leave the HKSAR for other countries, such as the UK and Canada, while many foreign countries were shocked by the hardline approach adopted by the PRC authorities over the HKSAR. Yet, the criticisms leveled by foreign states on China's policy toward the HKSAR have created the mutual distrust between them. The relations between China and those Western democracies, especially the allies of the US, have turned sour over the handling of the HKSAR since mid-2020. In fact, Hong Kong could also be regarded as a victim in the Sino-US struggles over technology, trade, and human rights. On the other hand, the rise of the new deep state in Hong Kong is accompanied by the prominence of the dual state, namely the central state in Beijing and the local state in the HKSAR. The central state further imposed its will on the local state in March 2021 when the electoral system was revamped, with the objectives of excluding the localist and pro-democracy factions from the LegCo, eliminating the influence of District Councils, empowering the patriotic or nationalistic factions, and yet stabilizing Hong Kong's political system.

3
Beijing's Comprehensive Jurisdiction, Sino-Western Value Clashes, and Hong Kong Elections from 2021 to 2023

Implications for Taiwan

The localist emergence in the HKSAR brought about tremendous challenges to the legitimacy of the Hong Kong government, especially as some of them were radicals who resorted to violence and populists who mobilized public opinion and citizen protests against the regime. Reaching the limits of its political tolerance, Beijing decided to realize its "comprehensive jurisdiction" over the HKSAR through a series of measures from 2020 onward: (1) SCNPC interpretation of the Basic Law in November 2016 on the oath-taking behavior of legislators-elect and public office holders; (2) the promulgation and implementation of the national security law since mid-2020; (3) the utilization of the SCNPC decision in November 2020 to clarify the allegiance requirement of LegCo members (see the next section); (4) the overhaul of the Hong Kong electoral system in March 2021 (see Table 3.1); (5) the holding of the March 2022 chief executive election; (6) the holding of the December 2022 LegCo elections; (7) the holding of the December 2023 District Council elections; (8) the implementation of national security education in all schools ranging from kindergartens to universities; (9) the enforcement of national education and Chinese cultural education in Hong Kong's kindergarten, primary, and secondary schools; (10) the establishment of the constitutional practice of requiring the chief executive to submit a duty report to Beijing annually in December (see section below); (11) the enactment of the local legislation of Article 23 of the Basic Law in the HKSAR in the year 2024; and (12) and the preparation and enactment of a cybersecurity law after the LegCo's approval of the legislation on Article 23 of the Basic Law.[1]

---

1. For education reform, see Sonny Shiu-hing Lo and Steven Chung-fun Hung, *The Politics of Education Reform in China's Hong Kong* (London: Routledge, 2022).

Table 3.1: Beijing's Comprehensive Responses to Localist Populism

Events of Localist Populism	Beijing's Responses
Oath-taking controversy of Yau Wai-ching and Baggio Leung on October 12, 2016.	SCNPC interpretation of Basic Law's Article 104 on November 7, 2016.
Anti-extradition movement, May to December 2019.	In August 2019, the People's Armed Police was sent to the Shenzhen border as a warning to Hong Kong protestors. On May 22, 2020, the NPC approved a decision to let the NPCSC pass a national security law for Hong Kong. On June 30, 2020, the SCNPC passed the law unanimously, and it is included in Appendix 3 of the Hong Kong Basic Law.
Localist populists held primary elections for the originally scheduled but later delayed LegCo elections. Localist legislators went to the US to lobby the US government for its support of Hong Kong during the 2019 anti-extradition movement.	The organizers of the primary elections were arrested and prosecuted under the national security law. On November 11, 2020, the SCNPC reached a decision to clarify the allegiance requirements of LegCo members, resulting in the HKSAR government's announcement of four legislators (Alvin Yeung, Dennis Kwok, Kwok Ka-ki, and Kenneth Leung) losing the status of being LegCo members. The four disqualified legislators had submitted nominations to run for the 2020 LegCo elections, but their nominations were invalidated by the returning officers, who found that all of them "solicited intervention by foreign governments or political authorities in relation to the HKSAR's affairs." They also "expressed an intention to indiscriminately vote down any legislative proposals, appointments, funding applications and budgets introduced by the HKSAR government after securing a majority in LegCo to force the government to accede to certain political demands."
The election of localist populists into the LegCo.	On March 11, 2021, the SCNPC passed a decision to change the electoral system of Hong Kong, especially the LegCo composition, in which the Election Committee will play a crucial role in returning LegCo members.

(continued on p. 182)

Table 3.1 (continued)

Events of Localist Populism	Beijing's Responses
Students and young people from secondary schools and universities participated in the 2012 anti-national education campaign, the 2014 Umbrella Movement, the 2016 Mongkok riot, and the 2019 anti-extradition movement. The 2019 anti-extradition bill movement turned violent—a kind of domestic "terrorism" unacceptable to the PRC.	The national security law had to be enacted in June 2020 to deter violent localism and domestic terrorism in the HKSAR. Under the national security law, national security education must be implemented in Hong Kong. Moreover, patriotic education was formulated and implemented by the HKSAR government at the primary and secondary schools, including the abolition of the liberal studies curriculum at the secondary school level. National education has been adopted in the HKSAR so that young people understand their motherland, China, in a deeper way.
Radical localists could be directly elected to the LegCo, while localist populists could be directly elected to District Councils, which could nominate candidates for the LegCo's super-seat elections. District Council members could also go into the Chief Executive Election Committee to select the chief executive.	A comprehensive electoral reform was approved by the NPC in March 2021. Annex 1 and Annex 2 of the Basic Law were amended by the SCNPC. The new electoral system eliminates the influence of District Council members, who will no longer be members of the Chief Executive Election Committee and who will no longer have the power to nominate from among themselves candidates to run in the LegCo's super-seat elections.
Prevent localist populists and radicals from participating in Hong Kong's LegCo elections.	The Candidate Eligibility Review Committee is set up in accordance with the amendments to the Basic Law. It will decide the eligibility of candidates running for the LegCo and chief executive elections after receiving reports from the police's national security department and from the Committee for Safeguarding National Security.
Overall, localist populism plunged the HKSAR into a serious crisis of legitimacy and governance from the anti-national education movement in 2012 to the anti-extradition bill movement in the latter half of 2019—moves that were perceived by Beijing as violating the national security of the central government in the HKSAR.	Beijing decided to promulgate the national security law in late June 2020 to stabilize the society and politics of Hong Kong, and it changed the electoral system in such a way as to ensure that "patriots" would be able to govern the HKSAR—a point emphasized by CCP General Secretary Xi Jinping in his speech delivered at the 20th Party Congress in Beijing on October 16, 2022. The HKSAR, according to the PRC leadership, had to be transformed from "chaos to governance" and then from "governance to prosperity."

Sources: "NPCSC Decision Explained," Hong Kong government press release, November 14, 2020, accessed March 23, 2021. https://www.news.gov.hk/eng/2020/11/20201114/20201114_124103_167.html. For CCP General Secretary Xi Jinping's speech delivered to the 20th Party Congress on October 16, 2022, see RTHK broadcast of the 20th Party Congress, October 16, 2022.

The Exercise of "Comprehensive Jurisdiction"

To remove the localist populists from the LegCo, the PRC authorities on November 11, 2020, utilized the SCNPC decision to clarify the allegiance requirement of Hong Kong LegCo members. According to the decision, LegCo members would be disqualified from the office once they were determined by law to fail to meet the legal requirements of upholding the Basic Law and honoring the pledge of allegiance to the HKSAR. Those circumstances "deemed failing to meet these requirements" included "advocating or supporting 'Hong Kong independence,' refusing to recognize the state's sovereignty and its exercise of sovereignty over Hong Kong, seeking interference in the HKSAR affairs by foreign countries or external forces, or committing other acts endangering national security."[2] The HKSAR government took immediate action to announce that four legislators failed to comply with the legal requirement, prompting all other democratic populists (except for two democrats) to resign from the LegCo. Their mass resignation paved the way for the LegCo to enact laws and approve policies, which in the eyes of Beijing stabilized the society and polity of Hong Kong.

The PRC authorities saw the roots of the Hong Kong political turbulence as stemming from the structure of the LegCo, thereby requiring the designing of a new electoral system for the HKSAR. Curbing the number of directly elected seats and reinjecting a large Election Committee to select legislators would allow the patriotic elites to govern Hong Kong. This new electoral system, as decided by the SCNPC on March 11, 2021, would have several advantages. First, the executive-led polity of Hong Kong would be restored, empowering the HKSAR government to deal with a relatively weak LegCo. Second, all the radical populists and localists would find it very difficult to enter the LegCo, except for the moderate democrats who are politically acceptable to the PRC. Third, voters would no longer easily vote those radicals into the LegCo, for they would understand the political bottom line of Beijing. Fourth, a powerful Candidate Eligibility Review Committee (CERC) would screen out those radical populists and localists while accepting the moderate elements for participation in LegCo elections. Fifth, most patriotic elites would occupy almost all the seats in both the Election Committee and functional constituencies of the LegCo, thereby playing a dominant role in Hong Kong's political superstructure. Sixth, after the political system was stabilized, the HKSAR government would be expected to enhance its governing capacity by putting forward bills and policies that would be easily approved by the cooperative legislature. Seventh, political violence

---

2. "China's Top Legislature Adopts Decision on HKSAR LegCo Members' Qualification," Xinhua, November 11, 2020, accessed March 22, 2021, http://www.npc.gov.cn/englishnpc/c23934/202011/d2a89c95fb3d4db5b8bedd5988445ad1.shtml.

would be curbed and intimidated, consolidating China's sovereignty and territorial integrity over Hong Kong. Eighth, in a new political system designed in favor of the patriotic elites, the mainland-born elites, like Professor Sun Dong who later became the secretary for innovation, technology, and industry, would have the realistic chance to climb up the political ladder far more easily than ever before because these people are the loyalists in a new patronage system. Ninth, the business and the landed elites would likely have their influence in functional constituencies curbed by the Election Committee, whose composition would still be under the control of the central authorities. In this way, if the HKSAR government would like to formulate and implement land and housing policies to address the plight of the poor and the needy, it would not encounter fierce opposition from the business and landed elites. Tenth, the new electoral system is legally buttressed by the SCNPC decision on March 11, 2020, its interpretation of the Basic Law's Article 104 in November 2016, and its decision on the qualifications of LegCo members in November 2020. Electoral reform is legitimized by a series of the SCNPC's interpretations and decisions, representing a mix of political-legal instruments to stabilize the Hong Kong polity. Altogether, they concretely constitute a blueprint for Beijing's "comprehensive jurisdiction" over Hong Kong, as mentioned ambiguously for the first time in the 2014 *White Paper* on the implementation of the Basic Law. Overall, the new design of the LegCo is meant to exclude the influence of the radical localists and pro-democracy populists while empowering the "patriots" to rule the HKSAR with stability and dominance.

As the loyal clients of the powerful patron Beijing, the patriotic LegCo members in March 2021 amended the house rules to limit speaking time and curb filibustering efforts inside the legislature. A penalty system that sees a legislator suspended for a week was installed if he or she breaks the rule.[3] Lawbreakers who ignore the house rules continuously would be suspended from two to four weeks. The only localist legislator, Cheng Chung-tai from Civic Passion, voted against the amendment. He said, "The NPC has already approved electoral changes in Hong Kong, where there will be panel to vet candidates running for LegCo in the future. Theoretically, anyone being able to speak in the LegCo in the future should be patriots, such a move is totally unnecessary."[4] According to the amended rules of procedures, lawmakers would not be able to easily move a motion to adjourn certain debates, such as the disqualification of a legislator from office. Any legislator who wished to present a petition to the LegCo

---

3. "Misbehaving Lawmakers Will Be Suspended from LegCo Meetings," *The Standard*, March 25, 2021, accessed April 5, 2021, https://www.thestandard.com.hk/breaking-news/section/4/168240/Misbehaving-lawmakers-will-be-suspended-from-LegCo-meetings.
4. "Misbehaving Lawmakers Will Be Suspended from LegCo Meetings," *The Standard*, March 25, 2021.

would have to give three days of prior notice to the LegCo president instead of informing the president on the eve of the meeting. Beijing's political loyalists in the LegCo followed the mainland example of utilizing Chinese legalism to tighten the house rules and punish any legislator who would violate the internal procedures.

Figure 3.1 demonstrates the old interactions between Beijing and the HKSAR before the enactment of the national security law in Hong Kong in June 2020, showing the role and influence of external actors in the political environment. Because of Beijing's concern about the prospects of a "color revolution" in the HKSAR, it was determined to cut off the political linkage between the external actors, like the US, and local political actors, including LegCo members, ExCo members, principal officials, civil servants, middlemen, interest groups, and mass media. In Figure 3.2, the new interactions between Beijing and the HKSAR have embraced two new political institutions since the promulgation of the national security law in June 2020: the central government's Office for Safeguarding National Security, which is stationed in the HKSAR, and the Hong Kong government's Committee for Safeguarding National Security. The new electoral system empowers the chief executive and the ExCo while making the LegCo far more politically "patriotic," loyal, and reliable than ever before. At the same time, the Central Coordination Committee on Hong Kong Affairs remains the supreme CCP body responsible for Hong Kong affairs, assisted by the HKMAO, Liaison Office, Ministry of Foreign Affairs (MFA), SCNPC, NPC, and CPPCC. If public opinion and political culture in the HKSAR were previously shaped by Western and pro-foreign influences, the new electoral system under the protection of the national security law aims at transforming public opinion and political culture from anti-governmental to more pro-establishment, pro-PRC, and pro-CCP than ever before. In short, political correctness and loyalty are the hallmarks of Hong Kong's new politics under the national security law.

The Constitutional Practice between Beijing and Hong Kong/Macau: Duty Visit and Report

Since the establishment of the Hong Kong and Macau special administrative regions, the chief executives of Hong Kong and Macau have annually visited the central authorities in Beijing and submitted their duty reports to the top leaders; nevertheless, the visits by Hong Kong Chief Executive John Lee and Macau Chief Executive Ho Iat Seng to Beijing in December 2023 revealed some significant continuities and changes that, altogether, are establishing the constitutional

186   *The New Politics of Beijing–Hong Kong Relations*

Figure 3.1: Beijing's Interactions with Hong Kong before the 2020 National Security Law

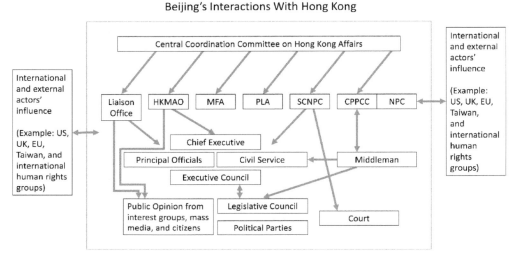

Note: → influences

Figure 3.2: Beijing's New Interactions with Hong Kong after the 2020 National Security Law

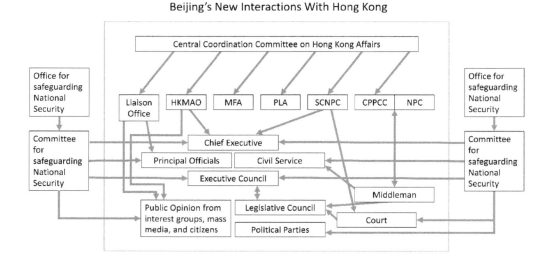

practices, and perhaps later the constitutional convention, of their duty reports submitted to the central government in Beijing.[5]

On December 18, 2023, when John Lee reported to President Xi Jinping on his work, the mainland officials sitting on the left hand side of the middle position of the president were of very high level, including Premier Li Qiang, the Central Secretariat Party-Secretary and Central Office Director Cai Qi, Vice Premier and convenor of the CCP Central Hong Kong and Macau Work Leading Small Group Ding Xuexiang, United Front Department Minister Shi Taifeng, and Political and Legal Affairs Commission Secretary Chen Wenqing. Sitting on the right-hand side of the president were Hong Kong Chief Executive John Lee, Hong Kong and Macau Office (HKMAO) Director Xia Baolong, HKMAO Deputy Director Zhou Ji, HKMAO Deputy Director and Liaison Office Director Zheng Yanxiong, and Hong Kong Chief Executive Office Director Carol Yip Man Kuen.[6] The mainland side was filled with top officials, including the Premier, Central Office director, convenor of the leading small group on Hong Kong and Macau, united front work minister, and political and legal affairs director. This meant that the central government attached immense importance to Hong Kong and Macau affairs, as the same line-up and sitting arrangement could be seen in the duty report made by Macau Chief Executive Ho Iat Seng. Furthermore, the elevation of the premier to accompany the president to meet the two chief executives from Hong Kong and Macau was unprecedented. In the past, the Hong Kong and Macau chief executives tended to meet the premier separately from the president. This time, the co-attendance of the president and the premier had two important implications: the accountability of the Hong Kong and Macau chief executives to the whole batch of the Chinese leadership in Beijing could be formalized and institutionalized. This set-up could also save the time of the premier in meeting the chief executives from Hong Kong and Macau separately.

Another significant phenomenon is that accompanying the chief executive of Hong Kong and Macau were, firstly, the HKMAO director, secondly, the HKMAO deputy director, thirdly, the Liaison Office director, and finally, the Chief Executive Office director. In the case of Ho Iat Seng's meeting with President Xi, the mainland side had the same line-up and seating arrangement, while the right-hand side of the President included firstly Ho Iat Seng, secondly Xia Baolong, thirdly Zhou Ji, fourthly Liaison Office Director Zheng Xincong, and finally Chief Executive Office Director Hoi Lai Fong. It is noteworthy that only the directors of the Chief Executive Office from Hong Kong and Macau

---

5. For constitutional conventions, see Sonny Shiu-Hing Lo, "The Emergence of Constitutional Convention in the Hong Kong Special Administrative Region," *Hong Kong Law Journal*, 35 (2005): 103–128.
6. *Ming Pao*, December 19, 2023; *Wen Wei Po*, December 19, 2023; TVB News, December 18, 2023.

attended the meeting as secretaries, and both sat beside the Liaison Office Director—an institutionalization of the accountability of the chief executive to the central authorities in Beijing and an accountability mechanism mentioned in the Basic Law and practiced during the December 2023 duty visit.

Both John Lee and Ho Iat Seng were praised by President Xi, who affirmed their work positively—a significant move pointing to how the central leadership supports the work of the two chief executives. John Lee presented a report that, according to him, talked about the work and achievements of the Hong Kong government and the forthcoming work about the legislation on Article 23 of the Basic Law. Ho Iat Seng was seen on television submitting two reports to President Xi, one report on Macau and the other on its economic diversification plan. President Xi praised Ho's good work, including the affirmation of the Macau government's amendment of the national security law, the legislation concerning the chief executive election and the Legislative Council election, the consolidation of management over the gaming industry, the economic diversification plan, the promotion of the construction work on the Hengqin-Macau Cooperation Zone, the expansion of Macau's external relations, and the economic recovery and societal stability of Macau.[7]

John Lee's report to the president covered the consolidation of national security work, the District Council election, and how Hong Kong dealt with post-COVID economic recovery. President Xi, according to the State Council press release on December 19, highly praised the chief executive, saying that he led the HKSAR government in not only shouldering the responsibilities and delivering satisfactory results, but also in restoring order and maintaining Hong Kong's distinctive status and advantages. President Xi was seen to shake hands with both John Lee and Ho Iat Seng in two separate photos—an indication that the central authorities highly lauded their performances.

Xia Baolong, the HKMAO director, and his deputy, Zhou Ji, as well as the Liaison Office directors of both Hong Kong and Macau, were sitting together with the two chief executives while facing the top five leaders of the central leadership—Li Qiang, Cai Qi, Ding Xuexiang, Shi Taifeng, and Chen Wenqing. This arrangement is politically significant: the HKMAO and the Liaison Office chiefs are directly accountable to the central leadership of the CCP. While the HKMAO and the Liaison Office chiefs are assisting the chief executives of both Hong Kong and Macau in terms of governance, they are simultaneously accountable to the central CPC leadership—an indication that the Party's authority has been strengthened and institutionalized in the recent revamp of the HKMAO,

---

7. Now TV News, December 18, 2023.

which has been reorganized as the Hong Kong and Macau Work Office under the Central Committee of the CCP.[8]

When the concept of the central government's "comprehensive jurisdiction" over Hong Kong was first mentioned in mid-2014, very few people understood what it meant. Nine years later, however, Beijing's "comprehensive jurisdiction" over Hong Kong and Macau is now realized through various mechanisms: the enactment and implementation of the national security law in Hong Kong, the amendment of the national security law in Macau, the revamp of the electoral system for the chief executives and Legislative Councils in Hong Kong and Macau, the reorganization of the District Council election in Hong Kong, the publication of the Master Plan on Macau's economic diversification by the State Council's State Planning and Reform Commission in December 2023, the implementation of the Guangdong-Macau In-Depth Cooperation Zone in Hengqin, and the economic integration of both Hong Kong and Macau into the Greater Bay Area.[9] All these measures have been taken to realize the central government's "comprehensive jurisdiction" over Hong Kong and Macau, bringing about the socio-political stability and economic prosperity of the two cities and realizing the uniqueness of the "one country, two systems."

The key to realize Beijing's "comprehensive jurisdiction" over Hong Kong and Macau is to ensure that the "patriots" can and will govern the two cities. As such, electoral systems in the two places were reformed so that the "patriotic" elites can enter the political system and govern with confidence and stability. This was why Xia Baolong, the HKMAO director, delivered a speech on December 22 in the meeting of the Hong Kong and Macau Study Association in front of a group of newly elected and appointed District Council members in Hong Kong. Xia appealed to the elected and appointed members of the District Councils on the need to maintain solidarity and to the civil servants on the necessity of sticking to patriotism.

Three days after the District Council election on December 10, the government's Civil Service Bureau published a consultative document on the Civil Service Code, covering the oath-taking and declaration requirement of civil servants, their core values and standard of conduct, and their relationship with the political appointment system. The draft Civil Service Code tends to emphasize the importance of national security in the psyche of civil servants, who are also expected to be responsive to the needs of the citizens and society and to be enthusiastic in the delivery of public services. Xia's message on December 22

---

8. Sonny Lo, "The New Structure of HKMWO and Its Political Implications," *Macau Business*, November 5, 2023, https://www.macaubusiness.com/opinion-the-new-structure-of-hkmwo-and-its-political-implications/.
9. For the details of the Cooperation Zone released by the State Council in September 2021, see https://www.hengqin-cooperation.gov.mo/en_US/shq, accessed January 2, 2024.

was clear: the people of Hong Kong from all walks of life, including elected and appointed office-bearers and civil servants, have to be united, to protect national security, and to support the central government's "comprehensive jurisdiction" over Hong Kong for the sake of contributing to the success of "one country, two systems."

The duty visits and reports made by the chief executives of Hong Kong and Macau to Beijing on December 18, 2023, could be regarded as a new chapter in the relationships between the two special administrative regions and the central government in Beijing. The annual visit and its related reports, as well as the seating arrangements, fully realized Beijing's "comprehensive jurisdiction" over Hong Kong and Macau. The duty visits and reports are the necessary and important mechanisms through which the chief executives of both Hong Kong and Macau are held accountable to Beijing in accordance with the requirement of the Basic Laws of Hong Kong and Macau. The seating arrangements illustrated the proper etiquette and formal reporting mechanism through which the CPC leadership oversees the work of the two chief executives, the two governments of Hong Kong and Macau, the HKMAO, and the Liaison Office directors who are appointed to deal with the affairs of both Hong Kong and Macau. In the study of law and politics, legal scholars have advanced the concept of constitutional convention to refer to a series of constitutional practices adopted for a sustained period. If so, the duty visits and reports made by the Hong Kong and Macau chief executives to Beijing on December 2023 were politically and constitutionally very significant because these are relatively new constitutional practices that, if they persist in the years to come, will become the constitutional conventions between Hong Kong and Macau on the one hand and the central government in Beijing on the other hand.

The Clashes of Sino-Western Political Civilizations

From 2003 to the present, the PRC has been consistently opposing the political internationalization of Hong Kong and seeing some democrats and localist populists as having collusion with Western countries and non-governmental organizations, especially human rights groups. Political internationalization is defined here as an attempt made by local human rights activists to form an alliance with foreign like-minded actors and organizations to push for democratic changes in the HKSAR. As a country experiencing foreign imperialism and national humiliation in its historical trajectory, the PRC has been traditionally anti-foreign in its international outlook. Its opposition to the political internationalization of Hong Kong explains why mainland authorities have adopted an increasingly hardline approach to dealing with Hong Kong matters, especially after the Occupy Central movement, which mainland officials saw as a sign of a "color revolution." The perception of localist populists fostering a "color revolution" with Western democratic states was reinforced in the anti–extradition bill movement from May to December 2019. When some civil society groups advocated for the political democratization of Hong Kong through the assistance of Western democracies, and when some localist protesters and activists waved the national flags of foreign countries, they were utterly ignorant of the PRC's anti-foreignism and strong reactions.[10] Many localist populists were politically insensitive to the deep-rooted xenophobic sentiment of PRC authorities, who are highly nationalistic and who are eager to wipe out foreign influences amid their profound memories of Western imperialism and the humiliation of China's Qing dynasty. The heated exchanges between Yang Jiechi, a state councilor and former foreign minister, and US Secretary of State Anthony Blinken in Alaska in March 2021 showed that the PRC side emphasized the co-existence of "Chinese democracy" with US democracy, that the rules-based order should not be dictated by the US, and that China confronted US hegemony in the world.[11] As Yang said, "The United States has its style—United States-style democracy—and China has the Chinese-style democracy. It is not just up to the American people, but the also the people of the world, to evaluate how the United States has done in advancing its own democracy."[12]

Given that PRC leaders emphasize that Chinese democracy is different from that of the West, they expect Hong Kong to develop its Hong Kong–style democracy suitable for the local circumstances,[13] as they argued for the necessity of the electoral reform decided by the NPC on March 11, 2021. Similarly, immediately after the promulgation of the national security law on Hong Kong, the PRC secured the support of fifty-two countries led by Cuba to assert that all states had the right to enact their national security laws.[14] In contrast, twenty-seven countries including the UK, the US, France, Canada, Australia, New Zealand, Japan, and Switzerland expressed their anxiety about Hong Kong because the

---

10. Some liberal activists and a very few academics even called for Hong Kong's civil society groups to form a "global civil society," even after the Occupy Central movement and before the anti-extradition movement—a move showing their ignorance of China's deep-rooted anti-foreignism.
11. "Washington Reveals Its True Color in Anchorage," *China Daily*, March 19, 2021, accessed March 24, 2021, https://www.chinadailyhk.com/article/a/160975.
12. "How It Happened: Transcript of the US-China Opening Remarks in Alaska," *Nikkei Asia*, March 19, 2021, accessed March 24, 2021, https://asia.nikkei.com/Politics/International-relations/US-China-tensions/How-it-happened-Transcript-of-the-US-China-opening-remarks-in-Alaska.
13. Sonny Lo, "Shenzhen as a New Economic Locomotive: Implications for Macau and Hong Kong," *Macau Business*, October 17, 2020, accessed March 24, 2021, https://www.macaubusiness.com/opinion-shenzhen-as-a-new-economic-locomotive-implications-for-macau-and-hong-kong/.
14. "中國硬推香港國安法 歐美27國反對 中國拉52國反擊" ["China pushes for the national security law for Hong Kong: 27 European and American countries oppose, but China mobilizes 52 countries to counterattack"], Radio Free Asia, July 1, 2020, accessed March 24, 2021, https://www.rfi.fr/tw/.

national security law was perceived as "undermining" Hong Kong's autonomy and the "one country, two systems." The PRC has displayed assertive nationalism, anti-foreignism, and Chinese exceptionalism in its handling of Hong Kong's political development.

The PRC's opposition to the political internationalization of Hong Kong does not mean that it rejects Hong Kong as an international financial center. Conversely, PRC authorities have been separating politics from economics, meaning that they believe the new electoral system designed by the NPC in March 2021 would make Hong Kong society recover from turbulence and let it retain its status as the financial center. Such a separation of politics from economics stems from the Marxist-Leninist view of the relationships between the superstructure and economic base, namely changing the political institutions at the superstructure level is and will be conductive to both the consolidation of the economic base and the development of productive forces in the HKSAR. If economic internationalization is defined as a process of accelerating the productive forces of both Hong Kong and mainland China, it is naturally encouraged and supported by the central authorities in Beijing. The economic internationalization of Hong Kong is politically acceptable to PRC authorities because they see the HKSAR as a window for China to speed up its economic modernization and to expand its Belt and Road Initiatives further. Hong Kong remains a renminbi offshore center for the PRC, which regards the capitalistic city as an international financial and monetary center characterized by its common law system. During President Xi Jinping's visit to Hong Kong on July 1, 2022, he emphasized Hong Kong as a place where the common law system persists. Clearly, the HKSAR remains a crucial economic window with its unique common law system for the PRC to enhance its global outreach and consolidate its economic rise.

An article published in *China Daily* as early as August 2019 amid the anti-extradition protests demonstrated the PRC's assertive nationalism on Hong Kong.[15] It argued that the struggle over Hong Kong's political reform was a "power struggle" between pro-democracy and pro-Western activists on the one hand and pro-government forces and China on the other, that the PRC's rapid rise challenged and hurt the superiority complexes of some Hong Kong people, that the failure of national education in Hong Kong brought about the anti-China sentiment of the young people, that "Western-style democracy was by no means a wise choice" for Hong Kong's political development, that the local opposition's forceful activities would necessitate the center's intervention, and that the

---

15. "看明白香港的现状，必须先搞懂这6个问题" ["Understanding Hong Kong's current situation, one has to clarify six questions"], 中国日报网 [*China Daily*], August 21, 2019, accessed March 24, 2021, https://cn.chinadaily.com.cn/a/201908/21/WS5d6e216da31099ab995ddb94.html.

HKSAR would not become "a city of creating turbulence and chaos."[16] Judging from all the responses of Beijing from the enactment of the national security law in June 2020 to the fundamental revamp of Hong Kong's electoral system in March 2021, all the six points mentioned in the article above were a testimony to the PRC's nationalistic perceptions of Hong Kong's localist populism.

To exercise its comprehensive jurisdiction, the PRC was determined to groom and consolidate the nationalistic or "patriotic populists" in the HKSAR by revamping the local electoral system. By reinstituting the Electoral Committee, which is comparable to the electoral college introduced by the British to Hong Kong's LegCo in the mid-1980s, "patriotic" elites would enjoy a privileged political position. Their political preponderance would be accompanied by the rapid growth of "patriotic" populist groups, which are composed of pro-Beijing clan groups, business associations, labor unions, women organizations, and district united front forces.[17] All of these patriotic groups advertised on the two pro-Beijing mouthpieces, *Ta Kung Pao* and *Wen Wei Po*, about 10 days before and after the SCNPC decision on the electoral system on March 11, 2021.[18] If populist authoritarianism is an enduring characteristic of Chinese politics, as Tang Wenfang has noted, then the HKSAR polity is increasingly punctuated by this mainland feature. However, the patriotic populists have class differences. Ng Chau-pei of the FTU openly criticized the business sector for exerting "landed hegemony" on Hong Kong, and he argued that such a situation of land developers accumulating land should be changed.[19] In response, a LegCo member representing the real estate sector, Abraham Shek Lai-him, said that it was like Ng was living in the 1960s, implying that the latter's remarks were reminiscent of the Maoists.[20] While Ng and his pro-Beijing labor activists are the left-wing "patriotic" populists, Shek and other businesspeople in the LegCo can be seen as the pro-Beijing conservative business elites.[21] As such, the division among the "patriotic" elites can be discerned in the LegCo.

The PRC has ignored not only foreign criticisms of its policy toward the HKSAR but also the sanctions against its officials after the enactment of the national security law. The UK criticized the PRC government for "violating" the Sino-British Joint Declaration four times: firstly, shortly after the disappearance

---

16. "Understanding Hong Kong's Current Situation, One Has to Clarify Six Questions."
17. For details, see Lo, Hung, and Loo, *China's New United Front Work in Hong Kong*.
18. See the extensive advertisements in these two newspapers from March 1 to 20, 2021.
19. "吳秋北4000字批「地產霸權」 發起「新工運」促懲罰囤地發展商" ["Ng Chau-pei 4,000 words criticizes 'land hegemony' and launches 'new labor movement' to advocate penalizing those land developers accumulating land"], hk01.com, March 24, 2021, accessed March 27, 2021, https://www.hk01.com/.
20. *Ming Pao*, March 26, 2021.
21. For left-wing populists, see Oscar Garcia Agustin, *Left-Wing Populism: The Politics of the People* (Bingley: Emerald, 2020).

of the book publishers in the Causeway Bay Bookstore in early 2016; secondly, for the enactment of the national security law for Hong Kong in June 2020; thirdly, the NPC decision to disqualify legislators in November 2020; and fourthly, the NPC decision to change the electoral system of Hong Kong.[22] However, the PRC government criticized the UK government for intervening in its domestic affairs in Hong Kong. In fact, PRC officials have rarely mentioned the Sino-British Joint Declaration over Hong Kong since the early 2000s, believing that Hong Kong matters belong to China's internal matters. As such, while foreign countries like the UK and the US have emphasized the importance of China sticking to the content of the Sino-British Joint Declaration and the rules-based international order, respectively, PRC authorities have seen these emphases as an outright interference with its internal political development. During the meeting between State Councilor Yang Jiechi and US Secretary of State Anthony Blinken in Alaska in March 2021, the former criticized the "rules-based international order" as being decided by a few countries in the world, implicitly referring to the US.[23] The tensions between the political internationalization of Hong Kong and the mainlandization of the HKSAR became prominent.

Hong Kong can be regarded as a battleground between the Chinese political civilization and Western civilization and between Chinese and Western political cultures. As Samuel Huntington said, the Sinic civilization, which is characterized by hierarchy, state authority, and mass obedience, would be in conflict with the Western civilization, which cherishes pluralism, civil liberties, and individual rights.[24] The Sinic civilization remains deep-rooted in the psyche of PRC leaders and officials, who firmly believe that the rights of the people of Hong Kong, including their civil liberties and voting rights, have been conferred upon them by the central state on the mainland. This conception fits into what Andrew

---

22. Chris Buckley, "Britain Accuses China of Violating Treaty in Hong Kong's Bookseller's Case," *New York Times*, February 13, 2016, accessed March 24, 2021, https://www.nytimes.com/2016/02/13/world/asia/britain-china-hong-kong-bookseller.html. "Foreign Secretary Declares Break of Sino-British Joint Declaration," UK government's press release, November 12, 2020, accessed March 24, 2021, https://www.gov.uk/government/news/foreign-secretary-declares-breach-of-sino-british-joint-declaration. See also "China Non-Compliant with Joint Declaration, Says UK," RTHK News, March 13, 2021, accessed March 24, 2021, https://news.rthk.hk/rthk/en/component/k2/1580434-20210313.htm.
23. Sonny Lo, "China's Pragmatism and Political Posturing to the US and Taiwan in the Era of Civilizational Clashes," Macau Business, March 27, 2021, accessed March 27, 2021, https://www.macaubusiness.com/opinion-chinas-pragmatism-and-political-posturing-to-us-and-taiwan-in-the-era-of-civilizational-clashes/.
24. Samuel P. Huntington, *The Clash of Civilizations and the Remaking of the World Order* (New York: Penguin, 1996). For an application of Huntington's argument to Hong Kong, see Sonny Shiu-hing Lo, *Governing Hong Kong: Legitimacy, Communication and Political Decay* (New York: Nova Science, 2001). See also Sonny Lo, "Hong Kong: A Battleground in a Clash of Political Civilisations," Asialink, July 29, 2020, accessed March 24, 2021, https://asialink.unimelb.edu.au/insights/hong-kong-a-battleground-in-a-clash-of-political-civilisations.

Nathan has long described as a "Chinese democracy" that treasures the values of paternalism, collectivism, and state dominance in social, economic, and political life. Governed by the British for 155 years from the Treaty of Nanking in 1842 to the retrocession in 1997, some Hong Kong people have been imbued with the strong values of pluralism and civil liberties as enjoyed by citizens in Western democratic states. As such, the clash of political cultures between PRC authorities and some pro-democracy and pro-Western Hongkongers has been fully demonstrated since the mass protests on July 1, 2003, and especially after the promulgation of the national security law in late June 2020.

From the Western perspective, the developments of Hong Kong since mid-2020 have undermined the "one country, two systems," ignored the Sino-British Joint Declaration, and curbed the autonomy and social freedom of the HKSAR—a view that has been constantly rejected by the PRC authorities. The clashes of political values and civilizations between the Western democratic countries and the PRC can be easily discerned in their divergent opinions and disputes over the HKSAR. Perceiving the national security law as a measure that "violated" the Sino-British Joint Declaration and as a tool to "suppress" the pro-democracy Hongkongers, the UK government in early 2021 allowed the holders of British National Overseas (BNO) passports to apply for British citizenship; nevertheless, the BNO passport holders were immediately not recognized by the PRC government—a contentious matter illustrating the UK's decision to provide a rescue route for some Hong Kong people and China's counter-reaction to such a measure.[25]

The clashes between the Chinese political civilization and Western civilization could be seen in the vote result of the United Nations Human Rights Council on Xinjiang in early October 2022. A total of nineteen countries voted down the motion on the alleged "abuses" against Uigur Muslims in China's Xinjiang province, while seventeen voted in favor of it and eleven abstained.[26] The vote could be seen as a victory for the PRC, which received support from Bolivia, Cameroon, Ivory Coast, Cuba, Eritrea, Gabon, Indonesia, Kazakhstan, Mauritania, Namibia, Nepal, Pakistan, Qatar, Senegal, Sudan, United Arab Emirates, Uzbekistan, and Venezuela. Countries that voted for the motion included the Czech Republic, Finland, France, Germany, Honduras, Japan, Lithuania, Luxembourg, Marshall Islands, Montenegro, Netherlands, Paraguay, South Korea, Somalia, the UK, and the US. The eleven countries that abstained were Argentina, Armenia, Benin,

---

25. Yew Lun Tian and William James, "UK offers Hong Kong residents route to citizenship, angering China," Reuters, January 30, 2021.
26. Latika Bourke, "China Wins Vote to Stop UN Human Rights Council from Debating Xinjiang Abuses," *Sydney Morning Herald*, October 7, 2022, accessed October 10, 2022, https://www.smh.com.au/world/europe/china-wins-key-vote-in-un-human-rights-council-to-prevent-debate-on-xinjiang-20221007-p5bnv6.html.

Brazil, Gambia, India, Libya, Malawi, Malaysia, Mexico, and Ukraine. The divided nature of the council members showed that human rights remain a controversial issue in the world, for its universal applicability has been challenged by state leaders who contend that different countries have varying political cultures, values, practices, and traditions.

The HKSAR government sent a delegation led by Erick Tsang, the former secretary for constitutional and mainland affairs, to the United Nations Human Rights Committee meeting in July 2022, emphasizing its full commitment to the protection of human rights.[27] Tsang concluded that human rights in the HKSAR "are guaranteed constitutionally by both the constitution of the PRC and the Basic Law of the HKSAR, and are underpinned by the rule of law and an independent judiciary."[28] Moreover, the "provisions of the International Covenant on Civil and Political Rights (ICCPR) as applied to the HKSAR have already been incorporated into local law by the Hong Kong Bill of Rights Ordinance."[29] Both the central government in Beijing and the HKSAR government "are determined to make 'one country, two systems' a continued success."[30] As such, the official position of Beijing and the HKSAR government is that human rights are fully protected in the HKSAR. These rights include, for instance, press freedom, freedoms of assembly and procession, freedom of association, and academic freedom. The national security law "does not undermine judicial independence or right to a fair hearing under Article 14 of the ICCPR."[31] Finally, the HKSAR government asserted that the decision of the SCNPC to change the electoral system in March 2021 "did not revise the ultimate aim of attaining universal suffrage in relation to Articles 45 and 68 of the Basic Law."[32]

The December 2021 LegCo Elections

The arrangements of the December 2021 LegCo elections and the May 2022 chief executive elections were politically significant to Beijing and the HKSAR government. The two elections would constitute a testimony to the smooth operation and "success" of "one country, two systems." In the words of President Xi Jinping on July 1, 2022, the HKSAR changed from chaos to governance from

---

27. "HKSAR Government Committed to Protecting Human Rights," Press Release, July 12, 2022, accessed October 10, 2022, https://www.info.gov.hk/gia/general/202207/12/P2022071200739.htm.
28. "HKSAR Government Committed to Protecting Human Rights."
29. "HKSAR Government Committed to Protecting Human Rights."
30. "HKSAR Government Committed to Protecting Human Rights."
31. "HKSAR Government Committed to Protecting Human Rights."
32. "HKSAR Government Committed to Protecting Human Rights."

2019 to 2021 and from governance to greater prosperity from 2022 onward.[33] In retrospect, the governance of the HKSAR was stabilized and consolidated by the LegCo elections in December 2021 and the chief executive election in May 2022.

The LegCo election results on December 20 were hailed by the pro-Beijing media as a "new chapter" in Hong Kong's democracy but regarded by moderate media as a "complete failure" of the non-establishment force, which merely acquired one out of ninety elected seats.[34] The voter turnout rate dropped significantly from 58.28 percent in 2016 to 30.2 percent in 2021—a decrease of 841,603 voters. Quite likely, many of the 841,603 voters did not cast their ballots because of a multiplicity of factors, including their dissatisfaction with the political transformations in the HKSAR, political apathy, and their loss of interest in the new electoral system.

Table 3.2: Number of Voters and Voter Turnout in Legislative Council Elections, 2008–2021

Year	Number of Registered Voters	Number of Voters	Turnout Rate (%)
2008	3,372,007	1,524,249	45.20
2012	3,466,201	1,838,722	53.05
2016	3,779,085	2,202,283	58.28
2021	4,472,843	1,350,680	30.20

Source: "Voter Turnout Rate," accessed October 11, 2022, https://www.elections.gov.hk/legco2021/eng/turnout.html.

Table 3.3 shows the results of the LegCo's direct elections in which the pro-Beijing DAB grasped ten seats, the FTU captured three seats, and the New People's Party (NPP) got two seats. Three elected FTU candidates—Tang Ka Piu, Ng Chau Pei, and Chan Wing Yan—acquired some 60,000 votes each, and they appeared to get a lot of "iron votes" from their core supporters. However, the DAB and FTU also competed with the NPP in the geographical constituency of Hong Kong Island East, where Edward Leung Hei from DAB and Ng Chau Pei from the FTU defeated Liu Ting Shing from the NPP. The democrats performed poorly in direct elections; none of the two Path of Democracy (PoD) candidates

---

33. Evelyn Cheng, "China's Xi Says Hong Kong Is Moving from 'Chaos to Governance,'" CNBC, July 1, 2022, accessed October 10, 2022, https://www.cnbc.com/2022/07/01/china-xi-says-hong-kong-is-moving-from-chaos-to-governance.html.
34. "New Electoral System Successfully Implemented, Hong Kong's Democracy Opened New Chapter," *Ta Kung Pao*, December 21, 2021, p. A1. Contrast it with "Tik Chi-yuen 1:89: Non-establishment Utterly Failed in Direct Elections," *Ming Pao*, December 21, 2021, A1.

Table 3.3: Results of the Legislative Council's Direct Elections in December 2021

Constituency	Candidate	Votes	Affiliation	Result
Hong Kong Island East	Edward Leung Hei	20,799	DAB	Elected
	Liu Ting Shing	23,171	NPP	Lost
	Ng Chau Pei	64,509	FTU	Elected
	Poon Cheuk Hung	14,435	Independent	Lost
Hong Kong Island West	Regina Ip	65,694	NPP	Elected
	Chan Hok Fung	36,628	DAB	Elected
	Fong Lung Fei	8,058	Independent	Lost
Kowloon East	Tang Ka Piu	65,036	FTU	Elected
	Ngan Man Yu	64,275	DAB	Elected
	Chan Chun Hung	2,999	PoD	Lost
	Wu Kin Wah	3,090	Independent	Lost
	Li Ka Yan	12,049	Independent	Lost
Kowloon West	Leung Man Kwong	36,840	WKNS	Elected
	Frederick Fung	15,961	Democrat	Lost
	Vincent Cheng	64,353	DAB	Elected
Kowloon Central	Starry Lee	95,976	DAB	Elected
	Yang Wing Kit	35,702	Independent	Elected
	Tam Heung Man	8,028	Democrat	Lost
New Territories South	Choi Ming Hei	6,718	Democrat	Lost
	Li Sai Wing	82,595	DAB/NTFA	Elected
	Lam So Wai	38,214	PPower	Elected
New Territories North	Zhang Xinyu	28,986	HKND	Elected
	Lau Kwok Fun	70,584	DAB	Elected
	Shum Ho Kit	17,839	Independent	Lost
	Judy Tzeng	3,498	Independent	Lost
New Territories North West	Holden Chow	93,195	DAB	Elected
	Michael Tien	40,009	Roundtable	Elected
	Wong Chun Long	4,006	Third Side	Lost
New Territories South West	Lau Cheuk Yu	12,828	Democrat	Lost
	Chan Han Pan	83,303	DAB	Elected
	Chan Wing Yan	62,690	FTU	Elected

Sources: "Election Results," accessed October 11, 2022, https://www.elections.gov.hk/legco2021/eng/rs_gc.html. See also *Oriental Daily*, December 21, 2021, p. A6.

Note: NPP = New People's Party; PoD = Path of Democracy; WKNS = West Kowloon New Synergy; DAB = Democratic Alliance for Betterment and Progress of Hong Kong; NTFA = New Territories Federation of Associations; PPower = Professional Power; HKND = Hong Kong New Direction.

got elected, while both Frederick Fung (15,961 votes) and Lau Cheuk Yu (12,828 votes) were defeated. The democrats showed loose organization in which Wong Sing Chi competed with Allan Wong in New Territories Northeast. Most of the supporters of democrats simply did not go to the polls on election day, leading to the phenomenon that none of the democrats were directly elected. Michael Tien from Roundtable was directly elected, for his image as a relatively independent pro-establishment politician attracted the support of many voters. The two surprising results included Zhang Xinyu from the Hong Kong New Direction (HKND), who got support from even some Hong Kong people who lived in Shenzhen and who returned to the HKSAR to vote for him, and Lam So Wai, who grasped 38,214 votes and who was from the Professional Power.[35] Overall, unlike the pre-2021 LegCo elections where the democrats performed strongly, the 2021 LegCo direct elections witnessed the easy victory of the pro-Beijing forces.

Table 3.4 shows that forty of the fifty-one candidates running in the LegCo elections through the Election Committee were elected. Those candidates with strong political and pro-Beijing backgrounds were easily elected, such as Leung Mei Fun, who was a member of the Basic Law Committee (BLC) and a core member of the Business Professionals Alliance (BPA). Five DAB heavyweights—Cheung Kwok Kwan, Elizabeth Quat, Chen Chung Nin, Nixie Lam, and Kwok Ling Lai—were elected, but not the young Chan Hoi Wing. Three members of the FTU—Alice Mak, Wong Kwok, and Luk Chung Hung—were elected, but not bus captain Choy Wing Keung. Many CPPCC members were also elected, including Tang Fei from the Federation of Education Workers (FEW), Lai Tung Kwok from the NPP, Ng Kit Chong from Youth Synergy, Peter Koon from the Anglican Church, and So Cheung Wing from the Hong Kong Island Federation of Association. The NPP got three members elected, namely Eunice Yung, Judy Chan, and Lai Tung Kwok—an indication that the pro-Beijing party led by Regina Ip secured the support of the members of the Election Committee. Apart from three FTU members being elected, the Federation of Hong Kong and Kowloon Labor Unions got Lam Chun Sing elected to the LegCo. Incumbent LegCo candidates, notably Paul Tse and Junius Ho, were comfortably elected. However, the pro-business Liberal Party only had one member, namely Lee Chun Keung, elected—its influence was weaker than the BPA, which had not only Priscilla Leung Mei Fun but also Luk Hon Man elected.

Some surprising results were seen. Mainland-born Sun Dong was elected, although he was a political unknown. Later, after the chief executive election

---

35. On election day, 18,000 registered Hong Kong voters who lived in Shenzhen returned to the HKSAR to vote at the voting stations near the border between Hong Kong and mainland China. See *Ming Pao*, December 8, 2021, A2.

Table 3.4: Results of the Election Committee in Legislative Council Elections, 2021

Candidate	Affiliation	Votes	Result
Leung Mei Fun	BPF/BLC member	1,348	Elected
Cheung Kwok Kwan	DAB/ExCo member	1,342	Elected
Tang Fei	FEW/CPPCC	1,339	Elected
Maggie Chan	NPC member	1,331	Elected
Alice Mak	FTU	1,326	Elected
Elizabeth Quat	DAB	1,322	Elected
Eunice Yung Hoi Yan	NPP	1,313	Elected
Simon Lee Hoey	China Resources	1,308	Elected
Stephen Wong	BHKF	1,305	Elected
Chen Chung Nin	DAB/CPPCC	1,297	Elected
Chan Hoi Yan	Former political assistant	1,292	Elected
Kan Wai Mun	Women's Federation	1,291	Elected
Judy Chan Ka Pui	NPP	1,284	Elected
Paul Tse Wai Chun	Incumbent LegCo member	1,283	Elected
Junius Ho	Incumbent LegCo member	1,263	Elected
Tan Yueheng	Bank of Communication	1,245	Elected
Ng Kit Chong	Youth Synergy/CPPCC	1,239	Elected
Chan Siu Hung	CLP Holdings Limited	1,239	Elected
Lai Tung Kwok	NPP/CPPCC	1,237	Elected
Ma Fung Kwok	New Century Forum	1,234	Elected
Lau Chi Pang	Lingnan University	1,214	Elected
Chan Pui Leung	Insurance Federation	1,205	Elected
Wong Kwok	FTU	1,192	Elected
Chan Yuet Ming	Rural Committee	1,187	Elected
Nixie Lam Lam	DAB	1,181	Elected
Luk Chung Hung	FTU	1,178	Elected
Leung Yuk Wai	Youth Federation	1,160	Elected
Lam Shun Chiu	NPC member	1,157	Elected
Wendy Hong Wen	New World Development	1,142	Elected
Sun Dong	City University	1,124	Elected
Kwok Ling Lai	DAB	1,122	Elected
Peter Koon Ho Ming	Anglican Church/CPPCC	1,102	Elected

(continued on p. 201)

Table 3.4 (continued)

Candidate	Affiliation	Votes	Result
Chow Man Kong	HKMSA	1,060	Elected
Lee Chun Keung	Liberal Party	1,060	Elected
Luk Hon Man	BPF	1,059	Elected
Doreen Kong Yuk Foon	Law Society	1,032	Elected
Lam Siu Lo	Former AAB chair	1,026	Elected
So Cheung Wing	HKIFA/CPPCC	1,013	Elected
Lam Chun Sing	FLU	1,002	Elected
Lam Chi Yuen	Accountancy sector Love Alliance	970	Elected
Ng Wang Wai	HKUST	958	Defeated
Gary Wong	GAW Capital Partners	956	Defeated
Allan Zeman	Lan Kwai Fong Group	955	Defeated
Chan Hoi Wing	DAB/Youth Association	941	Defeated
Tseng Chin I	Phoenix TV host	919	Defeated
Sun Wei Yung	Businessman	891	Defeated
Tu Hai Ming	CPPCC/COFA	834	Defeated
Choy Wing Keung	FTU/Bus Captain	818	Defeated
Fung Wai Kwong	Former Information Coordinator of the HKSAR Government	708	Defeated
Mike Rowse	Former Director-General of InvestHK	454	Defeated
Vincent Diu Sing Hung	Electrician	342	Defeated

Sources: "Election Results," accessed October 11, 2022, https://www.elections.gov.hk/legco2021/eng/rs_ecc.html. See also *Ming Pao*, December 21, 2021, p. A7.

Note: BLC = Basic Law Committee; BHKF = Better Hong Kong Foundation; HKMSA = Hong Kong and Macau Study Association; AAB = Antiquities Advisory Board; HKIFA = Hong Kong Island Federation of Associations; HKUST = Hong Kong University of Science and Technology; COFA = Chinese Overseas Friendship Association.

in May 2022, Sun was appointed to be the secretary for innovation, technology, and industry. Although there were expectations from some moderate democrats that Mike Rowse might have a chance of being elected, he got the least number of votes from the Election Committee members. Similarly, Allan Zeman failed to be elected. The defeat of Rowse and Zeman appeared to indicate that their support base in the Election Committee was relatively weak, although they got 454 and 955 votes, respectively. Rumors were rife that some pro-Beijing elites in the Election Committee did not vote for the relatively independent candidates. Subsequently, electrician Vincent Diu and bus captain Choy were defeated, although HKMAO Director Xia Baolong referred to the LegCo elections as having "glittering colors" and implied that candidates came from different class backgrounds and ethnic groups.[36]

Table 3.5 shows the results of the LegCo's functional constituency elections. The BPA became the largest pro-business group, capturing five seats, including the elected Kenneth Lau, Lo Wai Kwok, Jeffrey Lam, Andrew Leung, and Ng Wing Ka. The LP's performance was mediocre, with only two of its leaders, Peter Shiu Ka Fai and Tommy Cheung, elected to the LegCo. The party later witnessed a withdrawal of the elderly leaders, such as James Tien, Selina Chow, and Miriam Lau, from their honorary chair positions after they learnt that the central committee planned to cancel the honorary titles without consultation.[37] Tommy Cheung defended the LP's move to cancel the honorary titles for the sake of the party's development. Tien, Chow, and Lau co-founded the LP in 1993 together with the late Allen Lee Peng-fei and Stephen Cheong Kam-chuen. The decline of the LP was obvious as the BPA has become the most influential business party in the LegCo's functional constituencies. In the educational constituency, with the dissolution of the pro-democracy Professional Teachers Union in August 2021, as it had been regarded as being involved excessively in the socio-political movements of the HKSAR, the pro-Beijing Federation of Workers (FEW) rose up and filled the political vacuum; the victory of Chu Kwong Keung was a sign of this political metamorphosis. The pro-Beijing FTU grasped two seats in the labor constituency, together with the coopted FLU, especially after the dissolution of the pro-democracy Confederation of Trade Unions (CTU) in October 2021.[38] Another pro-Beijing party, the DAB, got three members elected, includ-

---

36. "Hong Kong People Are about to Enjoy Real Democracy: Xia Baolong," RTHK, December 6, 2021, accessed October 11, 2022, https://news.rthk.hk/rthk/en/component/k2/1623001-20211206.htm.
37. James Lee, "Exits Hammer Liberal Party," Hong Kong Standard, August 11, 2022, accessed October 12, 2022, https://www.thestandard.com.hk/section-news/section/11/244533/Exits-hammer-Liberal-Party.
38. The CTU was set up in 1990 and emerged from the Christian Industrial Committee, which was very active in the 1970s and 1980s. With the imprisonment of CTU leader Lee Cheuk-yan, who was involved in protests, and with the departure of its Chief Executive Mung Siu Tat from Hong Kong, members of the CTU voted for the union's disbandment in October 2021. See Pak Yiu, "Hong

Table 3.5: Results of the Legislative Council's Functional Constituency Elections, 2021

Sector	Candidate	Affiliation	Votes	Result
Heung Yee Kuk	Kenneth Lau	BPF	119	Elected
	Mok Kam Kwai	BPF	35	Lost
Agriculture and fisheries	Steven Ho	DAB	117	Elected
	Yeung Sheung Chun		53	Lost
Insurance	Chen Zhaonan		24	Lost
	Chan Kin Por		65	Elected
Transport	Alan Chan		56	Lost
	Frankie Yik		147	Elected
Education	Jessica Man		2,054	Lost
	James Lam		4,544	Lost
	Ting Kin Wa		2,533	Lost
	Lam Wing Sze		3,280	Lost
	Chu Kwok Keung	FEW	10,641	Elected
Legal	Lam Sun Keung		1,637	Elected
	Chen Xiaofeng		674	Lost
Accountancy	Wong Wang Tai		1,981	Lost
	Yung Kin		1,065	Lost
	Man See Yee		1,734	Lost
	Edmund Wong	DAB	3,175	Elected
Medical and health services	Chan Chi Chung		2,585	Lost
	Chan Wing Kwong	DAB	3,446	Lost
	Ho Sung Hon		1,631	Lost
	Scarlett Pong		2,719	Lost
	David Lam		5,511	Elected
Engineering	Wong Wai Shun		1,243	Lost
	Lo Wai Kwok	BPF	3,849	Elected
Architectural, surveying, planning, and landscaping	Tony Tse		2,266	Elected
	Chan Chak Bun		1,063	Lost
Labor	Leung Tze Wing	FTU	373	Elected
	Chau Siu Chung	FLU	371	Elected
	Lee Kwong Yu		116	Lost
	Kwok Wai Keung	FTU	398	Elected
Social welfare	Chu Lai Ling	DAB	872	Lost
	Yip Cham Kai		196	Lost
	Tik Chi Yuen	Third Side	1,400	Elected
Real estate and construction	Howard Chao		138	Lost
	Loong Hon Biu		242	Elected

(continued on p. 204)

Table 3.5 (continued)

Sector	Candidate	Affiliation	Votes	Result
Tourism	Ma Yat Chiu		13	Lost
	You Pak Leung		160	Elected
Commercial (First)	Yew Yat Ming		101	Lost
	Jeffrey Lam	BPF	628	Elected
Commercial (Second)	Martin Liao		176	Elected
	Yip Wing Shing		71	Lost
Commercial (Third)	Yim Kong		174	Elected
	Yau Wai Kong		110	Lost
Industrial (First)	Andrew Leung	BPF	235	Elected
	Leung Yat Cheong		67	Lost
Industrial (Second)	Ng Wing Ka	BPF	306	Elected
	Lo Ching Kong		65	Lost
Finance	Chan Chun Ying		51	Elected
	Chan Chi Fai		17	Lost
Financial services	Robert Lee		314	Elected
	Christopher Cheung		169	Lost
Sports, performing arts, culture, publishing	William So		29	Lost
	Kenneth Fok		195	Elected
Import and export	Michael Li		48	Lost
	Kennedy Wong		108	Elected
Textiles and garments	Sunny Tan		172	Elected
	Chung Kwok Pan	Liberal Party	82	Lost
Wholesale and retail	Lam Chi Wing		112	Lost
	Shiu Ka Fai	Liberal Party	1,116	Elected
Technology and innovation	Wu Chili		12	Lost
	Chiu Duncan		59	Elected
Catering	Rayman Chui		27	Lost
	Tommy Cheung	Liberal Party	101	Elected
Members of NPC/CPPCC	Chan Yung	DAB/NTFA	432	Elected
	Tse Hiu Hung		177	Lost

Sources: "Election Results," accessed date: October 12, 2022, https://www.elections.gov.hk/legco2021/eng/rs_fc.html. See also *Oriental Daily*, December 21, 2021, p. A7; *Hong Kong Economic Times*, December 21, 2022, p. A18.

ing Steven Ho, Edmund Wong, and Chan Yung; nevertheless, Chan Wing Kwong and Chu Lai Ling were defeated. Chu's defeat was politically significant as she could not check the moderate democrat Tik Chi Yuen, who acquired 1,400 votes in the social welfare constituency. In the past, the functional constituencies of social welfare, education, law, and technology and innovation were grasped by the democrats. However, under the new elections in December 2021, only the social welfare constituency was captured by the only democrat, Tik Chi Yuen—the reversal of the political tide and fortunes was prominent.

Table 3.6 sums up the new political landscape of the LegCo after its elections in December 2021. The largest political party in the LegCo is now the DAB, followed by the FTU, BPA, NPP, and LP—all politically "patriotic." The FLU has already been coopted with two seats, while each of the other small groups, like Roundtable, West Kowloon Synergy, Professional Power, Hong Kong New Direction, and Third Side, has one seat. In terms of occupational sectors, the business sector occupies one-third of the LegCo seats, followed by the law, education, trade union, social welfare, construction/engineering, accountancy, and medical and health sectors. Most importantly, thirty-three out of ninety LegCo members are affiliated with the NPC (seven), the CPPCC at the national level (fourteen), and the CPPCC at the provincial and municipal levels (twelve) on the mainland.[39]

From the PRC perspective, the LegCo elections on December 20 were a tremendous success for Hong Kong's "one country, two systems" and its "democracy." The HKMAO announced that the elections were a testimony to the establishment of a "democratic system" suitable for the HKSAR, that they created a new framework for Hong Kong's "good governance," and that the "one country, two systems" could be promoted further with "profound repercussions."[40] The Liaison Office added that the elections were "a successful realization of the Hong Kong style of democracy" and that the principle of "patriots governing Hong Kong" was implemented.[41] According to Chief Executive Carrie Lam, the LegCo in the past envisaged the phenomena that the "anti-China" elements who stirred up troubles" entered the political system of the HKSAR through elections and that they created "chaos" in the legislature and later even attempted to dominate it and "usurp the governing power."[42] All these activities generated "risks to the

---

Kong Opposition Trade Union Group to Disband," Reuters, September 19, 2021, accessed October 12, 2022, https://www.reuters.com/world/china/hong-kong-opposition-trade-union-group-disband-2021-09-19/. See also "CTU Latest Hong Kong Group to Disband," RTHK, October 3, 2021, accessed October 12, 2022, https://news.rthk.hk/rthk/en/component/k2/1613314-20211003.htm.

39. *Ming Pao*, December 21, 2021, A3.
40. "New Democracy Elects Our New Future," a special supplement of *Wen Wei Po*, December 21, 2021, 2.
41. "New Democracy Elects Our New Future," 2.
42. "New Democracy Elects Our New Future," 5.

Table 3.6: New Political Profile of the Legislative Council after the 2021 Elections

Political Groups/Parties	Seats	Occupation Sector	Seats
DAB	19	Business	30
FTU	8	Law	13
BPF	7	Education	9
NPP	5	Unionists	7
LP	4	Social welfare employees	5
FLU	2	Construction/engineering	4
Roundtable	1	Accountancy	3
West Kowloon Synergy	1	Medical and health	2
Professional Power	1	Religion	1
Hong Kong New Direction	1	Others	16
Third Side	1		
Total	90	Total	90

Source: *Ming Pao*, December 21, 2021, p. A3.

nation."[43] The 2021 LegCo elections rectified the chaos in the past and paved the way for "good governance" in the HKSAR.[44]

The Chief Executive Elections in May 2022: Political Implications for the HKSAR

On May 8, 2022, John Lee Ka-chiu, the secretary for security from 2017 until his announcement to participate in the 2022 chief executive election on April 6, 2022, was elected the chief executive of the HKSAR by grasping 1,416 out of 1,428 votes in the Election Committee.[45] On April 4, 2022, Chief Executive Carrie Lam announced that she would not run in the election. Two days later, once John Lee revealed his decision to run, the State Council approved his resignation from the position of chief secretary for administration on April 7—a clear signal that Beijing as the central government strongly supported him. On April 9, John Lee held his press conference on his electoral participation. Later, it was reported that PRC officials told some members of the Election Committee that John Lee would be the only candidate in this chief executive election, indicating that Beijing did not want to see any other contenders. On April 13, John Lee got

---

43. "New Democracy Elects Our New Future," 5.
44. "New Democracy Elects Our New Future," 5.
45. "John Lee Wins Chief Executive Election," Hong Kong Standard, May 8, 2022, accessed October 12, 2022, https://www.news.gov.hk/eng/2022/05/20220508/20220508_113345_467.html.

786 nominations from the 1,452 members of the Election Committee, meaning that he would surely become the next chief executive of the HKSAR.

John Lee's campaign platform was deliberately shaped in such a way as to focus on Beijing's concern about the consolidation of governance and the improvement of livelihood issues in the HKSAR.[46] He vowed to enhance the governing capability of the HKSAR by (1) improving executive-legislative relations, (2) exploring the reorganization of governmental secretaries, (3) strengthening the leadership role of senior officials, (4) formulating key performance indicators for government departments, (5) reviewing administrative regulations and improving efficiency, (6) strengthening the crisis management ability through a mobilization mechanism led by high-ranking officials, (7) establishing a civil service culture loyal to the PRC constitution and the Basic Law, (8) implementing and legislating on Article 23 of the Basic Law, (9) establishing multiple channels of connections with district organizations and volunteer groups, (10) maintaining the cohesiveness of governing talents who are "loving China and Hong Kong," and (11) embracing talents to elevate the policy research standards and the vitality of think tanks.

Lee's easy electoral victory had tremendous implications for the new politics of Hong Kong. First and foremost, Beijing strongly supported him because he was seen as a local official loyal to the central government's policy directives, especially the extradition bill that he promoted in 2019. Lee had also played a crucial role in the banning of the Hong Kong National Party in September 2018. Above all, Lee's strong record of serving as a security official as assistant police commissioner (2003–2011), undersecretary for security (2012–2017), and secretary for security (2017 to March 2021) fit the needs of Beijing in an era during which the securitization of the HKSAR is a must. In particular, the HKSAR was plunged into a crisis of governance and legitimacy by the anti-national education movement in 2012, the Occupy Central movement in September–December 2014, the Mong Kok riot in early 2016, and the anti–extradition bill movement in the latter half of 2019. As a Hong Kong official frequently interacting with the mainland security authorities, John Lee gained the political trust of the central government in Beijing. It was not surprising that some Hong Kong reports said he had been recommended by the Ministry of Public Security to the top leadership of the CCP for consideration to be the chief executive succeeding Carrie Lam.

Second, if John Lee performed well as a protector of the PRC's national security, he was seen by the mainland's conservative nationalists to be a like-minded

---

46. For his campaign platform, see John Lee, "Starting New Chapter for Hong Kong Together: Election Manifesto of Chief Executive Election 2022," accessed October 13, 2022, https://www.johnlee2022.hk/wp-content/uploads/2022/04/Election-manifesto.pdf.

member. As such, the dominant conservative nationalistic faction in Beijing did not want to witness any other contender competing with him. Rumors that were circulated by the Hong Kong media on the possible candidates, such as former Chief Executive C. Y. Leung and Financial Secretary Paul Chan, all turned out to be inaccurate. Paul Chan stated publicly on April 6 that he wished John Lee "smoothness in everything."[47] Similarly, when C. Y. Leung was elected as the vice chairman of the CPPCC in March 2017, his highly respectable position in the PRC's political system meant that it would be odd for him to "go down" and "return" to be the chief executive of the HKSAR again. As such, when C. Y. Leung was reportedly a senior convenor of the Election Committee that would select the chief executive, it was obvious that Beijing was eager to envisage political harmony and unity in the May election that would certainly bestow upon John Lee a high degree of legitimacy from both the central government and the "patriotic" elites.

Third, prior to John Lee's decision to participate in the chief executive election, the Hong Kong media kept circulating the "news" that Carrie Lam would run for election again—a report that turned out to be wrong for several reasons. The local media and especially Carrie Lam's staunch supporters took it for granted that she would undoubtedly run, but they ignored her occasional message in 2021 that whether she would continue to be in the political arena depended on her family's wishes. As early as 2019, there were reports saying that Lam toyed with the idea that she wanted to resign amid the fierce protests and opposition to the extradition bill.[48] The local media might not have noted that, during Carrie Lam's meeting with President Xi Jinping in December 2021, there was no handshaking gesture in the official photograph of the two leaders—a kind of body gesture that perhaps pointed to the fact that Lam might have already indicated her intention of discontinuing as the chief executive of the HKSAR.[49] Hence, once John Lee announced his decision to run in the election, the local media and some politicians were shocked. Some media commentators quickly pointed to Lee's lack of economic expertise, but they neglected the fact that Hong Kong's chief executives, such as Tung Chee-hwa, Donald Tsang, C. Y. Leung, and even Carrie Lam, did not really have specialized knowledge on how to deal

---

47. "Paul Chan Sends Best Wishes to John Lee Ka-chiu on His Chief Executive Election Endeavor," Hong Kong Standard, April 6, 2021, accessed October12, 2022, https://www.thestandard.com.hk/breaking-news/section/4/188900/Paul-Chan-sends-best-wishes-to-John-Lee-Ka-chiu-on-his-CE-election-endeavor.
48. James Pomfret and Greg Torode, "Exclusive: 'If I Have a Choice, The First Thing Is to Quit'—Hong Kong Leader Carrie Lam—Transcript," Reuters, September 3, 2019, accessed October 12, 2022, https://www.reuters.com/article/us-hongkong-protests-carrielam-transcrip-idUSKCN1VO0KK.
49. Sonny Lo, "An Analysis of John Lee's Participation in Hong Kong's Chief Executive Elections," Macau Business, April 9, 2022, accessed October 12, 2022, https://www.macaubusiness.com/opinion-an-analysis-of-john-lees-participation-in-hong-kongs-chief-executive-elections/.

with the local economy. Instead, all the previous chief executives delegated the economic task to the financial secretary.

Fourth, the chief executive election in May 2022 exhibited the hallmark of "democratic centralism" to a degree stronger than the previous elections.[50] In 1996, Tung Chee-hwa gained 320 votes out of 400 members of the Election Committee and became the first HKSAR chief executive, defeating former judge Yang Ti-liang (42 votes) and businessman Peter Woo (36 votes). The 2007 chief executive election was the most competitive in the political history of the HKSAR as two candidates—democrat Alan Leong and pro-establishment Donald Tsang—competed, and they created an atmosphere of political pluralism. On March 25, 2007, Tsang received 649 votes and defeated Leong, who got 123 votes. The 2012 chief executive election witnessed Leung Chun-ying grasping 777 votes and defeating former Financial Secretary Henry Tang (285 votes) and democrat Albert Ho (76 votes). The 2017 chief executive election, during which Carrie Lam was elected with 777 votes out of 1,163 votes and defeated both former Financial Secretary John Tsang (365 votes) and former judge Woo Kwok-hing (21 votes), showed a carefully orchestrated political game with heavy ingredients of mainland Chinese centralism.[51] The 2022 chief executive election showed a more centralist aspect in terms of disallowing other contenders to rival John Lee—a reflection of the CCP's foremost concern about the unquestionable legitimacy conferred on him. This kind of thrustful and centralist electoral dynamics was in conformity with the mainland's political development in which political power has been centralized by the top leadership in Beijing under Xi Jinping, who holds the "trinity" of positions as the state president, the CCP's general-secretary, and the chairman of the Central Military Commission (CMC). In short, the political development of Hong Kong as expressed in the 2022 chief executive election arguably reflected the parallel political development in the PRC, which turned from the previously "soft" authoritarian era to a much "harder" authoritarian one.

Fifth, in conformity with Beijing's expectation that the new political system in the HKSAR would strengthen its governance, Chief Executive-designate John Lee shortly after his electoral victory nominated a batch of principal officials and ExCo members to the central government for its approval. On June 19, 2022, the PRC's State Council approved the appointment of twenty-six principal officials, including the secretaries of fifteen bureaus and six secretaries and under-secretaries in three core positions: chief secretary for administration, secretary for justice, and financial secretary. Eric Chan, a former director of the Chief

---

50. Sonny Shiu-Hing Lo, "The Political Cultures of Hong Kong and Mainland China: Democratization, Patrimonialism and Pluralism in the 2007 Chief Executive Election," *Asia Pacific Journal of Public Administration* 29, no. 1 (January 2014): 101–128.
51. Sonny Shiu-Hing Lo, "Factionalism and Chinese-Style Democracy: The 2017 Chief Executive Election," *Asia Pacific Journal of Public Administration* 39, no. 2 (2017): 100–119.

Executive Office, was appointed as the chief secretary, and his undersecretary for administration was the former permanent secretary for innovation and technology, Cheuk Wing-hing. The secretary for justice is Paul Lam Ting-kwok, a former chairman of the Bar Association, and his undersecretary is Horace Cheung Kwok-kwan, a former DAB vice chairman. Cheung withdrew from the DAB after his appointment had been approved by the State Council. Financial Secretary Paul Chan remains in the same post, and his undersecretary is Wong Wai-lun, a former secretary for development.

Fifteen policy secretaries were nominated by John Lee and approved by the central government.[52] They include the Secretary for Food and Health Lo Chung-mau (former chief executive of the University of Hong Kong–Shenzhen Hospital), Secretary for Innovation and Technology Professor Sun Dong, Secretary for Home and Youth Affairs Alice Mak Mei-kuen (former vice-chairperson of the Federation of Trade Unions), Secretary for Development Bernadette Linn Hon-ho (former permanent secretary of development), Secretary for Civil Service Ingrid Yeung Ho Poi-yan (former permanent secretary for the civil service), Secretary for Environment and Ecology Tse Chin-wan (former undersecretary for the environment bureau), Secretary for Education Choi Yuk-lin (former undersecretary for education), Secretary for Housing Winnie Ho Wing-yin (former director of architectural services), Secretary for Transport and Logistics Lam Sai-hung (former permanent secretary for development), Secretary for Commerce and Economic Development Algernon Yau Ying-wah (former chief executive officer of Greater Bay Airlines), Secretary for Labor and Welfare Chris Sun Yuk-han (former commissioner for labor), Secretary for Culture, Sports and Tourism Kevin Yeung Yun-hung (former secretary for education), Secretary for Security Chris Tang Tang Ping-keung, Secretary for Constitutional and Mainland Affairs Erick Tsang Kwok-wai, and Secretary for Financial Services Christopher Hui Ching-yu.

Deflecting some criticisms that the chief executive himself lacked expertise and experience in economic affairs, John Lee announced his ExCo members on June 22, 2022, during which sixteen people were appointed, including nine from the Carrie Lam government and seven new members.[53] Regina Ip of the NPP

---

52. "State Council Approves Principal Officials of the Sixth-Term HKSAR Government," Xinhua, June 19, 2022, accessed October 12, 2022, https://www.chinadaily.com.cn/a/202206/19/WS62ae9945a310fd2b29e63811.html. See also Kari Soo Lindberg and Krystal Chia, "Here Are Hong Kong's Crackdown Leaders Rewarded in New Cabinet," Bloomberg, July 1, 2022, accessed October 12, 2022, https://www.bloomberg.com/news/articles/2022-06-30/who-s-in-new-hong-kong-leader-john-lee-s-cabinet-and-what-will-they-do.
53. Hillary Leung, "Hong Kong's Incoming Leader John Lee Reveals Members of Advisory Body Executive Council," Hong Kong Free Press, June 23, 2022, accessed October 12, 2022, https://hongkongfp.com/2022/06/23/hong-kongs-incoming-leader-john-lee-reveals-members-of-advisory-body-executive-council/.

took over from Bernard Chan as the ExCo convenor. As a LegCo member, she becomes a bridge between the ExCo and the LegCo. There are three members of the national committee of the CPPCC, including Hang Seng Bank executive Margaret Leung Ko May-yee, former secretary for food and health Ko Wing-man, and solicitor Eliza Chan Ching-har. Clearly, CPPCC members are playing a crucial role not only in the LegCo but also in the ExCo. Three new legislators joined ExCo: Gary Chan Hak-kan from the DAB replacing Horace Cheung, Stanley Ng Chau-pei from the FTU, and insurance representative Chan Kin-por. Other new ExCo members include Moses Cheng Mo-chi, formerly the chair of the Insurance Authority, with his rich legal expertise and knowledge. The reappointed ExCo members include Arthur Li, the former council chair of the University of Hong Kong, barrister Ronny Tong, and pediatric doctor and chair of the elderly and health affairs committee Lam Ching-chor. To maintain the influence of the business sector, John Lee retained Jeffrey Lam of the BPA and Tommy Cheung of the LP in the ExCo while maintaining the positions of Kenneth Lau from the rural advisory, Heung Yee Kuk, and pro-establishment Martin Liao. Overall, the rich experiences of ExCo members could appease the anxiety of those critics doubtful of the economic expertise of the newly elected chief executive.

The 2023 District Council Elections in Hong Kong

The first new District Council elections in Hong Kong were held on December 10, 2023, after the revamp of its composition and electoral methods. Overall, the elections could be seen as a success, as the patriotic camp mobilized many of its supporters to vote on voting day; nevertheless, there were considerable areas that call for further improvements in the future.

The voting turnout was 27.54 percent with 1.19 million voters—a satisfactory result demonstrating a full-scale mobilization of the pro-establishment forces (see Table 3.7). The voting patterns showed the morning time from 9:30 a.m. to 11:30 a.m. had almost 3 percent voter turnout every hour, but the voter turnout gradually declined from 11:30 a.m. onward until 4:30 a.m.—a period in which each hour witnessed about 2 percent of the voter turnout. The last few voting hours from 5.30 p.m. to 12 p.m. saw between 1 and 2 percent of the voter turnout. Overall, the voting patterns demonstrated the success of full-scale mobilization during the morning, but the late afternoon and nighttime witnessed a declining interest in voting. Compared with the voter turnout of 30 percent in the December 2021 Legislative Council elections in which 1.3 million voters went to the polling stations, the voter turnout in the 2023 District Council elections was a success with a figure approaching the 2021 mobilization.

If we analyze the election results by dividing the pro-establishment forces into four groupings—the long-time patriotic camp composed of the Democratic Alliance for Betterment and Progress of Hong Kong (DAB) and the Federation of Trade Unions (FTU); the moderate patriotic camp comprising the Liberal Party (LP), Business Professionals Alliance (BPA), the New People's Party (NPP), Professional Power (PP), and the Federation of Hong Kong and Kowloon Labor Unions (FHKKLU); the new patriotic camp including the Path of Democracy (PoD), Hong Kong New Direction (HKND), and the Bauhinia Party (BP); and the non-party independents—the overall results could be seen in the following Table.

Table 3.7 shows that while the DAB is the largest political group in the new District Councils, the FTU is trailing behind—a robust performance of the long-time patriotic camp. The moderate patriotic camp performed satisfactorily, including the LP, which got eight seats from all the elected seats, district committees and appointed seats (1.7 percent), the BPA, which got twenty-four seats in total (5.1 percent), and the NPP, which acquired twenty-five seats in total (5.3 percent). Professional Power (PP) captured one seat, and the pro-Beijing Federation of Hong Kong and Kowloon Labor Unions (FHKKLU) grasped only three seats—being relatively weak moderate patriotic groups. The new patriotic groups performed quite poorly, with the PoD having one member appointed and the Bauhinia Party (BP) without any elected or appointed members, even

Table 3.7: The December 2023 District Council Elections in Hong Kong

Groups	Elected	District Committees	Appointed	Ex Officio	Total	%
DAB	41	68	38	0	147	31.3
FTU	18	9	16	0	43	9.1
LP	3	2	3	0	8	1.7
BPA	4	8	10	2	24	5.1
NPP	5	10	10	0	25	5.3
PP	1	0	0	0	1	0.2
FHKKLU	0	1	2	0	3	0.6
HKND	1	0	0	0	1	0.2
PoD	0	0	1	0	1	0.2
BP	0	0	0	0	0	0
Independent	15	78	99	25	217	46.2

Source: *Ming Pao*, December 12, 2023, pp. 1–2.

though it had been founded under a strong media spotlight. The Bauhinia Party remains to be localized as its mainland-born leaders have not yet adapted to active participation in local electoral politics.

The non-party-affiliated independents became the largest fragment in the District Councils, having 217 members and occupying 46.2 percent of the seats. Given that the pro-government independents could secure enough nominations to participate in the elections, they are obviously the patriots contributing to the work of District Councils.

The DAB and FTU chairs, Gary Chan and Ng Chau-pei, said in the media before the elections that the two groups did not coordinate between themselves. It looked as if the pro-Beijing groups were encouraged to compete among themselves, while the moderate patriotic groups could nominate members to compete with the long-time patriotic groups. As such, the 2023 District Council elections witnessed a fragmentation of the patriotic forces—perhaps a deliberate ploy adopted by the mainland Chinese officials responsible for Hong Kong matters for the sake of creating a degree of pluralism within the patriotic camp.

Immediately after the elections, the Liaison Office, the Commissioner's Office of China's Foreign Ministry in Hong Kong, and the Hong Kong Macau Affairs Office congratulated the District Council election for being a success. This was understandable because, from the perspective of the central authorities, the elections represented an important event that not only guaranteed the success of the "patriots" governing Hong Kong but also laid a solid social and political foundation for the city's economic prosperity and stability. Most importantly, the screening of the candidates ensured that those "anti-China" Hong Kong people were excluded from participation in the District Council elections, unlike the situation in 2019 when many of them were successfully directly elected.

The ways in which the formerly pro-democracy candidates were excluded from being nominated in these 2023 District Council elections implied that they would have to change their political orientations to have a better chance of being nominated in future district elections. Several members of the Democratic Party (DP) failed to get nominations to run in the District Council elections. While the pro-Beijing official media did not reveal the reasons, it carried unofficial commentaries pointing to the "political unacceptability" of the DP's platform and stance, for the party in the past had criticized the national security law and new electoral system, including the Legislative Council elections in December 2021. If so, the DP may have to rethink whether its party platform would have to be revised in the future so that its members would stand a much better chance of being nominated.

The power of nominating candidates in the 2023 District Council elections was vested in the hands of the members of the three committees—District Committees, Fight Crime Committees, and Fire Prevention Committees.

Members of these three committees were influential and powerful; they could nominate candidates, they could vote for candidates running in the District Committees section, and they could get nominations from other members of the three committees if any of them might be interested in electoral participation. Before the elections, some members of the pro-democracy and other groups complained that the details of the members of the three committees were not easily publicly accessible. The government authorities replied that if candidates wished to contact members of the three committees, they could be a conduit. Overall, it remains to be seen how the government would make the contact methods, like emails, of the members of the three committees more easily accessible in future district elections.

In the 2023 District Council elections, 87 percent (409) of the District Council members came from the members of the three committees, including 75 directly elected members, 147 members elected from the three committees, 111 appointed by the government, and 13 members who are ex officio members (rural committee members). If so, members of the three committees are politically far more influential and powerful than any other group. In the new era of Hong Kong politics, they are expected to be the gatekeepers of the political system; nevertheless, the government may have to ensure that conflicts of role and interest will be best avoided or minimized in the future. For instance, appointed members of District Councils would ideally come from sectors other than the three committees, especially ethnic minorities. There are only two members of ethnic minorities being appointed as District Council members after the elections—a number that appears to be far less than the composition of ethnic minorities in the population of Hong Kong.

A computer glitch on the night of election day led to the extension of voting hours from 10.30 p.m. to 12 midnight—a situation that led to Chief Executive John Lee demanding a report from the electoral authorities within three months. It seemed that the database of voters was overcentralized in such a way that the cloud computing problem affected all 600 voting stations. If the database was decentralized and reorganized in accordance with the voting list in each of some 600 voting stations, such a sudden extension of voting hours might have been avoided. It was embarrassing, if not controversial, that voting hours were suddenly extended because of the computer problem. Indeed, rehearsals of voting should in the future embrace crisis management scenarios if electoral administration is expected to be smooth.

The government organized a carnival on the night of December 9 to boost the voter turnout. However, the content of the carnival could perhaps have been more concrete by emphasizing the size of different constituencies in direct elections, the number of candidates in each constituency, and their platform. Many voters got confused with the size of their constituencies, the number of candidates, and their platform. In the past, election forums were held in District Council elections so that voters understood the candidates, their platforms, and their party backgrounds in a much deeper manner. This time, only one pro-government organization held election forums, but the government itself did not hold any forum in the various townhalls of different districts. More work remains to be done if the government and its electoral authorities expect the voluntary participation of voters.

Overall, the District Council elections in Hong Kong on December 10, 2023, could be regarded as a success, as the official media and mainland perspectives have declared. However, there were considerable areas in need of further improvement, including electoral administration, crisis management in the voting process, the lack of election forums for deeper debate among candidates and groups, and the "excessive" power of the members of the three committees. The dilemma is how to balance the gatekeeping role of the members of three committees and to minimize their potential conflict of roles. Moreover, if some candidates were excluded from being nominated, a much clearer message could have been conveyed to them rather than leaving the nomination matter very difficult and ambiguous, unlike the clear position of some unofficial commentaries of pro-Beijing media. The results of the elections are clear: the long-time patriotic camp composed of the DAB and FTU constitutes the dominant force in Hong Kong's local elections, while the moderate pro-government camp is trailing behind, with the new patriotic force performing quite poorly. Still, most of the District Council members remain non-party-affiliated independents. It remains to be seen how the new District Council members will bring issues related to transport and the environment and other livelihood affairs to the attention of local-level officials, who are and will be expected to be responsive in the new era of Hong Kong–style democracy.

Can the Taiwan Model of "One Country, Two Systems" Be Attractive and Acceptable to the Taiwanese People?

If Hong Kong–style democracy has been established through the 2021 LegCo elections, the 2022 chief executive election, and the 2023 District Council elections, the challenge is whether the model of "one country, two systems" as practiced in Hong Kong and Macau can be applicable to solve the question of Taiwan's political future. In recent years, PRC officials have utilized the concept of the Taiwan model of "one country, two systems" to appeal to the people of Taiwan for reunification. The problems of promoting the applicability of "one country, two systems" to Taiwan are obvious, including (1) the internationally controversial implementation of "one country, two systems" in the HKSAR since late June 2020, (2) the strong localist identity of the Taiwanese people, some of whom are ever toying with the idea of "separatism," which is politically unacceptable to PRC leaders, and (3) the strong localist populism in Taiwan where the ruling Democratic Progressive Party (DPP) and the opposition Kuomintang (KMT) can be regarded as populist parties appealing to the support of public opinion in Taiwan.

The PRC's new authoritarian responses to Hong Kong's localist populism have tremendous implications for Beijing's relations with Taipei. The late Deng Xiaoping attempted to use the Hong Kong and Macau model of "one country, two systems" as a means to appeal to Taiwan for reunification in the long run. Yet, in his January 2019 speech delivered to the Taiwanese comrades, President Xi emphasized the usage of the Taiwan model of "one country, two systems" to appeal to Taiwan for reunification. He also said that this Taiwan model would be "explored" further, that both sides should promote China's rejuvenation and peaceful reunification, that the one-China principle should be followed, that integrated development should be deepened on the two sides, and that the mainland and Taiwan should "forge closer bonds of hearts and minds between people on both sides."[54] Xi's five points have marked a new PRC strategy on Taiwan, focusing on how to explore a Taiwan model of "one country, two systems" while calling for the Taiwan side to accept the 1992 consensus and achieve peaceful reunification.

Several obstacles to Beijing-Taipei relations remain to be resolved. First, the more hardline Beijing's policy toward Hong Kong, the stronger the reluctance of most Taiwanese people to accept the model of "one country, two systems." The ways in which the PRC has been coping with Hong Kong sets a negative example of whatever model of "one country, two systems" is to be promoted to the people of Taiwan. In July and August 2020, a survey of 1,071 Taiwanese people showed that 89 percent rejected the application of the model of "one country, two systems" to Taiwan.[55] The harder the PRC policy toward Hong Kong, the more political benefits the DPP would gain in Taiwan's politics. Mainly due to many Taiwanese voters' concerns about whether Taiwan would become another Hong Kong politically, DPP presidential candidate Tsai Ing-wen comfortably defeated KMT counterpart Han Kuo-yu on January 11, 2020, with the former grasping 8.17 million votes (57 percent) and the latter acquiring 5.52 million votes (39

---

54. Xi Jinping, "Working Together to Realize Rejuvenation of the Chinese Nation and Advance China's Reunification," speech at the Meeting Marking the 40th Anniversary of the Issuance of the Message to Compatriots in Taiwan, January 2, 2019, accessed March 23, 2021, https://www.news.gov.hk/eng/2020/11/20201114/20201114_124103_167.html.
55. "89 Percent of Taiwanese Oppose China's 'One Country, Two Systems:' Poll," Taiwan News, August 7, 2020, accessed March 23, 2021, https://www.taiwannews.com.tw/en/news/3982562.

percent).⁵⁶ If "one country, two systems" is effectively promoted by the PRC to Taiwan, Beijing's policy toward the HKSAR would arguably have to be softer.

Second, Taiwan's localist populism and identity are far much stronger than Hong Kong's, and the people of Taiwan see the "one country, two systems" as a backward step surrendering their own "sovereignty" over the island republic, although the PRC sees Taiwan as undoubtedly under its sovereignty. The Sunflower Movement in Taiwan from March to April 2014 was a repudiation of an attempt by the KMT government to forge a closer economic partnership with the PRC. It was also a challenge to the PRC's mandate of heaven.⁵⁷ The Taiwanese identity among the people of Taiwan is much stronger than the Hong Kong identity of Hongkongers, and as such, they do not share the same cultural-political identity with the mainlanders. In general, mainlanders tend to mix their culturally Chinese identity with the political identification with the ruling regime in power. Yet, the people of Taiwan tend to separate their cultural identity from their political identity, especially as Taiwan's democracy allows the rotation of the political parties in power. In recent years, although the PRC government has been providing all kinds of socio-economic privileges for the Taiwanese people to invest, work, and reside on the mainland, most Taiwanese people have a strong Taiwanese identity, and most of them do not really see the urgency of reunifying with the PRC. Most Taiwanese people prefer to maintain the status quo. Under these circumstances, the PRC needs to not only provide the incentives for the Taiwan side to enhance socio-economic and human interactions with the mainland but also to clarify and liberalize the content of the Taiwan model of "one country, two systems."

The nine points proposed by the late Marshal Ye Jianying in September 1981 to deal with the problem of Taiwan's future remain to be implemented or refined. His nine points were (1) the CCP's negotiation with the KMT, (2) direct air, shipping, mail, and trade links between the two sides, (3) Taiwan would enjoy a high degree of autonomy and keep its own military, (4) Taiwan's existing lifestyle and socio-economic system would remain unchanged, (5) Taiwan's representatives would be allowed to participate in the mainland's political institutions, (6) the central government would financially subsidize Taiwan if necessary, (7) there would be freedom of exit and entry for Taiwanese people and their minorities, (8) Taiwanese people would be welcome to invest and live on the mainland,

---

56. Matthew Strong, "Taiwan President Tsai Ing-wen Wins Election with Record 8.17 Million Votes," Taiwan News, January 11, 2020, accessed March 23, 2021, https://www.taiwannews.com.tw/en/news/3854958.
57. Ming-shuo Ho, *Challenging Beijing's Mandate of Heaven* (Philadelphia: Temple University Press, 2019).

and (9) the reunification of the motherland is the responsibility of all Chinese.[58] Forty-three years after Ye's nine-point proposal, the KMT remains an opposition party without the power to enforce any agreement with the mainland. Direct air, shipping, mail, and trade links remain limited on the two sides. Taiwan's military is actively trained by the US with US-made weapons. Without integration and reunification with the mainland, the people of Taiwan can still enjoy their existing lifestyle. Taiwan is uninterested in having its representatives participate in the mainland's political system. Nor is Taiwan interested in any financial subsidies given by the PRC regime. Although the PRC has been providing lots of incentives for the Taiwanese people to invest, work, and live on the mainland, most Taiwanese people do not see the urgency and necessity of reunifying with the mainland. As such, the think tanks of the PRC government must redesign a new Taiwan model attractive to the people of Taiwan.

Third, so long as the US provides military weapons for Taiwan to deter the PLA military threat, Beijing-Taipei interactions are complicatedly tied with the triangular relations with the US. The former Donald Trump administration was hostile toward the PRC militarily, technologically, and economically, with its Secretary of State Mike Pompeo openly criticizing the CCP. The Joe Biden administration of the US has been directing its focus on strategic competition with the PRC. However, President Biden and Secretary of State Anthony Blinken remain supportive of Taiwan ideologically, politically, and militarily.

The US claims adopt a two-point policy toward Taiwan, namely the resolution of Taiwan's future is a matter for the Chinese themselves to decide, but the US has an interest to see that resolution be peaceful.[59] This two-point policy has been allowing the US some degree of "strategic ambiguity," which makes it unclear how Washington would respond to a military conflict between the mainland and Taiwan.[60] Such strategic ambiguity allows the US to exercise its decision to sell the amount and types of military weapons to Taiwan that would deter the PRC military threat on the one hand and to rein in any Taiwanese extremism on the other hand. Some American analysts have called for a shift from "strategic ambiguity" to clarity.[61] Arguably, the sudden visit of House Speaker Nancy Pelosi

---

58. "Ye Jianying on Taiwan's Return to Motherland and Peaceful Reunification," September 30, 1981, accessed April 4, 2021, http://www.china.org.cn/english/7945.htm.
59. Dennis Van Vraken Hickey, "America's Two-Point Policy and the Future of Taiwan," *Asian Survey* 28, no. 8 (August 1988): 881–896, quoting the remarks of the former Assistant Secretary of State for East Asia and Pacific affairs, William A. Brown (881).
60. Michael E. O'Hanlon, "A Need for Ambiguity," Brookings, April 27, 2001, accessed March 23, 2021, https://www.brookings.edu/opinions/a-need-for-ambiguity/.
61. Richard Haass and David Sacks, "American Support of Taiwan Must Be Unambiguous," *Foreign Affairs*, September 2, 2020, accessed March 23, 2021, https://www.foreignaffairs.com/articles/united-states/american-support-taiwan-must-be-unambiguous.

to Taiwan on August 2, 2022, showed that the US government changed its one-China policy.

The sudden visit of House Speaker Nancy Pelosi to Taiwan in early August 2022 infuriated Beijing to such an extent that the PLA conducted military exercises in six zones near the island republic of Taiwan—a demonstration of the Chinese military capability of imposing an economic blockade on the island.[62] The Pelosi visit to Taiwan was militarily and politically provocative to Beijing; nevertheless, the Biden administration asserted that its one-China principle remains unchanged. On the surface, the Biden government has altered its policy from strategic ambiguity toward Taiwan to strategic clarity, namely the US would likely use its military to defend Taiwan if the PLA launches any attack on the island—a situation mentioned in public by President Biden in October 2021 and then in September 2022.[63] Above all, the failure of the Biden administration to stop Pelosi's visit to Taiwan intentionally or unintentionally created a fait accompli that Taiwan is de facto recognized diplomatically and politically by Washington as another political entity "separate" from mainland China. Under the circumstances in which both the US and the PRC see each other as a military threat, the future of Taiwan will remain a flashpoint testing how the two powers can and will manage their profound opinion differences.

From the perspective of realpolitik, any Beijing-Taipei negotiation and its outcome in the future will perhaps likely need tacit support from the US, even though Beijing is insistent that the Chinese themselves can and will settle the question of Taiwan's future. Perhaps US policymakers on Taiwan need to prepare for a contingency solution to bring the CCP and the Taiwanese government, whether it will be led by the DDP or KMT, together by studying the failure of George Marshall to do so peacefully in 1947. The late George Marshall wrote in January 1947:

> I think the most important factors involved in the recent breakdown of negotiations are these: On the side of the Nationalist Government, which is in effect the Kuomintang Party, there is a dominant group of reactionaries who have been opposed, in my opinion, to almost every effort I have made to influence the formation of a genuine coalition government . . . They were quite frank in publicly stating their belief that cooperation by the CCP in the government was inconceivable and that only a policy of force could definitely settle the issue.

---

62. Sonny Lo, "A Risk Assessment of Beijing-Taipei Relations after Pelosi's Visit," Macau Business, August 6, 2022, accessed October 12, 2022, https://www.macaubusiness.com/opinion-a-risk-assessment-of-beijing-taipei-relations-after-pelosis-visit/.
63. Stephen McDonell, "Biden Says Us Will Defend Taiwan If China Attacks," BBC News, October 22, 2021, accessed October 12, 2022, https://www.bbc.com/news/world-asia-59005300. See also Frances Mao, "Biden Again Says Us Would Defend Taiwan If China Attacks," BBC News, September 19, 2022, accessed October 12, 2022, https://www.bbc.com/news/world-asia-62951347.

This group includes military as well as political leaders. On the side of the CCP there are, I believe, liberals as well as radicals, though this view is vigorously opposed by many who believe that the CCP discipline is too rigidly enforced to admit of such differences of viewpoint.[64]

Seventy-seven years after Marshall wrote his note, the factional arrangements on both the PRC and Taiwan sides remain politically obstinate and ideologically dogmatic. The PRC side is ruled by an assertively nationalistic faction that does not renounce the use of military force to solve the Taiwan problem, while Taiwan is governed by the DDP that remains far more distanced emotionally and politically from the mainland than the opposition KMT. As such, if the US government prepares a contingency plan to intervene in Taiwan in case a military conflict erupts between the two sides, it would perhaps have to figure out the dominant factional arrangements in the PRC and Taiwan at that juncture and to suggest a temporary settlement conducive to a peaceful resolution of Taiwan's political future. However, the PRC sees any US interference with China's domestic affair of handling the Taiwan issue as politically unacceptable. This means that only a third country, for example, Singapore, which has friendly relations with both Beijing and Taipei, can and will be able to intervene in case a military conflict erupts between the PRC and Taiwan.

Fourth, if the Taiwanese government under the DPP leadership refuses to accept the 1992 consensus (which was, as reached by both the CCP and KMT, that there is only one China, but the meaning of one China is up to the interpretation of both sides),[65] it means that, for a breakthrough in Beijing-Taipei relations to take place, then the PRC would have to wait for the KMT to return to presidential power. So long as the DPP government is in power, Beijing's relations with Taipei remain stagnant. However, when the KMT was revived and rejuvenated under the leadership of Han Kuo-yu in the January 2020 presidential elections, he was unfortunately victimized by the anti-extradition movement in Hong Kong. Han had visited the PRC, Hong Kong, and Macau in March 2019, forging closer economic relations between the mainland and Kaohsiung city where he was a directly elected mayor. The outbreak of the anti-extradition movement plunged Han's popularity into a crisis, for many pro-Taiwan politicians and ordinary citizens saw him as being too pro-Beijing, and they feared that voting for him would be tantamount to making Taiwan more like Hong Kong politically. In January 2024, the DPP led by William Lai defeated the KMT led by Hou You-yi to maintain its grip on Taiwan's presidential leadership. Given

---

64. George Marshall, "Personal Statement, January 7, 1947," The George Marshall Foundation, accessed April 4, 2021, https://www.marshallfoundation.org/library/digital-archive/personal-statement1/.
65. "1992 Consensus Called Key to Cross-Straits Ties," *China Daily*, May 7, 2016, accessed May 9, 2016, http://www.china.org.cn/china/2016-05/07/content_38402457.htm.

that Taiwan's domestic politics are beyond the control of the PRC, Beijing would find it difficult to impose its Taiwanese version of the "one country, two systems" onto the people of Taiwan easily.

President Xi Jinping is eager to settle the question of Taiwan's future rather than leaving it to the next generation. The November 2015 meeting between President Xi and Taiwan's President Ma Ying-jeou of the Kuomintang demonstrated an attempt at institutionalizing the relationships between Beijing and Taipei, namely (1) a verbal peace consensus without a formal agreement between the two places and (2) the consent of both sides to continue the existing economic relations and interactions.[66] The historic meeting on November 7, 2015, represented a landmark peace consensus on both sides, even though no formal agreement was signed. This verbal peace consensus, however, had little impact on the Taiwanese government after the presidential election in January 2016, which saw DPP presidential candidate Tsai Ing-wen easily defeat KMT candidate Eric Chu.

Both Xi and Ma stressed in their historic political dialogue that peace was and would be essential to the Chinese people from both mainland China and Taiwan.[67] They pointed to the need to prosper the Chinese nation. This unprecedented two-point consensus established the basis for the economic and political development of Beijing and Taipei at least when Ma Ying-jeou remained the Taiwanese president until 2016. It established a solid framework for both sides to continue implementing their previous economic agreements. The Xi-Ma meeting in November 2015 was historic because both sides realized the necessity of having a political dialogue in the face of rapid transformations on both sides. President Xi's Taiwan think-tank advisers understood the imperative of reaching a peace consensus with the Taiwan side, especially in view of the inevitable defeat of the KMT in the 2016 presidential election. Ma was shrewd in raising the issue that the Taiwan side was concerned about the fact that some 1,500 missiles were stationed along the coast of mainland China. Although these missiles were by no means targeted at Taiwan, as President Xi said, Ma had made an appropriate political gesture that, under the 1992 consensus of having different interpretations on the meaning of "one China," the PRC should neither use military force nor deploy military threats to deal with the ROC.

Both Xi and Ma stressed the necessity of reviving the "Chinese nation," implying that Taiwan in the future would be able to join more international organizations by using the term "Chinese Taipei." Zhang Zhijun, the director

---

66. "Xi-Ma Meeting Turns Historic Page in Cross-Strait Relations: Official," Xinhua, November 9, 2015, accessed March 23, 2021, http://www.scio.gov.cn/32618/Document/1454345/1454345.htm.
67. For Xi's speech, see BBC News (Chinese version), November 7, 2015. For Ma's speech, see *Wen Wei Po*, November 8, 2015, A3. Their meeting was broadcast live on Hong Kong's Cable TV news on November 7, 2015.

of the Taiwan Affairs Office of the PRC State Council, stressed in his statement immediately after the Xi-Ma meeting that, according to President Xi, the PRC does not tolerate any independence move on the Taiwanese side. Xi's remarks aimed at sending a strong and clear message to the DPP. Any DPP move to drift toward independence would bring about havoc in Beijing-Taipei relations. Zhang also said that any turbulent Beijing-Taipei relations would make the Chinese people suffer. He stressed the need for both sides to set up telephone hotlines to deal with urgent matters.

During the last year of the Donald Trump administration in 2020, tensions between the PRC and Taiwan were running high.[68] PLA military planes often flew near Taiwanese airspace, triggering criticisms from the DPP government. While the gesture of the PLA planes created a new normality to flex their military muscles, the US military has been enhancing its cooperation with the Taiwanese military in the areas of intelligence sharing, training, and exchanges. Taiwan is occupying a key role in the US Indo-Pacific strategy, being a Western-style democracy supported by not only the US but also by Japan, South Korea, and the Philippines in forming a networked coalition of regional states vis-à-vis the perceived PRC military threat in the Asia-Pacific region.[69] Some American observers predicted the likelihood of military conflicts between the PRC and Taiwan. In March 2021, an outcoming Indo-Pacific US commander, Admiral Philip Davidson, asserted that China would "invade" Taiwan within six years, while his successor, Admiral John Aquilino, claimed that "this problem is much closer to us than most think and we have to take this on."[70] Their military perspective is understandable, but all those who believe in the imminent PRC military "invasion" into Taiwan have perhaps neglected the remarks made by President Xi Jinping, namely that the Chinese will not fight the Chinese, and peaceful resolution remains the ultimate objective unless Taiwan moves toward "independence." Even a week prior to the twentieth Party Congress in Beijing in mid-October 2022, PRC Foreign Ministry spokeswoman Mao Ning remarked:

> The root cause of the current tensions across the Taiwan Strait is that the DPP authorities have been acting with external forces to make provocations and seek independence. Only by resolutely deterring "Taiwan independence," separatism

---

68. Sonny Lo, "Will Military Accident or Skirmishes Occur Amidst Tense Beijing-Taipei-Washington Relations," Macau Business, July 25, 2020, accessed March 23, 2021, https://www.macaubusiness.com/opinion-will-military-accident-or-skirmish-occur-amidst-tense-beijing-taipei-washington-relations/.
69. Howard Wang, "Taiwan's Security Role in the US Indo-Pacific Strategy," The Diplomat, June 27, 2019, accessed March 23, 2021, https://thediplomat.com/2019/06/taiwans-security-role-in-the-u-s-indo-pacific-strategy/.
70. "China Threat to Invade Taiwan Is 'Closer Than Most Think,' Says US Admiral," The Guardian, March 23, 2021, accessed March 24, 2021, https://www.theguardian.com/world/2021/mar/23/taiwan-china-threat-admiral-john-aquilino.

and opposing external interference can peace and stability be ensured in the Taiwan Strait. I want to stress that peaceful reunification and "one country, two systems" is the basic principle for resolving the Taiwan question and the best way to realize national reunification. Provided that national sovereignty, security and development interests are ensured, Taiwan can adopt a high degree of autonomy as a special administrative region, Taiwan's social system and its way of life will be fully respected and the lawful rights and interests of our Taiwan compatriots will be fully protected. China's reunification will not undermine any country's legitimate interests. Instead, it will only bring development opportunities to other countries and inject more positive energy into the prosperity of the Asia-Pacific region and the world at large.[71]

According to the PRC's *White Paper on the Taiwan Question*, which was published on August 10, shortly after the Pelosi visit to Taipei, Beijing suggests that any negotiations with Taipei over reunification would proceed by stages, that there was no statement on whether the PLA would not be stationed in Taiwan after reunification, and that foreign countries would be allowed to establish diplomatic missions in Taiwan after its reunification with the PRC.[72] The *White Paper* says:

> We will continue working with our compatriots in Taiwan to explore a two systems solution to the Taiwan question and increase our efforts towards peaceful reunification. In designing the specifics for implementing "one country, two systems," we will give full consideration to the realities in Taiwan and the views and proposals from all walks of life on both sides, and fully accommodate the interests and sentiments of our compatriots in Taiwan.[73]

For the first time in China's official position on Taiwan, the *White Paper* raised the issue of stage-by-stage negotiations with Taiwan over reunification and mentioned that foreign states will be allowed to establish their missions on the island after reunification. These two elements, from the perspective of exploring the Taiwan model of "one country, two systems," are new and flexible, with a realistic prospect of having a breakthrough in mutual dialogue, if and only if the Taiwan side agrees with the 1992 consensus.

On October 16, 2022, when CCP General Secretary Xi Jinping delivered his report to the twentieth Party Congress, he mentioned that the PRC would

---

71. "Foreign Ministry Spokesperson Mao Ning's Regular Press on October 9, 2022," accessed October 12, 2022, https://www.fmprc.gov.cn/mfa_eng/xwfw_665399/s2510_665401/2511_665403/202210/t20221009_10780009.html.
72. "The Taiwan Question and China's Reunification in the New Era," The PRC Taiwan Affairs Office of the State Council and the State Council Information Office, August 10, 2022, accessed October 12, 2022, http://www.scio.gov.cn/zfbps/32832/Document/1728491/1728491.htm.
73. "The Taiwan Question and China's Reunification in the New Era."

have to finish the task of "complete reunification" with Taiwan.[74] The Pelosi visit to Taipei in early August 2022 stimulated and accelerated Beijing's determination to reunify Taiwan "completely" in the coming years. Although the timetable of Beijing in its "complete reunification" with Taiwan remains unclear, the PRC does not renounce the use of force, as reiterated by Xi Jinping in his speech and during his meeting with President Biden in San Francisco in November 2023. As such, the PRC's priority is to reunify Taiwan peacefully, but if this alternative fails, Beijing will consider the use of force to achieve its mission of "complete reunification."

From the perspective of factional politics, both the KMT and DPP have internal factions dealing with the PRC, shaping Beijing-Taipei relations in a complex and unpredictable way. The KMT, according to Han Kuo-yu, has at least three factions: one supportive of the 1992 consensus, another one supportive of the ROC on Taiwan but focusing on the interactions between the mainland and Taiwanese islands such as Penghu, Kinmen, and Matsu, and the third one supportive of de-mainlandization.[75] On the other hand, the DPP has been divided into three factions on its policy toward the PRC: one supportive of using the ROC constitution to engage the PRC side in their dialogue over the 1992 consensus and the one-China principle, the other one adopting an ambiguous approach to dealing with mainland China, and the third one rejecting the one-China principle.[76] At present, the DPP faction rejecting the one-China principle is the dominant one, while the KMT is divided into a struggle between the faction supporting the 1992 consensus and that advocating de-mainlandization. Johnny Chiang, the KMT chairman, remarked that "China is the main threat" to Taiwan, and his comment led to severe criticism from Lien Chan, the former KMT chairman from 2000 to 2005 and a "dark blue" politician supportive of the 1992 consensus.[77]

There are at least four scenarios in Beijing-Taipei relations. The first is a step-by-step process of socio-economic integration, negotiation, and reunification—a scenario that has already been provided by China's 2022 *White Paper* on Taiwan. The current socio-economic integration between the PRC and Taiwan will likely deepen, for the mainland government under the CCP leadership is keen to enhance human interactions across the two sides, especially as Beijing and many

---

74. RTHK Channel 32, October 16, 2022.
75. "結盟趙少康有內幕？韓國瑜遭爆曾斷言：國民黨剩三條路," 聯合新聞網 [United Daily News], February 3, 2021, accessed March 23, 2021, http://city.udn.com/54543/7106062?raid=7106842.
76. Liu Chin-Tsai, "The Observation of DPP's Mainland China Policy in 2013: Controversy and Development," *Prospect and Exploration* (Taiwan) 12, no. 2 (February 2014): 24–33. See also Yan Jiann-fa, "DPP's Current China Policy," *Prospect and Exploration* 12, no. 7 (July 2014): 15–20.
77. "叫戰江啟臣 中媒曝：江一席話連戰暴怒 推連勝文拼黨魁" ["Johnny Chiang's remarks alienated Lien Chan"], 新頭殼 [Newtalk], March 15, 2021, accessed March 23, 2021, https://newtalk.tw/news/view/2021-03-15/549259.

other provinces, especially Fujian and Guangdong, in recent years have come up with various policies and preferential treatments for the Taiwanese comrades to invest, study, work, and reside in the PRC. Intermediaries, such as the old members of the KMT (Ma Ying-jeou and Lien Chan) and younger leaders like Han Kuo-yu, will have tremendous potential to act as the key persons bridging the communication and expectation gaps between the two sides, leading to mutual dialogue. However, the negotiations over reunification will be difficult, partly because of the image of Beijing's "hardline" policy toward Hong Kong and partly because many Taiwanese people do not see any incentive to being integrated with the PRC economically and reunited with the mainland politically.

The second scenario is to maintain the status quo with both sides making verbal arguments, positioning themselves in a high-profile manner, and engaging in a kind of megaphone "diplomacy." The current situation of Beijing-Taipei relations fits into this scenario, which requires trust building to be made between the officials and politicians of the two sides. Since the people of Taiwan do not show their urgency or have any incentive to accept the Taiwan model of "one country, two systems," both sides will likely engage in a tug of war, with the mainland side eager to see Taiwan be economically integrated with at least Fujian, Guangdong, and the South China region. Yet, the Taiwan side will likely remain distanced and detached politically and socio-economically from the mainland.

The third scenario would be sudden military conflicts between the two sides. Under the condition that the Taiwanese government cannot do anything, like constitutional revision, that will certainly provoke the PRC side militarily, and that it will not declare "independence," it will be unlikely for the PRC to use military force, which remains a means of last resort. Ultimately, President Xi Jinping and his successor will likely emphasize the rejuvenation of the Chinese nation and the adoption of peaceful means of resolving the question of Taiwan's future. However, with the frequent patrol of PLA planes near the Taiwanese airspace and the dispatch of mainland warships approaching Taiwan's waters, there would be a real danger of military accidents, which would likely spark off a military crisis at once. At that juncture, the US responses would be a critical factor shaping how Beijing, Taipei, and Washington would manage their military accidents or conflicts. The Sino-US military-to-military communication may help to defuse a military crisis, but it remains to be seen how such a mechanism operates at the grassroots and the commanding levels on both sides.

The fourth scenario would be a mix of softline united work conducted by Beijing on Taipei, but if it fails and if the CCP has a timetable of reunifying Taiwan, then the PRC would likely resort to economic sanctions and even the application of swift military force. However, the timing of applying economic sanctions and military force would be crucial; the longer the period of application, the faster the Taiwanese and US responses. An unknown factor would be the

US policy toward Taiwan. Although President Biden mentioned twice that the US would defend Taiwan if mainland China attacks the island, it remains unclear whether this American position would remain unchanged. The Republican Party under Donald Trump's leadership was explicitly hawkish toward the PRC, seeing Beijing as the number one enemy of the US. This hardline US position has been inherited by the Biden administration, which does not show a fundamental departure from Trump's policy toward China. Clearly, the rapid economic, military, and political rise of China has challenged the hegemony of the US in the world. Under these circumstances, if Hong Kong has already become a pawn in the Sino-US struggles for power and influence in the world, Taiwan is destined to be increasingly a "protectorate" of the US, which supplies military weapons to the Taiwanese regime to deter any PLA attack. Yet, from Beijing's standpoint, any US move to "colonize" Taiwan would likely accelerate its pace of achieving the "complete reunification" of the island. CCP Secretary General Xi Jinping's remarks that China would resort to peaceful means first but retain the option of force in dealing with Taiwan fits into this fourth scenario—peaceful gestures and moves in cementing relations with Taiwan followed by a possible use of military force if the peaceful option is exhausted. In late 2023, some mainland Chinese videos stressed that the PLA would be able to target the strategic and military sites in Taiwan with precision, accuracy, and a speedy capability of destroying them in case of any decision to "reunify" the island—a scenario that pointed to a hawkish but swift approach to dealing with Taiwan's future.

In March 2021, the scenario of envisaging a step-by-step process of integration and negotiation witnessed a proposal from the dark blue camp of the KMT. Political scientist Chang Ya-chung suggested that if he were elected as the KMT party chair, he would negotiate a peace memorandum with the PRC side first, and then, it would be submitted to all KMT members for a vote.[78] After the vote of approval by KMT members, the peace memorandum would be put forward as a platform of the KMT in the 2024 presidential elections. If the KMT could return to presidential power in the 2024 elections, the ruling KMT would sign a peace agreement with the PRC side. Chang's proposal was bold.[79] He also proposed that both the PRC and Taiwan could form a "common union."[80]

78. "張亞中主張兩岸協商和平備忘錄　國民黨執政後再簽和平協議," 自由時報電子報 [*Liberty Times*], March 28, 2021, accessed March 28, 2021, https://news.ltn.com.tw/news/politics/breakingnews/3481037.
79. I also put forward an idea about both the PRC and ROC sides reaching a memorandum of understanding first before both sides would proceed to detailed negotiations. See *The Dynamics of Beijing-Hong Kong Relations: A Model for Taiwan?*
80. "張亞中拋「兩岸和平備忘錄」：台灣與中國成立共同體" ["Chang Ya-chung throws out 'peace memorandum for two sides: Taiwan and China set up a common union"], 三立新聞網 [setn.com], March 31, 2021, accessed April 4, 2021, https://www.setn.com/News.aspx?NewsID=918764.

In the short run, trust-building between the PRC and some Hong Kong people and the PRC and Taiwan sides must be enhanced to achieve a breakthrough in Beijing-Taipei relations. Given the relatively "hardline" and conservatively nationalistic policy adopted by Beijing over Hong Kong, it would take some years for trials of the lawbreakers of the 2019 anti-extradition protests and the national security law to be settled and completed. The legacy of the 2019 anti-extradition riots would likely linger, but its impacts on Beijing-Taipei relations would continue to be negative. Unless the pursuit of key leaders, organizers, and activists of the 2019 anti-extradition protests were relaxed and unless the PRC side adopts a more relaxed and more liberal version of the Taiwan model of "one country, two systems" with more autonomy than in the Hong Kong and Macau circumstances, the future of Beijing-Taipei relations would likely remain difficult, turbulent, and unpredictable.

Summary

The rise of localist populism constituted an increasingly serious national security threat to the HKSAR government and the central authorities in Beijing, which decided to introduce the national security law in June 2020, reinterpreted the allegiance requirements of LegCo members in November 2020, and revamped the electoral system in March 2021. All these measures were taken to stop, curb, and suppress the localist populists and radicals. Beijing changed the electoral system completely by reducing the section of directly elected seats in the LegCo and replacing it with the clientelist Election Committee. Beijing was determined to groom the patriotic populist faction to stabilize Hong Kong's political system and to nurture the political leadership of the HKSAR. The LegCo elections in December 2021, the chief executive election in May 2022, and the District Council elections in December 2023 symbolized Beijing's determination to exclude all localist populists from Hong Kong's political system, to empower the "patriotic" elites in governing the HKSAR, and to consolidate the central government's "comprehensive jurisdiction" over the capitalist enclave. The three elections were hailed as a victory of Hong Kong's style of democracy and the "one country, two systems." However, the mass participation rate in the LegCo and District Council elections was dampened as many eligible voters were either apathetic or uninterested in the new electoral system. Still, so long as the "patriotic" elites and core supporters of the HKSAR government and Beijing actively participated in legislative and district elections, the objective of ensuring the "patriots" governed the HKSAR was firmly achieved.

Unfortunately, Beijing's "positive" intervention in Hong Kong's political development has generated a "negative" boomerang effect in Taiwan, where the leaders, followers, and ordinary citizens do not find it urgent to see a united mainland and Taiwan by accepting the "one country, two systems." Although the PRC emphasizes that both sides can explore the Taiwan model of "one country, two systems," the relations between mainland China and Taiwan remain politically tense. Factional politics within the KMT and the CCP also complicate Beijing-Taipei relations. If Beijing cannot control the dynamic and complex factional politics in Taiwan, it is far more difficult to impose the "one country, two systems" onto Taiwan than its preferred model of governance onto the HKSAR. PRC authorities have put forward the Taiwan model of "one country, two systems." This Taiwan model is characterized by a high degree of autonomy given to Taiwan, including the preservation of the existing social lifestyle and the establishment of foreign missions on the island after reunification. However, the challenge is to lure the Taiwan side to integrate economically into the mainland first, followed by a stage-by-stage process of dialogue and punctuated by mutual concessions from both sides. Under the circumstances of tense Sino-US relations over Taiwan and the presidential dominance of the DPP that rejects the 1992 consensus, a breakthrough would not be easy unless intermediaries can and will help cement Beijing-Taipei relations in a positive way.

Conclusion

The promulgation of the national security law in the HKSAR in mid-2020 and its resultant revamp of the electoral system in March 2021 have transformed the political system from patron-client pluralism to paternalistic authoritarianism. I argued in my previous book on Beijing–Hong Kong relations in 2008 that the political system of the HKSAR was characterized by patron-client pluralism, meaning that the PRC as the most powerful political patron cultivated its clients in Hong Kong, where the political sphere was full of pluralistic actors competing among themselves. From 1997 to 2020, the pro-Beijing elites expanded their political influence through the patronage of both the HKSAR government and the PRC officials responsible for Hong Kong matters. Yet, they found it difficult to compete with the democrats electorally because the political system of Hong Kong remained relatively pluralistic with a comparatively strong civil society. However, since late June 2020, patron-client pluralism has gradually changed to patron-client and paternalistic authoritarianism. PRC authorities have seen political pluralism as excessively conflict-ridden and politically "subversive." The implementation of the national security law legitimized the HKSAR government to tame the civil society of Hong Kong, especially its "uncivil" aspect. If paternalism is defined as an ideology in which the ruling elites see themselves as the parents whose orders and directives should be obeyed by the masses like their sons and daughters, then it has become increasingly prominent in Beijing's policy toward the HKSAR, particularly after the latter half of 2019 when many Hong Kong people participated in the anti–extradition bill movement. The PRC leadership was infuriated by the 2019 protests and determined to exercise its "comprehensive jurisdiction" over the HKSAR to protect its national security and sovereignty. The key to achieve such a "comprehensive jurisdiction" is to ensure the "patriotic" or loyalist elites govern Hong Kong and to exclude all political "troublemakers" from the political system. The patron-clientelist ingredient of Hong Kong's polity persists in the form of grooming the pro-government and pro-Beijing loyalists, while the paternalistic and authoritarian aspects have been shown in how the core "troublemakers" were arrested, prosecuted, and punished. Paternalism, which has its deep-rooted Confucian political culture in mainland China, has become a new hallmark of Hong Kong's political development after the promulgation of the national security law in late June 2020.

Since the transfer of Hong Kong's sovereignty from Britain to the PRC on July 1, 1997, the ideological clashes between the HKSAR and the mainland have become increasingly more acute than ever before—a process complicated by the evolution of factional politics on both sides. The ideological shift from liberal nationalism to conservative nationalism on the PRC's ruling stratum since late 2012, on the one hand, and the increasingly vociferous localism and violent populism after the anti–national education movement in 2012, on the Hong Kong side, changed Beijing–Hong Kong relations to a far more confrontational and conflict-ridden situation than ever before. The conflict-ridden encounters between the two sides became apparent from 2016 to 2021, ranging from the SCNPC interpretation of Article 104 of the Basic Law over the improper oath-taking behavior of legislators-elect to its promulgation of the national security law for the HKSAR in June 2020 and from the SCNPC interpretation of the allegiance requirements of legislators in November 2020 to the redesign of Hong Kong's electoral system in March 2021. The SCNPC interpretations and the reform of Hong Kong's electoral system demonstrated the paternalistic aspect of how Beijing coped with the problem of governance in Hong Kong. To Beijing, the democrats and the localist populists plunged the HKSAR into an unprecedented crisis of legitimacy and governance, necessitating its decisive and positive intervention in Hong Kong's political development.

In short, factionalism is used as both an analytical framework and an empirical phenomenon in this book. It is extremely useful for us to comprehend the power struggles between the democrats/populists/localists and Beijing/the HKSAR government/pro-Beijing forces on the one hand and between Western democratic states and the PRC on the other. The power struggles between the West, notably the US, and the PRC have exacerbated the rivalries between the democrats/populists/localists and the Beijing/HKSAR government/pro-Beijing forces. Eventually, Beijing as the patron of the HKSAR government and pro-Beijing forces decided to take hardline action to struggle against the democrats, populists, and localists through its exercise of "comprehensive jurisdiction" over Hong Kong. The Hong Kong democrats, localists, and populists all failed to predict, assess, and understand China's political development, whose oscillation from "soft" authoritarianism to "hard" authoritarianism or even "neo-totalitarianism" has reversed the tide of democratization in Hong Kong in the form of making democratic change mainlandized or Sinified. Most importantly, when the Chinese ideologies of legalism, Marxism-Leninism, and paternalistic authoritarianism are combined with Beijing's dominant conservative nationalistic faction, Hong Kong's Western-style democratization had to be reversed in a Chinese manner.

The SCNPC's promulgation of the national security law for Hong Kong on June 30, 2020, was a watershed in the new politics of Beijing–Hong Kong relations. Patron-client politics is deepening and broadening in Hong Kong where the new electoral system established a 1,500-member Election Committee in which *guanxi* politics among the patriotic elites were inevitable. Beijing as the most powerful political patron decided who were eligible to join the 1,500-member Election Committee as the political kingmakers responsible for not only selecting the chief executive but also forty of the ninety LegCo members. Yet, as the late Lucian Pye reminded us, if *guanxi* politics are a crucial factor leading to political bargaining and compromise, the politics of nomination and election of the members of the Election Committee and LegCo run the risks of being characterized by inside bargaining and political horse-trading. Inside politics became natural in the selection of LegCo members through the Election Committee, while open competition remains the defining feature in the LegCo's direct elections and functional constituency elections. Inside politics and horse-trading were possible in the 2,500-member District Committees, which were composed of the District Committees, District Fight Crime Committees, and Fire Prevention Committees, and which selected 176 District Council members. Members of the District Committees could nominate candidates running for District Council elections and constituted a politically privileged group with the veto power of screening out any political "troublemakers." The new electoral system installed gatekeepers, who, however, may have hidden inside politics and whose mutual support or nominations could perhaps run the risk of having potential conflicts of roles.

Populist authoritarianism, as Tang Wenfang has argued, remains a hallmark of mainland Chinese politics.[1] It has been seeping into the HKSAR since June 30, 2020. The PRC authorities were determined to expel those legislators who challenged and threatened China's national security from the LegCo, culminating in the November 2020 SCNPC decision to clarify the allegiance requirements of LegCo members. The immediate announcement of the HKSAR government to disqualify four pro-democracy legislators was unprecedented, marking the swift and hardline way in which Beijing handled localist and populist legislators in Hong Kong. The new political system in Hong Kong is now characterized by deep concerns about national security, the arrests and prosecutions of the offenders violating national security, a stronger executive-led branch vis-à-vis

---

1. Tang Wenfang, *Populist Authoritarianism: Chinese Political Culture and Regime Sustainability* (New York: Oxford University Press, 2016).

a relatively weaker legislature, a much weaker civil society with the mass media more supportive of the government than before, an increase in the political influence of pro-Beijing and pro-establishment populists, the exclusion of radical and democratic populists from the LegCo and District Councils, and the substantial reduction in the political influence of directly elected members of the legislature and district advisory bodies. If localist populists have already been excluded and punished, the rise of "patriotic" populists is prominent. These pro-establishment populists are by no means anti-elitist. They are politically loyal to the HKSAR and central government; they make use of clan groups, townspeople (*tongxiang*) associations, district federations, women's federations, and labor unions to conduct extensive united front work to win the hearts and minds of more Hong Kong people than before. The politics of loyal opposition in the Hong Kong–style of democracy has emerged since late 2021.

From Beijing's perspective, the Hong Kong political system needs a fundamental overhaul to exclude all those "radical" localists—liberal, Marxist, confrontational, and separatist ones—from participation in the chief executive election, the LegCo, and District Councils. From a Marxist perspective, the superstructure in Hong Kong, including its education system, the political culture of many Hong Kong people, and political institutions, needs to be drastically revamped while retaining Hong Kong's economic base. National security and national education have to be formulated and implemented to transform the political culture of the young people from an "unpatriotic" attitude to a "patriotic" one. The March 2021 decision of the SCNPC to revamp the composition of the LegCo and the Chief Executive Election Committee was politically significant. By reinjecting a much larger and more influential Election Committee into the election of LegCo members than any previous electoral college of the British colonial legislature, Beijing was determined to empower the "patriotic elites" and legitimize the nationalistic populists, who are overwhelmingly occupying the LegCo seats. Moreover, all LegCo candidates and chief executive candidates are required to be screened by the Candidates Eligibility Review Committee, which is composed of local elites loyal to the central government and the CCP.[2] The committee's decision on the eligibility of candidates "is not subject to any judicial

---

2. In September 2022, Chief Executive John Lee appointed Eric Chan, the Chief Secretary, to be the chair of the Committee. Paul Chan, the Financial Secretary, ceased to be the chair. The Committee's official members include Secretary for Constitutional and Mainland Affairs Erick Tsang Kwok-wai, Secretary for Security Chris Tang Ping-keung, and Secretary for Home and Youth Affairs Alice Mak Mei-kuen. Three non-official members are Elsie Leung, Rita Fan, and Lawrence Lau. "Candidate Eligibility Review Committee Members Appointed," Hong Kong Standard, September 19, 2022, accessed October 13, 2022, https://www.thestandard.com.hk/breaking-news/section/4/194863/Candidate-Eligibility-Review-Committee-members-appointed. The Committee's decision on candidates' eligibility is "not subject to any judicial proceedings."

proceedings."[3] Under these circumstances, the political superstructure of Hong Kong has already been legally reformed and firmly controlled by the "patriotic" populists and nationalistic elites, thereby enhancing the executive-led nature of the HKSAR political system and consolidating the governance of Hong Kong.

Comparatively speaking, however, the pro-Beijing nationalistic populists are much weaker than the previously democratic localists and populists. Although the nationalistic populists could still mobilize a lot of people to vote for the pro-Beijing and pro-establishment candidates in the 2021 LegCo direct elections and 2023 District Council elections, they tended to be much weaker and could not create an exciting and highly competitive electoral atmosphere. After all, many eligible voters in support of the democratic populists and localists did not come out to vote on the election days in December 2021 and December 2023, leading to relatively lackluster legislative and district elections. Those who did not go to the polls appeared to be either politically apathetic, indifferent, or alienated. Still, the 2021 LegCo elections were hailed as a victory for not only Hong Kong's new era but also for the Hong Kong style of democracy where loyalists participate in elections enthusiastically.

If localists are regarded as the political "viruses" infiltrating Hong Kong's political system, such a "virus" was filtered out by Article 104 of the Basic Law and excluded from participation in the local political superstructure.[4] If localists are defined broadly as those Hong Kong people with a very strong local Hong Kong identity, their return to the political and electoral arena depends on two factors: firstly, whether the political and electoral atmosphere turns at least more relaxed and liberal and, secondly, whether the performance of the HKSAR government would become a stimulus to their electoral participation. If the political and electoral atmosphere turns less tense and if the pro-Beijing media tend to be more lenient toward the democratic localists, more localist candidates will likely return to participate in elections and more formerly pro-democracy voters will likely go to the polls. Ironically, if the HKSAR government's performance is deemed unsatisfactory, there will be a realistic possibility that some localist voters would likely cast their ballots for the pro-democracy candidates in the future—a phenomenon that could be seen in the pre-2022 LegCo elections. The above two conditions were not seen in the 2022 LegCo elections and 2023 District Council elections, which were characterized by a relatively low voter turnout compared with previous elections.

---

3. See "Candidate Eligibility Review Mechanism," May 1, 2021, accessed October 13, 2022, https://www.cmab.gov.hk/improvement/en/qualification-review/index.html.
4. "Hong Kong Troublemakers Are a Political Virus: Luo Huining," RTHK News, February 20, 2020, accessed April 4, 2021, https://news.rthk.hk/rthk/en/component/k2/1509714-20200220.htm.

The performance of the HKSAR government did influence voting. The 2019 District Council elections witnessed many pro-democracy localist voters going to the polls, directly leading to the victory of localist populists. However, PRC authorities believed that many of them failed to pledge allegiance to the Basic Law and the HKSAR government. Once the new electoral system of the LegCo was reformed in March 2021, all public officers holding elected positions were required to take the oath supporting the Basic Law, the national security law, and the HKSAR government. Many localist populists who were directly elected as District Council members in 2019 failed to go through the allegiance tests and were disqualified in 2021. Some left the HKSAR, opting to vote with their feet as they saw the promulgation of the national security law in mid-2020 as creating a "new" Hong Kong that they disliked. Identity, ideology, and political culture remain the crucial factors leading to the decision of some Hong Kong people to emigrate or to remain electorally apathetic in local elections.

In Samuel Huntington's terms, while the procedural legitimacy of the Hong Kong government has been revamped in a mainland Chinese manner, its performance legitimacy relies on the political leadership of the "patriotic" and nationalistic faction. The PRC has conferred upon the "patriotic" and nationalistic elites a strong degree of procedural legitimacy through the revamped chief executive election, LegCo elections, and District Council elections. On July 1, 2022, when President Xi Jinping visited the HKSAR, he emphasized the importance of improving governance in the city. The pressure was exerted on Chief Executive John Lee and his principal officials to perform well in dealing with the livelihood and housing issues, narrowing the gap between the rich and the poor, and addressing the problem of poverty. If the governance of the HKSAR can be improved in terms of delivering goods and services to ordinary people more effectively, its performance legitimacy will be enhanced. Otherwise, a relatively weak government combined with "unpopular" policies in the HKSAR, as with the situation of the Carrie Lam administration, would likely precipitate a sudden crisis of governance, especially as some liberal-minded Hong Kong people still harbor latent, cynical, and hidden discontent due to the tight political control over some localists and democratic populists after the promulgation of the national security law.

The first policy address unveiled by John Lee in October 2022 showed that he and his principal officials aptly focused on livelihood issues, notably housing and land supply. Given the fact that Hong Kong's socio-political movements, ranging from the anti–national security legislation in mid-2003 to the anti–national education movement in 2012 and from the Occupy Central movement in late 2014 to the anti–extradition bill movement in the latter half of 2019, were all directly triggered by unpopular government policies formulated without sufficient consultation and explanation, it remains imperative for the HKSAR government to handle controversial policy issues very carefully. Even though the imposition of the national security law in late June 2020 has acted as a deterrent against mass protests, it remains to be seen whether the existing weak resistance from isolated individuals would either fade away or snowball suddenly into a socio-political movement because of the government's mishandling of policy issues.

One objective of Beijing's efforts at revamping the LegCo and District Councils is to enhance the governing capability of the HKSAR government. However, it remains to be seen whether the government's capability will be substantially enhanced. The reasons are that governing capability depends on a multiplicity of factors, ranging from the ability of senior civil servants to provide expert advice to the appointed politicians at the top echelon and the political leadership to the unity of the patriotic factions and the political finesse of the chief executive and his or her followers. During the Carrie Lam administration, some middle-level and senior civil servants did not really perform well, as evidenced in the sluggishness of government officials to deal with the dead bodies of those citizens who died of the COVID-19 Omicron variant in March 2022 and the failure of government departments to mobilize elderly people to be vaccinated against Omicron—obvious performance gaps that led to public anger and criticisms. When John Lee revealed his election platform in April 2022, he vowed to transform the culture of civil servants; nevertheless, it remains to be seen how civil servants are stimulated and encouraged to perform more efficiently and accountably, especially as they are now the target of political reeducation.

Most civil servants have performed diligently, but the lax performance and weak leadership of a minority led to public discontent—an issue addressed by John Lee's emphasis on the need to conduct civil service reform by using key performance indicators. Unlike the pre-2019 era when the political "neutrality" of civil servants was regarded as a "virtue," the new Hong Kong polity since late June 2020 has called for civil servants to abandon using the concept of "neutrality" as an "excuse" to shun their responsibility of promoting and defending government policies. The draft code of conduct of civil servants in December 2023 called for bureaucrats to be politically loyal to the country.[5] While a majority of civil servants must adapt to the emphasis on political loyalty to the central authorities, it remains to be seen how civil service leadership and performance will be enhanced.

Nor did the appointed principal officials perform well in the final years of the Carrie Lam administration. Quite a number of principal officials performed in a mediocre way, including the lack of efforts at vaccinating the elderly people

---

5. *Updating the Civil Service Code: Draft for Consultation* (Hong Kong: Civil Service Bureau, 2023).

who stayed in care homes before the apex of the Omicron attacks in March and April 2022, leading to the deaths of several thousands of the elderly. Hong Kong appeared to be fortunate in avoiding the first several waves of the COVID-19 attacks in 2020 and 2021 until March and April 2022, when the relatively lax attitude of the government toward the mobilization of the elderly and children against COVID-19 and its variants was fully exposed. Other areas of policy failures were prominent, including the failure to reduce the long waiting time of five to six years for ordinary people who applied for accommodations in public housing units and the absence of a comprehensive land acquisition policy so that public housing units and low-cost housing would be massively built for the poor and the needy. Chief Executive John Lee and his ministers are tackling these baffling problems through the construction of transitional housing units and the shortening of the waiting time for public housing applicants to four and a half years. These moves are addressing the livelihood issues as expected by Beijing.

One problem of Hong Kong's governance is that the "patriotic" elites remain divided even though the Liaison Office has been conducting an extensive united front campaign targeted at them. Some newly elected pro-Beijing populist legislators have shown their critical attitudes toward the HKSAR government, playing the role of a loyal opposition. Yet, the "patriotic" elites are divided and competing against each other. The fragmentation of the "patriotic" elites is natural given their varying views on policy issues, thereby leading to a degree of pluralism within the "patriots." The divided "patriotic" elites have to demonstrate to the members of the public that they can check the power of the executive branch effectively and healthily. A relatively weak legislature alongside a powerful executive branch, however, cannot and will not guarantee that all government policies will be popular and satisfactory to the members of the public.

A structural problem of Hong Kong's political system is that, after the revamp of the LegCo's electoral system, the legislature may not fully reflect public opinion, especially as the directly elected members are now occupying only twenty out of ninety seats. If public opinion can be represented in the two sectors—functional constituencies and the Election Committee—then the non-directly elected legislators must do a better job in reflecting public opinion to the government. Otherwise, a new legislature with its politically "reorganized" and "correct" composition would run the risks of "narrowing" public opinion and producing "controversial" government policies. The late Samuel Huntington reminded us of the need to use the legislature to absorb social forces for the sake of maintaining political stability. Yet, if a legislature absorbs only political friends and patrons while excluding all the "enemies" from participation, there would be a real danger of ignoring any hidden social discontent in the new society and politics of Hong Kong.

Objectively speaking, before the Basic Law Article 23 legislation was approved unanimously by LegCo members on March 19, 2024, many legislators raised pertinent concerns and asked sharp questions, thereby improving the content of the legislation and demonstrating their ability to check the power of the executive branch of the government even without the presence of the "pan-democratic" camp. As such, the development of a Hong Kong–style democracy is continuing to evolve gradually. The Hong Kong–style of democracy is now characterized by a legislature with members voicing constructive criticisms; District Councils with new members showing their attendance in meetings and raising livelihood-related questions to officials; a more cooperative mass media whose criticisms of public housing, cage homes, and social policies are increasingly prominent; a more harmonious civil society in which interest groups are working in partnership with the government; and a changing mass political culture in which citizens are gradually divided into political activists, reluctant participants, apathetic materialists, neutral observers, and hesitant spectators. The new dominant politics of paternalistic authoritarianism in the HKSAR is interestingly intermingled with some elements of political pluralism and emergent democratic centralism—the hallmarks of Hong Kong–style democracy. If hybridity, as some scholars have asserted, was a feature of Hong Kong politics, it is currently displaying the dominant Chinese ideological mixture of paternalism, authoritarianism, and centralism with a relatively limited degree of Western pluralism.

Some degree of pluralism can be seen within the power elites, but it remains to be seen how the "patriotic" elites will reach consensus on livelihood issues, including a neglected policy of providing better comprehensive social welfare for the poor, the elderly, and the needy. Hong Kong's capitalism remains "exploitative" in that many lower-class citizens do not have sufficient social welfare benefits. With an aging population, the government does not want to spend too much on the provision of social welfare, on the one hand, and it has to encounter the danger of a decline in economic productivity and competitiveness on the other hand. As such, the importation of mainland talents, especially the younger ones, has become inevitable.

The politics of aging and social welfare gives rise to the question of tax reform. The tax system in Hong Kong has been traditionally biased in favor of rich people. Any tax reform is bound to be socially and politically controversial. The government may have to consider increasing its revenues in the future by imposing more tax on not only the very rich people but also on land transactions, focusing on the pockets of capitalists and land developers. Such a move, however, would encounter opposition from the rich landed elites and the big capitalist class. The politics of tax reform, which can practically be more progressive as it can have redistributive impacts, will likely become more evident and yet controversial from now to 2047, especially as the government's budget deficit is rising.

Another problem of governance in the HKSAR is how to balance the interests of the capitalist class and that of the lower-class citizens. The capitalist class remains a dominant political and economic actor in the top policy-making ExCo and law-making LegCo, which, however, are expected to come up with policies that can and will ideally improve the social welfare of the ordinary citizens. Class contradictions remain hidden in the HKSAR. Ideally, more members of the capitalist class should appreciate the value of enhancing social welfare rather than seeing it as a zero-sum game undermining business interests. The LegCo is dominated by many conservative-minded business elites, and its working-class representatives remain numerically weak, especially after all the democratic populists and welfarists were politically "purged." It remains to be seen how the government of the HKSAR can and will strike a delicate balance between the interests of the capitalists and those of the lower-class residents. Indeed, many capitalist elites are socially benevolent, making donations to society and contributing immensely to charity work. However, if any progressive tax reform were targeted at rich people, the politics of resistance from the rich will likely be a contentious issue, necessitating perhaps intervention from the central government in Beijing. If so, tax reform in the HKSAR will likely be piecemeal and limited, focusing more on indirect tax rather than progressive tax.

From a critical perspective, the ideological conflicts between Hong Kong and the mainland from the beginning of the Occupy Central movement in late 2014 to the anti-extradition movement in the latter half of 2019 stemmed partly from the ignorance, underestimation, and miscalculation of some Hong Kong democrats about the nature of the PRC regime and partly from the increasing dominance of the assertive and conservative nationalistic faction on the mainland. The ignorance of some Hong Kong democrats originated from a batch of young and radical localists, who were highly politically individualistic and perhaps excessively self-centered, who were imbued with a very strong sense of Hong Kong identity at the expense of giving face to PRC authorities, and who unfortunately lacked a profound knowledge of how the mainland's Marxist-Leninist and paternalistically authoritarian regime operates. Unlike the older generation of democrats who were calmer and moderate, the younger generation was more politically outspoken, defiant, and action-oriented. Some of them performed politically provocative acts, such as the oath-taking saga in October 2016, and some participated in violent protests in such a way that alienated PRC authorities. As a result, the political intervention from the PRC officials responsible for Hong Kong matters became inevitable.

From the Marxist-Leninist and paternalistic perspective, the "one country, two systems" in Hong Kong must respect the CCP on the mainland. As former

PRC President Jiang Zemin remarked in 1989, the well water (Hong Kong) should not mix with the river water (mainland China). His warning was not heeded carefully by a minority of Hong Kong localists and democratic populists, who kept on challenging and exceeding the political red lines of the central government in Beijing from 2016 to 2019. If Hong Kong's political system since March 2021 has suffered from a "retrogressive" move back to the polity of the twilight of the British colonial era, some radical localists and democratic populists had to shoulder the historical and political responsibility of unnecessarily provoking the mainland's direct rule over the HKSAR. They failed to appreciate the importance of giving "face" to the PRC authorities. Nor did they fully grasp the paternalistic hallmark of the PRC's elite political culture in dealing with Hong Kong.

The remarks made by HKMAO Director Xia Baolong in February 2021 that the people of Hong Kong should respect the CCP and that they should not engage in activities that undermine the mainland's socialist system led by the CCP are politically significant.[6] Unfortunately, the 2019 anti-extradition movement did undertake actions that disrespected the CCP, such as the acts of desecrating the national flag and the attacks on the Liaison Office headquarters and pro-Beijing organizations. The radical protestors utilized violent activities to plunge the legitimacy of the HKSAR government into a deeper crisis, dragging the central government into the necessity of legal and political intervention through the SCNPC interpretation and decisions on the Basic Law in November 2016, November 2020, and March 2021.

The moderate democrats miscalculated the intention of the PRC authorities after the unprecedented 2010 political compromise over the ways in which the LegCo should be reformed. The 2010 political compromise took place at a juncture when the PRC side was governed by the dominant faction led by liberal nationalists and when the HKSAR side was characterized by not only the split between radical and moderate democrats but also the determination of moderates to negotiate with PRC officials. This historic moment of opportunities, however, could no longer be replicated from the anti–national education campaign in mid-2012 to the enactment of the national security law for Hong Kong in March 2020. Coincidentally, the democratic localists and radical populists became more united after the Occupy Central movement in 2014, believing that the continuous pressure exerted on the HKSAR government and Beijing would bring about more political concessions over the pace and scope of political reform—an assumption that turned out to be totally wrong as the central

---

6. Bai Yunyi, "Relationship between Patriotism, Loving Hong Kong and Upholding the Leadership of the CCP, Fully Explained," *Global Times*, March 2, 2021, accessed March 28, 2021, https://www.globaltimes.cn/page/202103/1217074.shtml.

authorities became more conservatively nationalistic than ever before. Nor did the think tank members, including some intellectuals and academics, of pro-democracy populists and radical localists accurately assess the political ideology and orientation of the PRC authorities. Compounding this miscalculation on the part of democratic populists and radical localists was their deeply divided nature in which the younger new generation of "leaders" were competing among themselves. The so-called "leaderless" nature of the 2019 anti–extradition bill movement hid the fact that there were many small and young leaders competing among themselves and yet challenging the legitimacy of the HKSAR government and Beijing to an unprecedented but unacceptable degree. The political chaos within the pro-democracy camp in the HKSAR from 2012 to 2019 sounded its death knell in mid-June 2020 as the national security law was promulgated to regulate its behavior.

Tensions in "One Country, Two Systems": From Power Struggle to One Country's Victory

The implementation of "one country, two systems" entails at least ten major tensions that require the Hong Kong people and PRC authorities to adapt to each other and to engage in political learning of how their contradictions can be resolved peacefully through a trust-building process and dialogue. These tensions embrace (1) the vision of whether Hong Kong should be an international city or a Chinese city, (2) the clashes between the strong local Hong Kong identity and the mainland Chinese national identity, (3) the surging Hong Kong localism versus the increasing Chinese assertive nationalism, (4) the contradictions between democratization and national security, (5) the Western conception of democracy and the Chinese-style democracy, (6) Hong Kong's pluralism versus the PRC's paternalism, (7) the local political culture tolerant of protests and dissent and the PRC political culture intolerant of them, (8) Hong Kong's mass political culture of accepting an open and confrontational approach versus the mainland's political culture of attaching importance to face and harmony, (9) the lenient approach advocated by some Hong Kong people to deal with protestors and the philosophy of Chinese legalism adopted by PRC authorities, and (10) the PRC's preference of maintaining a powerful executive in Hong Kong versus the tendency of local democrats to support an increasingly representative and powerful legislature vis-à-vis the executive.

The acute contradictions above were expressed in the form of a series of socio-political movements and struggles, including the July 1 protests against the national security bill in 2003, the anti–national education campaign in 2012, the Occupy Central movement from September to December 2014, the Mong Kok riot in early 2016, the oath-taking controversy in October and November

2016, and the anti-extradition movement from June to December 2019. From the perspective of political science, all these movements represented ferocious power struggles between the localist populists and the pro-Beijing HKSAR government. Due to the fact that the pro-Beijing forces remained relatively weak not only in the direct elections held for the LegCo but also in terms of mass mobilization in support of the HKSAR government, PRC authorities sensed the urgency and necessity of controlling the opposition's power struggles by using legal and political instruments: (1) the SCNPC interpretation of the Basic Law's Article 104 on the oath-taking behavior of legislators-elect in November 2016; (2) the promulgation of the national security law in June 2020; (3) the SCNPC decision on the allegiance requirements of LegCo members in November 2020; (4) the SCNPC decision on the revamp of Hong Kong's electoral system in March 2021; (5) the requirement under the national security law that Hong Kong's education system needs to incorporate the ingredient of national security; (6) the HKSAR government's moves to disqualify four LegCo members immediately after the November 2020 decision made by the SCNPC; (7) the HKSAR government's move to transform the content of the liberal studies curriculum, which had been criticized for politicizing many young students; (8) the elevation of the traditionally weak "patriotic" populist faction to the echelons of political power through the LegCo elections in December 2021; (9) the empowerment of the police to arrest and of the legal apparatus to prosecute those offenders of the national security law; and (10) the powerful deterrent impacts of the national security law on the alleged law-breakers. The persistent power struggles between the localist populists on the one hand and the HKSAR government and PRC authorities on the other resulted in the swift, decisive, and authoritarian intervention from Beijing in Hong Kong's political development. From a realpolitik perspective, Beijing, as the most powerful political actor in Hong Kong's political development, has scored a resounding victory in its power struggles with the democratic populists and radical localists.

All the ten tensions mentioned above resulted in the victory of "one country" under the national security law. Except for the ongoing tension between Hong Kong as an international city or a Chinese city, all the other nine tensions have been shifted to the side of "one country"—the triumph of assertive Chinese nationalism over Hong Kong localism; the dominance of mainland Chinese national identity over local Hong Kong identity; the priority of national security over democratization; the triumph of Chinese-style democracy over Western democracy; the salience of PRC's paternalism instead of Hong Kong's pluralism; the increasing prominence of mainland Chinese political culture in the political system of the HKSAR; the primacy of face and harmony in Hong Kong politics; the hallmark of mainland Chinese legalism in Hong Kong's political development; and the prominence of a more powerful executive in the HKSAR.

Some Hong Kong people have underestimated the likelihood that the PRC's authoritarian polity can be diffused to the HKSAR across the border. The authoritarian diffusion from the PRC to the HKSAR shows that Hong Kong's political system has been mainlandized to some extent. The efforts of some localist populists to internationalize Hong Kong politically and to form a "global" civil society proved to be "subversive" to PRC authorities, who decided to crack down on them. The crux of the problem was that some radical localists and democratic populists were politically unwise, continuing to challenge and test the PRC's political red lines. Beijing believes that although the HKSAR continues to be a financial and monetary center, it cannot and should not become a political city susceptible to foreign influences. In short, Hong Kong cannot and should not become a Trojan horse in which foreign forces seek to influence the political systems of the HKSAR and the mainland. This Trojan horse mentality of PRC authorities is deep-rooted, for the Marxist-Leninist regimes in the world, including China, Cuba, and North Korea, are all vigilant to the likelihood that Western democracies would instigate "color revolutions" to change and "subvert" the socialist systems through collaboration with civil society groups. Believing that the Hong Kong LegCo was filled with elements with linkages to foreign forces, Beijing decided to crack down these "supporters" of foreign forces, change the electoral system of Hong Kong, and eliminate all "unpatriotic" localist populists from the legislature.

Critics of Beijing's policy toward the HKSAR have said that the PRC's red lines on Hong Kong remain "unclear." Nonetheless, a sober analysis of Beijing's policy toward the HKSAR shows that the red lines are increasingly clear under the national security law: the four areas of subversion, secession, terrorism, and collusion with foreign forces. Moreover, when some democrats continued to organize the so-called "primary elections" after the enactment of the national security law in June 2020, the move was clearly politically provocative as they put forward ten steps: (1) democrats had an alternative plan if some of them were disqualified to run in the September LegCo elections; (2) the objective of grasping at least thirty-five out of the seventy LegCo seats; (3) the democrats would become a majority in the LegCo; (4) the democrats would veto government bills in the LegCo; (5) the LegCo would veto the government budget and the chief executive would be forced to dissolve the LegCo; (6) the democrats would run in LegCo elections again and capture over thirty-five seats out of the seventy LegCo seats; (7) the LegCo would veto the financial budget of the government, and then, the chief executive would resign; (8) the SCNPC would announce that the HKSAR would enter the emergency period, dissolve the LegCo, and replace it with a provisional LegCo; (9) the HKSAR would witness street protests and mass strikes; and (10) the Western states would implement political and economic sanctions on the PRC.[7] These steps were criticized by the pro-Beijing media as a plot to "paralyze the government, usurp the LegCo and subvert the political regime."[8] From a critical perspective, some democrats politically provoked PRC authorities even immediately after the promulgation of the national security law.[9] If the plan were revised to get fewer than thirty-five LegCo seats and to work with the HKSAR government harmoniously in the LegCo, a conciliatory message to PRC authorities could have depoliticized the very tense atmosphere. Unfortunately, the continuous radicalization of some localist populists proved to be politically lethal and costly. The lesson for the Hong Kong localist and democratic populists is clear: if they want to participate in the new politics of Hong Kong, they must be politically wise and become a loyal opposition. They failed to understand mainland Chinese politics and assumed wrongly that Hong Kong was a "separate" political entity.

Perhaps the most influential impact of the national security law on the society of Hong Kong is that some sectors of the society have been exercising self-censorship. The educational sector has been affected to some extent. While teachers at the primary, secondary, and tertiary levels have already accepted the importance and necessity of protecting national security, a certain degree of strategic self-censorship is inevitable. Such self-censorship has been spreading to other sectors, like the mass media, arts, and the cultural sector. Since the national security law was implemented in late June 2020, a certain degree of the "mainlandization" of Hong Kong, politically and socially, has become irreversible. The challenge is for the people of Hong Kong to adapt to the changing circumstances and learn how to strike a balance between the exercise of their civil liberties and the protection of China's national security. However, from the realist perspective of maintaining law and order, the introduction of the national security law and the legislation on Article 23 of the Basic Law can and will safeguard the civil liberties enjoyed by the people of Hong Kong, establish a comprehensive security legal regime, and buttress Hong Kong's social stability and economic prosperity.

---

7. "'Primary Elections' Seek to Paralyze the Government, Usurp the Legco and Subvert the Political Regime," in *A Call in the Era of Patriots Ruling Hong Kong: Perfection of Hong Kong's Electoral System* (Hong Kong: Tai Kung Pao, March 12, 2021), a special issue, 10–11.
8. "'Primary Elections' Seek to Paralyze the Government, Usurp the Legco and Subvert the Political Regime," 10–11.
9. Zen Soo, "Hong Kong Arrest 53 Activists under National Security Law," Associated Press, January 6, 2021, accessed March 28, 2021, https://apnews.com/article/legislature-primary-elections-democracy-hong-kong-elections-25a66f7dd38e6606c9f8cce84106d916.

The New Politics of Beijing–Hong Kong Relations

Chapter 1 delineates all the features of Chinese politics that are applicable to the new politics of Beijing–Hong Kong relations. China's authoritarian diffusion into Hong Kong is the most prominent feature of the mainlandization of the polity in the HKSAR. The PRC is determined to groom and empower the patriotic populist faction to govern the HKSAR and to exclude those "unpatriotic" localists and populists from infiltration into the power structures, including the LegCo and District Councils. The civil society of Hong Kong was perceived by Beijing as too strong and too dangerous, especially as it had "uncivil" or violent aspects during the anti-extradition movement in 2019 and, particularly, some groups and individuals had linkages with foreign forces. The "explosion" of civil society in the HKSAR during the anti-extradition movement from June to December 2019 was met with authoritarian response from the increasingly authoritarian local state in Hong Kong.[10] In mainland Chinese politics, the state is consistently strong vis-à-vis a weak civil society. Conversely, Hong Kong's civil society challenged not only the legitimacy of the local state but also that of the central state. As the legitimacy of the dual states was challenged and questioned in the political game of power struggles, the CCP as the ruling party on the mainland had to take action to salvage and re-empower the weak local state in the HKSAR. In the PRC, a process of securitization has taken place since the establishment of the National Security Commission in November 2013; nevertheless, Hong Kong's localist populists were ignorant of the mainland political development, and they kept challenging the bottom line of tolerance of the central state. The imposition of the national security law for Hong Kong in June 2020 has empowered the local state in the HKSAR, where the police and the legal apparatuses have been empowered to protect Beijing's national security. The enactment of the national security law for Hong Kong was a testimony to Beijing propping up the weak local state, which failed to legislate on Article 23 of the Basic Law from mid-2003 to mid-2019. In a sense, the weak local state in the HKSAR necessitated the direct rule of the central state over Hong Kong's security-related matters.

If Samuel Huntington emphasized the important function of political institutions to absorb political dissent and social forces, then some dissenting social forces would likely remain politically excluded and yet alienated in the HKSAR. If the governing capacity of Hong Kong can be improved, as the PRC authorities hope, then social discontent and political dissent will continue to be contained. However, if the governing capacity of the Hong Kong executive

---

10. The "explosion" of civil society could be a turning point in democratization, but Hong Kong proved that it could trigger authoritarian responses. See Guillermo O'Donnell and Philippe C. Schmitter, *Transitions from Authoritarian Rule: Tentative Conclusions about Uncertain Democracies* (Baltimore: Johns Hopkins University Press, 1986).

remains controversial with the formulation of unpopular policies, as with the case of the national security bill in 2003 and the extradition bill in early 2019, any sudden eruption of mass discontent would likely occur, even though the scale of such discontent would likely be much smaller because the national security law remains like a sword hanging over the heads of protestors. Many Hong Kong people possess a traditionally far more critical and participatory political culture than their Macau counterparts, but the political culture and traditions of Hongkongers can gradually change under the national security law to make them become a more politically passive and apathetic citizenry. Still, their passiveness and apathy will not guarantee absolute political stability and social tranquility in the HKSAR, especially if the local economy enters any period of fluctuation and decline and if the PRC's political development changes into a more liberal atmosphere. Economic change in Hong Kong and political development in mainland China will shape the politics of discontent in the HKSAR in the coming decades.

A certain degree of political convergence between Hong Kong and Macau is looming. Hong Kong's LegCo direct election component is even smaller compared with Macau's counterpart. The "patriotic" elites in both Hong Kong and Macau are destined to be politically influential and powerful. Both political systems are designed to have a strong executive vis-à-vis a relatively weak legislature. Still, the Hong Kong model of electoral reform in March 2021 did not exclude the likelihood that, if the "patriotic" front can prove its leadership and is determined to push for the re-democratization of Hong Kong, then a return to the political parameter of the August 31, 2014, decision made by the SCNPC would still be possible. Specifically, if the PRC feels more politically secure about Hong Kong's political development, it would perhaps reconsider the possibility of allowing two to three chief executive candidates to be screened out by a Beijing-controlled Nomination Committee and then permit them to compete for the people's votes in direct elections.

However, democratization of the LegCo would be politically more difficult, not to mention the possibility of having a fully directly elected legislature, because the Election Committee will likely continue to play a powerful role in legislative politics, and it will likely become a conservatively nationalistic force hindering any return of Western-style democratization along the path of double direct elections—direct elections of the entire LegCo and direct election of the chief executive through universal suffrage. If the HKSAR is going to re-democratize its polity, it can be anticipated that the direct election of the chief executive after the candidates are screened by the Nomination Committee would likely be much faster and easier than the increase in the proportion of direct elections in the LegCo.

The imposition of the national security law in Hong Kong in late June 2020 can be regarded as a second transition of the HKSAR. The first transition of Hong

Kong to mainland China from 1997 to 2019 was fraught with tremendous difficulties, socio-political conflicts, and political disputes. Beijing was determined to use the imposition of the national security law to change the political landscape of Hong Kong, stabilize its society, and utilize Shenzhen as a locomotive in south China to trigger the economic development of Hong Kong. To some Hong Kong people with a very strong sense of Hong Kong identity, this is a "new" Hong Kong that they cannot accept easily. Those who rejected the second transition and the creation of a new Hong Kong have opted for emigration. Those who accept the second transition are staying in the HKSAR and adapting to the political and legal changes under the umbrella of the national security law. Those who have been traditionally "patriotic" and nationalistic are politically happier in the new Hong Kong. Those who are politically opportunistic are learning to be part of the "patriotic," loyalist, and nationalistic front, climbing up the political ladder quickly in the coming years.

The revamped electoral system in Hong Kong carries a risk factor. As the political system of Hong Kong is moving toward paternalistic authoritarianism, patron-client politics are increasingly prominent in the cooptation of "patriotic" elites to govern the city. Because patron-client politics are vulnerable to electoral bribery and corruption,[11] it remains to be seen whether the new political system of Hong Kong will be free from corruption in the coming decades. If patron-clientelist politics entails secret dealings, inside politics could be a phenomenon suddenly emerging and endangering the legitimacy of the HKSAR leadership, thereby directly shaping public discontent with the regime. After all, if the "patriotic" populist faction is composed of class contradictions, their internal rivalries and power struggles would perhaps necessitate the intervention from the most powerful political patron, namely the PRC officials responsible for Hong Kong affairs. Fortunately, the Independent Commission Against Corruption (ICAC) remains a crucial agency, having educated the candidates of LegCo elections in 2022 and those in District Council elections in 2023 about the importance of clean elections. As such, clean elections will persist.

Although Hong Kong's LegCo composition has experienced a process of "reverse democratization," to borrow from Huntington's term, since the SCNPC decision in March 2021, the controlled political system of the HKSAR would ironically have a demonstration effect on mainland China, especially if the PRC

---

11. James C. Scott, "Patron-Client Politics and Political Change in Southeast Asia," *American Political Science Review* 66, no. 1 (March 1972): 91–113. Scott wrote: "One can classify similarly officeholders in colonial or contemporary settings whose discretionary powers over employment, promotion, assistance, welfare, licensing, permits and other scare values can serve as the basis of a network of personally obligated followers. Politicians and administrators who exploit their office in this way to reward clients while violating the formal norms of public conduct are, of course, acting corruptly" (98).

undergoes a process of gradual political liberalization and democratization in the future. Chinese politics have a tradition of operating in a cycle of political control and relaxation. Beijing's political control over Hong Kong could be easily discerned in the period from late 2016 to 2023. However, if China liberalizes and democratizes its system in the future, the Hong Kong model of a relatively strong executive, a weak legislature, a moderately critical but slightly curbed mass media, and most importantly the possibility of selecting a chief executive through the carefully controlled Election Committee would likely become an important reference and a political experiment for the PRC, especially in the Greater Bay Area where a mayor could be practically elected by imitating the Hong Kong model of selecting the chief executive.

For the Hong Kong democrats, they need to understand and study Chinese politics in a deeper way than ever before. In March 2021, the Democratic Party began to establish a committee to enhance the awareness of its members of China's political development. Some of its leaders were interested in becoming loyal oppositionists joining the "patriotic" front in the new politics of Hong Kong. Trust-building between the moderate democrats on the one hand and PRC officials and "patriotic" elites on the other hand will have to be enhanced. Doing so requires the moderate democrats to abandon their biases against the PRC, to adopt a new engagement policy to participate in local elections, and to create more opportunities for dialogue with PRC authorities. Otherwise, the democrats are destined to be politically marginalized and sidelined. China's united front work on Hong Kong distinguishes its friends from the enemies; for those who want to participate in the "bird-caged democracy" in Hong Kong, they have to be far more politically realistic than before and to accept the necessity of becoming the loyal opposition. Communication is a two-way process in which the moderate democrats and PRC authorities will have to be less politically dogmatic and more mutually interactive than ever. Realpolitik will emerge as a hallmark of the new politics of Beijing–Hong Kong relations.

For the Hong Kong exiles who seek to promote the city's democratization outside of the HKSAR, their influence is bound to be minimized and banned under the extraterritorial reach of the Hong Kong national security law. Any Hong Kong person who collaborates with the political activists in exile or with foreign governments would likely run the high risk of being blacklisted. If intellectuals critical of the state and participative in opposition politics easily become the enemies of the mainland's socialist state, then those local "organic intellectuals" who forge networks with the outside forces are bound to play a risky political game. Under the national security law, the democracy movement outside Hong Kong is seen as subversive, and it would be very difficult to promote changes in Hong Kong unless political liberalization and democratization in mainland China would trigger political change and reform in the HKSAR.

The political development of Hong Kong was mainly the outcome of factional struggles between the mainland and Hong Kong; it was also the result of the civilizational clashes between China and the West. If the Chinese political civilization is characterized by hierarchy, obedience to the authority, harmony between state interests and individual interests, and the supremacy of the state over individuals and groups, all these features are in conflict with the Western values of cherishing human rights, individualism, group autonomy, and civil liberties. The rise of China has already constituted a serious threat to Western states politically, economically, technologically, and militarily. The China threat is real to many Western states, just as the Western-inspired "color revolution" is threatening Beijing's national security in the psyche of PRC authorities. Underlying these mutual perceptions is the tremendous pressure on Hong Kong as an international city or a mainland Chinese city. Those people from Hong Kong and foreign states who wish to internationalize the HKSAR politically are bound to be seen as "subversive" under the national security law, while those people who attempt to turn Hong Kong into a mainland Chinese city are destined to be conservative nationalists with a far more paternalistic and obedient political culture than the liberal democrats.

In a nutshell, Hong Kong's political transformation from 2019 to 2023 illustrated that the city became a victim in the clashes of political civilizations between China and the West, especially the US, of the conflicts between Chinese-style democracy and Western-style democracy, and of the mutual threat perceptions between China and the West. In recent years, unfortunately, the Sino-US rivalries in the military, political, and economic spheres have plunged the HKSAR into becoming a political pawn and a target of power struggles. Geopolitical struggle for power and influence between Beijing and Washington in the international world politicized, complicated, polarized, and victimized some Hong Kong people, especially those residents whose political culture and values tend to embrace the values of Westernization rather than those of Sinification.

The rise of China has benefited Hong Kong economically, but it has impinged on the governance of the HKSAR. The PRC's assertive nationalism was increasing by leaps and bounds, culminating in the promulgation of the national security law for Hong Kong in June 2020. This assertive Chinese nationalism has been accompanied by the PRC's tendency of relying on Chinese legalism to deal with the protest activists and core leaders of the 2019 anti-extradition movement. Penalties rather than pardons were used—a feature of Chinese legalism. New laws and the existing local laws were utilized to pursue lawbreakers. These practices were reflective of Chinese political paternalism combined with Leninism, in which the ruling party remains the vanguard organization whose legitimacy cannot be challenged. Yet, some Hong Kong protestors in the 2019 anti-extradition movement were politically naïve, believing that the localist and populist movement could challenge the authoritarian regime in the PRC and push Hong Kong along the path of Western-style democratization. However, the PRC's authoritarian regime remains very resilient, politically stable, and ideologically strong, perceiving the Hong Kong protest activists as fostering the "color revolution." Some scholars have argued that the PRC regime has even become "neo-totalitarian," as its mobilization of the masses to effectively contain the spread of COVID-19 throughout 2020 showed. Regardless of whether the PRC system has become "neo-totalitarian," its authoritarian diffusion to the HKSAR has become prominent, inevitable, and irreversible since mid-2020. The China factor has arguably become both an external and an increasingly internal factor in Hong Kong's political development, especially as the mainland's assertive nationalism has been rising quickly and as the Hong Kong localists and populists continued to challenge the legitimacy of the dual states—the local Hong Kong state and the central Chinese state. The result was China's determination to exercise its "comprehensive jurisdiction" in the HKSAR through the SCNPC's interpretations of the Basic Law in November 2016, November 2020, and March 2021, the promulgation of the national security law in late June 2020, the implementation of national security education and national education, the mobilization of local civil servants to understand the Basic Law and China more deeply than ever before, the empowerment of the local "patriotic" elites and populists to enter and dominate the LegCo, the full support of John Lee as the sole candidate running in and winning the chief executive election in April and May 2020, and the exclusion of all liberal democrats from District Council elections in 2023. In the entire process of China's exercise of its "comprehensive jurisdiction," the mainland Chinese concept of sovereignty over Hong Kong is absolute and ancient, reflecting Beijing's deep-rooted political tradition and culture of paternalistic authoritarianism.

If dependent development refers to the phenomenon of the PRC's economic reliance on Hong Kong as a window for its modernization from the mid-1970s to the 1990s, such dependent development is no longer significant. The rapid economic rise of China has changed Hong Kong to become increasingly dependent on the mainland's capital, investment, tourists, and expertise since the early 2000s. The China model of development is characterized by its strong developmental state. It can be a model for Hong Kong, whose government after July 1, 1997, remained relatively weak in the formulation and implementation of land policies, the slow construction of public housing units, and the inadequate provision of social welfare. To force the government of Hong Kong to be more capable, Beijing redesigned the political system in the HKSAR in March 2021—a phenomenon reflective of the mainland's mentality of altering the superstructure of Hong Kong in a fundamental way to correct all the political aberrations. Hence, there has been some degree of convergence in the governing philosophy of both mainland China and Hong Kong. Hong Kong is expected to learn from the PRC's strong developmental state and relatively socialist policies to the benefit of the poor and the needy. Still, Hong Kong has its economic utility to mainland China. The HKSAR is seen as a crucial offshore renminbi center where the common law system can protect the city's status as a financial and monetary hub to attract foreign capital and investment. The common law system remains intact, while political cases are handled by the courts through the implementation of the national security law.

The business sector in the HKSAR is resistant to the implantation of mainland socialism into the city, for its business interests and lucrative profits would be deeply undermined. The business sector grasps the golden opportunity of China's united front work to lobby PRC authorities against the implementation of the anti-sanction law in the HKSAR—a lobby that was eventually successful in August 2021.[12] The government-business relations in Hong Kong are politically dynamic. On the one hand, businesspeople can voice their deep concern and show their resistance to any unpopular policy, like the anti-sanctions law. Both the HKSAR government and Beijing did listen to the views of the business elites. Nevertheless, there is a limit to business lobbying for both the local government and Beijing. Prior to the mid-October twentieth Party Congress in Beijing, some businesspeople in Hong Kong tried to lobby the HKSAR government to open its doors to outside visitors by using the so-called 0 + 0 policy (no compulsory quarantine in designated hotels and no need for medical surveillance on visitors staying at home). However, the HKSAR government insisted that the 0 + 3 policy (three-day stay for visitors) would remain in the short run, while Beijing announced that the mainland would continue to adopt its dynamic zero-COVID policy. The messages to the business elites were clear: they should no longer push for the further relaxation of Hong Kong's anti-COVID policy and entry restrictions on outside visitors. Moreover, the HKSAR government and its leaders were reminded by President Xi Jinping during his speech on July 1, 2022, that the Hong Kong leadership should keep a certain distance from the elements of vested interests—an implicit message referring to the need for the HKSAR to maintain, to borrow from Marxist terminology, its relative autonomy vis-à-vis the capitalist class.

The relatively non-interventionist governing philosophy of the HKSAR government is now regarded as outdated; it must learn more from the ways in which the mainland has been governed. As such, the John Lee administration is under pressure to demonstrate its competence, apart from the necessity of protecting

---

12. Sonny Lo, "The Dynamics of Delaying Anti-Sanctions Laws for Hong Kong," *Macau Business*, August 21, 2021, accessed October 14, 2022, https://www.macaubusiness.com/opinion-the-dynamics-of-delaying-anti-sanctions-law-for-hong-kong/.

the national security of Beijing and maintaining its autonomy from the influence of capitalist elites. Yet, the loose coalition supportive of the HKSAR government remains politically divided with diverse interests. It remains to be seen how Beijing can conduct a more thrustful united front work on all the "patriotic" elites, who have different interests, class backgrounds (members of the capitalist class versus the working-class representatives), and political calculations.

The concept of the dual states as advanced by Ernst Fraenkel can be seen in Beijing–Hong Kong relations. Beijing can be seen as a "prerogative state" exercising its "comprehensive jurisdiction" over the HKSAR, while Hong Kong's "normative state" executes the national security law and maintains the legal and political order as instructed by the central government. Within the HKSAR, a deep state composed of the police and legal apparatus has emerged to implement the national security law. By having the chief executive select court judges to deal with national-security-related cases, the PRC authorities expect that this personnel arrangement can safeguard the center's national security interests. Even though the implementation of the national security law may have affected Hong Kong's political autonomy to some extent, PRC authorities believe that this is a necessary and small sacrifice for the sake of protecting national security. Above all, PRC leaders, as with President Xi's speech on July 1, 2022, have emphasized the persistence of the common law system in Hong Kong—a perception that the legal system in Hong Kong remains effective in buttressing the financial, monetary, and international status of the capitalist enclave.

The PRC's ideology of reunification can be regarded as a kind of regime inclusion, embracing not only Hong Kong and Macau but also Taiwan. Any separatist elements in Hong Kong must be cracked down on. Radical localists and democratic populists can be anarchists, while violent terrorists are "subversive" and must be punished under the national security law. District Council election results that led to the infiltration of radical localists and democratic populists into Hong Kong's political superstructure could be overturned by disqualifying district councilors and by eliminating their role of electing LegCo members, according to the March 2021 decision made by the SCNPC. In short, PRC authorities have seen localist populism as practically dangerous and politically subversive.

Paradoxically, Beijing's positive intervention in Hong Kong's political development has negative impacts on Taiwan, where the leaders and citizens do not find the "one country, two systems" politically attractive.[13] Although the PRC side emphasizes that both sides can explore the Taiwan model of "one country, two systems," the current relations between mainland China and Taiwan remain

---

13. Remarks made by KMT core leaders like Eric Chu and dark blue member Jaw Shaw-kong. See *Liberty Times*, March 28, 2021.

rocky. So long as Beijing cannot control factional politics in Taiwan, it is very difficult for the PRC to impose the "one country, two systems" onto the island province. Unless PRC authorities soften their policy toward Hong Kong, and unless they spell out more details of the Taiwan model of "one country, two systems" in a way that gives more autonomy to the Taiwanese people, the political gap between the two sides of the Taiwan Strait remains a huge one.

If Beijing cherishes a peaceful solution as a priority to settle the question of Taiwan's political future, several elements will be critical to its united front work on the people of Taiwan. First, there have to be some intermediaries working as peaceful "ambassadors" to the two sides of the strait, trying to look for possibilities for semi-official and official dialogue, even though the DPP would likely be a "permanent" ruling party in Taiwan. Second, the spirit of agreeing to disagree—a principle essential to the Sino-British negotiations over Hong Kong's political future from 1982 to 1984—remains applicable to Beijing-Taipei relations and their possible breakthrough. Third, the US as a foreign actor backing up Taiwan should perhaps rethink whether it has unduly hardened the DPP stance on the mainland. In other words, the US may have to rein in the "separatist" tendency of the DPP if it really wishes to see a peaceful resolution of Taiwan's political future. Fourth, the stage-by-stage process of negotiations and dialogue as suggested by China's *White Paper* on Taiwan in August 2022 will likely be an important breakthrough in mutual contacts and discussions. In this stage-by-stage process, both sides must exchange their conditions, such as the Taiwan side accepting the 1992 consensus in exchange for Beijing's consensus to abandon the use of force on the island. Moreover, a memorandum of understanding, as Chang Ya-chung suggested, would have to be reached quickly by both sides so that stage one would have a real breakthrough. Indeed, the existence of political will from both sides to reach a common understanding will be the key factor leading to any success in the quest for a peaceful resolution of Taiwan's political future.

In a nutshell, the new politics of Beijing–Hong Kong relations has been deeply affected by the changing nature of factions from both sides, their intense power struggles, and the absence of a profound knowledge of China on the part of some Hong Kong localists and populists. Although Hong Kong's new politics are now characterized by paternalistic authoritarianism, a limited degree of pluralism can be seen in the pro-establishment and pro-Beijing factions, thereby making China's united front work on the HKSAR remain challenging. China's "comprehensive jurisdiction" over Hong Kong has been fully exercised by a series of SCNPC interpretations over Hong Kong's Basic Law and electoral arrangement, the implementation of the national security law, the formulation and implementation of national security education and national education, and the exclusion of all political "troublemakers" from participation in the political superstructures of the HKSAR. Although Hong Kong's new politics have emerged as an unattractive model to most people in Taiwan, the spirit of "one country, two systems"—the principle of agreeing to disagree—remains applicable to Beijing-Taipei relations. If Beijing is keen to utilize a peaceful solution as the priority to deal with Taiwan's political future, the mixture of intermediaries, a stage-by-stage process of dialogue, mutual concessions, and the utilization of the memorandum of understanding to come up with the key elements of consensus from both sides will hopefully be the essential ingredients leading to a new breakthrough in Beijing-Taipei relations in the years to come.

During the twentieth Party Congress in Beijing on October 16, 2022, CCP General Secretary Xi Jinping said that the central government is determined to implement its "comprehensive jurisdiction" over the HKSAR and to ensure the "patriots" rule the capitalist enclave.[14] He pointed to the need for Hong Kong to resolve its "deep contradictions" in the society, implying that the HKSAR government must work harder to improve the livelihood issues of ordinary people and to maintain its autonomy vis-à-vis any social forces, including the capitalists who are now expected to contribute their profits for the good of the society and the previously democratic localists who were ignorant of China's political culture and who saw the Westernization of the political system as a panacea of democratization. From now onward, the capitalist class in the HKSAR must and should ponder how its members can and will help Hong Kong generate a more equitable and just society in which the welfare of the poor and the needy can and will be addressed. An "exploitative" capitalistic system in Hong Kong is not what the central leadership in Beijing would like to witness. Similarly, the localists and democrats in Hong Kong must change their political culture from Western idealism to a more realistic perspective of developing a Hong Kong style of democracy, focusing on how to improve government policies instead of dreaming of a speedy achievement of the so-called double direct elections (direct elections of the chief executive and the entire LegCo). Double direct elections cannot and will not solve all the social contradictions and governing problems of the HKSAR. Instead, the democrats should no longer be nostalgic of their "good old days" in the past two decades; they should pluck up their courage to participate actively in local LegCo and district elections, showing that the people of Hong Kong can strike a balance between Hong Kong–style democratization on the one hand and the protection of mainland China's national security on the other in the new era of Beijing-HKSAR relations.

When CCP General Secretary Xi Jinping mentioned during the October 16 Party Congress that "complete reunification" with Taiwan would be an important objective and that the PRC would not renounce the use of force, it was crystal

---

14. Speech delivered by CCP General Secretary Xi Jinping to the 20th Party Congress on October 16, 2022. RTHK Channel 32 Broadcast, October 16, 2022, 10:00 am to 11.50 am.

clear that Beijing-Taipei relations would sooner or later go through ordeals and challenges. However, with the spirit of agreeing to disagree with issues relating to reunification, Beijing-Taipei relations would perhaps have the potential for a real breakthrough if both sides proceed with their economic and cultural exchanges in the first stage, followed by mutual exchanges and concessions in the second stage and by a memorandum of understanding laying out the essential elements of consensus from both sides. The PRC leadership has made it clear that foreign intervention in China's domestic affairs, especially in Taiwan, will not be tolerated. If so, the US must rethink how it can and will facilitate both Beijing and Taipei to come to a peaceful resolution rather than make any moves that can be construed as abandoning the one-China principle and supporting a minority of Taiwan separatists. An indispensable element in the success of the Sino-British negotiations from 1982 to 1984 over Hong Kong's political future—agreeing to disagree but looking for consensus on issues of common concern—can be applied to Beijing-Taipei relations in the coming years. If all sides cherish the principle of agreeing to disagree over issues over which they need to look for constructive solutions, then the future of Beijing-Taipei relations remains hopeful amid highly politically uncertain, economically volatile, and militarily unstable developments. If ideological conflicts and factional power struggles have increasingly characterized Beijing–Hong Kong relations since 2003, and especially from 2012 to 2023 when Beijing's conservative nationalist victory was eventually sealed, ideological contentions and power politics can also be prominently seen in the evolving Beijing-Taipei relations.

Bibliography

"1992 Consensus Called Key to Cross-Straits Ties." *China Daily*, May 7, 2016, accessed May 9, 2016, http://www.china.org.cn/china/2016-05/07/content_38402457.htm.

"4 Lawmakers Disqualified." November 11, 2020, accessed March 21, 2021, https://www.news.gov.hk/eng/2020/11/20201111/20201111_130632_671.html.

"89 Percent of Taiwanese Oppose China's 'One Country, Two Systems:' Poll." *Taiwan News*, August 7, 2020, accessed March 23, 2021, https://www.taiwannews.com.tw/en/news/3982562.

"A Review Document of Xi Led to the Event of the Causeway Bay Bookstore." March 2, 2018, accessed March 1, 2021, https://www.rti.org.tw/news/view/id/398146.

"中共權貴家族幾乎全部在香港洗錢" [Almost all of mainland rich and powerful families laundered money in Hong Kong]. June 11, 2018, accessed January 3, 2021, https://www.epochtimes.com/b5/18/6/10/n10472449.htm.

"Andy Li's Lawyer Not Hired by Family, Says Sister." RTHK, March 31, 2021, accessed April 2, 2021, https://www.infocushongkong.com/breaking-news/andy-li-s-lawyer-not-hired-by-family-says-sister.

"Candidate Eligibility Review Committee Members Appointed." *Hong Kong Standard*, September 19, 2022, accessed October 13, 2022, https://www.thestandard.com.hk/breaking-news/section/4/194863/Candidate-Eligibility-Review-Committee-members-appointed.

"Candidate Eligibility Review Mechanism." May 1, 2021, accessed October 13, 2022, https://www.cmab.gov.hk/improvement/en/qualification-review/index.html.

"Chan Hin-shing Returns to Hong Kong after Holidays and Gives the Clients' Data to Lam Wing-kee." June 17, 2016, accessed March 1, 2021, https://theinitium.com/article/20160617-hongkong-hkbooksellers07/.

"張亞中拋「兩岸和平備忘錄」：台灣與中國成立共同體" [Chang Ya-chung throws out 'peace memorandum' for two sides: Taiwan and China set up a common union." 三立新聞網 [setn.com], March 31, 2021, accessed April 4, 2021, https://www.setn.com/News.aspx?NewsID=918764.

"Cheng Chung-tai and Pierre Chan Remains in LegCo." *The Standard*, November 11, 2020, accessed March 16, 2021, https://www.thestandard.com.hk/breaking-news/section/4/158912/Cheng-Chung-tai-and-Pierre-Chan-remains-in-Legco.

"China Corruption: Life Term for Ex-security Chief Zhou." BBC, June 11, 2015, accessed February 21, 2021, https://www.bbc.com/news/world-asia-china-33095353.

"China Non-compliant with Joint Declaration, says UK." RTHK News, March 13, 2021, accessed March 24, 2021, https://news.rthk.hk/rthk/en/component/k2/1580434-20210313.htm.

"中國硬推香港國安法 歐美27國反對 中國拉52國反擊" [China pushes for the national security law for Hong Kong: 27 European and American countries oppose, but China mobilizes 52 countries to counterattack]. Radio Free Asia, July 1, 2020, accessed March 24, 2021, https://www.rfi.fr/tw/%E4%B8%AD%E5%9C%8B/20200701-%E4%B8%AD%E5%9C%8B%E7%A1%AC%E6%8E%A8%E9%A6%99%E6%B8%AF%E5%9C%8B%E5%AE%89%E6%B3%95-%E6%AD%90%E7%BE%8E27%E5%9C%8B%E5%8F%8D%E5%B0%8D-%E4%B8%AD%E5%9C%8B%E6%8B%8952%E5%9C%8B%E5%8F%8D%E6%93%8A.

"China Replaces Its Hong Kong and Macau Affairs Office Chief Zhang Xiaoming." Reuters, February 13, 2020, accessed March 7, 2021, https://www.straitstimes.com/asia/east-asia/china-replaces-head-of-its-hong-kong-and-macau-affairs-office.

"China Threat to Invade Taiwan Is 'Closer Than Most Think,' Says US Admiral." AFP, March 23, 2021, accessed March 24, 2021, https://www.theguardian.com/world/2021/mar/23/taiwan-china-threat-admiral-john-aquilino.

"China's Top Legislature Adopts Decision on HKSAR LegCo Members' Qualification." Xinhua, November 11, 2020, accessed March 22, 2021, http://www.npc.gov.cn/englishnpc/c23934/202011/d2a89c95fb3d4db5b8bedd5988445ad1.shtml.

"Decision of the Standing Committee of the National People's Congress on Issues Relating to the Methods for Selecting the Chief Executive of the HKSAR in the Year 2007 and for Forming the LegCo of the HKSAR in the Year 2008." Adopted by the Standing Committee of the Tenth National People's Congress at Its Ninth Session on April 26, 2004, accessed March 7, 2021, https://www.basiclaw.gov.hk/en/materials/doc/2004_04_26_e.pdf.

"Demosisto Drops 'Self-Determination' Clause." RTHK News, January 11, 2020, accessed March 21, 2021, https://news.rthk.hk/rthk/en/component/k2/1502283-20200111.htm?spTabChangeable=0.

"Ex-Hong Kong Lawmaker Baggio Leung Seeks Asylum in US." AFP, December 11, 2020, accessed March 14, 2021, https://hongkongfp.com/2020/12/11/ex-hong-kong-lawmaker-baggio-leung-seeks-asylum-in-us/.

"Ex-Stand News Editors Denied Bail." RTHK, December 30, 2021, accessed October 2, 2022, https://news.rthk.hk/rthk/en/component/k2/1626644-20211230.htm.

"Fact Sheet on China's Foreign NGO Law." November 1, 2017, accessed January 1, 2021, https://www.chinafile.com/ngo/latest/fact-sheet-chinas-foreign-ngo-law.

"Foreign Ministry Spokesperson Mao Ning's Regular Press on October 9, 2022." Accessed October 12, 2022, https://www.fmprc.gov.cn/mfa_eng/xwfw_665399/s2510_665401/202210/t20221009_10780009.html.

"Foreign Secretary Declares Break of Sino-British Joint Declaration." UK government's press release, November 12, 2020, accessed March 24, 2021, https://www.gov.uk/government/news/foreign-secretary-declares-breach-of-sino-british-joint-declaration.

"Former China Leader Jiang Zemin and Supporters in Chairman Xi's Sights." July 9, 2019, *Taiwan News*, accessed February 28, 2021, https://www.taiwannews.com.tw/en/news/3741630.

Bibliography

"Gui Minhai: Hong Kong Bookseller Gets 10 Years Jail." BBC News, February 25, 2020, accessed March 1, 2021, https://www.bbc.com/news/world-asia-china-51624433.

"Highlights of Xi's Speech at Taiwan Message Anniversary Event." *China Daily*, January 2, 2019, accessed February 17, 2021, https://www.chinadaily.com.cn/a/201901/02/WS5c2c1ad2a310d91214052069.html.

"HKMAO Chief Zhang Xiaoming Demoted." RTHK, February 13, 2020, accessed April 2, 2021, https://news.rthk.hk/rthk/en/component/k2/1508301-20200213.htm.

"HKSAR Government Announces Disqualification of Legislators Concerned in Accordance with NPCSC's Decision on Qualification of Legislators." November 11, 2020, accessed October 3, 2022, https://www.info.gov.hk/gia/general/202011/11/P2020111100779.htm.

"HKSAR Government Announces Disqualification of Legislators Concerned in Accordance with SCNPC's Decision on the Qualification of HKSAR Legislators." Hong Kong government press release, November 11, 2020, accessed March 16, 2021, https://www.info.gov.hk/gia/general/202011/11/P2020111100779.htm.

"HKSAR Government Committed to Protecting Human Rights." Press release, July 12, 2022, accessed October 10, 2022, https://www.info.gov.hk/gia/general/202207/12/P2022071200739.htm.

"Hong Kong Boat Activists: China Jails Group for up to Three Years." BBC News, December 30, 2020, accessed March 16, 2021, https://www.bbc.com/news/world-asia-china-55481425.

"Hong Kong Court Upholds Decision for No Jury at First National Security Trial." Reuters, June 22, 2021, accessed September 30, 2022, https://www.cnbc.com/2021/06/22/hong-kong-court-upholds-decision-for-no-jury-at-first-national-security-trial.html.

"Hong Kong People Are about to Enjoy Real Democracy: Xia Baolong." RTHK, December 6, 2021, accessed October 11, 2022, https://news.rthk.hk/rthk/en/component/k2/1623001-20211206.htm.

"Hong Kong Troublemakers Are a Political Virus: Luo Huining." RTHK News, February 20, 2020, accessed April 4, 2021, https://news.rthk.hk/rthk/en/component/k2/1509714-20200220.htm.

"Hong Kong's New Bishop Faces Delicate Balancing Act." Union of Catholic Asia News, December 4, 2021, accessed September 28, 2022, https://www.ucanews.com/news/hong-kongs-new-bishop-faces-delicate-balancing-act/95231.

"Hong Kong's University Entrance Exam Question Triggers Outcry, Exposes Education Flaws." Xinhua, May 17, 2020, accessed March 16, 2021, https://www.shine.cn/news/nation/2005178307/.

"How It Happened: Transcript of the US-China Opening Remarks in Alaska." Nikkei Asia, March 19, 2021, accessed March 24, 2021, https://asia.nikkei.com/Politics/International-relations/US-China-tensions/How-it-happened-Transcript-of-the-US-China-opening-remarks-in-Alaska.

"Hu Jintao Paid High Attention to Hong Kong's Political System Development." In *The Discussion and Dispute over Patriotism* (*Aiguo Luncheng*), edited by Ming Pao. Hong Kong: Ming Pao Publisher, April 2004.

"Hu Jintao's Speech in Hong Kong on July 1, 2007." accessed April 13, 2018, http://www.locpg.hk/2015-03/18/c_127594820.htm.

hk01 interview with Emily Lau. "專訪｜傳「超區」將取消　劉慧卿：2010年後北京與民主派再無溝通". hk01.com, March 10, 2021, accessed March 14, 2021, https://www.hk01.com/.

"John Lee Wins Chief Executive Election." *Hong Kong Standard*, May 8, 2022, accessed October 12, 2022, https://www.news.gov.hk/eng/2022/05/20220508/20220508_113345_467.html.

"叫戰江啟臣 中媒曝：江一席話連戰暴怒 推連勝文拼黨魁" [Johnny Chiang's remarks alienated Lien Chan." 新頭殼 [Newtalk], March 15, 2021, accessed March 23, 2021, https://newtalk.tw/news/view/2021-03-15/549259.

"Kevin Yeung: Doubts on Liberal Studies Revamp 'Unnecessary.'" *The Standard*, December 5, 2020, accessed March 16, 2021, https://www.thestandard.com.hk/breaking-news/section/4/160448/Kevin-Yeung:-doubts-on-liberal-studies-revamp-%22unnecessary%22.

"北大教授孔庆东骂'部分香港人是狗'" [Kong Qingdong scolded some Hong Kong people as 'dogs.'" 网易新闻中心, January 21, 2012, accessed March 16, 2021, archive.org.

"Law of the People's Republic of China on Safeguarding National Security in the Hong Kong Special Administrative Region." Accessed November 8, 2020, https://www.gld.gov.hk/egazette/pdf/20202448e/egn2020244872.pdf.

"LCQ2: Espionage activities Conducted by Foreign Governments in Hong Kong." LegCo, January 26, 2022, accessed September 29, 2022, https://www.info.gov.hk/gia/general/202201/26/P2022012600473.htm.

"LCQ5: Enacting Legislation on Article 23 of the Basic Law." LegCo, May 11, 2022, accessed September 29, 2022, https://www.info.gov.hk/gia/general/202205/11/P2022051100512.htm.

"LegCo General Election Postponed for a Year." HKSAR government press release, July 31, 2020, accessed March 14, 2021, https://www.info.gov.hk/gia/general/202007/31/P2020073100898.htm.

"Li Keqiang Going South, Xi Jinping Going North: What Signals Are Released?" Yahoo News, August 18, 2022, accessed August 21, 2022, https://tw.news.yahoo.com/.

"Method for Selecting the Chief Executive by Universal Suffrage: Consultation Report and Proposals." April 2015, accessed April 13, 2018, http://www.2017.gov.hk/filemanager/template/en/doc/report_2nd/consultation_report_2nd.pdf.

"Misbehaving Lawmakers Will Be Suspended from LegCo Meetings." *The Standard*, March 25, 2021, accessed April 5, 2021, https://www.thestandard.com.hk/breaking-news/section/4/168240/Misbehaving-lawmakers-will-be-suspended-from-LegCo-meetings.

"New Democracy Elects Our New Future." *Wen Wei Po*, December 21, 2021.

"New Electoral System Successfully Implemented, Hong Kong's Democracy Opened New Chapter." *Ta Kung Pao*, December 21, 2021, A1.

"吳秋北4000字批「地產霸權」　發起「新工運」促懲罰囤地發展商" [Ng Chau-pei 4,000 words criticizes 'land hegemony' and launches 'new labor movement' to advocate penalizing those land developers accumulating land." hk01.com, March 24, 2021, accessed March 27, 2021, https://www.hk01.com/.

"Non-jury Trial Ordered for Hong Kong's Largest National Security Case: AFP." *The Standard*, August 16, 2022, accessed September 30, 2022, https://www.thestandard.com.hk/breaking-news/section/4/193545/Non-jury-trial-ordered-for-Hong-Kong's-largest-national-security-case:-AFP.

"On Beijing's Imposition of National Security Legislation on Hong Kong: Press Statement, Michael R. Pompeo, U.S. Secretary of State." June 30, 2020, https://hk.usconsulate.gov/n-2020063001/.

"'One Country, Two Systems' at Risk, Jasper Tsang Says." August 31, 2015, accessed October 11, 2017, https://tsangyoksing.hk/2015/08/31/one-country-two-systems-at-risk-jasper-tsang-says/.

"Open Letter Relating to Universities Service Centre for China Studies." CUHK, December 30, 2020, accessed January 17, 2021, https://www.cpr.cuhk.edu.hk/en/press_detail.php?id=3460&t=open-letter-relating-to-the-universities-service-centre-for-china-studies-usc&s=).

"Paul Chan Sends Best Wishes to John Lee Ka-chiu on His Chief Executive election endeavor." *Hong Kong Standard*, April 6, 2021, accessed October12, 2022, https://www.thestandard.com.hk/breaking-news/section/4/188900/Paul-Chan-sends-best-wishes-to-John-Lee-Ka-chiu-on-his-CE-election-endeavor.

"【香港要聞】王滬寧、令計劃舊部接管，鳳凰衛視或成港版央視" [Phoenix TV may become the CCTV version of Hong Kong], February 9, 2021, accessed April 2, 2021, https://gnews.org/articles/403740.

"'Primary Elections' Seek to Paralyze the Government, Usurp the LegCo and Subvert the Political Regime." In *A Call in the Era of Patriots Ruling Hong Kong: Perfection of Hong Kong's Electoral System*. Hong Kong: Tai Kung Pao, March 12, 2021.

"Report on the Public Consultation on Constitutional Development and on Whether There Is a Need to Amend the Methods for Selecting the Chief Executive of the HKSAR and for Forming the LegCo of the HKSAR in 2012." December 12, 2007, accessed March 7, 2021, https://www.cmab.gov.hk/doc/issues/Report_to_NPCSC_en.pdf.

The Standing Committee of the National People's Congress. "Report on Whether There Is a Need to Amend the Methods for Selecting the Chief Executive of the HKSAR in 2007 and for Forming the LegCo of the HKSAR in 2008." April 15, 2004, accessed March 7, 2021, https://www.cmab.gov.hk/cd/eng/executive/pdf/cereport.pdf.

"Report to the State Council Concerning the Submission of a Request to the SCNPC Regarding the Interpretation of Article 53(2) of the Basic Law of the HKSAR of the PRC." April 6, 2005, accessed March 7, 2021, https://www.info.gov.hk/gia/general/200504/06/04060198.htm.

"State Council Appoints Principal Officials of the Sixth-Term HKSAR Government." Xinhua, June 19, 2022, accessed October 12, 2022, https://www.chinadaily.com.cn/a/202206/19/WS62ae9945a310fd2b29e63811.html.

"Sydney Academic Feng Chongyi Allowed to Leave China." BBC, April 2, 2017, accessed January 25, 2021, https://www.bbc.com/news/world-australia-39471670.

"The Basic Law of the HKSAR of the PRC." Adopted by the NPC on April 4, 1990 and Promulgated by Order No. 26 of the PRC President on April 4, 1990, and Effective as of July 1, 1997, accessed September 29, 2022, https://www.basiclaw.gov.hk/en/basiclaw/chapter2.html.

"The Basic Law of the Hong Kong Special Administrative Region." Article 45, accessed March 2, 2021, https://www.basiclaw.gov.hk/pda/en/basiclawtext/chapter_4.html.

"The Interpretation by the Standing Committee of the National People's Congress of Annex 7 of Annex I and Article III of Annex II to the Basic Law of the HKSAR of the PRC." L.N. 54 of 2004, B431, April 6, 2004, accessed March 7, 2021, https://www.basiclaw.gov.hk/en/materials/doc/2004_04_06_e.pdf.

"The Law of the People's Republic of China on Safeguarding National Security in the Hong Kong Special Administrative Region." G.N. (E.) 72 of 2020, accessed September 29, 2022, https://www.elegislation.gov.hk/fwddoc/hk/a406/eng_translation_(a406)_en.pdf.

"The Law of the PRC on Safeguarding National Security in the HKSAR." Accessed October 2, 2022, https://www.elegislation.gov.hk/fwddoc/hk/a406/eng_translation_(a406)_en.pdf.

"The National Security Law Is Used Retrospectively, Ray Wong Says." *The Standard*, August 1, 2020, accessed March 28, 2021, https://www.thestandard.com.hk/breaking-news/section/4/152207/The-national-security-law-is-used-retrospectively,-Ray-Wong-says.

"The Taiwan Question and China's Reunification in the New Era." The Taiwan Office of the State Council, August 10, 2022, accessed September 11, 2022, http://www.scio.gov.cn/zfbps/32832/Document/1728491/1728491.htm.

"The Taiwan Question and China's Reunification in the New Era." The PRC Taiwan Affairs Office of the State Council and the State Council Information Office, August 10, 2022, accessed October 12, 2022, https://english.news.cn/20220810/df9d3b8702154b34bbf1d451b99bf64a/c.html.

"Therapists Convicted over Seditious Children's Books." RTHK English News, September 7, 2022, accessed September 29, 2022, https://news.rthk.hk/rthk/en/component/k2/1665940-20220907.htm.

"Those Banned Books That Have to Be Pursued and Investigated." Post852.com, June 17, 2016, accessed March 1, 2021, https://www.post852.com/161892/.

"Tik Chi-yuen 1:89: Non-Establishment Utterly Failed in Direct Elections." *Ming Pao*, December 21, 2021, p. A1.

"Tung Chee-hwa Resigns as Hong Kong Chief Executive." *China Daily*, March 11, 2005, accessed March 7, 2021, https://www.chinadaily.com.cn/english/doc/2005-03/11/content_424042.htm.

"Two Examination Authority Staff Resigned amid DSE Question Controversy." *Hong Kong Standard*, May 16, 2020.

"看明白香港的现状，必须先搞懂这6个问题" [Understanding Hong Kong's current situation, one has to clarify six questions]. 中国日报网 [*China Daily*], August 21, 2019, accessed March 24, 2021, https://cn.chinadaily.com.cn/a/201908/21/WS5d6e216da31099ab995ddb94.html.

"Washington reveals its true color in Anchorage." *China Daily*, March 19, 2021, accessed March 24, 2021, https://www.chinadailyhk.com/article/a/160975.

"What Does Benny Tai's Illegal 'Primary Election' Bring to Hong Kong." Xinhua, March 2, 2021, accessed March 14, 2021, http://www.xinhuanet.com/english/2021-03/02/c_139778675.htm.

"White Paper on Hong Kong's Democratic Development." The State Council's Information Office, December 20, 2021, accessed September 11, 2022, https://www.chinadailyhk.com/article/252582#Full-text:-White-paper-on-Hong-Kong's-democratic-development.

"Xi Jinping Mentions Struggles 14 times in His New Speech at the Party School." March 3, 2021, accessed March 30, 2021, https://www.rfi.fr/tw/.

"Xi Jinping Named President of China." BBC News, March 14, 2013, accessed March 30, 2021, https://www.bbc.com/news/world-asia-china-21766622.

"Xia Baolong: Comprehensively Implement the Principle of 'Patriots Governing Hong Kong' and Promote the Stable and Smooth Process of Realizing the 'One Country, Two Systems.'" *Ta Kung Pao*, March 2, 2021, p. A10.

"夏寶龍：愛國就要愛中華人民共和國　不允損中共領導社會主義制度" [Xia Baolong: Loving the country is to love the PRC and the act of undermining the CCP-led socialist system is not allowed]. hk01.com, February 22, 2021, accessed April 2, 2021, https://www.hk01.com/.

"【中共權鬥】外媒：「江澤民白手套」肖建華最快今月上海受審" [Xiao Jianhua who was a "white glove" of Jiang Zemin is going to be on trial in Shanghai this month]. 自由亞洲電台粵語部 [Radio Free Asia], June 10, 2022, accessed September 18, 2022, https://www.rfa.org/cantonese/news/xiao-06102022060216.html.

"Xi-Ma Meeting Turns Historic Page in Cross-Strait Relations: Official." Xinhua, November 9, 2015, accessed March 23, 2021, http://www.scio.gov.cn/32618/Document/1454345/1454345.htm.

"Xinjiang: China Defends 'Education' Camps." BBC News, September 17, 2020, accessed March 30, 2021, https://www.bbc.com/news/world-asia-china-54195325.

"Ye Jianying on Taiwan's Return to Motherland and Peaceful Reunification." September 30, 1981, accessed April 4, 2021, http://www.china.org.cn/english/7945.htm.

2007 Chief Executive Election: Electoral Affairs Commission Report on the 2007 Chief Executive Election. Report submitted to the Honorable Donald Tsang Yan-kuen, Chief Executive of the HKSAR of the PRC, June 22, 2007, accessed May 18, 2014, http://www.eac/pdf/chief/en/2007_CE_Report/2007ce_ch12.pdf.

A Call in the Era of Patriots Ruling Hong Kong: Perfection of Hong Kong's Electoral System, Hong Kong: Tai Kung Pao, March 12, 2021.

Anderson, Benedict. *Imagined Communities: Reflections on the Origin and Spread of Nationalism*. London: Verso, 2006.

Apple Daily. Hong Kong Chinese newspaper.

Applebaum, Anne. "The Leninist Roots of Civil Society Repression." *Journal of Democracy* 26, no. 4 (October 2015): 21–27.

Au-yeung, Allen. "What Is One Belt, One Road Strategy All About?" *South China Morning Post*, January 13, 2016, accessed April 13, 2018, http://www.scmp.com/news/hong-kong/economy/article/1900633/what-one-belt-one-road-strategy-all-about.

Baehr, Peter. "Hong Kong Universities in the Shadow of the National Security Law." *Society* 59 (2022): 225–239, accessed July 24, 2022, https://doi.org/10.1007/s12115-022-00709-9.

Bai, Yunyi. "Relationship between Patriotism, Loving Hong Kong and Upholding the Leadership of the CCP, Fully Explained." *Global Times*, March 2, 2021, accessed March 28, 2021, https://www.globaltimes.cn/page/202103/1217074.shtml.

Baker, Hugh D. R. "Life in the Cities: The Emergence of the Hong Kong Man." *China Quarterly*, no. 95 (September 1983): 469–479.

Barney, Darin David. "The Role of Intellectuals in Contemporary Society." *Transforms: Insurgent Voices in Education* 1, no. 1 (1994): 89–105.

BBC News. "Shanghai Lockdown: Residents Protest after Five Weeks of Zero-Covid Measures." BBC News, April 29, 2022, accessed August 21, 2022, https://www.bbc.com/news/av/world-asia-china-61270616.

Beja, Jean-Philippe. "Xi Jinping's China: On the Road to Neo-totalitarianism." *Social Research* 86, no. 1 (Spring 2019): 203–230.

Bell, Daniel A. *The China Model: Political Meritocracy and the Limits of Democracy*. Princeton, NJ: Princeton University Press, 2016.

Bhattacharya, Abanti. "Chinese Nationalism and China's Assertive Foreign Policy." *Journal of East Asian Affairs* 21, no. 1 (April 2007): 235–262.

Bourke, Latika. "China Wins Vote to Stop UN Human Rights Council from Debating Xinjiang Abuses." *Sydney Morning Herald*, October 7, 2022, accessed October 10, 2022, https://www.smh.com.au/world/europe/china-wins-key-vote-in-un-human-rights-council-to-prevent-debate-on-xinjiang-20221007-p5bnv6.html.

Brasher, Keith. "Hong Kong Retreats in National Education Plan." *New York Times*, September 8, 2012.

Buckley, Chris. "Britain Accuses China of Violating Treaty in Hong Kong's Bookseller's Case." *New York Times*, February 13, 2016, accessed March 24, 2021, https://www.nytimes.com/2016/02/13/world/asia/britain-china-hong-kong-bookseller.html.

Bugaric, Bojan. "The Two Faces of Populism: Between Authoritarian and Democratic Populism." *German Law Journal* 20 (2019): 390–400.

Burns, John P. "The Structure of Communist Party Control in Hong Kong." *Asian Survey* 30, no. 8 (August 1990): 749–763.

Buscaneanu, Sergiu. *Regime Dynamics in EU's Eastern Neighborhood: EU Democracy Promotion, International Influences, and Domestic Contexts*. Switzerland: Springer, 2016.

Bush, Richard C. *Hong Kong in the Shadow of China: Living with the Leviathan*. Washington: Brookings Institution Press, 2016.

Buzogany, Aron. "Illiberal Democracy in Hungary: Authoritarian Diffusion or Domestic Causation?" *Democratization* 24, no. 7 (2017): 1307–1325.

Cable TV News. Hong Kong.

Cao, Erbao. "Hong Kong's Governing Forces under the condition of 'One Country, Two Systems.'" *Study Times*, vol. 422 (January 29, 2008), accessed February 17, 2021, https://www.legco.gov.hk/yr08-09/chinese/panels/ca/papers/ca0420cb2-1389-2-c.pdf.

Chan, Ho-him. "Hong Kong's Public Universities Should Reflect National Security Law in Curricula by New Academic Year, Be Ready to 'Suppress' Acts That Violate It: Education Minister." *South China Morning Post*, March 3, 2021, accessed March 16, 2021, https://www.scmp.com/news/hong-kong/education/article/3124228/hong-kongs-public-universities-must-reflect-national.

Chan, Ho-him. "Teachers to Drop Sensitive Subjects." *South China Morning Post*, March 22, 2021, A1.

Chan, Ho-him, and Gary Cheung. "Beijing Blasts 'Poisonous' Hong Kong Exam Question on Whether Japan Did More Good Than Harm to China during First Half of the Last Century and Warns of 'Rage' of the Chinese People." *South China Morning Post*, May 15, 2020, accessed March 16, 2021, https://www.scmp.com/news/hong-kong/education/article/3084523/beijings-foreign-ministry-takes-aim-hong-kong-exam.

Chan, Kelvin. "Chinese Shoppers Latest Target of Hong Kong Protest Anger." Associated Press, March 2, 2015.

Chan, Ming K., and Kent P. K. Wan. "Uncertain Prospects for Democracy in China's Hong Kong." *Journal of East Asian Studies* 18 (2018): 117–126.

"Chan Wai-yip's Team in New Territories West." Accessed May 28, 2014, http://www.chanwaiyip.com/policypaper/electionmail.pdf.

Chang Liao, Nien-Chung. "The sources of China's Assertiveness: The System, Domestic Politics or Leadership Preferences?" *International Affairs* 92, no. 4 (2016): 817–833.

Chau, Candice. "Hong Kong Media Tycoon Jimmy Lai Again Refused Bail over Alleged National Security Law Violations." *Hong Kong Free Press*, February 19, 2021, accessed March 17, 2021, https://hongkongfp.com/2021/02/19/hong-kong-media-tycoon-jimmy-lai-again-refused-bail-over-alleged-national-security-law-violations/.

Chau, Candice. "47 Democrats Charged with 'Conspiracy To Commit Subversion' over Legislative Primaries." *Hong Kong Free Press*, February 28, 2020, accessed March 14, 2021, https://hongkongfp.com/2021/02/28/47-democrats-charged-with-conspiracy-to-commit-subversion-over-legislative-primaries/.

Chau, Candice. "Hong Kong National Security Police Explain Why Children's Picture Books about Sheep Are Seditious." *Hong Kong Free Press*, July 22, 2021, accessed September 29, 2022, https://hongkongfp.com/2021/07/22/hong-kong-national-security-police-explain-why-childrens-picture-books-about-sheep-are-seditious/.

Chen, Lulu, and Coco Liu. "China Targets Jack Ma's Alibaba Empire in Monopoly Probe." Bloomberg, December 24, 2020, accessed April 3, 2021, https://www.bloomberg.com/news/articles/2020-12-24/china-launches-probe-into-alibaba-over-monopoly-allegations.

Chen, Yu-his. "Dependent Development and Its Sociopolitical Consequences: A Case Study of Taiwan." PhD thesis, University of Hawaii, 1981.

Chen, Zhonghai. "The Chinese People's Concept of *Dayitong*." *Observations on China's Development* 6 (2017): 62–64 [in Chinese].

Cheng, Edmund W. "Street Politics in a Hybrid Regime: The Diffusion of Political Activism in Post-colonial Hong Kong." *China Quarterly* 226 (June 2016): 383–406.

Cheng, Evelyn. "China's Xi Says Hong Kong Is Moving from 'Chaos to Governance.'" CNBC, July 1, 2022, accessed October 10, 2022, https://www.cnbc.com/2022/07/01/china-xi-says-hong-kong-is-moving-from-chaos-to-governance.html.

Cheng, Joseph Y. S. "Challenge to Pro-democracy Movement in Hong Kong." *China Perspectives* 2 (July 2011): 44–60.
Cheng, Joseph Y. S. "Introduction: Causes and Implications of the July 1 Protest Rally in Hong Kong." In *The July 1 Protest Rally: Interpreting a Historic Event*, edited by Joseph Cheng, 1–69. Hong Kong: City University Press of Hong Kong, 2005.
Cheng, Kris. "Beijing Discouraged Me from Entering Leadership Race, Says Ex-LegCo President Jasper Tsang." *Hong Kong Free Press*, March 15, 2017, accessed October 11, 2017, https://www.hongkongfp.com/2017/03/15/beijing-discouraged-me-from-entering-leadership-race-says-ex-legco-president-jasper-tsang/.
Cheng, Selina. "Activists in Exile Launch '2021 Hong Kong Charter' Solidarity Movement to Unite Hongkongers Overseas." *Hong Kong Free Press*, March 15, 2021, accessed April 5, 2021, https://hongkongfp.com/2021/03/15/activists-in-exile-launch-2021-hong-kong-charter-solidarity-movement-to-unite-hongkongers-overseas/.
Cheng, Teresa. "Prosecutorial Independence Assured." April 15, 2022, accessed October 2, 2022, https://www.news.gov.hk/eng/2022/04/20220415/20220415_121410_161.html.
Cheung, Gary. "Beijing's U-Turn 'to Thwart radicals.'" *South China Morning Post*, June 22, 2010, accessed March 14, 2021, https://www.scmp.com/article/717745/beijings-u-turn-thwart-radicals.
Cheung, Gary. "Hong Kong 'Separation of Powers': Why Beijing Is Laying Down the Law on Who's In Charge." *South China Morning Post*, September 16, 2015, accessed February 22, 2021, https://www.scmp.com/news/hong-kong/politics/article/1858535/why-beijing-laying-down-law-whos-charge-hong-kong.
Cheung, Gary Ka-wai. *Hong Kong Watershed: The 1967 Riots*. Hong Kong: Hong Kong University Press, 2009.
Cheung, Jane. "Office Partnership Falls Apart for Two Lawmakers." *Hong Kong Standard*, October 11, 2022, accessed October 13, 2022, https://www.thestandard.com.hk/section-news/section/47381906/246273/Office-partnership-falls-apart-for-two-lawmakers.
Cheung, Tommy. "'Father' of Hong Kong Nationalism? A Critical Review of Wan Chin's City-State Theory." *Asian Education and Development Studies* 4, no. 4 (2015): 460–470.
Ching, Cheong. "The Fall of Hong Kong: China's Strategic Plan to Conquer Hong Kong and Purge of Its People." *China: Inquiry and Analysis Series*, no. 1560 (February 21, 2021), accessed March 21, 2021, https://www.memri.org/reports/fall-hong-kong-chinas-strategic-plan-conquer-hong-kong-and-purge-it-its-people.
Chung, Kimmy, and Tony Cheung. "Political Storm in Hong Kong as Activist Agnes Chow Banned from By-election over Party's Call for City's 'Self-Determination.'" *South China Morning Post*, January 27, 2018, accessed April 13, 2018, http://www.scmp.com/news/hong-kong/politics/article/2130714/hong-kong-activist-agnes-chow-banned-legco-election.
Churchill, Owen, and Alvin Lum. "Hong Kong's Former No. 2 Anson Chan Meets Mike Pence in Washington as US Report Criticizes Beijing's 'Intervention' in City's Affairs." *South China Morning Post*, March 23, 2019, accessed December 25, 2019,

https://www.scmp.com/news/hong-kong/politics/article/3002953/hong-kong-lawmakers-and-former-no-2-hit-us-capital-report.

Cohen, David. "China's Factional Politics." *The Diplomat*, December 8, 2012, accessed February 21, 2021, https://thediplomat.com/2012/12/chinas-factional-politics/.

Deng, Jinting, and Pinxin Liu. "Consultative Authoritarianism: The Drafting of China's Internet Security Law and E-Commerce Law." *Journal of Contemporary China* 26, no. 107 (2017): 679–695.

Dirlik, Arif. *The Origin of Chinese Communism*. New York: Oxford University Press, 1989.

Dittmer, Lowell. "Chinese Factional Politics under Jiang Zemin." *Journal of East Asian Studies* 3, no. 1 (January-April 2003): 97–128.

Domes, Jurgen. "Intra-Elite Group Formation and Conflict in the PRC." In *Groups and Politics in the People's Republic of China*, edited by David S. G. Goodman, 28–35. New York: M. E. Sharpe, 1984.

Dong, Lin. "The Space Concept of Confucius' 'Great Unity' Thought." *Journal of Xinyang Normal University* 38, no. 5 (September 2018): 12–15.

Drucker, H. M. *The Political Uses of Ideology*. London: Palgrave, 1974.

Editorial. "Following the Basic Law Interpretation, the High Court's Ruling on Leung and Yau Makes People Happy." *Ta Kung Pao*, November 22, 2016, accessed February 21, 2021, http://www.takungpao.com.hk/paper/2016/1122/39949.html.

Editorial. "Speeding Up the Local Legislation on the Law of National Anthem." *Ta Kung Pao*, October 11, 2017, A3.

Education Bureau Circular No. 3. 2021. "National Security: Maintaining a Safe Learning Environment Nurturing Good Citizens." February 2, 2021, accessed April 2, 2021, https://applications.edb.gov.hk/circular/upload/EDBC/EDBC21003E.pdf.

Electoral Affairs Commission: Report on the 1998 Legislative Council Elections, accessed May 18, 2014, http://www.info.gov.hk/info/98eac-e.htm.

Evans, Peter B. *Dependent Development: The Alliance of Multinationals, State and Local Capital in Brazil*. Princeton, NJ: Princeton University Press, 1979.

Fong, Brian C. H. "State-Society Conflicts under Hong Kong's Hybrid Regime: Governing Coalition Building and Civil Society Challenges." *Asian Survey* 53, no. 1 (2013): 854–882.

Fong, Tak Ho. "Shanghai Court Jails Tycoon Xiao Jianhua for 13 Years for Financial Crimes." Radio Free Asia, August 19, 2022, accessed September 18, 2022, https://www.rfa.org/english/news/china/tycoon-jailing-08192022150411.html.

Fraenkel, Ernst. *The Dual State: A Contribution to the Theory of Dictatorship*. Toronto: Oxford University Press, 1941.

Frank, Andre Gunder. *Capitalism and Underdevelopment in Latin America*. New York: Monthly Review Press, 1969.

Frantz, Erica. *Authoritarianism: What Everyone Needs to Know*. New York: Oxford University Press, 2018.

Froissart, Chloe. "Changing Patterns of Chinese Civil Society: Comparing the Hu-Wen and Xi Jinping eras." In *Routledge Handbook of the Chinese Communist Party*, edited by Willy Wo-lap Lam, 352–370. London: Routledge, 2017.

Fu, Diana. "Fragmented Control: Governing Contentious Labor Organizations in China." *Governance* 30 (2017): 445–462.

Fu, Hualing. "Autonomy, Courts and the Politico-Legal Order in Contemporary China." In *The Routledge Handbook of Chinese Criminology*, edited by Liqun Cao, Ivan Sun, and Bill Hebenton, 76–88. London: Routledge, 2013.
Gardel, Nathan. "Why China Fears a "Color Revolution" Incited by the West." *New Perspectives Quarterly* 4 (November 2016): 8–14.
Gargan, Edward A. "Taiwan Could Buy Arms Abroad after Reunification, Deng Asserts." *New York Times*, August 21, 1983, accessed March 24, 2021, https://www.nytimes.com/1983/08/21/world/taiwan-could-buy-arms-abroad-after-reunification-deng-asserts.html.
Gilley, Bruce. "Did Bush Democratize the Middle East? The Effects of External-Internal Linkages." *Political Science Quarterly* 128, no. 4 (2013–2014): 653–685.
Gold, Thomas B. "Dependent Development in Taiwan." PhD thesis, Harvard University, 1981.
Gracie, Carrie. "Power Politics Exposed by Fall of China's Security Boss." BBC News, June 11, 2015, accessed March 28, 2021, https://www.bbc.com/news/world-asia-china-33098442.
Grant, Kevin Douglas. "China Clampdown: Hong Kong Issues Warrant for Samuel Chu, an American Citizen, Activist and the Pastor's Son." *Sight*, August 30, 2020, accessed March 23, 2021, https://www.sightmagazine.com.au/features/16930-china-clampdown-hong-kong-issues-warrant-for-samuel-chu-an-american-citizen-activist-and-pastor-s-son.
Green Paper on Constitutional Development. Hong Kong: Constitutional and Mainland Affairs Bureau, July 2007.
Greene, Martin, and Chris Chang. "Interview with Former Hong Kong Legislator Baggio Leung." *Taiwan News*, February 27, 2021, accessed March 14, 2021, https://www.taiwannews.com.tw/en/news/4137938.
Grieder, Jerome B. *Intellectuals and the State in Modern China: A Narrative History*. New York: Free Press, 1981.
Gupta, Sarthak. "Hong Kong Court Grants Bail to Ex-lawmaker in National Security Case." *Jurist: Legal News and Commentary*, August 24, 2022, accessed October 2, 2022, https://www.jurist.org/news/2022/08/hong-kong-court-grants-bail-to-ex-lawmaker-in-national-security-case/.
Guriev, Sergei. "Gorbachev versus Deng: A Review of Chris Miller's The Struggle to Save the Soviet Economy." *Journal of Economic Literature* 57, no. 1 (2019): 120–146.
Haas, Benjamin. "Hong Kong Court Bans Pro-independence Politicians from Office." *The Guardian*, November 15, 2016, accessed February 17, 2021, https://www.theguardian.com/world/2016/nov/15/hong-kong-bans-pro-democracy-politicians-after-beijing-rewrites-oath-law.
Haass, Richard, and David Sacks. "American Support of Taiwan Must Be Unambiguous." *Foreign Affairs*, September 2, 2020, accessed March 23, 2021, https://www.foreignaffairs.com/articles/united-states/american-support-taiwan-must-be-unambiguous.
Harding, Harry. *China's Second Revolution: Reform After Mao*. Washington: The Brookings Institution, 1987.
He, Baogang. "Why Is Establishing Democracy So Difficult in China?" *Contemporary Chinese Thought* 35, no. 1 (Fall 2003): 71–92.

He, Peng. "The Difference of Chinese Legalism and Western Legalism." *Frontiers of Law in China* 6 (2011): 645–669.
Headline News. Hong Kong Chinese newspaper.
Hickey, Dennis Van Vraken. "America's Two-Point Policy and the Future of Taiwan." *Asian Survey* 28, no. 8 (August 1988): 881–896.
Hinsley, Francis H. *Sovereignty*. London: Cambridge University Press, 1986.
Ho, Ming-shuo. *Challenging Beijing's Mandate of Heaven*. Philadelphia: Temple University Press, 2019.
Hong Kong Commercial Daily. Hong Kong Chinese newspaper.
Hong Kong Economic Journal. Hong Kong Chinese newspaper.
Hong Kong TVB News.
Howard, Michael C., and John King. *A History of Marxian Economics, Volume 1: 1883–1929*. Princeton, NJ: Princeton University Press, 2016.
Howell, Jude, and Tim Pringle. "Shades of Authoritarianism and State-Labor Relations in China." *British Journal of Industrial Relations* 57, no. 2 (June 2019): 223–246.
Hu, Taige. "SCNPC Clarifies 'Allegiance' Requirements for Hong Kong Legislators, Disqualifies Pro-Democracy Legislators." November 11, 2020, accessed March 16, 2021, https://npcobserver.com/2020/11/11/npcsc-clarifies-allegiance-requirements-for-hong-kong-legislators-disqualifies-pro-democracy-legislators/.
Huang, Yufan. "中共智囊王滬寧的集權政治見解" [Wang Huning's view of centralized politics]. *New York Times: Chinese Version*, September 30, 2015, accessed April 2, 2021, https://cn.nytimes.com/china/20150930/c30sino-adviser/zh-hant/.
Hui, Sophie, and Erin Chan. "Focus on Pluses in Liberal Studies." *The Standard*, February 8, 2021, accessed March 16, 2021, https://www.thestandard.com.hk/section-news/section/4/227346/%27Focus-on-pluses-in-liberal-studies%27.
Human Rights in China. "In Full: Charter 08 – Liu Xiaobo's Pro-Democracy Manifesto for China That Led to His Jailing." *Hong Kong Free Press*, July 14, 2017, accessed January 28, 2021, https://hongkongfp.com/2017/07/14/full-charter-08-liu-xiaobos-pro-democracy-manifesto-china-led-jailing/.
Huntington, Samuel P. *Political Order in Changing Societies*. New Haven, CT: Yale University Press, 1968.
Huntington, Samuel P. *The Clash of Civilizations and the Remaking of the World Order*. New York: Penguin, 1996.
Huntington, Samuel P. *The Third Wave: Democratization in the Late Twentieth Century*. Norman: University of Oklahoma Press, 1991.
Hwang, Kwang-Kuo. "Leadership Theory of Legalism and Its Function in Confucian Society." In *Leadership and Management in China: Philosophies, Theories, and Practices*, edited by Chao Chuan Chen and Yueh Ting Lee, 108–142. Cambridge: Cambridge University Press, 2008.
Information Office of the State Council, People's Republic of China. *The Practice of the "One Country, Two Systems" Policy in the Hong Kong Special Administrative Region*. Beijing: Foreign Languages Press, 2014.
Interview with Peter Martin. "Understanding Chinese 'Wolf Warrior Diplomacy.'" The National Bureau of Asian Research, October 22, 2021, accessed October 9, 2022, https://www.nbr.org/publication/understanding-chinese-wolf-warrior-diplomacy/.

Johnson, Chalmers. "The Mousetrapping of Hong Kong: A Game in Which Nobody Wins." *Asian Survey* 24, no. 9 (September 1984): 887–909.
Johnston, Alastair Iain. "Is Chinese Nationalism Rising?" *International Security* 41, no. 3 (Winter 2016–17): 7–43.
Jowitt, Kenneth. "Inclusion and Mobilization in European Leninist Regimes." *World Politics* 28, no. 1 (October 1975): 69–96.
Kang, Xiaoguang. "Moving toward Neo-Totalitarianism: A Political-Sociological Analysis of the Evolution of Administrative Absorption of Society in China." *Nonprofit Policy Forum* 9, no. 1 (2018): 1–8.
Karagiannis, Nikolaos, Moula Cherikh, and Wolfram Elsner. "Growth and Development of China: A Developmental State 'with Chinese Characteristics.'" *Forum for Social Economics* (2020), accessed February 20, 2021, https://doi.org/10.1080/07360932.2020.1747515.
Ken, Suzuki. "China's New 'Xi Jinping Constitution': The Road to Totalitarianism." November 27, 2018, accessed February 21, 2021, https://www.nippon.com/en/in-depth/a05803/.
King, Gary, Jennifer Pan, and Margaret E. Roberts. "How Censorship in China Allows Government Criticism but Silences Collective Expression." *American Political Science Review* 107, no. 2 (May 2013): 326–343.
Kuan, Hsin-chi. "Power Dependence and Democratic Transition: The Case of Hong Kong." *China Quarterly*, no. 128 (December 1991): 774–793.
Kuru, Ahmet T. "Authoritarianism and Democracy in Muslim Countries: Rentier States and Regional Diffusion." *Political Science Quarterly* 129, no. 3 (2014): 399–427.
Kwok, Rowena, Joan Leung, and Ian Scott, eds. *Votes without Power: The Hong Kong Legislative Council Elections, 1991.* Hong Kong: Hong Kong University Press, 1992.
Kwong, Ying-ho. "Political Repression in a Sub-national Hybrid Regime: The PRC's Governing Strategies in Hong Kong." *Contemporary Politics* 24, no. 4 (January 2018): 361–378.
Lague, David, James Pomfret, and Greg Torode. "How Murder, Kidnappings and Miscalculation set off Hong Kong's Revolt." Reuters, December 20, 2019.
Lam, Jeffie. "Influential Hong Kong Business Body Calls for Extra Safeguards in Government's Controversial Extradition Bill." *South China Morning Post*, May 27, 2019, accessed December 25, 2019, https://www.scmp.com/news/hong-kong/politics/article/3012007/influential-hong-kong-business-body-calls-extra-safeguards.
Lam, Kim. "What Implications of the Big Drop of Voter Turnout in Macau Legislative Elections for Hong Kong?" hk01.com, September 12, 2021, accessed October 8, 2022, https://www.hk01.com.
Lau, Justin. "China Concession in Hong Kong Spurs Reform Plan." *Financial Times*, June 21, 2010.
Lau, Stuart. "'Blinded by Desire for High Life,' Hui Jailed 7 and a Half Years; Kwok Sentenced to Five Years." *South China Morning Post*, December 24, 2014.
Lau, Wai Kwan, Zhen Li, and John Okpara. "An Examination of Three-Way Interactions of Paternalistic Leadership in China." *Asia Pacific Business Review* 26, no. 1 (2020): 32–49.

Law, Wing Sang. *Collaborative Colonial Power: The Making of the Hong Kong Chinese.* Hong Kong: Hong Kong University Press, 2009.
Lee, John. "Starting New Chapter for Hong Kong Together: Election Manifesto of Chief Executive Election 2022." April 2022, accessed October 13, 2022, https://www.johnlee2022.hk/wp-content/uploads/2022/04/Election-manifesto.pdf.
Lee, Shiu-hung. "The SARS Epidemic in Hong Kong: What Lessons Have We Learnt?" *Journal of the Royal Society of Medicine* 96 (August 2003): 374–378.
Leung, Hillary. "Hong Kong's Incoming Leader John Lee Reveals Members of Advisory Body Executive Council." Hong Kong Free Press, June 23, 2022, accessed October 12, 2022, https://hongkongfp.com/2022/06/23/hong-kongs-incoming-leader-john-lee-reveals-members-of-advisory-body-executive-council/.
Levitsky, Steven, and Lucan Way. "Elections Without Democracy: The Rise of Competitive Authoritarianism." *Journal of Democracy* 13, no. 2 (April 2002): 51–65.
Levitsky, Steven, and Lucan Way. "The New Competitive Authoritarianism." *Journal of Democracy* 31, no. 1 (January 2020): 51–65.
Li, Cheng. "The End of the CCP's Resilient Authoritarianism? A Tripartite Assessment of Shifting Power in China." *China Quarterly*, no. 211 (September 2012): 595–623.
Li, Hou. *Historical Journey of Sovereignty Return.* Hong Kong: Joint Publishing, 1997.
Li, Lifan. "Evolution of Western NGOs in CIS States after the 'Color Revolution.'" *China International Studies* 29, no. 4 (July–August 2011): 158–170.
Li, Pang-kwong. "Elections and Political Mobilization: The Hong Kong 1991 Direct Elections." PhD thesis, University of London, 1995.
Li, Yongqiao. "Understanding Qin Shihuang's Implementation of 'Great Unity.'" *Culture Journal* 7 (July 2017): 222–230 [in Chinese].
Li, Zhiting. "A Study of the Political Concept of the Great Unity Advocated by the Emperors of the Qing Dynasty." *Journal of Yunnan Normal University* 47, no. 6 (2015): 1–9 [in Chinese].
"張亞中主張兩岸協商和平備忘錄 國民黨執政後再簽和平協議." 自由時報電子報 [Liberty Times], March 28, 2021, accessed March 28, 2021, https://news.ltn.com.tw/news/politics/breakingnews/3481037.
Lim, Hyun-chin. *Dependent Development in Korea, 1963–1979.* Seoul: Seoul National University Press, 1985.
Lin, Feng. "The 2018 Constitutional Amendments: Significance and Impact on the Theories of Party-State Relationship in China." *China Perspectives*, no. 1 (2019): 11–21.
Lin, Paul. "Hong Kong Caught in the Middle." *Taipei Times*, September 7, 2019, accessed February 28, 2021, http://www.taipeitimes.com/News/editorials/archives/2019/09/07/2003721845.
Lindberg, Kari Soo. "Hong Kong Court Keeps Jimmy Lai in Jail on Security Charges." Bloomberg, February 18, 2021, accessed March 16, 2021, https://www.bloomberg.com/news/articles/2021-02-18/hong-kong-court-keeps-jimmy-lai-in-jail-on-security-charges.
Lindberg, Kari Soo, and Krystal Chia. "Here Are Hong Kong's Crackdown Leaders Rewarded in New Cabinet." Bloomberg, July 1, 2022, accessed October 12, 2022,

https://www.bloomberg.com/news/articles/2022-06-30/who-s-in-new-hong-kong-leader-john-lee-s-cabinet-and-what-will-they-do.

Liu, Chin-Tsai. "The Observation of DPP's Mainland China Policy in 2013: Controversy and Development." *Prospect and Exploration* (Taiwan) 12, no. 2 (February 2014): 24–33.

Liu, Peng. "A Framework for Understanding Chinese Leadership: A Cultural Approach." *International Journal of Leadership in Education* 20, no. 6 (2017): 749–761.

Lo, Shiu-Hing. "An Analysis of Sino-British Negotiations over Hong Kong's Political Reform." *Contemporary Southeast Asia* 16, no. 2 (September 1994): 178–209.

Lo, Shiu-hing. "Decolonization and Political Development in Hong Kong: Citizen Participation." *Asian Survey* 28, no. 6 (June 1988): 613–629.

Lo, Shiu Hing. *Political Development in Macau*. Hong Kong: Chinese University of Hong Kong Press, 1995.

Lo, Shiu-hing. "The Chinese Communist Party Elite's Conflicts over Hong Kong, 1983–1990." *China Information* 7, no. 4 (Spring 1994): 1–14.

Lo, Sonny Shiu-Hing. *Casino Capitalism, Society and Politics of China's Macau*. Newcastle upon Tyne: Cambridge Scholars Publishing, 2020.

Lo, Sonny Shiu-Hing. *Competing Chinese Political Visions: Hong Kong vs. Beijing on Democracy*. Santa Barbara: Praeger Security International, 2010.

Lo, Sonny Shiu-Hing. "Factionalism and Chinese-Style Democracy: The 2017 Chief Executive Election." *Asia Pacific Journal of Public Administration* 39, no. 2 (2017): 100–119.

Lo, Sonny Shiu-hing. *Governing Hong Kong: Legitimacy, Communication and Political Decay*. New York: Nova Science, 2001.

Lo, Sonny Shiu-Hing. *Hong Kong's Indigenous Democracy: Origins, Evolution and Contentions*. London: Palgrave Macmillan, 2015.

Lo, Sonny Shiu-Hing. "Hong Kong in 2019: The Anti-Extradition, Anti-Mainlandization and Anti-Police Movement." *Asian Survey* 60, no. 1 (February 2020): 34–40.

Lo, Sonny Shiu-Hing. "Ideology and Factionalism in Beijing-Hong Kong Relations." *Asian Survey* 58, no. 3 (2018): 392–415.

Lo, Sonny Shiu-hing, ed. *Interest Groups and the New Democracy Movement in Hong Kong*. London: Routledge, 2017.

Lo, Sonny Shiu-Hing. "Interest Groups, Intellectuals and New Democracy Movement in Hong Kong." In *Interest Groups and the New Democracy Movement in Hong Kong*, edited by Sonny Shiu-Hing Lo. London: Routledge, 2018.

Lo, Sonny Shiu-Hing. "The Chief Executive and the Business." In *The First Tung Chee-hwa Administration*, edited by Lau Siu-kai. Hong Kong: Chinese University of Hong Kong Press, 2002.

Lo, Sonny Shiu-Hing. *The Dynamics of Beijing–Hong Kong Relations: A Model for Taiwan?* Hong Kong: Hong Kong University Press, 2008.

Lo, Sonny Shiu-Hing. *The Politics of Controlling Organized Crime in Greater China*. London: Routledge, 2015.

Lo, Sonny Shiu-Hing. *The Politics of Crisis Management in China: The Sichuan Earthquake*. Lanham, MD: Lexington Books, 2014.

Lo, Sonny Shiu-Hing. "The Political Cultures of Hong Kong and Mainland China: Democratization, Patrimonialism and Pluralism in the 2007 Chief Executive Election." *Asia Pacific Journal of Public Administration* 29, no. 1 (January 2014): 101–128.

Lo, Sonny Shiu-Hing. *The Politics of Policing in Greater China*. London: Palgrave, 2016.

Lo, Sonny Shiu-hing, and Steven Chung-fun Hung. *The Politics of Education Reform in China's Hong Kong*. London: Routledge, 2022.

Lo, Sonny Shiu-Hing, Steven Chung-Fun Hung, and Jeff Hai-Chi Loo. *China's New United Front Work in Hong Kong: Penetrative Politics and Its Implications*. London: Palgrave Macmillan, 2019.

Lo, Sonny Shiu-Hing, Steven Chung-Fun Hung, and Jeff Hai-Chi Loo. *The Dynamics of Peaceful and Violent Protests in Hong Kong: The Anti-Extradition Movement*. London: Palgrave Macmillan, 2020.

Lo, Sonny Shiu-Hing, Steven Chung-Fun Hung, Jeff Hai-Chi Loo, and Cody Wai-Kwok Yau. *The Politics of District Elections and Administration in Hong Kong*. Hong Kong: City University of Hong Kong Press, forthcoming.

Lo, Sonny Shiu-hing, and Jeff Hai-chi Loo. "An Anatomy of the Post-Materialistic Values of Hong Kong Youth: Opposition to China's Rising 'Sharp Power.'" In *Youth: Global Challenges and Issues of the 21st Century*, edited by Stan Tucker and Dave Trotman. New York: Nova Science, 2018.

Lo, Shiu-hing, and Yu Wing-yat. "The Politics of Electoral Reform in Hong Kong." *Commonwealth and Comparative Politics* 39, no. 2 (July 2001): 98–123.

Lo, Sonny. "An Analysis of John Lee's Participation in Hong Kong's Chief Executive Elections." *Macau Business*, April 9, 2022, accessed October 12, 2022, https://www.macaubusiness.com/opinion-an-analysis-of-john-lees-participation-in-hong-kongs-chief-executive-elections/.

Lo, Sonny. "A Risk Assessment of Beijing-Taipei Relations after Pelosi's Visit," *Macau Business*, August 6, 2022, accessed October 12, 2022, https://www.macaubusiness.com/opinion-a-risk-assessment-of-beijing-taipei-relations-after-pelosis-visit/.

Lo, Sonny. "China's Pragmatism and Political Posturing to the US and Taiwan in the Era of Civilizational Clashes." *Macau Business*, March 27, 2021, accessed March 27, 2021, https://www.macaubusiness.com/opinion-chinas-pragmatism-and-political-posturing-to-us-and-taiwan-in-the-era-of-civilizational-clashes/.

Lo, Sonny. "Defining Patriotism in Hong Kong: Implications for Political Opposition." *Macau Business*, November 14, 2020, accessed October 3, 2022, https://www.macaubusiness.com/opinion-defining-patriotism-in-hong-kong-implications-for-political-opposition/.

Lo, Sonny. "Hong Kong: A Battleground in a Clash of Political Civilisations." Asialink, July 29, 2020, accessed March 24, 2021, https://asialink.unimelb.edu.au/insights/hong-kong-a-battleground-in-a-clash-of-political-civilisations.

Lo, Sonny. *Hong Kong, 1 July 2003: Half a Million Protestors – The Security Law, Identity Politics, Democracy and China*. Toronto: Canadian Institute of International Affairs, 2004.

Lo, Sonny. "Hong Kong in 2020." *Asian Survey* 61, no. 1 (February 2021): 34–42.

Lo, Sonny. "'New' Cross-Border Crime between Hong Kong and China." Asia Dialogue, August 2, 2016, accessed March 14, 2021, https://theasiadialogue.com/2016/08/02/new-cross-border-crime-between-hong-kong-and-china/.

Lo, Sonny. "Shenzhen as a New Economic Locomotive: Implications for Macau and Hong Kong." *Macau Business*, October 17, 2020, accessed March 24, 2021, https://www.macaubusiness.com/opinion-shenzhen-as-a-new-economic-locomotive-implications-for-macau-and-hong-kong/.

Lo, Sonny. "The Dynamics of Delaying Anti-Sanctions Laws for Hong Kong." *Macau Business*, August 21, 2021, accessed October 14, 2022, https://www.macaubusiness.com/opinion-the-dynamics-of-delaying-anti-sanctions-law-for-hong-kong/.

Lo, Sonny. "Will Military Accident or Skirmishes Occur Amidst Tense Beijing-Taipei-Washington Relations." *Macau Business*, July 25, 2020, accessed March 23, 2021, https://www.macaubusiness.com/opinion-will-military-accident-or-skirmish-occur-amidst-tense-beijing-taipei-washington-relations/.

Lo, Wai-chung. "A Review of the Housing Policy." In *The July 1 Protest Rally: Interpreting a Historic Event*, edited by Joseph Y. S. Cheng, 337–362. Hong Kong: City University of Hong Kong Press, 2005.

Loh, Christine. *Underground Front: The Chinese Communist Party in Hong Kong*. Hong Kong: Hong Kong University Press, 2010.

Lum, Alvin. "Advisers to Hong Kong Leader Carrie Lam Dismiss Idea of Amnesty for All Protestors Involved in Clashes over Extradition Bill." *South China Morning Post*, July 4, 2019, accessed April 2, 2021, https://www.scmp.com/news/hong-kong/politics/article/3017329/advisers-hong-kong-leader-carrie-lam-dismiss-idea-amnesty.

Ma, Joanne. "Hong Kong Pro-democracy Group Demosisto Disbands." *Young Post*, June 30, 2020, accessed March 21, 2021, https://www.scmp.com/yp/discover/news/hong-kong/article/3091186/hong-kong-pro-democracy-group-demosisto-disbands.

Ma, Miranda Lai Yee. "Framing Processes and Social Media: A Frame Analysis of the Tsoi Yuen Resistance Movement." A paper presented at the World Association for Public Opinion Research Conference, University of Hong Kong, June 14–16, 2012.

Ma, Ngok. *Political Development in Hong Kong: State, Political Society, and Civil Society*. Hong Kong: Hong Kong University Press, 2007.

Mao, Frances. "Biden Again Says US Would Defend Taiwan If China Attacks." BBC News, September 19, 2022, accessed October 12, 2022, https://www.bbc.com/news/world-asia-62951347.

Marsh, Christopher. "Learning from Your Comrade's Mistakes: The Impact of the Soviet Past on China's Future." *Communist and Post-Communist Studies* 36 (2003): 259–272.

Marshall, George. "Personal Statement, January 7, 1947." The George Marshall Foundation, accessed April 4, 2021, https://www.marshallfoundation.org/library/digital-archive/personal-statement1/.

Matsuzato, Kimitaka. "The Rise and Fall of Ethnoterritorial Federalism: A Comparison of the Soviet Union (Russia), China, and India." *Europe-Asia Studies* 69, no. 7 (2017): 1047–1069.

McDonell, Stephen. "Biden Says US Will Defend Taiwan If China Attacks." BBC News, October 22, 2021, accessed October 12, 2022, https://www.bbc.com/news/world-asia-59005300.

Meisner, Maurice. *Mao's China and After: A History of the People's Republic*. New York: Free Press, 1986.
Mertha, Andrew. "'Fragmented Authoritarianism 2.0': Political Pluralization in the Chinese Policy Process." *China Quarterly* 200 (December 2009): 995–1012.
Metro Radio. "王滬寧指國家的命運 與香港息息相關." March 6, 2018, accessed April 2, 2021, metroradio.com.hk.
Meyer, Alfred G. "Theories of Convergence." In *Change in Communist Systems*, edited by Chalmers Johnson. Stanford, CA: Stanford University Press, 1970.
Miller, Alice. "More Already on the Central Committee's Leading Small Groups." *China Leadership Monitor* 44 (July 28, 2014), accessed February 21, 2021, https://www.hoover.org/sites/default/files/research/docs/clm44am.pdf.
Ming Pao. Hong Kong Chinese newspaper.
Mok, Ka-ho. *Intellectuals and the State in Post-Mao China*. New York: Macmillan 1998.
Moral and National Education Curriculum Guide (Primary 1 to Secondary 6). Hong Kong: Curriculum Development Council, 2012.
Moura, Nelson. "2021 Legislative Assembly Election with Lowest Voter Turnout in SAR History." September 12, 2021, accessed October 8, 2022, https://www.macaubusiness.com/2021-legislative-assembly-election-with-lowest-voter-turnout-in-sar-history/.
Mulrenan, Stephen. "Business Navigates Hong Kong's New National Security Law." International Bar Association, September 25, 2020, accessed February 18, 2021, https://www.ibanet.org/article/ACD909C3-15D4-4817-8D2A-0EE0D39D3028.
Naseemullah, Adnan, and Paul Staniland. "Indirect Rule and Varieties of Governance." *Governance: An International Journal of Policy, Administration, and Institutions* 29, no. 1 (January 2016): 13–30.
Nathan, Andrew. *Chinese Democracy*. Berkeley: University of California Press, 1986.
Next Magazine, February 8, 2017, accessed January 3, 2021, "中南海金手指 追蹤肖建華姊弟幫洗錢網絡." nextmgz.com.
Northern Metropolis Development Strategy: Report, October 6, 2021. Hong Kong: Information Services Department of the HKSAR Government, 2021. Accessed October 9, 2022, https://www.policyaddress.gov.hk/2021/eng/pdf/publications/Northern/Northern-Metropolis-Development-Strategy-Report.pdf.
O'Donnell, Guillermo, and Philippe C. Schmitter. *Transitions from Authoritarian Rule: Tentative Conclusions about Uncertain Democracies*. Baltimore: Johns Hopkins University Press, 1986.
O'Hanlon, Michael E. "A Need for Ambiguity." Brookings, April 21, 2001, accessed March 23, 2021, https://www.brookings.edu/opinions/a-need-for-ambiguity/.
Olar, Roman-Gabriel. "Do They Know Something We Don't? Diffusion of Repression in Authoritarian Regimes." *Journal of Peace Research* 56, no. 5 (2019): 667–681.
Oriental Daily News. Hong Kong Chinese newspaper.
Ortmann, Stephan, and Thompson, Mark R., "China and the 'Singapore Model.'" *Journal of Democracy* 27, no. 1 (January 2016): 39–48.
Otjes, Simon, and Tom Louwerse. "Populists in Parliament: Comparing Left-Wing and Right-Wing Populism in the Netherlands." *Political Studies*, accessed November 20, 2013, https://doi.org/10.1111/1467-9248.12089.

Our Hong Kong Foundation. "Mr. Tung Chee Hwa, GBM." Accessed October 11, 2017, https://www.ourhkfoundation.org.hk/en/node/551.
Ouyang, Iris. "China Jails Tycoon Xiao Jianhua for 13 Years, Slapping an Unprecedented US$8 Million Fine on His Tomorrow Group." *South China Morning Post*, August 19, 2022, accessed September 29, 2022, https://www.scmp.com/business/banking-finance/article/3189498/tomorrow-groups-xiao-jianhua-sentenced-13-years-prison.
Pak, Yiu. "Hong Kong Opposition Trade Union Group to Disband." Reuters, September 19, 2021, accessed October 12, 2022, https://www.reuters.com/world/china/hong-kong-opposition-trade-union-group-disband-2021-09-19/.
Pang, Jessie, and James Pomfret. "Hong Kong Court Lifts Reporting Restriction on National Security Case." Reuters, August 17, 2022, accessed October 2, 2022, https://www.reuters.com/world/china/hong-kong-court-lifts-reporting-restriction-national-security-case-2022-08-17/.
Parton, Charles. "China and Hong Kong: One Country, One and a Half Systems." July 23, 2020, accessed July 24, 2022, https://www.rusi.org/explore-our-research/publications/commentary/china-and-hong-kong-one-country-one-and-half-systems.
Patapan, Haig, and Wang Yi. "The Hidden Ruler: Wang Huning and the Making of Contemporary China." *Journal of Contemporary China* 27, no. 109 (2018): 47–60.
Pei, Minxin. *China's Crony Capitalism: The Dynamics of Political Decay*. Cambridge, MA: Harvard University Press, 2016.
Pei, Minxing. "Xi Jinping's Dilemma: Back Down or Double Down." *China Leadership Monitor*, December 1, 2018, accessed January 3, 2021, https://www.prcleader.org/xi-s-dilemma.
Pepper, Suzanne. "A Tale of Two SARs and Beijing's Puzzle: Why Can't Hong Kong Be More Like Macau?" *Hong Kong Free Press*, May 20, 2017, https://hongkongfp.com/2017/05/20/tale-two-sars-beijings-puzzle-cant-hong-kong-like-macau/.
Pepper, Suzanne. "The Tong Ying-kit Case: First Show Trial of Hong Kong's New Mainland-Style Legal Regime." *Hong Kong Free Press*, August 21, 2021, accessed September 28, 2022, https://hongkongfp.com/2021/08/15/the-tong-ying-kit-case-first-show-trial-of-hong-kongs-new-mainland-style-legal-regime/.
Perry, Elizabeth J. "Educated Acquiescence: How Academia Sustains Authoritarianism in China." *Theory and Society* 49 (2020): 1–22.
Plattner, Marc F. "Populism, Pluralism and Liberal Democracy." *Journal of Democracy* 21, no. 1 (January 2010): 81–92.
Pomfret, James. "Beijing Breaks Ice with Hong Kong Opposition." Reuters, May 24, 2010. https://www.reuters.com/article/us-hongkong-democracy-idUSTRE64N1ZQ20100524.
Pomfret, James. "Hong Kong Tycoon Jimmy Lai Denied Bail in National Security Case." Reuters, February 9, 2021, accessed October 2, 2022, https://www.reuters.com/article/us-hongkong-security-idUSKBN2A907P.
Pomfret, James, and Jessie Pang. "Four Hong Kong 'Occupy' Leaders Jailed for 2014 Democracy Protests." Reuters, April 14, 2019, accessed March 14, 2021, https://www.reuters.com/article/us-hongkong-politics-idUSKCN1S004R.
Pomfret, James, and Greg Torode. "Exclusive: 'If I Have a Choice, The First Thing Is to Quit' - Hong Kong Leader Carrie Lam - Transcript," Reuters, September 3, 2019,

accessed October 12, 2022, https://www.reuters.com/article/us-hongkong-protests-carrielam-transcrip-idUSKCN1VO0KK.

Poon, Alice. *Land and the Ruling Class in Hong Kong*. Hong Kong: Enrich Professional Publishing, 2010.

Putnam, Robert D. *The Comparative Study of Political Elites*. Englewood Cliffs, NJ: Prentice-Hall, 1976.

Pye, Lucian W. *The Spirit of Chinese Politics*. Cambridge, MA: Harvard University Press, 1992.

Schmidt, Blake. "Fortune of Jailed Chinese Billionaire's Family Survives in Exile." Bloomberg, September 6, 2022, accessed September 18, 2022, https://www.bloomberg.com/news/articles/2022-09-05/jailed-chinese-billionaire-xiao-jianhua-s-family-fortune-survives-in-exile.

Schram, Stuart. *The Thought of Mao Tse-Tung*. London: Cambridge University Press, 1989.

Scott, Ian. *Political Change and the Crisis of Legitimacy in Hong Kong*. Hong Kong: Oxford University Press, 1989.

Scott, James C. "Patron-Client Politics and Political Change in Southeast Asia." *American Political Science Review* 66, no. 1 (March 1972): 91–113.

Selvin, Clarie. "Hong Kong's M+ Museum Promises to Comply with National Security Law Amid Pushback from Pro-Beijing Figures." ARTnews, March 24, 2021, accessed April 2, 2021, https://www.artnews.com/art-news/news/m-plus-museum-hong-kong-ai-weiwei-1234587731/.

Shambaugh, David. "Contemplating China's Future." *The Washington Quarterly* 39, no. 3 (2016): 121–130.

Shen, Zuowei. "Creating a Modern Nation of Great Unification." *Century (Shiji)*, no. 4 (2017): 1–5.

Shukla, Srijan. "The Rise of the Xi Gang: Factional Politics in the Chinese Communist Party." Occasional paper, Observer Research Foundation, February 20, 2021, accessed February 21, 2021, https://www.orfonline.org/research/the-rise-of-the-xi-gang/.

Shum, Lok-kei. "Hong Kong's Annual Tiananmen Vigil, Banned for the First Time in 30 Years: What You Need to Know about June 4 Event in the City." *South China Morning Post*, June 4, 2020, accessed April 4, 2021, https://www.scmp.com/news/hong-kong/politics/article/3087431/banned-first-time-30-years-heres-what-you-need-know-about.

Sing Tao Daily. Hong Kong Chinese newspaper.

Sing, Ming. *Hong Kong's Tortuous Democratization: A Comparative Analysis*. London: RoutledgeCurzon, 2004.

Siu, Phila and Natalie Wong. "Pro-mainland Chinese Financiers Based in Hong Kong Launch New Bauhinia Party Aimed at Reforming LegCo, Restraining Extremist Forces." *South China Morning Post*, December 6, 2020, accessed March 14, 2021, https://www.scmp.com/news/hong-kong/politics/article/3112771/mainland-born-hong-kong-based-financiers-launch-new.

Smilov, Daniel, and Ivan Krastev. "The Rise of Populism in Eastern Europe: A Policy Paper." In *Populist Politics and Liberal Democracy in Central and Eastern Europe*, edited by Grigorij Meseznikov, Olga Gyarfasova, and Daniel Smilov, 7-12. Bratislava: Institute for Public Affairs, 2008.

So, Alvin. *Hong Kong's Embattled Democracy: A Societal Analysis*. Baltimore: Johns Hopkins University Press, 1999.

So, Alvin. "The Development of Post-Modernist Social Movements in the HKSAR." In *East Asian Social Movements: Power, Protest and Change in a Dynamic Region*, edited by Jeffrey Broadbent and Vicky Brockman, 365–384. New York: Springer Science, 2011.

So, Alvin Y. "The Chinese Model of Development: Characteristics, Interpretation, Implications." *Perspectives on Global Development and Technology* 13 (2014): 444–464.

Soo, Zen. "Hong Kong Arrest 53 Activists under National Security Law." Associated Press, January 6, 2021, accessed March 28, 2021, https://apnews.com/article/legislature-primary-elections-democracy-hong-kong-elections-25a66f7dd38e6606c9f8cce84106d916.

South China Morning Post. Hong Kong Chinese newspaper.

Stockmann, Daniela, and Mary E. Gallagher. "Remote Control: How the Media Sustain Authoritarian Rule in China." *Comparative Political Studies* 44, no. 4 (2011): 436–467.

Strong, Matthew. "Taiwan President Tsai Ing-wen Wins Election with Record 8.17 Million Votes." *Taiwan News*, January 11, 2020, accessed March 23, 2021, https://www.taiwannews.com.tw/en/news/3854958.

Stuart, James B. *Deep State: Trump, the FBI, and the Rule of Law*. New York: Penguin Books, 2019.

Sum, Lok-kei. "Five Stand Trial for Sedition in Hong Kong over Children's Books about Sheep." *The Guardian*, July 6, 2022, accessed September 29, 2022, https://www.theguardian.com/world/2022/jul/06/hong-kong-sedition-trial-childrens-books-sheep-wolves-china.

Ta Kung Pao. Hong Kong Chinese newspaper.

Ta Kung Pao. "王沪宁：增强香港同胞的国家意识爱国精神." March 7, 2018, accessed April 2, 2021, http://news.takungpao.com/mainland/focus/2018-03/3549139_wap.html.

Tai, Benny. "The Most Lethal Weapon of Civil Disobedience." *Hong Kong Economic Journal*, January 16, 2013.

Tan, Su-Lin. "Chinese Academic Accused of Being an Australian Spy Slams 'Outrageous Slander' in Beijing-Run Tabloid." *South China Morning Post*, July 3, 2020, accessed January 25, 2021, https://www.scmp.com/economy/china-economy/article/3091586/chinese-academic-accused-being-australian-spy-slams.

Tang, Wenfang. *Populist Authoritarianism: Chinese Political Culture and Regime Sustainability*. New York: Oxford University Press, 2016.

Teets, Jessica C. "Let Many Civil Societies Bloom: The Rise of Consultative Authoritarianism in China." *China Quarterly* 213 (March 2013): 19–38.

Teng, Biao. "The Political Meaning of the Crime of 'Subverting State Power.'" In *Liu Xiaobo, Charter 08 and the Challenges of Political Reform in China*, edited by Jean-Philippe Beja, Fu Hualing, and Eva Pils, 271–288. Hong Kong: Hong Kong University Press, 2012.

The China Model: A Teaching Booklet on the Special Topic of National Circumstances. Hong Kong: National Education Service Center, 2012.

Bibliography

The Practice of the "One Country, Two systems" Policy in the Hong Kong Special Administrative Region, 《"一国两制"在香港特别行政区的实践》白皮书（英文）. June 10, 2014, accessed March 14, 2021, http://www.scio.gov.cn/zfbps/ndhf/2014/Document/1373163/1373163.htm.

Tian, Feilong (田飛龍). ""愛國者治港：香港民主的新生" [Patriots ruling Hong Kong: The new life of Hong Kong democracy." *Ming Pao*, March 3, 2021, accessed March 14, 2021, https://news.mingpao.com/ins/%E6%96%87%E6%91%98/article/20210303/s00022/1614528449160/%E6%84%9B%E5%9C%8B%E8%80%85%E6%B2%BB%E6%B8%AF-%E9%A6%99%E6%B8%AF%E6%B0%91%E4%B8%BB%E7%9A%84%E6%96%B0%E7%94%9F%EF%BC%88%E6%96%87-%E7%94%B0%E9%A3%9B%E9%BE%8D%EF%BC%89.

Tolstrup, Jakob. "Studying a Negative External Actor: Russia's Management of Stability and Instability in the 'Near Abroad.'" *Democratization* 16, no. 5 (2009): 922–944.

Tolstrup, Jakob. "When Can External Actors Influence Democratization? Leverage, Linkages, and Gatekeeper Elites." *Democratization* 20, no. 4 (2013): 716–742.

Tong, Elson. "Four More Pro-democracy Law-Makers to Be Ousted Following Hong Kong Court Ruling." *Hong Kong Free Press*, July 14, 2017, accessed October 11, 2017, https://www.hongkongfp.com/2017/07/14/breaking-4-elected-pro-democracy-lawmakers-ousted-following-hong-kong-court-ruling/.

Tonry, Michael. "Prosecutors and Politics in Comparative Perspective." *Crime and Justice* 41, no. 1 (August 2012): 1–33.

Torode, Greg. "Nuns Arrested as Beijing Turns Up Heat on Church in Hong Kong." Reuters, December 30, 2020, accessed January 17, 2020, https://www.reuters.com/investigates/special-report/hongkong-security-church/.

Torre, Carlos de la. "Hugo Chávez and the Diffusion of Bolivarianism." *Democratization* 24, no. 7 (2017): 1271–1288.

Torre, Carlos de la. "In the Name of the People: Democratization, Popular Organizations and Populism in Venezuela, Bolivia and Ecuador." *European Review of Latin American and Caribbean Studies*, no. 95 (October 2013): 27–48.

Truex, Rory. "Consultative Authoritarianism and Its Limits." *Comparative Political Studies* 50, no. 3 (2017): 329–361.

Tsang, Daniel C. "After Winning Asylum in Germany, Resistance Is Fertile, Not Futile, for Hong Kong Activist Ray Wong." Hong Kong Free Press, June 8, 2019, accessed March 16, 2021, https://hongkongfp.com/2019/06/08/winning-asylum-germany-resistance-fertile-not-futile-hong-kong-activist-ray-wong/.

Tsang, Steve. "Consultative Leninism: China's New Political Framework." *Journal of Contemporary China* 16, no. 62 (2009): 865–880.

Tucker, Nancy Bernkopf. "China as a Factor in the Collapse of the Soviet Empire." *Political Science Quarterly* 110, no. 4 (Winter 1995–1996): 501–518.

TVB News. "王滬寧出席港區人大代表小組會 稱中央對港獨零容忍". March 6, 2018, accessed April 2, 2021, https://news.tvb.com/tc/local/5a9e4428e60383796599f9ba/%E6%B8%AF%E6%BE%B3-%E7%8E%8B%E6%BB%AC%E5%AF%A7%E5%87%BA%E5%B8%AD%E6%B8%AF%E5%8D%80%E4%BA%BA%E5%A4%A7%E4%BB%A3%E8%A1%A8%E5%B0%8F%E7%B5%84%E6%9C%83-%E7%A8%B1%E4%B8%

B8%AD%E5%A4%AE%E5%B0%8D%E6%B8%AF%E7%8D%A8%E9%9B%B6%E5%AE%B9%E5%BF%8D.

Tyson, Adam, and Wu Xinye. "Ethnic Conflict and New Legalism in China." *Nationalism and Ethnic Politics* 23 (2016): 373–392.

United Daily News. "結盟趙少康有內幕？韓國瑜遭爆曾斷言：國民黨剩三條路". 聯合新聞網 [city.udn.com]. February 3, 2021, accessed March 23, 2021, http://city.udn.com/54543/7106062?raid=7106842.

Walker, Ignacio. "Democracy and Populism in Latin America." Working paper no. 347, the Helen Kellogg Institute for International Studies (April 2008). https://kellogg.nd.edu/documents/1655.

Walker, Tommy. "5 in Hong Kong Sentenced to Prison Over Sheep Book." VOA News, September 10, 2022, accessed September 29, 2022, https://www.voanews.com/a/in-hong-kong-sentenced-to-prison-over-sheep-book-/6739620.html.

Wang, Hongying. "From 'Taoguang Yanghui' to 'Yousuo Zuowei': China's Engagement in Financial Multilateralism." CIGI Papers, no. 52 (December 2014): 1–10.

Wang, Howard. "Taiwan's Security Role in the US Indo-Pacific Strategy." *The Diplomat*, June 27, 2019, accessed March 23, 2021, https://thediplomat.com/2019/06/taiwans-security-role-in-the-u-s-indo-pacific-strategy/.

Wang, Klavier Jie Ying. "Mobilizing Resources to the Square: Hong Kong's Anti-Moral and National Education Movement as a Precursor to the Umbrella Movement." *International Journal of Cultural Studies* 20, no. 2 (March 2017): 127–145.

Wang, Way Weichieh. "China's Wolf Warrior Diplomacy Is Fading." *The Diplomat*, July 27, 2022, accessed October 9, 2022, https://thediplomat.com/2022/07/chinas-wolf-warrior-diplomacy-is-fading/.

Wen, Qing. "'One Country, Two Systems:' The Best Way to Peaceful Reunification." *Beijing Review*, May 26, 2009, accessed March 24, 2021, http://www.bjreview.com.cn/nation/txt/2009-05/26/content_197568.htm.

Wen Wei Po. Hong Kong Chinese newspaper.

Weyland, Kurt. *Revolution and Reaction: The Diffusion of Authoritarianism in Latin America.* Cambridge: Cambridge University Press, 2019.

White, Lynn T. *Democratization in Hong Kong – and China?* Boulder, CO: Lynne Rienner, 2016.

Whiting, Allen S. "Assertive Nationalism in Chinese Foreign Policy." *Asian Survey* 23, no. 8 (August 1983): 913–933.

Wilber, Charles, ed. *The Political Economy of Development and Underdevelopment.* New York: Random House, 1979.

Williams, Michael C. "Words, Images, Enemies: Securitization and International Politics." *International Studies Quarterly*, no. 47 (2003): 511–531.

Winckler, Edwin A. "Institutionalization and Participation on Taiwan: From Hard to Soft Authoritarianism?" *China Quarterly* 99 (September 1984): 481–499.

Wingerden, Pieter van. "The National Security Law, 'One Country, Two Systems,' and Hong Kong's National Security Apparatus: The Coup De Grace to Hong Kong's Ideological Independence and Democratic Autonomy." *The Yale Review of International Studies*, April 2022, accessed July 24, 2022, http://yris.yira.org/essays/5696.

Wong, Edward, and Jonathan Ansfield. "China Grooming Deft Politician as New Leader." *New York Times*, January 23, 2011, accessed February 21, 2021, https://www.nytimes.com/2011/01/24/world/asia/24leader.html.

Wong, Joshua with Jason Ng. *Unfree Speech*. London: Penguin, 2020.

Wong, Matthew Y. H. "Party Models in a Hybrid Regime: Hong Kong, 2007–2012." *China Review* 15, no. 1 (Spring 2015): 67–94.

Wong, Natalie. "Stricter Bail Conditions to Apply to Offenders under Hong Kong's Future National Security Law, Justice Minister Says." *South China Morning Post*, July 17, 2022, accessed October 2, 2022, https://www.scmp.com/news/hong-kong/politics/article/3185585/stricter-bail-conditions-apply-offenders-under-hong-kongs.

Xi, Jinping. "新时代中国共产党的历史使命" [The historical mission of the Chinese Communist Party in the new era]. 求是网 [qstheory.cn], September 30, 2022, accessed October 9, 2022. http://www.qstheory.cn/dukan/qs/2022-09/30/c_1129040825.htm.

Xi, Jinping. "Working Together to Realize Rejuvenation of the Chinese Nation and Advance China's Reunification." Speech at the Meeting Marking the 40th Anniversary of the Issuance of the Message to Compatriots in Taiwan. January 2, 2019, accessed March 23, 2021, https://www.news.gov.hk/eng/2020/11/20201114/20201114_124103_167.html.

Xiao, Gongqing. "China's Four Decades of Reforms: A View from Neo-Authoritarianism." *Man and the Economy* 6, no. 1(2019): 1–7.

Xiao, Lao. "正告美国反华乱港势力：立即住手！——粉碎香港颜色革命，坚决捍卫国家统一" [Asking the US and anti-China forces that create chaos in Hong Kong to stop: Dismantling Hong Kong's color revolution and resolutely defending the nation's reunification]. 红旗 [Red Flag Association Website], July 3, 2019, accessed March 14, 2021. http://www.hongqi.tv/zatan/2019-07-03/15616.html.

Xiao, Weiyun. "The Center Has to Control the Development of Political Reform." *The Discussion and Dispute over Patriotism*. Hong Kong: Ming Pao Publisher, 2004.

Xie, Yu. "Hong Kong Opposition Demands 'May Hurt Dialogue.'" *China Daily*, March 12, 2010, accessed March 14, 2021, http://www.chinadaily.com.cn/china/2010npc/2010-03/12/content_9577171.htm.

Xu, Hui, and Stefan Schmalz. "Socializing Labor Protest: New Forms of Coalition Building in South China." *Development and Change* 48, no. 5 (2017): 1031–1051.

Xu, Jiatun. *Xu Jiatun Xianggang Huiyilu* (*Xu Jiatun's Hong Kong Memoirs*). Taipei: Lianhebao, 1993, Part 1 and Part 2.

Yan, Jiann-fa. "DPP's Current China Policy." *Prospect and Exploration* 12, no. 7 (July 2014): 15–20.

Yan, Qing, and Ping Weibun. "'*Dayitong*' and the Formation of the Common Entity Ideology of the Chinese Nation." *Minzu lilun yu zhengze* [The theory and policy of nationalities] 5 (2018): 14–18.

Yang, Dali. "China's Developmental Authoritarianism: Dynamics and Pitfalls." In *Routledge Handbook of Democratization in Asia*, edited by Tun-jen Cheng and Yun-han Chu, 122–141. London: Routledge, 2017.

Yang, Nianqun. "On the Modern Transformation of China's Traditional Unification View." *Journal of the People's University* 1 (2018): 117–131.

Yeung, S. C. "Cosco Takeover of Orient Overseas Fits a Pattern." *EJ Insight*, July 11, 2017, accessed October 12, 2017, http://www.ejinsight.com/20170711-cosco-takeover-of-orient-overseas-fits-a-pattern/.

Yilmaz, Gozde, and Nilgun Elikucuk Yildirim. "Authoritarian Diffusion or Cooperation? Turkey's Emerging Engagement with China." *Democratization* 27, no. 7 (2020): 1202–1220.

Yu, Po-sang. "Citizen Curation and the Online Communication of Folk Economics: The China Collapse Theory in Hong Kong Social Media." *Media, Culture & Society* 42, no. 7–8 (2020): 1392–1409.

Zeng, Vivenne. "The Curious Tale of Five Missing Publishers in Hong Kong." *Hong Kong Free Press*, January 8, 2016, accessed March 1, 2021, https://hongkongfp.com/2016/01/08/the-curious-tale-of-five-missing-publishers-in-hong-kong/.

Zhai, Keith. "China Replaces Head of Hong Kong Liaison Office amid Ongoing Protests." Reuters, January 4, 2020, accessed March 7, 2021, https://www.reuters.com/article/uk-hongkong-protests-china-liaison-idUSKBN1Z30AD.

Zhang, Laney. "China: 2018 Constitutional Amendment Adopted." Global Legal Monitor, March 18, 2018, accessed January 3, 2021, https://www.loc.gov/item/global-legal-monitor/2018-05-18/china-2018-constitutional-amendment-adopted/.

Zhang, Qianfan. "An Analysis of the Constitution of 'One Country, Two Systems.'" *Yanhuang Chunqiu* 3 (2016): 12–19.

Zhang, Qiang. "Great Unity Thinking as Constitutional System: Discussion of Ancient China's Constitutional Order under the Idea of Unification." *The Journal of South China Sea Studies* 1, no. 1 (March 2015): 44–49.

Zhao, Suisheng. "Foreign Policy Implications of Chinese Nationalism Revisited: The Strident Turn." *Journal of Contemporary China* 22, no. 82 (2013): 535–553.

Zheng, Jin, and Fang Yuanyuan. "Between Poverty and Prosperity: China's Dependent Development and the 'Middle-Income Trap.'" *Third World Quarterly* 35, no. 6 (2014): 1014–1031.

Zheng, William, and Jun Mai. "Is China's Police Chief Playing a New Part in Beijing's Handling of Hong Kong?" *South China Morning Post*, September 13, 2019, accessed March 16, 2021, https://www.scmp.com/news/china/politics/article/3027188/chinas-police-chief-playing-new-part-beijings-handling-hong.

Zhi, Zhiqun. "Interpreting China's 'Wolf-Warrior' Diplomacy: What Explains the Sharper Tone to China's Overseas Conduct Recently?" *The Diplomat*, March 15, 2020, accessed February 21, 2021, https://thediplomat.com/2020/05/interpreting-chinas-wolf-warrior-diplomacy/.

Ziegler, Charles E. "Great Powers, Civil Society and Authoritarian Diffusion in Central Asia." *Central Asian Survey* 35, no. 4 (2016): 549–569.

Zong, Daoyi, ed. *Zhou Nan's Oral Narratives*. Hong Kong: Joint Publishing, 2007.

Index

accountability, 59, 140, 187–188
accountable, 41, 84, 133, 188, 190
agreeing to disagree, 252–254
Alibaba, 167
allegiance, 7, 100, 170, 180–183, 227, 230–231, 234, 241, 267
Alliance for Universal Suffrage, 95
amnesty, 106
anarchists, 174, 251
ancient concept of sovereignty, 47
anti-corruption, 22
anti-extradition movement, 35, 55, 64, 124–125, 149, 157, 182, 220, 238, 241, 244, 248
anti-foreignism, 191–192
anti-intellectualism, 20
anti-mainlandization, 63
Anti-Mask Law, 126
anti-national education, 4, 14, 46, 82, 96–98, 103, 107–109, 119, 182, 207, 230, 234, 239–240
anti-sanctions law, 32, 250
Article 45 of the Basic Law, 90
Article 68 of the Basic Law, 90
Article 104 of the Basic Law, 15, 17, 47, 63, 156–157, 173, 181, 184, 230, 233, 241
Article 158 of the Basic Law, 101
assertive nationalism, 7, 11, 13–15, 47, 63, 175, 192, 240, 248–249, 278, 281
August 31 parameters, 110, 114, 168–169
authoritarian diffusion, 9, 38
authoritarianism, 26
autonomy vis-à-vis the business elites, 167

Bar Association, 129
bargaining, 94–95
Bauhinia Party, 166, 212–213
Basic Law, 6, 82–96, 100–101, 109, 157, 170, 173, 182, 188, 196, 207, 234, 241, 243–244, 249, 252, 258
Basic Law Committee, 199
Beijing, 105–107, 109–118, 120–127, 130–142, 144, 146–147, 150, 152–157, 164–169, 172–190, 192–199, 207–211, 216–222, 224–228, 229–254
Beijing–Taipei relations, 57–58, 216, 220, 222, 224–225, 227–230, 239, 241–242, 244, 246–247, 250–254, 263
Belt and Road, 104, 176, 192
Biden, Joe, 116, 218–219, 224, 226
Bill of Rights Ordinance, 196
bishop, 139
Blinken, Anthony, 191, 194, 218
Bo, Xilai, 72
Boomerang effect, 26, 170, 227
bourgeois democratization, 119
British citizenship, 195
British National Overseas (BNO) passports, 195
business elites, 40, 61, 129, 167, 172, 193, 238, 250
business factions, 165
business interests, 80, 167, 238, 250
Business Professionals Alliance, 199, 212
business tycoons, 115

Cao, Erbao, 48, 262

Candidate Eligibility Review Committee, 157–159, 162–163, 169, 182–183, 232
candidate for the chief executive, 161
capitalism, 37, 59, 110, 174, 237
capitalist class, 118, 238, 250–251, 253
capitalist system, 87, 177
Cardinal Joseph Zen, 140
Catholic, 139–140
Central Committee, 174, 189
Central Coordination Group for Hong Kong and Macau Affairs, 106
central government, 2, 5, 24, 48, 54, 83, 85–86, 100, 102–103, 105, 109, 126, 133–134, 156, 165, 174, 182, 185, 187, 189–190, 196, 206–210, 217, 227, 232, 238–239, 251, 253
centralism, 161, 169–170, 178, 209
Central-local relations, 48, 57, 63, 84, 114
Central Military Commission, 36, 72, 209
central state, 34, 62, 96, 150, 152, 154, 169, 172–174, 177, 179, 194, 244
Chan, Kin-man, 107
Chang, Ya-chung, 226, 252, 255
Chen, Shui-bian, 115
Chen, Yun, 71
Cheung, Anthony Bing-leung, 106
Cheung, Man-kwong, 112
chief executive elections, 182, 196, 206–211, 232
chief executive office, 187
China, 1–9, 23, 190–196, 229–254
China threat, 248, 256
China-US rivalries, 65, 116
China model, 57–58
China's concept of national security, 108
Chinese Communist Party, 5, 8–9, 13, 48, 72–73, 104–195, 123, 174, 265, 270, 272, 275, 279
Chinese democracy, 157–167, 171, 191, 195
Chinese exceptionalism, 192
Chinese legalism, 8, 15–17, 63, 67–68, 150, 185, 240–241, 248
Chinese nation, 50–53, 221, 225

Chinese national identity, 7, 67–68, 240–241
Chinese nationalism, 98
Chinese People's Political Consultative Conference (CPPCC), 157
Chinese politics, 10, 168
Chinese renaissance, 50
Chinese-style democracy, 105, 168, 170, 172, 191, 240–241, 248, 270
Choi, Peter, 139
Chow, Stephen Sau-yan, 131
Chu, Yiu-ming, 107
Civic Party, 94, 112
Civic Passion, 137
civil liberties, 43, 97–98, 118, 122, 128–129, 150, 194–195, 243, 248
Civil Service Code, 189
civil society, 29–30, 33, 38, 44–46, 58, 64–65, 67, 80, 115, 123, 191, 229, 232, 237, 242, 244, 261, 265
civil society groups, 45, 123, 191, 242
clan groups, 193, 232
clashes of Sino-Western political civilizations, 190–196
class struggle, 27
clients, 63, 65, 162, 164, 184, 229
coat-tail effect, 81
collective leadership, 72
colonial, 7, 45, 49, 59, 64–65, 80–81, 105, 158, 176, 178, 232, 239, 246, 263, 269
colour revolution, 7, 9, 21, 25–26, 30, 45, 63, 65, 109, 130, 132, 175–177, 185, 191, 242, 248–249
Commission on Strategic Development, 92
Committee for Safeguarding National Security, 135, 185–186
common law system, 67, 150, 192, 249, 250–251
Communist Youth League, 72
complete reunification, 57, 224, 226, 253
comprehensive jurisdiction, 6, 102, 109–110, 146, 172–173, 180, 183–190, 193, 227, 229–230, 249, 251–253

Index 283

compromise, 95–96
concessions, 92, 94, 95–96, 111, 115–116
confrontational localists, 118, 120
conservative, 90
conservative business elites, 193
conservative nationalism, 107, 109, 122, 174, 176, 230
conservative nationalists, 100–102, 104, 106–107, 110, 114–116, 118, 120, 122, 124, 127, 142, 153, 176–177, 207, 248
conspiracy, 2, 65, 108, 146–147, 153–155, 174
constitutional conventions, 187, 190
continuous showdown, 178
convenor, 162
convergence, 12, 57, 65, 68, 171, 245, 249, 273
cooptation, 49, 96, 246
court judges, 141, 147–148, 177, 251
Court of Final Appeal, 147, 149, 170
COVID-19, 127, 154
crisis of governance, 207, 234
crisis of legitimacy, 64, 182, 230
cultural identity, 97
cultural-political identity, 97, 217
cyclical pattern of control and relaxation, 168

deep contradictions, 253
deep state, 150–152, 178–179, 251, 276
Democratic Alliance for Betterment and Progress of Hong Kong (DAB), 80–81, 111, 113, 128, 197–198, 212, 200, 203–204
democratic centralism, 161, 169–170, 178, 209
Democratic Party, 20, 81, 94–95, 106, 165, 213, 247
democratic populists, 183, 232–233, 238, 234, 238–243, 251
democratization, 7, 40, 42–44, 46, 55, 58, 67, 108, 115–116, 119, 158, 171, 178, 191, 245–247, 253

democrats, 2, 4–5, 8, 64–65, 81–83, 92–96, 111–114, 116, 123, 137, 152–155, 161, 165–166, 170–172, 183, 199, 202, 229–230, 238–240, 242–243, 246–247
Demonstration effect, 116
dependent development, 57–58, 60, 65, 249
Deng, Xiaoping, 24, 48, 50–51
Deng, Zhonghua, 160
deter, 144, 182, 218, 226
deterrence, 65, 132
developmental interest, 18, 103
developmental state, 58–59, 249–250, 268
Ding, Xuexiang, 187–188
direct elections, 81
disqualification, 159, 165, 170–171, 184
District Committees, 162
District Council elections, 127, 211–215, 227, 233–234
District Councils, 92, 153
district federations, 115
Dongsha Islands, 136
double direct elections, 82
dual state, 62, 172–173, 179
duty visit, 185–190

economic base, 66–67, 174–175, 178, 192, 232
economic blockade, 4, 219
economic diversification, 188–189
economic expertise, 208, 211
economic integration, 40–41, 118, 121, 189
economic internationalization, 192
economic modernization, 36, 60, 62, 65–66, 192
education system, 177, 232, 241
egalitarian society, 119
Election Committee, 91, 157–159, 161, 169
elections, 161
electoral reforms, 157
eligibility test, 162
elite political culture, 67, 238

Emperor Qin Shihuang, 52–53
engagement, 40, 247
espionage, 144–145
ethnic minorities, 24, 214
ethnoterritorial federalism, 23–24
etiquette, 190
Examination Authority, 137
executive-led, 8, 67, 84, 89, 120, 233
executive-legislative relations, 169
extradition bill, 128–129
extraterritorial, 135

face, 8, 32, 67–68, 94, 221, 238–241, 257, 262
factional fragmentation, 99
factionalism, 28, 70, 81, 96, 98–99, 127, 150, 157, 165, 168, 172, 178, 230
factional politics, 1–2, 28, 70, 72–82, 90–91, 96–98, 123, 128, 166, 224, 228, 230, 252, 275
factional struggles, 99
factions, 73–82, 152–178
fear, 139
Federation of Education Workers, 199
Federation of Hong Kong and Kowloon Labor Unions, 199, 212
Federation of Trade Unions (FTU), 166, 197–201, 203, 206, 212
Fight Crime Committees, 162
filibustering, 103, 120, 184
Foreign Ministry, 6, 12, 24, 213, 222
fragmentation, 82, 99, 118–123, 165–166, 213, 236
fragmentation of democrats, 165
fragmentation of patriotic elites, 166
functional constituencies, 161

Gao, Siren, 75
gatekeeper, 44–46, 162, 214
general-secretary, 71–74, 182, 209, 223, 253
geographical constituencies, 161
geopolitical struggle, 248
golden goose, 9
governing capability, 207, 235

governing capacity, 183, 207, 244
government-business relations, 250
government performance, 233–234
gradual and orderly manner, 88–90
gray areas, 101
Greater Bay Area, 7, 19, 62, 168, 171, 189, 246
great unification, 50–56
guanxi, 3, 19–20, 99, 231
Gui, Minhai, 76–77, 122

Han Chinese, 100
Han, Kuo-yu, 131, 216, 220, 224–225
Han, Zheng, 100–101
harmony, 8–9, 67–68, 117, 171, 208, 240–241, 247
Hengqin, 188–189
Ho, Albert, 94, 112, 148, 151, 209
Ho, Iat Seng, 185–186, 187–188
Hong Kong and Macau Work Office, 189
Hong Kong identity, 5, 40, 66, 82, 96, 99, 217, 233, 238, 240–241, 246
Hongkongism, 99, 119
Hong Kong Macau Affairs Office (HKMAO), 73, 88, 160, 187–188, 213
Hong Kong National Party, 131, 207
Hong Kong New Direction, 198–199, 205–206, 212
Hong Kong-style democracy, 7, 168, 170, 191, 215
house rules, 184–185
housing shortage, 131
Hu, Jintao, 83, 88, 95, 107, 112
Hu, Yaobang, 71
human rights, 8, 24, 26, 37, 80, 126, 128–129, 133, 149, 179, 190, 195–196, 248, 257, 262, 267

ideological clashes, 1, 98–118, 230
ideological conflicts, 11, 119, 150, 174, 178, 238, 254
ideological contentions, 254
ideologically dogmatic, 178, 220
ideologies, 40, 65, 68, 70, 175, 230
imperialism, 33, 39, 64, 174, 175, 190–191

individual visit scheme, 98
institutionalization, 188
intellectuals, 20, 33–35, 71
internal actor, 43–49
International Covenant on Civil and Political Rights (ICCPR), 133, 196
international financial and monetary center, 192
internationalization, 61, 190, 192, 194
interpreting the Basic Law, 87, 101
Ip, Regina, 199, 210

Ji, Pengfei, 73
Jiang, Enzhu, 75
Jiang, Zemin, 21–23, 36, 72, 74–76, 78, 175, 239

Kaohsiung, 136
Kuomintang (KMT), 12, 56, 116, 219, 221

Lai, Jimmy, 103, 115
Lai, William, 220
Lam, Carrie, 40, 105–107, 125–126, 129, 131, 135–136, 140–141, 156, 177, 205–210, 234–235, 272
Lam, Wing-kee, 76–78, 122, 255
land and housing policies, 167
land developer, 167
landed elites, 184, 237
landlord, 167
Lau, Emily, 94, 112
Law Society, 129
leading small groups, 72
League of Social Democrats, 81–82
Lee, Bo, 76
Lee, John, 11, 19, 62, 129, 135, 185, 187–188, 206–211, 214, 232, 234–236, 249–250, 258–259, 269–271
Lee, Martin, 118
legalism, 15–17, 53, 63, 68, 230, 240–241, 248, 267, 278
legalist conservatives, 90
legalists, 90
Legislative Affairs Commission, 88

Legislative Council (LegCo) elections, 172, 181–182, 196–206
legislative elections (Hong Kong), 170, 197, 211, 214, 233
legislative elections (Macau), 170
legitimacy, 2, 5, 15, 28, 77, 83, 106, 122, 169, 180, 182, 207–209, 230, 234, 239–240, 244, 275, 246, 248–249
Leninism, 17, 21, 37, 63, 65, 67, 69, 174–175, 230, 248, 277
Leong, Alan, 112, 209
Leung, C. Y., 14, 105, 107–108, 114, 208–209
Li, Gang, 94
Li, Hou, 74
Li, Peng, 74
Li, Qiang, 187–188
Liaison Office, 75, 94–95, 100, 111–113, 123–125, 134, 151–152, 187–188, 205, 213
liberal democrats, 8
liberal faction, 93, 95
liberal localists, 123
liberal nationalism, 119, 230
liberal nationalists, 5, 105–106, 116–117, 124, 178, 239
Liberal Party, 80, 111, 199, 201, 204, 212
liberal studies, 137–139, 182, 241, 258, 267
liberalization, 23
limited pluralism, 172
linkage, 44
livelihood issues, 19, 83, 207, 234, 236–237, 253
localism, 29, 63, 68, 96, 98–119, 230
localist populism, 181–182, 193, 216–217, 227, 251
localist populists, 154, 181–183, 190–191, 227, 230, 232, 234, 241–244
localists, 15
Loh, Christine, 106
lower-class citizens, 238, 302
loyal opposition, 32, 165, 172, 232, 236, 243, 247
loyal oppositionists, 165
loyalty, 19, 100, 185, 235

Luo, Huning, 100

Ma, Ying-jeou, 58, 116, 221, 225
Macau, 127, 169–170
Macau Electoral Affairs Commission, 170
Macau national security law, 171
Macaunize, 169
mainlandization, 34, 63–64, 121, 125, 130–131, 194, 224, 244, 270
mainstream democrats, 82, 95–96
mandate of heaven, 50, 53, 217
Marshall, George, 219
Marxist, 5, 26, 66, 117–120, 123, 157, 174, 232, 238, 242, 250
Marxism-Leninism, 174–175, 230
Marxist localists, 118, 119
mass participation, 227
memorandum of understanding, 226, 252–254
military exercises, 4, 219
military weapons, 218, 226
Ministry of Foreign Affairs, 134
Ministry of National Security, 26, 107, 207
Ministry of Public Security, 107
miscalculation, 5, 113, 128, 238, 240, 268
mobilization, 30, 33, 43, 55, 81, 108, 111, 115, 128, 207, 211, 236, 241, 249
moderate democrats, 5, 94–96, 112–113, 123–124, 165–166, 172, 178, 183, 202, 239, 247
moderate reformers, 71
modern concept of sovereignty, 47
money-laundering activities, 125
Mong Kok riots, 122

naïve, 9, 22, 116, 124, 248
national dignity, 9
national education, 14, 34–35, 97–98, 107, 117, 138–139, 175, 182, 192, 207, 230, 232, 234, 239–240, 249, 252, 262, 273, 276, 278
national flags, 5, 124, 191
nationalistic populists, 2–3, 232–233
National People's Congress (NPC), 10

national security, 1–9, 56–57, 64, 68, 82, 108, 132–134, 138–140, 192–196, 207, 213, 227, 229–254
national security adviser, 133
National Security Commission, 107–109, 244
national security education, 35, 139
national security law, 1–9, 11, 31, 46, 56, 61, 127, 132–152, 154, 229–252, 256, 260, 262–263, 273, 275–279
neutrality, 141
New China News Agency, 73
New Macau Association, 170
New People's Party, 197, 212
Ng, Kuok Cheong, 170
1992 consensus, the, 51, 116, 216, 220–224, 228, 252
Nomination Committee, 110
nominations, 161
non-interventionist governing philosophy, 250
normative state, 173, 176, 250

oath-taking, 4, 15, 17, 21, 47, 82, 101, 156, 178, 180–181, 189, 238, 240–241
Occupy Central Movement, 5, 21, 46, 58, 108–110, 114, 119, 123, 135, 143, 176–177, 190–191, 207, 234, 238–240
Office for Safeguarding National Security, 134, 145, 185–186
Official Secrets Ordinance, 145
one-China principle, 216, 219, 224, 254
one country, two systems, 3–6, 52, 56–57, 63, 65–66, 68–69, 101, 109, 131, 157, 169, 189, 196, 205, 215–228, 238, 240, 251–253, 255, 259, 261–262, 267, 277–278, 280

party authority, 188
party-state, 33, 60, 64, 116
paternalism, 8, 17, 63, 229–230, 237, 240–241, 248
paternalistic authoritarianism, 2, 229, 237, 246, 249, 252

Path of Democracy, 165–166, 197, 212
patriotic, 110
patriotic elites, 2–3, 6, 20, 40, 147, 160–162, 165–166, 171–172, 237, 245–247, 249, 251
patriotic populists, 193
patriotism, 87
patron, 162, 184, 230
patronage, 39–40, 115, 184, 229
patron-clientelist, 229
patron-client pluralism, 2–3, 229
Patten, Christopher, 81
peace consensus, 221
peace memorandum, 226
Pelosi, Nancy, 4, 57, 218–219
Pence, Mike, 128
Peng, Qinghua, 75, 112
People's Armed Police (PAP), 126
People's Liberation Army, 134
Pingtung, 136
pluralism, 2, 115, 194, 229
police power, 125
policy research, 207
political actors, 141
political climate, 123
political compromise, 5, 95, 118, 123–124, 239
political concessions, 239
political convergence, 244
political correctness, 106, 137–138, 185
political culture, 8, 17–21, 66–68, 185, 194, 230, 232, 234, 237, 239–241, 245, 248, 253, 271, 276
political development, 10, 15, 35, 68, 89, 110, 116, 123, 137, 168, 171, 176, 209, 227, 241, 244–245, 247–249, 251, 270, 272
political divergence, 176
political harmony, 208
political identity, 97
political ideology, 5, 240
political liberalization, 43–44, 70–71, 119, 168, 172, 247
political loyalty, 100
political opposition, 92

political party, 91
political patron, 3, 40, 162, 229, 231, 246
political patronage, 115
political pawn, 65
political provocation, 178
political red lines, 9, 17, 63, 124, 139, 239, 242
political reform, 23, 95, 110
political trust, 96, 207
political will, 252
political winds, 113
politically converge, 169
Pompeo, Michael, 134, 149, 218
populist authoritarianism, 3, 193, 231
positive intervention, 227, 230
poverty, 22, 26, 59, 131, 167, 234
power dependence, 62
power politics, 73, 254, 266
power structures, 155, 244
power struggles, 9, 80, 230, 241, 244, 246, 248, 252, 254
prerogative state, 173, 176, 251
pro-Beijing forces, 111–112, 114, 127, 178, 199, 230, 241
pro-Beijing nationalism, 100
pro-democracy candidate, 136–137, 170–171
pro-democracy faction, 92
pro-democracy forces, 81
productive forces, 174, 192
pro-establishment forces, 5, 211–212
progressive tax, 238
pro-Hong Kong localism, 100
proportional representation system, 81, 161
protests, 5, 8–10, 13, 15, 17, 19, 21, 23–24, 30, 32, 37, 46, 56, 61, 64, 67, 68, 75, 80, 82–83, 103, 106, 108, 114–115, 118, 125–132, 140–141, 152–153, 162, 167–168, 176–177, 180, 192, 195, 202, 208, 227, 229, 235, 238, 240, 242, 271, 274, 280
public nuisance, 108
public opinion, 88, 93
Pye, Lucian, 12, 17–20, 70

radical democrats, 95–96
radical localists, 9, 63, 82,102, 153, 162, 165, 167, 182, 238, 242, 251
radical reformers, 71
Radio Television Hong Kong, 140
realpolitik, 64, 219, 241, 247
Red Flag, 176–178
referendum, 93–94
reformers, 71
relative autonomy, 167
renminbi, 61, 192, 250
renminbi offshore center, 192
residual power, 48
reunification, 3–4, 51–52, 54–58, 65–68, 176, 215–216, 218, 223–226, 251, 253–254, 260–261, 266, 278–279
right of abode, 101
rise of China, 61, 68, 226, 247–249
rotation of political parties in power, 217
rules-based international order, 194

sanctions, 32, 40, 133, 135, 153, 155, 193, 225, 243
Scholarism, 109
self-censorship, 139
separating politics from economics, 192
separation of powers, 9, 26, 75, 84, 101, 120
separatist localists, 117–123
Severe Acute Respiratory Syndrome (SARS), 98
Shanwei, 134
Shenzhen, 42, 71, 83, 126, 136, 181, 199, 210, 246
Singapore model, 58
Sinic civilization, 194
Sinification, 121
Sino-British Joint Declaration, 6, 193–195
Sino-British negotiations over Hong Kong, 118
Sino-US struggles, 179, 226
sinologists, 10
socialism, 16, 104, 110, 174, 250
Sou, Sulu, 170

sovereignty, 3–4, 8–9, 11, 23, 47–48, 86, 109, 124, 217, 223, 230
Soviet-style collapse, 21
speedboat, 136
stage-by-stage negotiations, 57, 66, 223
Standing Committee of the National People's Congress (SCNPC), 87, 91, 101, 110
State Council, 91
state-society relations, 8
status quo, 14, 23, 89–90, 100, 111, 217, 225
strategic ambiguity, 218–219
strategies, 18, 25, 40, 172
strong executive, 245, 247
strong state, 29, 64
subvert, 2, 9, 26, 34, 36–37, 44, 46, 64–65, 104, 127, 143, 153, 160, 174, 176, 242–243, 259, 276
superstructure, 66, 174–175, 177–178, 183, 192, 232–233, 249, 251–252
Szeto Wah, 118

Tai, Benny, 103, 107–108
Taiwan, 215–227, 251–256, 260–261, 263, 266, 270–272, 276, 278–279
Taiwan link in Hong Kong protests, 131
Taiwan model of "one country, two systems," 52, 56–57, 65–66, 69, 215–227
Taiwan's political future, 50–51, 56–57, 68, 215, 220, 252–253
Taiwan's presidential elections, 116
Taiwanese identity, 217
Tang, Chris, 132, 135, 143, 145, 210, 232
Tang, Henry, 140, 209
taxes, 167
teargas, 129
term of office of the chief executive, 91
territorial integrity, 9
terrorism, 9
Tian, Feilong, 165
Tibet, 55
Tik, Chi-yuen, 20, 106, 205
tolerance, 9

Tong, Hon, 139
Treaty of Nanking, 195
Trojan horse, 9, 26, 36, 108, 127, 241
Trump, Donald, 116, 126, 150–151, 126, 218, 222
trust-building, 225, 227, 240, 246
Tsai, Ing-wen, 58, 116, 131, 216, 221
Tsang, Donald, 86, 91, 93, 95, 112, 209
Tsang, Jasper Tak-sing, 105, 110, 131
Tsang, John, 209
Tsang, Yok-sing, 105
Tung, Chee-hwa, 83, 88, 90, 104, 209
Tung, Chao-yung, 104
turbulence, 60, 170, 178, 183, 192–193
two-point policy, 218

uncivil aspect of civil society, 33, 229, 243
United Democrats of Hong Kong, 118
united front, 34, 74–75, 80, 94, 96, 104, 113–115, 131, 140, 151–152, 167, 171–172, 187, 193, 232, 236, 247, 250–252, 271
united front groups, 114–115
united front work, 34, 74, 80, 94, 96, 113, 131, 140, 152, 167, 177, 187, 193, 232, 247, 250–252, 271
United Nations Human Rights Council, 195
United States, 126
United States–style democracy, 191
universal suffrage, 85, 87, 90, 93, 108, 160, 196
US Indo-Pacific strategy, 222

Vatican, 139–140
vested interest, 166
veto power, 88
victim, 19, 116, 128, 220, 248
victory, 195, 199, 241
violence, 5, 9, 103, 117, 120, 143, 173, 180, 183
violent populism, 230
voter turnout, 170, 197, 211, 214, 233

Wang, Huning, 102

Wang, Zhimin, 100, 124
weak legislature, 236, 245, 247
weak local state, 67, 244
weak society, 29, 64
welfarist approach, 167
Wen, Jiabao, 83, 90, 105
Western concept of human rights, 8
Western democracy, 38, 86, 241
Western idealism, 253
Westernization, 71, 101, 248, 253
Western states, 2, 24–25, 46, 153, 174, 242, 247
Western-style democratization, 7, 68, 176, 192, 231, 245, 249
White Paper on the implementation of the Basic Law, 109
wolf-warrior diplomacy, 12–13
women, 30, 98, 121, 162, 193
women organizations, 193
Wong, Joshua, 103, 109, 119
Woo, Kwok-hing, 209
Woo, Peter, 209
Wu, Bangguo, 88, 91
Wu, Jianfan, 83
Wukan village, 134

xenophobic, 191
Xi, Jinping, 5, 16, 22, 27, 36, 59, 72, 77, 90, 109, 112, 127–128, 175–176, 182, 187, 192, 196, 208–209, 216, 221, 226, 234, 250, 253, 258, 261–262, 265, 268, 274, 279
Xia, Baolong, 100, 103, 113, 135, 151, 187–189, 202, 239, 257, 261
Xia, Yong, 83, 85
Xiao, Weiyun, 83–84
Xinjiang, 24, 53, 130, 195
Xu, Chongde, 83–85
Xu, Jiatun, 73, 105, 124

Yang, Jiechi, 151–152, 191, 194
Yang, Shangkun, 73
Ye, Jianying, 217

Zhang, Dejiang, 100–101

Zhang, Xiaoming, 75, 100, 113, 124, 160
Zhao, Kezhi, 132
Zhao, Ziyang, 71
Zheng, Yanxiong, 134, 151, 187
Zhou, Ji, 187–188
Zhou, Nan, 74
Zhou, Yongkang, 72

Milton Keynes UK
Ingram Content Group UK Ltd.
UKHW022308050524
442188UK00002B/11